Technology and Innovation Management

Edited by **Ed Diego**

New York

Published by Willford Press,
118-35 Queens Blvd., Suite 400,
Forest Hills, NY 11375, USA
www.willfordpress.com

Technology and Innovation Management
Edited by Ed Diego

© 2016 Willford Press

International Standard Book Number: 978-1-68285-061-9 (Hardback)

Printed in the United States of America.

Contents

Preface

This book was inspired by the evolution of our times; to answer the curiosity of inquisitive minds. Many developments have occurred across the globe in the recent past which has transformed the progress in the field.

Technology and innovation management is an interdisciplinary field of study which incorporates concepts from various fields like entrepreneurship, organisational behaviour, resource management, etc. under one branch. This book consists of contributions made by an international panel of experts that will help to provide information on topics like business model innovations, knowledge management, managing emerging technologies and innovations, creating opportunities for entrepreneurship, strategic decision making, etc. The extensive content of the book will help provide innovative insights to the students and academicians engaged in this field.

This book was developed from a mere concept to drafts to chapters and finally compiled together as a complete text to benefit the readers across all nations. To ensure the quality of the content we instilled two significant steps in our procedure. The first was to appoint an editorial team that would verify the data and statistics provided in the book and also select the most appropriate and valuable contributions from the plentiful contributions we received from authors worldwide. The next step was to appoint an expert of the topic as the Editor-in-Chief, who would head the project and finally make the necessary amendments and modifications to make the text reader-friendly. I was then commissioned to examine all the material to present the topics in the most comprehensible and productive format.

I would like to take this opportunity to thank all the contributing authors who were supportive enough to contribute their time and knowledge to this project. I also wish to convey my regards to my family who have been extremely supportive during the entire project.

Editor

Collaborative Idea Management:
A Driver of Continuous Innovation

Jesper Bank and Adnan Raza

" *Collaboration is important not just because it's a better* "
way to learn. The spirit of collaboration is penetrating
every institution and all of our lives. So learning to
collaborate is part of equipping yourself for effectiveness,
problem solving, innovation, and life-long learning in
an ever-changing networked economy.

Don Tapscott
Business executive, author, and speaker

Despite the critical importance of innovation to most companies' ongoing success, many organizations fail to develop sustainable innovation management processes. The article explores the application of collaborative idea management to drive continuous innovation in large organizations based on our experience at Waabii, an innovation software and consulting service provider. First, we identify the key roadblocks faced by organizations in managing their innovation processes. Next, we describe the innovation model created at Waabii to help implement a sustainable innovation process, and we present a case study of an innovation management software solution, Exago Idea Market, which was implemented to create a collaborative and sustainable innovation environment in a large global telecommunications company. Finally, we offer recommendations for implementing this model of collaborative idea management. This article is particularly relevant to managers in larger organizations and practitioners of organizational change seeking to identify inhibitors of growth and business innovation and how to combat the roadblocks and create a sustainable innovation environment.

Introduction

Innovation is often touted as "the lifeblood of business", and yet many companies struggle to keep the continuous flow of innovation that is required to sustain long-term health. But why? What are the key factors that prevent companies from being the innovation engines they strive to be? In this article, we examine the major inhibitors of innovation, and then propose collaborative idea management as an approach that companies can use to drive continuous innovation by harnessing the creativity of their employees.

Our perspective is based on our experiences at Waabii (waabii.com), an innovation software and consulting service provider in the Greater Toronto Area of Ontario, Canada. We help companies overcome barriers to in-

novation by tapping into the knowledge of their employees using an approach called "collaborative idea management". In this article, we explore the concept of collaborative idea management with the aim of providing managers with insights to overcome roadblocks to innovation and harness the innovation capabilities of their employees on an ongoing basis. First, we identify the major inhibitors of innovation in large organizations. Second, we introduce collaborative idea management as a means of creating a sustainable environment for innovation. Third, we discuss the three essential components that must be considered when implementing a collaborative idea management process: strategy, leadership, and culture. Fourth, we highlight the benefits of the approach through a case study of a large global telecommunications company. Finally, we close with recommendations and conclusions.

Inhibitors of Innovation

Based on consulting interviews we conducted with executives from a wide mix of global corporations active in the telecommunications, banking, life science, utilities, and resource-extraction domains we have identified three major inhibitors of innovation: i) growing size, ii) operation silos, and iii) lack of employee motivation.

1. Growing size

Increasing size of an organization has created a disconnect between the organization's strategy and its core-level executors: its employees. Increasingly, companies are busy creating high-level strategies to steer the company to increase profitability but face challenges in involving key resources to execute the plan. In many cases, the major reason identified is not the dearth of skill to execute the high-level strategy but a lack of communication initiatives to drive and manage the core message to the primary contributors to help them work towards the primary goal. This challenge becomes even more evident when the company wants to drive "targeted" innovation (i.e., innovation aimed at a common or particular goal). It becomes virtually impossible to control the direction of innovation from high up in the leadership chain. Today, most companies plough resources into established R&D or innovation centres directed to churn out innovation; the major drawback in this innovation model is that we are leveraging a very small section of the company's intellectual capital. Moreover, one of the key resources is rarely involved in the innovation cycle: the front-end employees, who serve as the connection points between the organization and its customers. We have observed that these problems become particularly acute when companies are growing in size.

2. Operational silos

As growing companies create various new lines of business and numerous sub-divisions, they tend to become increasingly compartmentalized. Each section of the group becomes disconnected from its peers and respective divisions. Because each division is so busy competing and is focused on completing their given task, "tunnel vision" may begin to inhibit innovation. These effects may be further worsened by geographic expansion, because regional divisions become preoccupied by their own local challenges. In such an environment, innovating towards a common goal becomes challenging.

To overcome the negative impact of operational silos, many companies establish distributed innovation centres. However, a major drawback of this approach is typically a lack of sync between solutions developed in each of these distributed silos. More importantly, a lack of proper methodology to select the most applicable of best ideas undermines these efforts. Indeed, Vermeulen (2013; tinyurl.com/lvcsczz), reports that the act of selecting ideas is a key challenge faced by most large organizations today. He highlights that, in terms of innovation, most business executives place a high value on variation, but do not put enough thought or management effort into deliberately selecting which ideas are worth pursuing. The act of selecting ideas has become a subjective process, wherein political interests and personal preferences determine which projects are funded and which are terminated. Companies need to devise a systematic idea-selection process that is free from any personal bias and incorporates a smart and efficient selection framework.

3. Lack of employee motivation

The other underlying key reason for a dearth in corporate innovation is the lack of sufficient motivation for the employees to participate in innovation processes. We have observed that, even if employees are keen to participate in innovation processes or projects hosted by their company, the level of engagement is hard to maintain for a long period of time.

One of the main contributors to such behaviour is an ill-defined "innovation to implementation" process, or "idea journey". A typical idea journey has four stages: i) creating ideas, ii) sorting the submitted ideas, iii) selecting the top ideas, and iv) implementing the selected ideas. Companies must follow through on each of these stages. After the idea creation stage, it is equally important to communicate to the participants on the progress of subsequent stages, through the sorting and selecting stages to the final implementation of the shortlisted ideas. Most of the innovation projects organized by organizations fail in the last stage of the idea journey: implementing the shortlisted idea in a structured timeline process. To motivate employees for ongoing participation in innovation activities, companies need to develop processes and mechanisms that allow for the establishment of teams capable of executing the shortlisted ideas and monitoring the step-by-step progress from start to execution. This full-cycle approach is crucial for gaining and maintaining employee participation.

Collaborative Idea Management

To overcome these three inhibitors of innovation – growing size, operational silos, and lack of motivators for employees – we encourage our clients to adopt collaborative idea management within their organizations. In essence, collaborative idea management involves soliciting ideas from within an organization, empowering employees to work collaboratively to define better solutions for a given problem, and managing and communicating the progression of the ideas through the full cycle of the idea journey up to implementation. Thus, collaborative idea management is a systematic approach to gathering and channeling ideas that enables an organization to:

- foster innovation by tapping into the diverse knowledge and collective creativity of its employees

- ensure that the "right ideas" actually end up meeting the organization's relevant innovation needs

- measure and drive front-end innovation activities

- engage employees across the organization in business innovation and improvement

- provide participants with feedback and recognition

- communicate corporate strategy in a consistent and relevant manner to the entire organization

- create transformational change to an innovation-driven culture

Collaborative idea management should be supported by appropriate processes and tools for managing the submission, sorting, and selection of ideas, as well as their implementation. This approach not only overcomes the inhibitors of innovation described earlier but also improves the efficiency of the innovation process.

As an example, the innovation management solution we typically use at Waabii is the Idea Market by Exago (exagomarkets.com), which is illustrated in the case study described in Box 1.

Box 1. Case study: Portugal Telecom

Portugal Telecom (telecom.pt) was founded in 1994 and is headquartered in Lisbon, Portugal. As of January 2014, the company is the largest telecom provider in Portugal with a market cap of $4 Billion, $6.6 Billion in revenues, and more than 11,000 employees.

Challenge
- To define a transversal innovation strategy shared by the company's 11,000+ employees

Solution
- A structured innovation program open to entire organization
- Exago Idea Market used as the fundamental collaborative idea management tool to support this program, providing a solution to capture and collate ideas, enrich suggestions through comments, and help identify the best ideas
- The tool integrates an evaluation engine that mimics the functioning of a stock market, with virtual credits being invested by the participants to help select the best ideas

Benefits
- More than 7,000 employees joined the platform
- More than 5,000 ideas have bee validated so far.
- $38 Million in annual savings from employee's ideas on business process improvements
- 44% improvement in employee engagement over four years (from 58% in 2008 up to 84% in 2012)
- 67% of all employees engaged in business innovation
- Decentralized and transparent evaluation process brings efficiency and flexibility to the innovation process
- The Exago Idea Market helped increase employee satisfaction by providing them a platform to voice their creativity

The Idea Market enables an organization to "broadcast" a business problem or broad question relating to corporate strategy to its employees and "call" for innovative thinking and cross-company cooperation to find solutions to the problem. Employees from all business units can then offer insights in three ways:

1. Present their own ideas about how to address the business challenges that management put forward

2. Offer comments to discuss and build upon ideas presented by others

3. Indicate their support (or lack thereof) for a particular idea by choosing how to "invest" their virtual currency in the market

The Idea Market functions as a traditional stock market in that investor (i.e., employee) confidence drives results – the ideas that receive the most investment are the ideas that rise to the top. Top ideas are then assessed by the management team in order to decide which ideas move forward for implementation. This process helps the organization reach its broad employee base with ease, connects different operational departments, and engages everyone to work towards a common goal.

Most importantly, this type of approach to collaborative idea management increases employee engagement and promotes innovation. At Waabii, we provide our clients with the innovation platform, we support strategic management, and we actively assist in the implementation of supporting processes. The goal is to establish a collaborative idea management process that continuously drives innovation by empowering employees to better define problems and to propose and refine solutions.

Key Components of a Collaborative Idea Management Process

Underpinning our approach to collaborative idea management at Waabii is what we call the "innovation triangle". The innovation triangle highlights three components that are essential to establishing a successful and sustainable collaborative idea management process: strategy, culture, and leadership.

1. Strategy
Strategy in its broadest definition outlines the direction the company takes to comply with the vision of the organization. Communicating the strategy and the role of individual employees in "the big picture" is very import-ant; it allows the organization to harness the active participation of its employees. As underlined earlier, fast-growing companies face a challenging problem of communicating their strategy to their internal audience. But beyond simply communicating the direction the company is headed, the organization must also identify and communicate the roles each employee will play in executing this strategy. The concept of collaborative idea management helps the company direct strategic challenges aligned to the core strategy of the company or even to a specific business unit, and it helps engage the employees in innovating around the centrally defined problem. The key idea behind the success of this component is the empowerment of employees by providing them a platform to create innovative solutions and collectively evaluate and select the best solutions for the company-defined challenges.

2. Leadership
The other key aspect of implementing a successful innovation program is applying executive support for the process, which in turn will make respective lines of business/departments engage in the company-designed innovation program. A strong and engaged leadership structure helps the employee stay motivated and helps increase the active participation rate for the designed innovation program. Without support from leadership, an otherwise perfectly designed innovation process or program is bound to fail. In addition, it is imperative that the innovation program is pushed and supported by the top manager of the company/department leading this process. It not only gives a face to the innovation program but also increases the perceived importance of such program.

3. Culture
Lastly, the culture of the organization must be aligned with the innovation process. In the challenges identified above, we highlighted that companies are becoming compartmentalized and operate as silos, with each unit concentrating on its respective objectives. This compartmentalization limits the employees' ability to understand and effectively participate in initiatives that transcend their departments. The concept of collaborative idea management not only helps connect the employees, but helps the organization bring varied skilled individuals to converse about the potential solution to "sticky problems". Our experiences with large organizations indicate that employees emphasize problem solving and creating innovative solutions. The collaborative idea management process aligns the need of the organization to the want of the employees, thereby enhancing the workforce experience.

To further catalyze employee participation and embed innovation within the culture of the organization, an organization needs to motivate its workforce by rewarding participation through tangible or intangible awards. Tangible awards may include real goods or benefits, such as monetary awards, physical prizes, and so forth. Our interactions with organizations with a higher proportion of knowledge-based workforce has shown that, compared to tangible rewards, intangible awards are deemed more valuable even though they are not monetary. Examples of intangible awards include an opportunity to have breakfast with the CEO of the company or a coaching session with the senior manager of the employee's choice.

Key Takeaways

The concept of collaborative idea management helps an organization progress in its innovation process by aligning the three spokes of the innovation triangle: strategy, leadership, and culture. As illustrated earlier, collaborative idea management is based on the concept of designing a solution collectively, hence the primary step of the process is to design a problem broad enough but aligned to the central strategy of the organization. This problem can be a high-level problem or can be a problem designed to address a functional component of the larger puzzle.

The second component of collaborative idea management is to invite employees and potentially other stakeholders (e.g., suppliers, customers, academia, graduate students) to engage in a conversation to drive collaborative innovation. For example, the Exago Idea Market innovation solution can be used as an interface to engage various stakeholders around potential challenges faced by the company. The platform will thereafter help the company identify top ideas or solutions selected by the population at large. These top ideas can be further evaluated by the leadership team to prioritize development of the selected solution in isolation or combination, thereby driving groundbreaking innovation for the organization.

Finally, to increase employee participation exponentially and to instill innovation in the very core values of the workforce, the company needs to motivate the employees by rewarding them through a mix of tangible and intangible awards.

Conclusion

Collaborative idea management empowers an organization to efficiently leverage its prized intellectual capital: its employees. An organization has to be mindful of the three components in the innovation triangle – strategy, leadership, and culture – while implementing a collaborative idea management solution. Each of the three parameters helps in establishing a sustained innovation environment. Lastly, to instill an engaged participants, the organization has to reward participation. The reward mix has to be strategically composed of both tangible and intangible awards to attract participation from all areas of the workforce.

About the Authors

Jesper Bank is CEO and Co-Founder of Waabii Limited, where he is responsible for the company's strategic direction and partnership development in North America. He works with leaders in public and private sector organizations around the world to help increase collaboration, engage employees in idea generation, and convert great ideas into value. For over a decade, Jesper has helped companies achieve profitable growth through business process improvement, and he currently provides counsel in the areas of strategy clarification, innovation management, and business-process redesign. He also provides idea management software and consulting services that enable firms to identify and prioritize the winning ideas within their organizations. Jesper holds a TRIUM Global Executive MBA from New York University Stern School of Business, London School of Economics and Political Science, and HEC School of Management in Paris, and he has substantive international experience having lived and worked in both North America and Europe.

Adnan Raza is an Innovation Consultant for Waabii Limited, where he provides business support advice and consultancy for Waabii's idea management solutions. He works with innovation teams in global organizations to improve their business and product innovation processes through novel insights and analysis. He has worked for more than four years in helping global organizations manage innovation through competitive market analysis, as well as the management and protection of intellectual property portfolios. He holds a BASc in Electrical Engineering from the University of Windsor, Canada, and an MBA from Rotman School of Management at the University of Toronto, Canada.

Keywords: collaborative idea management, collaboration, innovation, open innovation, crowdsourcing, culture, strategy, leadership

2

Does Social Innovation Require Social Entrepreneurship?

Asceline Groot and Ben Dankbaar

" *Nobody talks of entrepreneurship as survival,* "
but that's exactly what it is.

Anita Roddick (1942–2007)
Founder of The Body Shop

Social innovation is now considered an important element in the search for solutions to pressing social problems. Inspired by Schumpeter's conceptualization of innovation, "social" entrepreneurship is thought to contribute to "social" innovation in more or less the same way that "normal" entrepreneurship consists of the introduction of "normal" innovations. In the literature as well as in practice, the definition of concepts such as social innovation and social entrepreneurship has led to considerable confusion. We aim to bring clarity to the debate, arguing that every entrepreneurial action results in some measure of intended or unintended social innovation, regardless of whether the entrepreneurs in question are considered or consider themselves "social" or not. We test our insights in an investigation of 20 social enterprises that have a commercial business model.

Introduction

In the European Union, social innovation is currently widely debated and considered an important element in all efforts to meet the "grand challenges" advanced societies are facing today: environmental degradation, climate change, declining birth rates, high levels of immigration, the rising costs of healthcare, the increasing number of elderly people, rising costs of healthcare, poverty and social exclusion, security of the citizenry, protection of critical infrastructures against terrorist attacks, etc. Given the complexity of these problems, no simple and politically uncontroversial solutions are available. Efforts to introduce major changes in the social welfare system, in healthcare and pensions, and in energy and mobility systems become bogged down in political conflict or end up in compromises that satisfy no one.

In contrast to such efforts toward reform undertaken by the public sector, social innovation is seen as a matter of private initiative. All over Europe, private initiatives that aim to tackle social problems and contribute to a more inclusive, more secure, and more sustainable society are flourishing. Social innovation is seen as complementary and sometimes as corrective to changes in public arrangements, but also as a source of inspiration, experimentation, and a catalyst for change, forcing the public as well as private actors to change their behaviour. Against this background, there is also a growing interest in what is called "social entrepreneurship" (Dees, 2001; Peredo & McLean, 2006; Seelos & Mair, 2005; Short et al., 2009). As we demonstrate later, there are many different definitions of social entrepreneurship, but they all concentrate on entrepreneurial action with social intentions.

In this article, we focus on the connection between social entrepreneurship and social innovation. In the first two sections, we discuss the concepts of social innovation and social entrepreneurship in more detail. In the third section, we argue that the distinction between social entrepreneurship and "normal" entrepreneurship is far from clear, especially if the focus lies on actual social impact instead of intentions. In the fourth section, we test our insights by looking at the characteristics of 20 enterprises in The Netherlands that are generally considered to be "social". In a final section, we offer our conclusions and suggestions for further research.

Social Innovation

Considerable literature on social innovation has come into existence over the past two decades, recently culminating in *The International Handbook on Social Innovation* (Moulaert et al., 2013). In North America, social innovation is usually associated with initiatives in and by the public sector, sometimes also in the form of public-private partnerships. In the European context, the concept of social innovation usually refers to private initiatives to solve specific problems and fulfil specific needs, originally mainly in the field of social care and security (Leadbeater, 1998). Some of these problems and needs had come to the surface as a consequence of the retreat of the welfare state starting in the 1980s. Others had never been adequately covered or solved by the institutions of the welfare state: loneliness among the elderly, petty crime and violence among high school dropouts, or diminishing social cohesion in multi-cultural neighbourhoods. Social innovation took the form of local initiatives to tackle these problems, often at the level of a single neighbourhood.

The International Handbook on Social Innovation argues that social innovation "means fostering inclusion and wellbeing though improving social relations and empowerment processes: imagining and pursuing a world, a nation, a region, a locality, a community that would grant universal rights and be more socially inclusive" (Moulaert et al., 2013). The European Union, which has recently supported various activities in the area of social innovation, defines social innovations as "new ideas (products, services, and models) that simultaneously meet social needs (more effectively than alternatives) and create new social relationships or collaborations" (Dro et al., 2011). This definition is very similar to textbook definitions of innovation with the addition of the adjective "social". The reference to "new social relationships" brings it close to the definition from the handbook. However, in the handbook approach, social innovation tends to be located in the so-called "third sector", which consists of non-governmental and non-profit organizations. Texts published by the European Commission, however, show that the meaning of social innovation is expanding in two directions (European Commission, 2010; Dro et al., 2011). On the one hand, it is argued that social innovation can be initiated everywhere in the economy, not just in the non-profit sector, but also in the public and private sectors. On the other hand, social innovation is, in these texts, not limited to issues of welfare and social inclusion, but may also be concerned with issues of environmental protection and sustainable development. Thus,

a program matching students looking for accommodation with older people living on their own in Oporto, Portugal, is considered just as much a social innovation as a cooperative enterprise set up to revive beekeeping in Copenhagen, Denmark (European Commission, 2010). Social innovation is seen to be concerned with "the development of what are currently viewed as assets for sustainable development: environmental, human and social capital" (Dro et al., 2011).

What are measures of success for social innovation? Obviously, an innovation needs to survive for some period of time in order to be recognized as successful and indeed to be recognized as a social innovation in the first place. But is survival enough? Shouldn't there be some kind of diffusion of the innovation, a spreading to other locations and maybe even other countries? And what about funding? What if the social innovation only has survived because it has attracted public funding? Social innovation has attracted interest because it was based on private initiative and promised to supplement and even replace public arrangements. It would become less interesting if it were to depend on public funding. On the other hand, one can argue that an important measure of success for privately initiated social innovation is that it becomes institutionalized. Institutionalization can involve public funding of similar initiatives in other places and communities, outside its original place of invention. But, institutionalization can also take the form of a change in behaviour by a substantial number of people (e.g., refusing plastic bags in supermarkets) or a new code of conduct for multinational corporations (e.g., purchasing textiles in developing economies). Successful social innovation will indeed be characterized by some form of formalization, institutionalization, or by changes in behaviour by a substantial number of people or companies. Differences may arise with regard to questions of scale. How many people should be involved in a local initiative before it can be called social innovation? What share of the population must change their behaviour before we speak of successful social innovation?

Social Entrepreneurship

As noted, social innovation is usually a result of private initiative. The initiative can also come from people working in the public sector, but new social legislation initiated by politicians is usually not seen as social innovation – however innovative it may be. The people engaged in social innovation have an idea – a product, service, or model (Dro et al., 2011) – to meet an unfulfilled need. In line with Schumpeter (1934), who argued that innovation is the essence of entrepreneurship, social innovation is therefore associated with "social entrepreneurship".

There is a considerable literature on social entrepreneurship, which partly overlaps with the literature on social innovation. However, although definitions of social innovation have been relatively uncontroversial, there is considerable debate on the definition of social entrepreneurship (Mair & Marti 2006; Dacin et al., 2010). For some authors, social entrepreneurship is by definition not for profit (Dees et al., 2002; Weerawardena & Mort, 2006), whereas others argue that there is no such thing as entrepreneurship without profit (Acs et al., 2011; Marshall, 2010; Wilson & Post, 2011). Some authors emphasize that the concept should not be constrained by the profit/not-for-profit discussion (Dees & Battle Anderson, 2006; Kramer, 2005; Santos, 2009). Moreover, on closer inspection, the meaning of "non-profit" appears far from clear. Does it imply living off charity and subsidies? Does it include making no profits, but generating income to cover costs? Or making profits, but sharing profits with stakeholders?

Circular definitions abound in the literature, with "social" appearing on both sides of the equation. Social entrepreneurs are, for instance, defined as producers of social value – where social value remains largely undefined. Sometimes, social value is considered purely separate from economic value, but in other cases, economic value is seen as a type of social value, and then there are various options in between (Auerswald, 2009; Lumpkin et al., 2013). Obviously, there is no metric scale for happiness, active aging, social cohesion, or security. Some authors therefore underline that "social entrepreneurs" and "business entrepreneurs" have different ways of measuring performance. Contrary to business entrepreneurs, social entrepreneurs have a "double bottom line" in which social value appears next to financial value (Acs et al., 2013; Lumpkin et al., 2013). Other authors emphasize that social entrepreneurship is also a question of governance: both in the business process and in performance measurement, all stakeholders should play a role. Social entrepreneurship is then closely related to economic democracy.

Because of the lack of clear definitions, the literature is full of examples and case studies that are used to illustrate the authors' understanding of social entrepreneurship (Dees, 2001; Mort et al., 2003). Others criticize this approach (Mair & Marti, 2006; Peredo & McLean, 2007; Seelos & Mair, 2005) because it tends to focus on successful "heroes" and therefore fails to include the countless initiatives that falter or fail. Central to the discussion is the use of the adjective "social". In practice, people have different ideas of what is social and what is not. The term social appears to be inherently subjective. The meaning can differ between countries, but even between different regions of one country. It is negotiable and stakeholders can agree on what it is and what it is not (Lumpkin et al., 2013; Santos, 2009).

Social Entrepreneurs and "Normal" Entrepreneurship

Here, we focus on social entrepreneurs, who aim to be independent of public funding, charity, or gifts. They may receive some initial public funding or soft loans from a supportive patron, but they have a business model that aims at long-term survival without such support. In fact, we agree with other authors that, only in such cases, it is justifiable and interesting to speak of entrepreneurship. These social entrepreneurs aim to bring about change in society and support movement towards sustainable development by means of activities that raise so much income that all costs are covered and the enterprise remains financially independent. Looking at these social entrepreneurs, two important observations can be made.

First, these entrepreneurs need to be profitable in order to survive. Social entrepreneurs want to meet social needs, stimulate social change, or induce responsible behaviour. Therefore, making a profit may seem less relevant to them (Dees & Battle Anderson, 2006; Kramer, 2005; Santos, 2009). However, just like other entrepreneurs, they must find resources for their business: human capital, money, knowledge, etc. (Austin et al., 2006). Acquiring these resources involves costs. Social entrepreneurs will need to make some sort of profit in order to run a sustainable business, cover their costs, and manage their own risks and the risks of their investors, even while they are constantly led by their social mission. They have indeed a "double bottom line" with social and commercial purposes. Social entrepreneurs may need investors who step in for the long run and support them until they are able to pay the money back – but they do have to pay it back. From this perspective, social entrepreneurs do not differ very much from normal business entrepreneurs. Making profit is not their main aim, but they need to be profitable, or at least cover all relevant costs, in order to survive. In fact, there is a category of "social" enterprises that have been explicitly set up to make maximum profits for the benefit of some specific charity, for example, the commercial activities undertaken by the United Nations Children's Fund (UNICEF).

A second observation is that quite a few business entrepreneurs may not see themselves as social entrepreneurs, but are similarly less interested in profits and are more interested in, for instance, selling their invention or maintaining jobs in the business they have built up or inherited from their parents. The adjective "social" suggests that normal "business" entrepreneurs are not social or are even anti-social – something most of them would emphatically deny. And, what to do with "normal" entrepreneurs, who realize innovations with positive social impact? Take the Internet service Skype. A large number of elderly people have been able to be in regular contact with their children and grandchildren and even see them on screen without having to pay expensive telephone bills. For eliminating the isolation of elderly people, Skype could be called a social innovation. However, it is seldom classified as such, because its creators did not have "social" intentions. Unless we want to define social entrepreneurship purely in terms of declared intentions, it turns out to be far from easy to distinguish the social entrepreneur from the normal business entrepreneur.

These two observations lead us to the conclusion that distinguishing social entrepreneurs from business entrepreneurs is not very useful if not impossible, because the two categories show considerable overlap. We also reject the idea that social businesses have a double bottom line, whereas normal businesses do not. Instead, we think it is far more useful to acknowledge that every business has a financial as well as a social bottom line. Every company has some social and environmental impact (positive or negative), regardless of whether it is intended or not. Moreover, many "ordinary" enterprises today want to behave in a "socially responsible" way or, for example, have set themselves targets to reduce their CO_2 footprint or mitigate other negative environmental impacts. If we move away from intentions and towards actual impact, some "normal" enterprises may turn out to be more social than some "social" enterprises. Arguing along similar lines, Pol and Ville (2009) have argued that social innovations and what they call business innovations show considerable overlap. However, they insist on maintaining the distinction. Our point is that it is more useful to consider "social" and "business" as dimensions of all innovations. Some innovations may score low on social and high on business or the other way around and many may score high on both, but any effort to draw a line between the two is arbitrary.

Two important implications can be drawn from this line of reasoning. First, there is no a priori reason why social entrepreneurs should be less profitable than normal entrepreneurs. Second, if social entrepreneurs want to receive special treatment because of their social goals, it is useful and indeed necessary to judge them on their impact, not their intentions, and to compare their impact with that of normal business entrepreneurs.

Examining Twenty "Social" Enterprises

With these implications in mind, we have taken a closer look at 20 Dutch social enterprises with a business model based on generating revenue through sales to customers. All of them are widely considered as "social" enterprises. The cases were selected from the network of the online community of ASN Bank (asnbank.nl), a medium-sized Dutch bank that focuses on sustainable investments, and the website of the Dutch organisation Social Enterprise NL (social-enterprise.nl). The mission of the consumer bank ASN is to promote sustainability in society. The economic conduct of the bank (i.e., investing the savings entrusted to it by its clients) is guided by that principle and is based on three criteria: i) promoting and defending human rights (people); ii) preventing climate change; and iii) maintaining biodiversity on the planet. The bank does not lend money to enterprises, it only invests in various securities, but it provides social entrepreneurs with network linkages, knowledge, training, and some start-up money through its online community of over 50,000 members and 1,000 projects and startups. We selected enterprises with paying customers and a business-to-consumer strategy from four different areas, which relate to the themes of the online community: i) fashion and design; ii) food; iii) social cohesion; and iv) energy and technology. The enterprises vary in scope and scale from local to national and international.

We are interested in three questions:

1. What is the social impact of these enterprises?

2. Is their social impact considerably higher than that of similar "ordinary" enterprises active in the same market?

3. Are these enterprises financially viable? An enterprise that is financially viable, but has no extraordinary social impact, cannot be called a "social" enterprise; an enterprise that aims to achieve an extraordinary social impact, but fails to survive without permanent financial support, stops being an enterprise.

In this article, we focus mainly on questions 1 and 3; question 2 is an area of ongoing research.

We base our analysis primarily on information available on the websites of these enterprises, but we contacted the companies if their website did not include some of the information needed (e.g., figures on turnover and number of sales transactions). Table 1 provides a brief overview of the cases.

All of these enterprises have paying customers. Although some of the companies also engage in business-to-business activities, they all operate in the consumer market. The number of customers varies greatly, as measured by the number of consumers buying the company's product in shops or through other sales channels. Because some of the enterprises did not want precise figures to become public, we distinguish three different ranges: small (up to 5,000 customers); medium (between 5,000 and 25,000); and large (more than 25,000 customers per year). These ranges allow rough, relative comparisons; but of course, it is easier to reach a large number of customers selling chocolate bars than solar lights.

Looking at the aims of the enterprises, we distinguish between "people" (e.g., social cohesion, human rights) and "planet" (e.g., saving energy, recycling, improving biodiversity) on the one hand and between enterprises aiming to change the behaviour of individual consumers and enterprises promoting institutional change (e.g., influencing large corporations or policy makers). Based on these two dimensions, we have placed the 20 enterprises in a 2x2 matrix (Figure 1) based on their primary focus. Obviously, some of these enterprises aim to help people as well as the planet, and it is not always easy to say where their primary focus lies. However, we use this matrix only as a heuristic device, to see if grouping enterprises along these lines leads to additional insights. The enterprises with a large number of customers (i.e., more than 25,000) or that are operating on an international level are printed in bold and italics.

Fourteen of the enterprises studied aim to influence consumer behaviour as their primary focus and they include several large enterprises with over 25,000 customers a year. Six enterprises focus primarily on influencing institutions, three of which have an international scope. First, note that there are large enterprises in each section of the matrix. Size (i.e., turnover, number of customers, international presence) is obviously a measure of social impact. Apparently, it is possible to be successful regardless of whether the primary focus of the enterprise is on people, the planet, influencing behaviour, or effecting institutional change. A second observation is that there are many more enterprises combining a focus on the planet and influencing behaviour. Of course, this bias may be a result of our selection, and we cannot claim to present a representative sample. Nevertheless, we do not think this finding is a coincidence. It seems to be far easier to convince con-

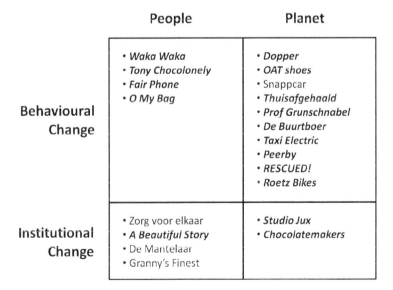

Figure 1. Primary focus of the 20 enterprises in this study.
(The names of large or international enterprises are printed in bold and italics.)

Table 1. Details of the 20 enterprises in this investigation *(continued on next page...)*

Theme	Enterprise	Mission Statement	Type	Customer Base*	Scale
Food	**Tony Chocolonely** www.tonychocolonely.nl	Crazy about chocolate, serious about people	For profit	Large	National
	Chocolatemakers chocolatemakers.nl	(Not mentioned on the website)	For profit	Large	International
	De Buurtboer debuurtboer.nl	To stimulate the use of biological, local, and seasonal products in company canteens.	For profit	Large	National
	Professor Grunschnabel grunschnabel.nl	Natural vegetable ice cream	For profit	Large	International
Fashion & Design	**Studio Jux** studiojux.nl	Studio JUX = design + eco + fair (people, planet, profit). Sustainability is in our DNA.	For profit	Large	International
	A Beautiful Story abeautifulstory.nl	A beautiful story improves fair trade by creating opportunities for producers in a difficult economic environment.	For profit	Large	International
	O My Bag omybag.nl	We, at O My Bag make great bags that will not only make you happy, but also the world around you. We aim to harness the power of business to create social change.	For profit	Large	International
	Granny's Finest grannysfinest.nl	Kickstart young designer talent and improve the well being of elderly people.	Non-profit /hybrid	Small	National
	RESCUED! rescued.nl	RESCUED! Stands for the indoor and outdoor products that are made of used materials, with respect for their original beauty.	For profit	Medium	International
	OAT Shoes oatshoes.com	Our future lies in a reconciliation between industry and nature, between mankind and nature. We have to close the loop, come full circle and realize we're an integral part of the whole thing.	For profit	–	International
	Roetz Bikes roetz-bikes.com	Roetz-Bikes makes stylish city bikes with hands and heart, bikes with a history that are ready for a second life.	For profit	Small	International
	Dopper dopper.nl	Dopper stops plastic waste.	For profit	Large	International

Table 1. Details of the 20 enterprises in this investigation *(...continued from previous page)*

Theme	Enterprise	Mission Statement	Type	Customer Base*	Scale
Social Cohesion	**Mantelaar** demantelaar.nl	Mantelaar is the second-best solution for elderly people in need.	For profit	Small	National
	Zorg voor Elkaar zorgvoorelkaar.com	Zorg voor Elkaar is an online marketplace for volunteers and professionals who want to help others.	Co-operative	Medium	National
	Taxi Electric taxielectric.nl	Our mission is to be the most client oriented and cleanest taxi service in the Netherlands.	For profit	Large	National
	Thuisafgehaald thuisafgehaald.nl	Thuisafgehaald improves the social cohesion in neighbourhoods by making it possible to share food and reduces waste.	Founda-tion	Large	International
	Peerby peerby.nl	80% of the products we own are used only once a month. Why buy if you can borrow for free?	Profit	Large	International
	Snappcar snappcar.nl	Snapp car tries to reduce the number of cars by making it possible to share your car with others and as a by-product meet new people too.	For profit	N/A	National
Energy & Technology	**Waka Waka** waka-waka.com	Waka Waka makes the world's most efficient lights and chargers on solar energy. High tech, cheap and a solution for people without electricity all over the world.	For profit	Large	International
	Fair Phone fairphone.com	Fairphone is a social enterprise working to create a fairer economy and change how things are made. We open up supply chains, solve problems and use transparency to start debate about what's truly fair.	For profit	Large	International

* Small = up to 5,000; Medium = 5,000 – 25,000; Large = > 25,000 customers

sumers to buy products with a positive environmental story than products with a story that focuses on people. For the latter purpose, consumers are more inclined to think in terms of either donations and charity or in terms of state responsibilities. Similarly, there are fewer enterprises having a primary focus on institutional change than on influencing individual behaviour, but it is interesting to note that promoting institutional change can be the focus of profitable entrepreneurial activities and not just of non-governmental organizations and non-profit organizations.

The 20 enterprises clearly differ in their social impact. Apart from the number of customers they reach, they differ in geographical scope and in the breadth of their impact on people, the environment, or both. Waka Waka, for instance, scores high on all of these points. It has distributed 97,209 solar lights and chargers in 25 countries. Its product is environmentally friendly and allows people to (learn to) read in the evening hours in places where no electricity is available. An enterprise such as Granny's Finest has a far more limited scale and scope, but we do not argue here that Waka Waka is more social than Granny's Finest. It would be easy to develop a scale on which Waka Waka could be shown to be more social, but it would probably be as controversial as earlier efforts in that direction. The point we would like to make here, is that such scales should and can be applied to ordinary enterprises just as well as to so-called social enterprises. It should be possible to measure the social impact of normal enterprises with, for instance, an ambitious corporate social responsibility strategy just as easily as measuring the impact of social enterprises.

Conclusions

The main contribution of this article is a clarification of the concept of social entrepreneurship. We propose that "social" should not be used as an adjective to entrepreneurship, which suggests that some entrepreneurs are social and others are not, but as a dimension of the results of entrepreneurial action. Entrepreneurship can have social results, intended (by what are often called social entrepreneurs), but also unintended (when a business idea leads to social change) or maybe half-intended. New ideas, new products, or new services, may turn out to be social innovations regardless of any social impact intended by the inventor. It may well be far easier to define, distinguish, and compare the social impact of enterprises than to come up with a solid criterion to distinguish "social" enterprises from "regular" enterprises. At the same time, focusing on impact instead of on intentions makes it far easier to treat "social" entrepreneurs as "normal" entrepreneurs, who have to meet certain standards to stay in business.

Our investigation of 20 social enterprises shows that these companies with a variety of social intentions can be successful in terms of their customer base, their turnover, and indeed their profitability. Conversely, we argue that "normal" enterprises can also be successful in terms of their actual impact on human rights, climate, biodiversity, etc. Therefore, social enterprises should allow themselves to be compared with normal businesses with regard to their impact. If they are truly "social", they should perform much higher on various indicators of social impact than ordinary businesses, while at the same time showing a financial performance that guarantees survival. The aim of this article is therefore to put an end to considerable confusion in the literature concerning the definition of social entrepreneurship. At least for the category of social entrepreneurs that do not want to depend on charity or government subsidies, we have shown that it is more fruitful for all stakeholders to consider "social" as a "normal" dimension of all entrepreneurship, regardless of the intentions or self-image of the entrepreneur.

We see several important practical implications arising from our research. First of all, it is important to encourage would-be social entrepreneurs to learn from "normal" entrepreneurs. Instead of thinking of themselves as incomparable, the social entrepreneurs should learn to see themselves as not that much different from ordinary entrepreneurs. This perspective will in all likelihood lead to more attention for the financial aspects of the business and therefore contribute to the viability and success of the social enterprise.

Second, "normal" entrepreneurs should be encouraged to think about possibilities to engage in social innovation instead of thinking that social innovation is something for government, foundations, charity, or non-profit organizations. By uncovering the social dimension of their activities, companies may find ways to increase their impact and at the same time improve their competitive performance.

Third, political actors have been encouraged to think of social change as the result not just of legislative action, but also of social entrepreneurship. It is important for them to realize that social innovation can also be a product of normal business entrepreneurship.

Finally, further research is needed to compare avowed social enterprises with normal enterprises. For this purpose, efforts to create valid indicators for the social impact of enterprises need to be intensified. Such efforts can build on the work done in the fields of corporate social responsibility, quality of work, fair trade, and sustainability.

Social innovation is apparently happening in many places: in the public sector, in the non-profit sector, and also in the private sector. It can result from actions undertaken by public authorities and political actors as well as from private initiatives, both profit and non-profit. Thus, the answer to the question raised in the title of this paper should be "no". Social innovation does not require social entrepreneurship, because there are other sources of social innovation. And, if we limit ourselves to the private sector, we have seen that social innovation can also be a product of normal business entrepreneurship. Social innovations should not be considered hugely different and separate from other innovations that are constantly being introduced by businesses. Thus, also in the private sector, social innovation does not require social entrepreneurship, but like any other innovation it does require entrepreneurship.

Acknowledgements

An earlier version of this paper was presented at the first ISPIM Americas Innovation Forum in Montreal, Canada, on October 5–8, 2014. The International Society for Professional Innovation Management (ISPIM; ispim.org) is a network of researchers, industrialists, consultants, and public bodies who share an interest in innovation management. The authors are grateful for comments received at the conference as well as from anonymous reviewers.

About the Authors

Asceline Groot is Senior Communications Officer at ASN Bank, a Dutch consumer bank that focuses on sustainable investments. She is responsible for the online community of ASN Bank "Voor de Wereld van Morgen| (For the World of Tomorrow). She is also a part-time PhD candidate at the Institute of Management Research of the Radboud University Nijmegen, The Netherlands. Her research is concerned with the effects of social entrepreneurs on society. She is the author of the books *Het Nieuwe Groen* (The New Green) and *Dromen voor Altijd* (Dreams for Ever).

Ben Dankbaar is Emeritus Professor of Innovation Management at Radboud University Nijmegen, The Netherlands. He is currently a part-time professor at the Automotive Institute of the HAN University of Applied Sciences in Nijmegen, The Netherlands, and he is partner in InnoTeP (Innovation in Theory and Practice). He studied social sciences and economics at the University of Amsterdam and has a PhD in Economics from the University of Maastricht in The Netherlands. Ben Dankbaar has published widely on issues of technical change, work organization, innovation management, and industrial policy. He is also an expert on developments in the automobile industry.

References

Acs, Z. J., Boardman, M. C., & McNeely, C. L. 2013. The Social Value of Productive Entrepreneurship. *Small Business Economics*, 40(3): 785–796.
http://dx.doi.org/10.1007/s11187-011-9396-6

Auerswald, P. 2009. Creating Social Value. *Stanford Social Innovation Review*, Spring 2009: 50–55.

Austin, J., Stevenson, H., & Wei-Skillern, J. 2006. Social and Commercial Entrepreneurship: Same, Different or Both? *Entrepreneurship Theory and Proactive*, 30(1): 1–22.
http://dx.doi.org/10.1111/j.1540-6520.2006.00107.x

Dacin, P. A., Dacin, M. T., & Matear, M. 2010. Social Entrepreneurship: Why We Don't Need a New Theory and How We Move Forward from Here. *Academy of Management Perspectives*, 24(3): 37–57.

Dees, J. G. 2001. *The Meaning of "Social Entrepreneurship"*. Stanford, CA: Stanford Graduate Business School.

Dees, J. G., Emerson, J., & Economy, P. (Eds). 2002. *Strategic Tools for Social Entrepreneurs: Enhancing the Performance of Your Enterprising Nonprofit*. New York: John Wiley & Sons, Inc.

Dees, J. G., Battle Anderson, B. 2006. Framing a Theory on Social Entrepreneurship: Building on Two Schools of Practice and Thought. *ARNOVA Occasional Paper Series*, 1(3). Aspen, CO: Aspen Institute.

Dro, I., Therace, A., & Hubert, A. 2011. *Empowering People, Driving Change: Social Innovation in the European Union*. Brussels: European Commission.
http://dx.doi.org/10.2796/13155

European Commission. 2010. *This is European Social Innovation*. Brussels: European Commission.
http://dx.doi.org/10.2769/825

Kramer, M. 2005. *Measuring Innovation: Evaluation in the Field of Social Entrepreneurship*. Boston, MA: Foundation Strategy Group.

Leadbeater, C. 1999. *Living on Thin Air*. London: Penguin Books.

Lumpkin, G. T., Moss, T. W., Gras, D. M., Kato, S., & Amezcua, A. S. 2013. Entrepreneurial Processes in Social Contexts: How Are They Different, If at All? *Journal of Small Business Economics*, 40(3): 761–783.
http://dx.doi.org/10.1007/s11187-011-9399-3

Mair, J., & Marti, I. 2006. Social Entrepreneurship Research: A Source of Explanation, Prediction, and Delight. *Journal of World Business*, 41(1): 36–44.
http://dx.doi.org/10.1016/j.jwb.2005.09.002

Marshall, R. S. 2010. Conceptualizing the International For-Profit Social Entrepreneur. *Journal of Business Ethics*, 98(2): 183–198.
http://dx.doi.org/10.1007/s10551-010-0545-7

Mort, G. S., Weerawardena, J., & Carnegie, K. 2003. Social Entrepreneurship: Towards Conceptualisation. *International Journal of Entrepreneurial Behaviour & Research*, 8(1): 76–88.
http://dx.doi.org/10.1002/nvsm.202

Moulaert, F., MacCallum, D., Mehmood, A., & Hamdouch, A. (Eds.). 2013. *The International Handbook on Social Innovation*. Cheltenham: Edward Elgar

Peredo, A. M., & McLean, M. 2006. Social Entrepreneurship: A Critical Review of the Concept. *Journal of World Business*, 41(1): 56–65.
http://dx.doi.org/10.1016/j.jwb.2005.10.007

Pol, E. & Ville, S. 2009. Social Innovation: Buzz Word or Enduring Term? *The Journal of Socio-Economics*, 38(6): 878–885.
http://dx.doi.org/10.1016/j.socec.2009.02.011

Santos, F. M. 2012. A Positive Theory on Social Entrepreneurship. *Journal of Business Ethics*, 111(3): 335–351.
http://dx.doi.org/10.1007/s10551-012-1413-4

Schumpeter, J. A. 1934. (Reprinted in 1980.) *The Theory of Economic Development*. London: Oxford University Press.

Short, J. C., Moss, T. W., & Lumpkin, G. T. 2009. Research in Social Entrepreneurship: Past Contributions and Future Opportunities. *Strategic Entrepreneurship Journal*, 3(2): 161–194.
http://dx.doi.org/10.1002/sej.69

Seelos, C., & Mair, J. 2005. Social Entrepreneurship: Creating New Business Models to Serve the Poor. *Business Horizons*, 48(3): 241–246.
http://dx.doi.org/10.1016/j.bushor.2004.11.006

Thompson, J. 2002. The World of the Social Entrepreneur. *International Journal of Public Sector Management*, 15(5): 412–431.
http://dx.doi.org/10.1108/09513550210435746

Weerawardena, J., & Mort, G. S. 2006. Investigating Social Entrepreneurship: A Multidimensional Model. *Journal of World Business*, 41(1): 21–35.
http://dx.doi.org/10.1016/j.jwb.2005.09.001

Wilson, F., & Post, J. E. 2013. Business Models for People, Planet (& Profits): Exploring the Phenomena of Social Business, a Market-Based Approach to Social Value Creation. *Journal of Small Business Economics*, 40(3): 715–737.
http://dx.doi.org/10.1007/s11187-011-9401-0

Keywords: social innovation, social entrepreneurship, Schumpeter, social change, institutional change, sustainability, entrepreneurship

Table 1. Most popular TIM Review articles published from October 2013 to September 2014*

Rank	Article (http://timreview.ca/article/)	Author(s)	Issue
1	**From Idea Crowdsourcing to Managing User Knowledge** (timreview.ca/article/750)	Rajala et al.	December 2013 *Living Labs and Crowdsourcing*
2	**Risk Management in Crowdsourcing-Based Business Ecosystems** (751)	Kannangara & Uguccioni	December 2013 *Living Labs and Crowdsourcing*
3	**3D Printing: A Revolutionary Advance for the Field of Urology?** (772)	Neu	March 2014 *Emerging Technologies*
4	**Formulating an Executive Strategy for Big Data Analytics** (773)	Palem	March 2014 *Emerging Technologies*
5	**The Businesses of Open Data and Open Source: Some Key Similarities and Differences** (757)	Lindman & Nyman	January 2014 *Open Source Business*
6	**Corporate Lifecycles: Modelling the Dynamics of Innovation and Its Support Infrastructure** (733)	Koplyay et al.	October 2013 *Managing Innovation*
7	**Developing a Social Network as a Means of Obtaining Entrepreneurial Knowledge Needed for Internationalization** (827)	Han & Afolabi	September 2014 *Insights*
8	**Collaborative Idea Management: A Driver of Continuous Innovation** (764)	Bank & Raza	February 2014 *Seeking Solutions*
9	**Open Innovation Processes in Living Lab Innovation Systems: Insights from the LeYLab** (743)	Schuurman et al.	November 2013 *Living Labs*
10	**Using Boundary Management for More Effective Product Development** (734)	Thomson & Thomson	October 2013 *Managing Innovation*
11	**A Living Lab as a Service: Creating Value for Micro-enterprises through Collaboration and Innovation** (744)	Ståhlbröst	November 2013 *Living Labs*
12	**Linking Living Lab Characteristics and Their Outcomes: Towards a Conceptual Framework** (748)	Veeckman et al.	December 2013 *Living Labs and Crowdsourcing*
13	**IT Consumerization: A Case Study of BYOD in a Healthcare Setting** (771)	Marshall	March 2014 *Emerging Technologies*
14	**Innovation in Services: A Literature Review** (780)	Morrar	April 2014 *Service and Innovation*
15	**Actor Roles in an Urban Living Lab: What Can We Learn from Suurpelto, Finland?** (742)	Juujärvi & Pesso	November 2013 *Living Labs*
↑	**The Government of India's Role in Promoting Innovation through Policy Initiatives for Entrepreneurship Development** (818)	Abhyankar	August 2014, *Innovation and Entrepreneurship in India*
↑	**Widening the Perspective on Industrial Innovation: A Service-Dominant-Logic Approach** (791)	Korhonen	May 2014 *Service and Innovation*
↑	**Entrepreneurship Education in India: A Critical Assessment and a Proposed Framework** (817)	Basu	August 2014, *Innovation and Entrepreneurship in India*
↑	**Conceptualizing Innovation in Born-Global Firms** (826)	Zijdemans & Tanev	September 2014 *Insights*
↑	**Product and Service Interaction in the Chinese Online Game Industry** (789)	Ström & Ernkvist	May 2014 *Service and Innovation*

*The rankings are based on website traffic to timreview.ca from October 1, 2013 to September 30, 2014. The list also includes 5 recently published articles (denoted by ↑) that would appear in the main list if only traffic from June 1, 2014 to November 30, 2014 were considered.

3

From Idea Crowdsourcing to Managing User Knowledge

Risto Rajala, Mika Westerlund, Mervi Vuori, and Jukka-Pekka Hares

" Crowdsourcing will shift its focus from individuals " solving individual problems to a more collaboration-based model. Groups of people will be engaged to solve more complex problems, and the power of the crowdsourcing engine will be used to create crack virtual teams that you can build locally.

Chris McNamara
COO, DesignCrowd
tinyurl.com/k7gorac

This article explores how technology companies can benefit from user knowledge in product and service innovation beyond mere idea generation through crowdsourcing. We investigate a case from the telecommunications sector to discover the ways a company can overcome the challenges of motivating users to participate in innovation activity and gaining from their knowledge in the innovation process. In particular, we seek to learn how the company has created understanding about the future uses of technology and the developments of the market with the lead users. In addition, we analyze the key means of capturing value from the knowledge gathered from the users, including the essential organizational practices that support user innovation and the ways the company makes sense of the vast volume and variety of user knowledge. Our empirical inquiry increases the understanding of how technology companies can complement and use crowdsourcing to effectively utilize knowledge resident in user communities.

Introduction

There is a growing appreciation for the value of resources that lie beyond a firm's organizational boundaries and can be tapped into for innovation purposes and R&D collaboration with suppliers, universities, customers, or even competitors (Un et al., 2010; tinyurl.com/mlcbg5t). Users can be considered as one important source of innovation, and user innovation has been recognized as one central research stream within the open innovation phenomenon (Gassman, 2006; tinyurl.com/n5fq3gs). The unique knowledge held by users is perceived as a valuable resource for innovation because it improves understanding of real-life situations where the company's product or service is used (Poetz and Schreier, 2012; tinyurl.com/lgham7n). Previous research shows that innovations created by lead users

have been regarded commercially attractive. Moreover, it has been shown that the needs of lead users indicate how the market is to change in the future (von Hippel, 2005; tinyurl.com/57xp5x). Also, Piller and Walcher (2006; tinyurl.com/m9nkb4r) show that innovations developed with lead users can be successfully commercialized. Hence, it is reasonable to think that, from an innovation management perspective, companies should engage users – especially lead users – in ideation processes to devise desirable solutions.

Given that the knowledge needed for innovation is becoming increasingly distributed across organizational boundaries (Swan et al., 1999; tinyurl.com/cgy3gje), the task of capturing user ideas and transforming them into commercialized innovations poses a challenge for companies. Although many companies have resorted to user design toolkits to capture users' ideas (Thomke and von Hippel, 2002; tinyurl.com/l6vb5gq), crowd-sourcing has become an increasingly popular tool for acquiring external knowledge and ideas (Djelassi and Decoopman, 2013: tinyurl.com/lqfbrxg; Feller et al., 2012: tinyurl.com/l8oxsle). Crowdsourcing is characterized by the voluntary participation of a diverse crowd in a problem-solving initiative from a sponsoring organiza-tion that chooses from among the generated ideas and solutions (cf. Estellés-Arolas and Gonzales-Ladron-de-Guerva, 2012; tinyurl.com/ma8ohjg). A company that initi-ates a crowdsourcing initiative is usually exploring in-novative solutions that may include new sources of revenue in the form of new products, new services, or even new business models (Dahlander and Gann, 2010: tinyurl.com/chacrs9; Djelassi and Decoopman, 2013: tinyurl.com/lqfbrxg).

But does crowdsourcing lead to increased or improved innovation? Leimeister and colleagues (2009; tinyurl.com/adzjqv6) argue that idea contests promoting the competitive nature of idea crowdsourcing may ac-tually lead to less collaboration and information shar-ing among contributors. Likewise, the absence of discourse – the ability to share various perspectives and build on each other's knowledge amongst crowd-sourcing participants – can inhibit co-creation in innovation (Majchrzak and Malhotra, 2013; tinyurl.com/mu6ypck). Although these challenges relate to the incent-ives associated with the implementation of crowd-sourcing, the issue of how a company can actually transform knowledge generated by crowdsourcing into viable innovations that outperform the competition re-mains a major challenge for any organization. Thus, there is a need for more research on the mechanisms, concepts, and tools to manage the wisdom of crowds, as well as on filling the conceptual gap between the generation and the selection of ideas and their trans-formation into innovations (Ebner et al., 2009; tinyurl.com/mwm2yfm).

This study aims to increase the understanding on *how technology companies can move beyond using crowd-sourcing to collect ideas to a more systematic and nu-anced way of using crowdsourcing to manage user knowledge*. In particular, the study focuses on the ways an organization can utilize crowdsourcing to gather knowledge from the users and subsequently comple-ment and use this knowledge in new product and ser-vice development. In doing so, the study examines: i) which motivations companies perceive as essential for users to share their knowledge for innovation pur-

poses, ii) what the key organizational practices are that support effective user innovation management, and iii) what the key challenges are from a knowledge manage-ment perspective. We believe that addressing these questions through an empirical inquiry is of interest to scholars and practitioners of innovation.

The New Role of Users as Innovators

External contributors are becoming ever more import-ant sources of knowledge and innovation for commer-cial product and service development. The literature on innovation management links customers to the success of product and service innovation (e.g., Von Hippel et al., 2011: tinyurl.com/cc98mlb; Coviello and Joseph, 2012: tinyurl.com/lkuu2qj) and suggests that users constitute a great potential source of innovation, because the com-petence and experience of users is not limited to the early idea generation: they can contribute throughout the innovation development process (Edvarsson et al., 2012; tinyurl.com/mvv2jbw). Through user innovation, companies can find new ideas more rapidly and at a lower cost than through traditional internal innovation. However, profiting from user innovation is difficult (Bogers et al., 2010; tinyurl.com/nxdeyb6) because user knowledge is considered complex and challenging to manage effectively.

Prior research has viewed users in different ways. An early work by Eason (1987; tinyurl.com/m4s5ewb) classifies users into three categories: i) primary users: those likely to be frequent users of the product or service; ii) sec-ondary users: those who use the product or service through an intermediary; and iii) tertiary users: those af-fected by the introduction of the product or service or who will influence its purchase. Later works (e.g., Sharp et al., 2007; tinyurl.com/kpqdbot) have defined users as those who interact directly with the product to achieve a task. However, companies must not only understand the interactions of users with their products; it is also important to understand *non-user* behaviour, such as the reasons behind a customer's intentional decision not to take on a product or service. Also, it is important to understand the situation of people who are not yet users to possibly help them benefit from the value of use. Indeed, several scholars have stressed the import-ance of mobilizing a mix of users in the innovation activity. For instance, Surowiecki (2005; tinyurl.com/ld49o4) suggests that diversity among members of the crowd, independent thought on the part of the actors, and decentralization in the organization of the activity are keys to success in crowdsourcing.

Von Hippel (1986; tinyurl.com/kxznqq3) underscores that lead users take part in successful innovation. Congruently, the study of Coviello and Joseph (2012; tinyurl.com/lkuu2qj) highlights that successful user innovation often engages lead users; they are keen to participate in the innovation activity because there is potential value created for their own needs in the innovation process. In addition to engaging lead users, Coviello and Joseph (2012; tinyurl.com/lkuu2qj) suggest that those users that are technically eager, open to learning, and willing to commit to the nascent innovation are equally relevant. They show that tech-savvy users seem to be willing to learn during the innovation process and, thus, are capable to adapt to changes and provide new ideas and relevant feedback in changing situations. Moreover, Edvarsson and colleagues (2012; tinyurl.com/mvv2jbw) demonstrate the potential for experienced users to provide context-specific expertise to the innovation process.

Crowdsourcing as a Form of User Innovation

Various community-engineering techniques leverage the potential of crowds by fostering an online user community for innovation, which provides a major opportunity for R&D (Ebner et al., 2009; tinyurl.com/mwm2yfm). Consequently, many approaches have been used to interact with users for innovation, including living labs and crowdsourcing. Companies use a variety of techniques to maximize returns from their interactions with users, and each approach has its strengths and weaknesses. In general, posting business problems in large communities – for example through "challenge driven innovation" (Bingham and Spradlin, 2011; tinyurl.com/kw7yey9) – may expose sensitive information and strategic intent to a wide audience, but crowdsourcing offers a possibility for more focused user innovation. Pisano and Verganti (2008; tinyurl.com/luw84un) suggest that, in company-led innovation approaches, innovating with a small number of contributors is appropriate when:

• one knows the knowledge domain from which the best solution to the problem is likely to emerge

• having the best experts is important and one has the capability to pick them

• one can define the problem and evaluate the proposed solutions

Conversely, Pisano and Verganti (2008; tinyurl.com/luw84un) suggest that a larger community of innovators may prove beneficial when:

• one requires ideas from many parties and the best ideas may come from unexpected sources

• participating in the network is easy

• the problem is small or, if large, can be broken into modular parts

• one can evaluate many proposed solutions cheaply

In its pure form, crowdsourcing is a manifestation of the latter approach. According to Pisano and Verganti (2008; tinyurl.com/luw84un), such an approach may be applicable in situations where a company is able to present a problem, anyone can propose solutions, and the company wishes to choose the solutions it likes best. However, large communities imply remarkable challenges for managing user knowledge. Knowledge in online user communities is characterized by mobility, appropriability, and stability that need to be orchestrated to make benefit of crowdsourcing (Feller et al., 2012; tinyurl.com/l8oxsle). Gibbert, Leibold, and Probst (2002; tinyurl.com/mbryalo) point out that the major challenges in making use of the knowledge resident in user communities include understanding and supporting users' motivations to participate in collaboration with a commercially oriented company. Community members' social orientations typically depart from the host organization's commercial focus, which can lead to unresolved tensions and to the failure of the initiative (Kelleher et al., 2011; tinyurl.com/ld8fecy).

In addition, users' knowledge and experiences are often tacit by nature and therefore difficult to share (Bonner, 2010; tinyurl.com/lddau6n). Users may find it challenging to share their knowledge in a meaningful way to support innovation. Moreover, Smith and McKeen (2005; tinyurl.com/kfxv927) show that structural challenges in the innovator's organization may hinder user participation. On the other hand, Jeppesen and Molin (2003; tinyurl.com/k2h6o4r) argue that user innovation can be structured, motivated, and organized by a company that provides the infrastructure for user participation. To this end, Boudreau and Lakhani (2009; tinyurl.com/khrzmnl) argue that executives need to consider whether users are motivated to participate by intrinsic motives such as enjoyment, status, and identity that participants can gain through their interactions with others (Deci et al., 1999; tinyurl.com/k6zambt) or by extrinsic motives such as financial benefits. In all, these notions on benefiting from online user communities call for more research on capturing, managing, and utilizing user knowledge for new product and service development.

Methodology

Our study follows the research design of an explorative single-case study where data collection took place using interviews. Extant literature on user innovation and crowdsourcing were used to guide the study; they provided us with an initial understanding of managing external innovation and users' roles in the innovation process. The inductive phases were conducted using an interpretive case study method (Walsham, 1995; tinyurl.com/nyca4vj), including seven semi-structured interviews with innovation and user community managers in the case organization (Table 1). In the interviews, the managers of the case organization were asked to share their views regarding the methods, knowledge gained, and the outcomes of crowdsourcing with their user communities. Given that we intend to improve the understanding of how the case company

may benefit from the knowledge gained through crowdsourcing, the managers involved in the crowdsourcing initiatives within the case company were considered feasible informants. The interpretations and meanings given to the different subjects by the interviewees were taken into consideration in our analysis of the data as suggested by Denzin and Lincoln (2011; tinyurl.com/levjb4g). In addition to the interviews, we also had access to a variety of secondary data, including company reports, white papers, articles, and studies.

The company investigated in our single case study is a globally operating manufacturer of mobile phones and related devices and software. In 2010, the company employed 60,000 people from 115 different nationalities. We selected this company because it has reportedly shown interest in benefiting from their customers' knowledge in service innovation. The case company has applied crowdsourcing to make use of the skills and creativity of the users in its product and service innovation activity. It has established a separate business unit to manage user insight in its innovation activity. This unit conducts crowdsourcing projects among other user-centered innovation activities. The case provides us with an opportunity to analyze the factors that facilitate large-scale user-knowledge management through crowdsourcing. What is more, it reveals some of the lessons to be learned from the challenges of transforming crowdsourcing initiatives away from idea generation to mastering knowledge gained from the users.

We provide illustrative excerpts from the interviews to demonstrate the key findings. After transcribing the interviews, we coded the contents and organized the data to discrete yet connected blocks that describe the key themes discovered from the data. Initially, we identified four general themes in user knowledge management: i) users' motivations for knowledge sharing, ii) diversity of the participating users, iii) facilitators of user innovation, and iv) challenges in deriving business value from user knowledge. That is, the analysis revealed those motives that companies perceive as essential to support to enhance users' knowledge sharing for innovation. Moreover, the differences between the types of users surfaced in the analysis and emphasized the importance of focusing on the lead users. Finally, the analysis separates the practices that foster user innovation through crowdsourcing and the challenges faced by companies in deriving business value from users' knowledge.

Table 1. List of interviews with the managers of the case organization

Interview	Title	Area of Responsibility	Years at the Organization
1	Manager	Manager of Beta Labs	7
2	Senior Manager	Innovation and benchmarking	7
3	Senior Manager	Strategy planning and dialogue	2
4	Senior Manager	Customer culture and innovation	9
5	Trend Specialist	Opportunity identification	10
6	Manager	Service creation product quality and delivery	7
7	Senior Manager	Customer insight initiative	5

Theme 1: Users' Motivations for Knowledge Sharing

Product giveaways

The willingness of users to participate in knowledge sharing and developing products and services is not connected with financial incentives. Instead, the users participate because they are interested in the products themselves: *"[We] have not given [direct] monetary compensations to individual lead users, but we may have rewarded them with a [rather small] promotional product gifts (such as a phone, headset, or something like that)"* (Interview 3). Monetary compensation is not among the important motivators they use to support knowledge sharing, because active participants want to be the first ones who see and get to use the new products. In addition, our interviewees underscored that users desire better and newer products and are willing to learn something new. Hence, small tangible rewards, such as the company's latest mobile devices, were seen to motivate users more than other rewards. For example, enthusiastic users submitted more than 2,500 new ideas related to mobile phones over a five-week period, just for the chance to win one of 15 new devices given away in the contest. Documents from the case show that small tangible rewards, such as the latest mobile devices, motivate people more than any other reward (tinyurl.com/k952yjs).

Meritocracy

The lead users are seen to be motivated to contribute to knowledge sharing, product development, and collaboration with a technology company in order to gain peer-to-peer recognition, for example, in the voting of user-generated ideas within the community: *"The feeling of bonding with the community and possibility to influence are significant motivators"* (Interview 1). The opportunity to participate and share their own thoughts and ideas was found to be an essential user incentive that company managers support. Moreover, the feeling of being part of the user community is considered an important motivator for users to share their knowledge in the user community. In addition, gaining credit, acknowledgement, and support from others in the user community were found to be effective motivators.

Credibility and trust

Users seem to be motivated to participate in the development of products that have a strong brand image. A good corporate reputation helps recruit voluntary users to cooperate with the company. Moreover, strong brands are seen to enhance the users' motivation to share their ideas and knowledge, because users can feel they are being given an exclusive opportunity to influence the products of a recognized brand: *"The credibility of our brand is so strong that a bank under our corporate brand could be easily established, assuming that the bank would be a culmination of a very high level of trust"* (Interview 3). One of the interviewees underscored that most of the community users she had been in contact with wanted to cooperate with the company and take part in its innovation process because they loved the brand. However, she noted that it was difficult to identify the lead users: *"Seeking the lead users is harder than head hunting -- there are even firms specialized in finding lead users from blogospheres and elsewhere on the web"* (Interview 3). Corporate credibility and brand image were considered to influence even the non-users given that some of the users of other brands have been willing to participate in the case company's innovation activity.

Theme 2: Diversity of the Participating Users

The role of lead users

Lead users are the primary target of user innovation in our case organization. The interviewed managers stressed that lead users are also most willing to participate in projects with the company: *"The target group needs to be clear and feedback should not be collected randomly from random people"* (Interview 2). The interviewees highlighted that lead users are not only enthusiastic about collaborating with the company, but they are also very interested in the latest technology and eagerly seek emerging programs because they want to try everything new. The lead users are highly capable in using the products and they have a good insight into the products: *"They seem to know more about the products than what we do"* (Interview 1). Users' ideas about the potential use of products go far beyond technological thinking about the future evolution of the products. Because lead users bring out novel ways to use the product in the future, it is important to understand the character and living context of the lead users: *"pure ideas are not important, the people behind them are"* (Interview 3).

User needs reflecting future trends

Lead users' perceptions were deemed important in the case organization because they are considered to represent the future needs of the mainstream users. However, sometimes the needs of lead users are so advanced that their behaviours never become mainstream. The preferences of lead users and the mainstream may differ significantly; some features that lead users may rate highly may be of no interest to the average user. Companies must take this into account when working with lead users. Crowdsourcing can significantly benefit from a mix of users given that it aims to collect a variety of ideas and knowledge. However, *"lead users are the ones who most often volunteer to participate in the projects with the company"* (Interview 3) and *"it is more difficult to reach the mainstream"* (Interview 6). Thus, it is tempting to focus on lead users that form their own homogenous community; they share ideas and thoughts with each other and want to be members in communities with like-minded others having similar interests. They are opinion leaders about technology and are considered to not only affect the innovation, but also the social behaviour of their friends and peers.

Theme 3: Facilitators of User Innovation

Mechanisms of participation

Our interviewees underscored the importance of paying attention to the ways of participating, gathering, and processing ideas. In addition to crowdsourcing, the case company has used various methods to collect customer knowledge, including workshops, interviews, ethnography, anthropology, consumer feedback, online events, forums, blogs, communities, focus groups, consumer testing, tracking, quantitative methods, open source, design reviews, and surveys. Furthermore, they use toolkits for involving consumers in the development process: *"We have invited lead users to the brainstorming events. They come there of their own accord and we pay the expenses, and of course we're trying to make it a 'wow'-experience"* (Interview 3). Users share their experiences, and the company tries to capture an impression of their everyday lives. One of the informants found that this is a way to identify important details, which the users may not even be conscious of or perceive as important. Therefore, it is important for an observer to have an analytical eye for the tacit knowledge embedded in the practices of everyday life.

Selection of relevant knowledge

Recognizing and picking relevant information is a major concern in large-scale crowdsourcing: *"How do we obtain the right knowledge, and on which level should the relevant user information be brought in so that it matches the needs of our in-house innovation? We can understand the world but we cannot control its needs so to say, because they are emerging and changing all the time. That is a big problem"* (Interview 5). It is also not always clear which part of the user input should be taken seriously. As disclosed by one of our informants (Interview 3), people may overstate their expertise in or-

der to become chosen into the crowdsourcing program. Another consideration is that the participants may represent only a small fraction of the users and that the most enthusiastic users may be overrepresented. *"Some people like our brand so much they participate in these events eagerly"* (Interview 3). The company was seen as the leader of the process of recognizing and deciding the needs behind the users' behaviour, because the users do not usually care about the expenses or how large a customer segment their idea would serve: *"We must be the brains that decide what customers need; we cannot assume they tell themselves about the needs the customer is not even aware of yet"* (Interview 4). Yet, the interviewees emphasized the importance of being able to put oneself in the user's shoes: *"You need to have a correct mindset all the time; you need to have a user in mind. Moreover, you need to use different sources of information and then decide and pick the relevant points. It's more a matter of competence than matter of the volume of information"* (Interview 4).

Continuity of interaction

The analysis shows that, in order to gain long-haul innovation outcomes, collaboration with the users should run on a continual basis. Conversely, the knowledge should be used promptly by the company. The interviewees all felt that the crowdsourcing processes must be kept simple and straightforward: *"The process should not go like this: you first plan a study and then order it and then get it sometime in the future. No way, that would be too slow"* (Interview 2). The innovation development process should be as quick as possible and users' ideas should be utilized soon after capturing them. The process of collecting feedback should be continuous so that the company has the newest ideas available all the time. That way, the whole process becomes closer to a partnership and makes the best use of crowdsourcing. Users should be engaged in the innovation process throughout the product lifecycle.

Theme 4: Challenges in Deriving Business Value from User Knowledge

Contingencies of knowledge

The tacit nature of knowledge poses major challenges to making use of users' knowledge. Tacit knowledge is probably the most challenging to collect due to its ambiguity and implicit characteristics. Tacit knowledge gathered from users can be best utilized when obtained in person. One of the interviewees said that, in her business unit, user knowledge is exploited effectively because they are doing ethnography research where the knowledge is gained mostly by personal involvement:

"I am not sure to what degree this kind of tacit knowledge is exploited in other firms at the moment" (Interview 5). The tacit nature of knowledge was seen as one reason why data repositories are not a feasible solution from the effective-utilization perspective. Tacit knowledge was considered to be best gained in face-to-face interaction and all of the interviewees mentioned that the only ways to collect tacit knowledge are personal interaction and working with users and observing them in action.

Sharing the acquired knowledge internally

To derive business value from the user-induced knowledge, the organization should be capable of utilizing the knowledge in its innovation process: *"There are people who want to collaborate with us to develop our devices and services and they have many ideas, but we need a system to make use of their input."* (Interview 2). The company's internal knowledge-sharing practices and cross-functional integration were perceived important in effective utilization of external knowledge.

Making sense of the data gained

The case company has conducted a large-scale project to make sense of all the knowledge obtained from the users. The sensemaking activities include data visualization where the outcome is a two-dimensional "idea map" (tinyurl.com/k952yjs). The visualization is based on advanced text-mining combined with clustering and regression analysis (Vuori, 2012; tinyurl.com/lbn3c2c). Through the idea map, a company can, for example, spot weak signals and megatrends: *"The visualizations of user-generated ideas on a map allow us to concentrate on the most relevant knowledge. For the organization's strategy people and R&D specialists, the visualized map of user knowledge is a refined view of the continuously evolving ideas and contributions from users."* (Interview 7). The idea map also contributes to deepening the understanding of the lifecycle of a certain segment. Such an understanding supports decisions regarding the technology roadmap.

Discussion

The findings discussed above provide a rationale to suggest that capturing and making use of knowledge resident in online user communities comprises four interlinked processes: management of community, management of ideas, management of innovation, and management of knowledge. Furthermore, management of information exchange between these processes is crucial, because the company assigns tasks and design challenges to the crowd and then reaps the rewards of

their contributions to the processes. Whereas crowdsourcing is an effective method to promote and collect user ideas in large communities, our findings suggest that there is a need to proceed from mere collection of ideas through crowdsourcing to management of user knowledge. To capture the value of user-induced knowledge, researchers and practitioners should consider the following key takeaways of this study:

1. Users value easy sharing of their knowledge for user innovation. There are several methods available to collect knowledge from users, including workshops, interviews, crowdsourcing, netnography, living labbing, web analytics, and online market research techniques. In addition, there are a myriad of channels for gathering user input, such as idea competitions, and different ways to organize online events and focus groups, observation of user communities, consumer testing, tracking, design reviews, opinion polls, and toolkits for involving users in the development process. Those channels that have best fit with individuals' behaviour are the most effective regarding quality, credibility, and relevance of the knowledge gathered.

2. Continuous interaction with the lead users and acknowledging the users for their ideas are vital in effective user innovation. The findings highlighted that continuous interaction between the firm and its user community is crucial for innovation, and collected ideas should be assessed and implemented quickly. Furthermore, our findings show that gaining tacit knowledge from the users requires profound collaboration with the users. Therefore, we suggest that users should be engaged in the innovation process throughout the whole product lifecycle, or for a prolonged period instead of through separate encounters.

3. Good internal knowledge management practices are important. Critical processing of the acquired knowledge is vital. In practice, the experiences of the company underlined that unitary data repositories fail to make a viable solution to user knowledge management, as they cannot scale to large volumes of data. Moreover, the variety and velocity of user knowledge is often immense and cannot be standardized. According to our findings, the tacit nature of knowledge is a reason for the major challenges of user-knowledge management practices in crowdsourcing. Hence, it calls for advanced data analytics capabilities.

4. Making sense of the data gained is a key to creating value with user knowledge. Data visualization is one of the key activities pursued by our case company in its effort to make sense of the areas of knowledge and in the practical aim of sharing the relevant knowledge with those intra-firm actors that need it most. This activity has proven to be one of the keys to create value with the ideas and knowledge gained from the users. The case company has made a great use of data mining and clustering techniques to provide both the strategy process and individual R&D projects with relevant ideas to support their specific needs out of the bunch of data collected.

Conclusion

How do the findings improve our understanding of using crowdsourcing in online user communities to source user knowledge for innovation? Although crowdsourcing is an effective way to collect ideas from large communities of heterogeneous users, our study shows that companies need to think about user-knowledge management in a more holistic way to complement and make benefit of users' knowledge. Furthermore, the study suggested four key lessons to move beyond mere idea crowdsourcing. First, technology companies need to understand and support users' motives for knowledge sharing. Although users are willing to share their ideas for free, effective incentives include the opportunity to gain access to the latest products or services, and the possibility of receiving token gifts as a reward. Second, given that user-knowledge management is often time-consuming and requires considerable effort, companies should pay attention to choosing the right users for collaboration. The case organization valued lead users, but recognized their potential bias in representing average users. Third, companies need to implement processes and practices that support user innovation and knowledge sharing. Companies can improve their innovation performance by sharing user knowledge in social action between those actors participating in the innovation process instead of collecting all data in one repository. Fourth, companies need to focus on how to visualize the data and make sense of the relevant information when using large-scale user ideation methods such as crowdsourcing in order to derive business value from users' knowledge.

Acknowledgments

The authors wish to express their gratitude to the Future Industrial Services (FutIS) research program. Also, the support of the Finnish Funding Agency for Technology and Innovation (Tekes) and the Finnish Metals and Engineering Competence Cluster (FIMECC) is gratefully acknowledged.

About the Authors

Risto Rajala, D.Sc. (Econ) is an Assistant Professor in the Department of Industrial Engineering and Management at Aalto University in Helsinki, Finland. Dr. Rajala holds a PhD in Information Systems Science from the Aalto University School of Business. His recent research has dealt with management of complex service systems, development of digital services, service innovation, and business model performance. Rajala's specialties include management of industrial services, collaborative service innovation, knowledge management, and design of digital services.

Mika Westerlund, D. Sc. (Econ) is an Assistant Professor at Carleton University's Sprott School of Business in Ottawa, Canada. He previously held positions as a Postdoctoral Scholar in the Haas School of Business at the University of California Berkeley and in the School of Economics at Aalto University. Mika earned his doctoral degree in Marketing from the Helsinki School of Economics. His doctoral research focused on software firms' business models and his current research interests include open and user innovation, business strategy, and management models in high-tech and service-intensive industries.

Continued on next page...

About the Authors (continued)

Mervi Vuori, M. Sc. (Econ) is a researcher and doctoral candidate at Department of Industrial Engineering and Management at Aalto University in Helsinki, Finland. Since 2010, she has acted as a principal researcher in several research projects in the field of purchasing and innovation management. She is currently working on her doctoral dissertation on "Innovating and collaborating with external resources: crowds, communities and suppliers". Her research is centered on the use of external resources, related management interfaces, as well as integration mechanisms in service and business model innovation.

Jukka-Pekka Hares, M. Sc. (Econ) received his master's degree from the Aalto University School of Economics in Helsinki, Finland. His master's thesis focused on crowdsourcing and user knowledge management in online user communities. He is currently working at the public relations agency Manifesto as a communications consultant.

Keywords: crowdsourcing, user innovation, online communities, knowledge management, lead users

4

Innovation in Services: A Literature Review

Rabeh Morrar

" The increasingly prominent role being played by "
service activities in productive systems have
combined to make innovation in the service
sector an issue of great importance.

Faiz Gallouj
Professor of Economics

The article reviews the literature relevant to innovation in services, which has flourished since the 1990s. We discuss the definition of service and to what extent the characteristics of service output have influenced the conceptualization of innovation in services. Then, based on the literature review, we develop a conceptual framework for innovation in service sector, which classifies innovation in service sector into three main approaches: i) assimilation, where innovation in the service sector is assimilated from innovation in manufacturing sector; ii) demarcation, which differentiates innovation in service sector from the traditional conceptualization of innovation in manufacturing sector; and iii) synthesis, which aggregates both assimilation and demarcation approaches within a common conceptual framework. We discuss the relationship between innovation in services and economic performance using productivity and employment as two indicators of performance.

Introduction

Awareness of the importance of service innovation as an engine for the economic growth is a recent phenomenon. Previously, services were considered as non-innovative activities, or innovations in services were reduced to the adoption and use of technologies. The innovation literature was focused on the manufacturing sector, technological product development, and process innovation, and thus, innovation in services was addressed from a manufacturing perspective. Indeed, the corresponding literature "assimilated services within the consolidated framework used for manufacturing sectors and manufactured products" (Gallouj & Savona, 2009). The risk of such a bias towards manufacturing is the underestimation of innovation in services and its effects, because innovation in services includes invisible or hidden innovations that are not captured by the traditional indicators of innovation in the manufacturing sector.

However, the traditional approach has been increasingly challenged, mainly because the underestimation of the dynamics of the service sector was seen as incon-sistent with the rise of the service economy, which now accounts for nearly 70% of gross domestic product and employment in member countries of the Organisation for Economic Co-operation and Development (OECD, 2005). Accordingly, the discussion about innovation in services should be extended beyond the traditional (technological) perspective.

A number of studies have shed light on the specificities of innovation in services beyond the traditional biased point of view, which constrained it to the adoption and use of technology (Gallouj & Weinstein 1997; Sundbo & Gallouj, 1999; Tether, 2005). These studies take into account the main characteristics of the service product – its intangibility, its co-production, and its co-terminality – which makes it efficient to define innovation in services.

The objective of this article is to review the extant literature on service innovation in order to identify and evaluate different models of the innovation process in services. The article also aims to show how the unresolved issues relative to the definition of service output have contributed to the underestimation of the performance of service innovation in terms of productivity and employment. First, the characteristics that are important for defining and measuring innovation in services are discussed. Next, the main theoretical perspective mobilized in the literature to account for innovation in services is presented. This discussion addresses the main theoretical inferences associated with each perspective accompanied with a survey of the most important pertinent application in each perspective. Finally, we discuss the relationship between innovation in services, including productivity and employment as indicators of economic performance.

Defining Service Output

The characteristics of services have largely been neglected by the innovation literature. There is a particular analytical problem of the definition of service output, which reflects on the definition of service innovation. When analyzing service innovation, scholars have merely analytical tools designed for manufacturing within the traditional technological view of innovation. This approach has led to the misunderstanding and the underestimation of innovation activities in services. Gallouj and Savona (2009) argue that it has also led to a wrong conclusion that innovation in services has a relatively small effect on economic performance in terms of productivity and value added, compared to innovation in manufacturing

Therefore, a clear definition of services and their characteristics is a key factor for the correct measuring of innovation output in services and the estimation of the real economic effect of services. However, "the study of services innovation immediately poses the question of how a 'service' should be defined" (DTI, 2007). Service production is an action, or a treatment protocol, that leads to a change of state, not the creation of a tangible good (Gallouj, 1998). Because of its fuzzy nature or intangibility, its heterogeneity and unstable character, a service is difficult to define, and therefore it is also difficult to measure its output and productivity (Melvin, 1995).

Arriving at a definition of a service is useful before discussing the problem of defining innovation in the service sector and measuring the productivity impact of innovation on services. However, there is no consensus today among economists about the theoretical characterization of service activities and their output (i.e., "services") (Gadrey, 2000). Therefore, this section of the article sets out to discuss, from a critical perspective,

the most prominent arguments about the distinctions between goods and services, with a focus on the definition of services.

Early definitions of services were based on technical criteria derived from classical economists. Three main definitions were adopted by those favouring a technical characterization. The first definition, advanced by Smith (1776) and Say (1803), views a service as a product that is consumed in the instant of production. The second definition, pioneered by Singelmann (1974) and Fuchs (1968), takes the notion of co-production, in other words, the interaction between consumer and producer in producing services. The third approach describes services as non-storable and non-transportable, which distinguishes services from goods (Stanback, 1980).

Hill (1977) introduced the most widely cited definition of services: "a change in the condition of a person, or a good belonging to some economic unit, which is brought about as a result of the activity of some other economic unit, with the prior agreement of the former person or economic unit". With this definition, Hill sought "to set forth a characterization of 'service situations' and of their outcomes that is both socio-technical and more synthetic" (Gadrey, 2000). Gadrey (2000) expanded Hill's definition by putting forward what is known as the "service triangle". In this view, "a service activity is an operation intended to bring about a change of state in a reality C that is owned or used by consumer B, the change being effected by service provider A at the request of B, and in many cases in collaboration with him / her, but without leading to the production of a good that can circulate in the economy independently of medium C". In other words, Gadrey introduced services as a process or a set of processing operations that are implemented through interactions (i.e., the intervention of B on C, the intervention of A on C, and service relations or interactions) between three main elements: service provider, client, and a reality to be transformed. The medium C in Gadrey's definition may be material objects (M), information (I), knowledge (K), or individuals (R). An important point in Gadrey's definition compared to Hill's is that the output cannot circulate economically and independently from C.

Inspired by Lancaster (1966) and Saviotti and Metcalfe (1984), Gallouj and Weinstein (1997) developed a conceptual framework for the provision of products (i.e., goods and services) that describe service output in terms of a set of characteristics and competences, which reflects both the internal structure of products and external properties. The delivery of services in this framework depends on the simultaneous mobilization of competences (from service provider and clients) and (tangible or intangible) technical characteristics. In a more detailed description, the service provision may require the interactions between four main vectors: service provider competencies [C], consumers' competencies [C*], tangible and intangible technical characteristics [T], and finally, the vector of characteristics of final service output [Y]. This framework has been used in a large extent to define innovation in service within the synthesis approach, which is discussed later in this article.

One of the most well-known conceptualizations of services in the last decade is the service-dominant logic by Vargo and Lusch (2004). Their approach was to redress the model of exchange in marketing, which had a dominant logic based on the exchange of "goods", which are mainly manufactured outputs. In the new marketing-dominant logic, service provision rather than goods is fundamental to economic exchange.

The main proposition of service-dominant logic is that:

"...organizations, markets, and society are fundamentally concerned with exchange of service – the applications of competences (knowledge and skills) for the benefit of a party. That is, service is exchanged for service; all firms are service firms; all markets are centered on the exchange of service, and all economies and societies are service based. Consequently, marketing thought and practice should be grounded in service logic, principles, and theories" (Lusch & Vargo, 2004).

Thus, the service-dominant logic highlights the role of producer and consumer in the production of a service (i.e., value is co-created).

In similar work, Grönroos (2006) makes a comparison between service logic and good logic. He found that service logic best fits the context of most goods-producing businesses today. Goods are one of several types of resources functioning in a service-like process, and it is this process that is the service that customers consume.

Four main criteria, commonly referred to as the "IHIP criteria", have been used to distinguish services from products: intangibility, heterogeneity, inseparability, and perishability (Fisk et al., 1993). Services are considered intangible because, unlike products, they can-

not be perceived physically nor can the results be fully preconceived by the customer before delivery (Biege et al. 2013). In other words, service products and processes are characterized by a "fuzzy", information-rich, and intangible nature, which means that they are not embedded in material or physical structures. Heterogeneity describes the variability of the results when providing services. Inseparability refers to the simultaneous provision and consumption of services; the customer is a co-producer and has to be included in the processes of both providing and consuming a service. Finally, perishability refers to "the transitory nature of services since these cannot be kept, stored for later utilization, resold, or returned" (Biege et al. 2013).

As mentioned earlier, a clear definition of services promotes understanding of service innovation. Due to the IHIP criteria, the dichotomy, or classification, of innovation into product and process innovation is not easy to apply to services in comparison with that in the manufacturing sector. For example, inseparability or co-terminality blurs the dividing line between product and process innovation (Bitran & Pedrosa, 1998). And, it highlights the role of clients in service innovation. The client plays an important role in the development of new services (Kline & Rosenberg, 1986; De Brentani, 2001). In any service innovation, feedback provided through the consumers of services is an important source of incremental service innovation (Riedl et al., 2008). In manufacturing, conversely, the clients are independent of the production process; they are just users of final products, and they do not participate in the production and delivery of the product.

The intangibility of services confirms the key role that information technology plays in innovation activities in services (Sirilli & Evangelista, 1998). However, the intangibility of service products hinder the measurement of the service output. Some scholars (Gallouj & Weinstein, 1997; Windrum & Garcia-Goni, 2008) have tried to overcome the ill-defined nature of service outputs by developing a new approach that is applicable to both tangible and intangible products. This integrative approach is discussed later in this article.

The low levels of capital equipment used in many services indicate that the technological competences and physical capital that play a major role in the production of industrial goods are less consistent with the "fuzzy" or immaterial outputs of services. Service firms are considered to be rather highly dependent on competences embedded in human capital as a key competitive factor and strategic element in the organization and delivery of service products (Sirilli & Evangelista, 1998). Thus, services may need special innovation that is not dependent on physical artifacts or complex technological changes (i.e., formalized R&D) or modes in which training activities and organizational changes are central dimensions of the innovation process (Castellacci, 2006).

Conceptual Perspectives for Innovation in Service

Service innovation studies have tried to go beyond the manufacturing-based perspective (e.g., Gallouj; 2002; Gallouj & Weinstein 1997). They have sought to address the peculiarities of service activities in terms of innovation. In this view, the service-based approach (Gallouj, 1994) and integrative approach (Gallouj & Weinstein, 1997) are considered two prominent conceptualization frameworks that extend beyond the traditional perspective, which is represented by the assimilation approach. Table 1 summarizes the three conceptual approaches to innovation in services: assimilation, demarcation, and integration.

Assimilation

In the assimilation approach, innovation in services is perceived as fundamentally similar to innovation in manufacturing. This traditional approach to innovation in services only considers technological or visible modes of product and process innovation. It ignores other non-technological or invisible modes of innovation, which are likely to include several types of innovation-like "social innovations, organizational innovations, methodological innovations, marketing innovations, innovations involving intangible products or processes, etc." (Djellal & Gallouj, 2010b). Therefore, the assimilation approach underestimates innovation in service activities, which is characterized by its intangible (invisible) and information-based nature.

The theoretical and empirical works favoring an assimilation approach are the most numerous. Within this perspective, Barras' reverse product lifecycle (Barras, 1986) is one of the most prominent works devoted to the adoption of information and communication technologies in service activities and their effects on innovation. The reverse product lifecycle, in contrast to the tradi-

Table 1. Conceptual perspective for innovation in services

Theoretical Perspective	Assimilation	Demarcation	Integration
Type of innovation	• technological	• non-technological	• complex • architectural
Characteristics of innovation	• equates or reduces innovation in services to the adoption and use of technology • considers technological or visible modes of product and process innovation	• leads to new typologies for innovation in services: non-technological types of innovation such organizational innovation, ad-hoc innovation, and marketing innovation	• shows convergence between manufactured goods and services in regards of innovation • includes technological and non-technological innovation
Innovation framework	• attempts to assimilate services within the consolidated framework used for manufacturing sectors and manufactured products	• attempts to develop a specific framework for service innovation, while attempting to highlight all the specificities in service product and production processes	• attempts to develop a common conceptual framework, able to account for an enlarged view of innovation that is applicable to any tangible or intangible product • proposes a new taxonomy of innovation in services based on a new definition of product

tional product lifecycle model (Abernathy & Utterback, 1975), starts with the introduction of incremental process innovations that aim to improve the efficiency of the service produced. In the second phase, more radical process innovations are implemented to improve the quality of services. In the final phase, new product innovations are produced.

Another important illustration of the assimilation approach is provided by the construction of new evolutionary taxonomies for innovation in services, which emphasize different trajectories for different groups of activities according to their technological intensive aspect (Evangelista, 2000; Miozzo & Soete, 2001; Soete & Miozzo, 1989). Soete and Miozzo's taxonomy (1989) distinguishes the following trajectories: supplier-dominated, scale-intensive, science-based, information intensive, and specialized suppliers.

Innovation systems and networks are also other important concepts for discussing the innovation activities in an interactive and dynamic process (Edquist 1997; Lundvall, 1992; Manley, 2002; Nelson, 1993). These innovation networks also reflect a technology bias when they address service innovation.

Demarcation
The demarcation approach considers that it is inappropriate to study service innovation activities by only mobilizing conceptual and empirical tools that are mainly developed for technical-based activities (e.g., R&D, patents, and accumulation of capital). In Gallouj and Savona's (2009) natural lifecycle of theoretical concern, the assimilation approach represents the maturity phase.

The demarcation perspective seeks to consider any specific characteristics of the nature and modes of organization of innovation in services (Gallouj & Savona, 2009), and it emphasizes the importance of service trajectories, taking into account the characteristics of service output (i.e., immateriality, interactivity, and co-production). It focuses on non-technological (service-based) and invisible innovation output (e.g., service customization, problem solving, new solutions, new methods, and new organizational structures). These innovation activities contribute to the economic development.

The demarcation approach leads to the production of new typologies for innovation in services; these typologies are innovation indicators dedicated to services that include non-technological types of innovation such as

organizational innovation, ad-hoc innovation, and marketing innovation. For example, Gadrey and Gallouj (1998) developed a new topology for consultancy that breaks down the product/process technological taxonomy for service innovation and includes three service specific types of innovation: ad-hoc innovation, new-expertise fields of innovation, and formalization innovation. McCabe (2000) has focused on organizational innovation (e.g., work organizations and standardized methods of management control) in financial services. In similar work, Van der Aa and Elfring (2002) developed a taxonomy of three modes of organization innovation: multi-unit organizations, new combinations of services, and customers as co-producers.

Integration
The integrative, or synthesizing, approach aggregates both the assimilation and demarcation approaches within a common conceptual framework that enlarges the view of innovation. This new perspective encompasses both services and goods and technological and non-technological modes of innovation (Gallouj & Savona, 2009; Gallouj & Windrum, 2009). It represents the emerging and expanding phase of the natural lifecycle of theoretical development in the service innovation discussion. The most important contribution in the integrative approach is provided by Gallouj and Weinstein (1997), who apply a characteristics-based representation to the product. As mentioned earlier, in such a representation, the product is represented by four main vectors, and "innovation can be defined accordingly as the changes affecting one or more elements of one or more vectors of characteristics (both technical and service) or of competences" (Gallouj & Savona, 2009).

The importance of the synthesis framework is also associated with the fact that the boundaries between goods and services have become blurred. This framework is motivated by the convergence between service and manufacturing, where the distinction between innovation in services and manufacturing is becoming more difficult due to the service dynamic and innovation blurring. In this new context, two main changes are taking place: manufacturing is becoming more like services and services are becoming more like manufacturing. In the former case, manufacturing firms produce more service products related to the main industrial products, and therefore, higher portions of their turnovers are becoming achieved through selling services (Howells, 2006). This process is summed up as the "servitization" of the manufacturing industry (Quinn et al., 1990). In the latter case, services firms become more innovative and greater parts of their innovative output are reflected by the traditional technological innovation in manufacturing. In other words, "services become more manufacturing-like in innovation" (Howells, 2006). Therefore, the synthesis framework is required to "redefine the product in such a way that it offers a relatively solid framework to generalize a theory of innovation for material and immaterial product" (Gallouj & Savona, 2009). The synthesis approach "highlights the increasing complex and multidimensional character of modern services and manufacturing, including the increasing bundling of services and manufacturing into solutions" (Salter & Tether, 2006).

The integrative approach is broadly used in the recent literature of innovation in services. In recent years, most of the conceptual frameworks and empirical tests addressing innovation in services apply an integrative approach in which both technological and non-technological innovation are emphasized (Gebauer, 2008; Hipp et al., 2000; Tidd, 2006; Ulaga & Reinartz, 2011).

Service Innovation and Economic Performance

In a service economy, defining and identifying the whole range of innovation is not easy, and it requires us to go beyond the assimilation, technology-biased perspective. Anyhow, in services as in manufacturing, innovation is a major source of economic performance. However, the link between innovation in services and economic variables such as productivity should be clarified. Indeed, in the service economy, the innovation gap is associated with a performance gap.

Innovations in services and productivity
Conceptually, there is no specific answer to the question of the degree and sign of the relationship between innovation in services and productivity, but it is related to the service specificities that "influence the definition and measurement of productivity" (Djellal & Gallouj, 2009).

The use of a technological or industrial approach for measuring innovation activities in services will lead to the under-estimation of both innovation and economic performance. And, it will lead to two gaps: an innovation gap and a performance gap (Djellal & Gallouj, 2010a). According to Djellal and Gallouj (2010b), "the innovation gap indicates that our economies contain invisible or hidden innovations that are not captured by the traditional indicators of innovation, while the performance gap is reflected in an underestimation of the efforts directed towards improving performance (or certain forms of performance) in those economies".

Measuring the productivity of immaterial and non technology-based services might need different methods from those employed to measure the productivity of material and technical activities in the manufacturing sector. For example, Biege and colleagues (2013) denoted that characteristic features of services were detected as reasons for the gap in measuring productivity in services. In addition to IHIP, Biege underlined four requirements when measuring productivity in services:

1. The innovativeness of the output has to be included to adequately measure productivity in knowledge-intensive business services. Innovativeness is measured by differentiating "services new to the company" from "services new to the market".

2. The "internal output of a service process has to be included to adequately measure service productivity.

3. Input figures in productivity measurement concepts for innovative services have to include interactive inputs that are not expressed by provider's and customer's inputs, especially time and cost induced by interactive loops in service processes mainly in knowledge-intensive business services.

4. Knowledge, competencies, and skills are central resources in many services, and they should be included in a productivity measurement concept.

Corsten (1994) measured service productivity based on an approach from production theory, which consists of factor combinations between inputs and corresponding outputs. In other words, service productivity is measured using multiple stages of a service delivery process.

Johnston and Jones (2004) proposed two perspectives for measuring service productivity: i) operational productivity, which is measured by the ratio of operational outputs to inputs of a period of time, and ii) customer productivity, which is measured by the ratio of customer output, such as experience and outcome, to value-to-customer inputs, such as time, effort, and costs.

Effect of service innovation on employment
The relationship between innovation and employment has been the subject of abundant literature. This de-

bate originated in manufacturing sector to analyze the effect of technological change on employment (Freeman & Soete, 1987; Hicks,1973; Pasinetti, 1981). In this context, two counter-arguments are put forth. The first argument anticipates a reduction in employment due to technological advancement. The second argument assumes that market-compensation mechanisms are able to overcome the negative effect on employment caused by labour-saving process innovation (Vivarelli, 2007; Vivarelli & Pianta, 2000).

In services, the technological trajectories are not the main form of innovation. Innovation activities include other non-technological elements. Therefore, the product/process dichotomy in the analysis of the effect on employment is not always consistent with service sector. The employment debate in the manufacturing sector is unlikely to sufficiently explain the effect on employment by non-technological forms of innovation in services. For example, new market strategies make important changes to consumer preferences and increase the market demands for new services, which in turn affect the employment rate. In addition, some of the compensation mechanisms (e.g., lower prices, new investments, and new machines) in manufacturing industries cannot always be applied directly to services. For example, because of the immateriality and co-productivity of many service outputs, it is not always easy to fix their prices and measure their intangible investment. In many services, there is an overlap between types of innovation, and it is not easy to disentangle them and distinguish labour-saving from labour-using effects.

Consequently, new methodological and conceptual frameworks might be needed to explain the employment effect of immaterial and invisible activities beyond the product/process dichotomy. New proxies are needed, provided that they are developed on the basis of the industrial sector, such as R&D and patents. In addition, new compensation and contradictory mechanisms need to be envisaged. These new mechanisms must challenge the manufacturing sector's traditional views that product innovation has a labour-using effect and that process innovation has a labour-saving effect.

Conclusion

In this article, the literature on innovation in services was reviewed using the assimilation-differentiation-integration framework. In addition to the discussion of the service concept, we emphasized the importance of both demarcation and integrative approaches as im-

portant tools to focus on non-technological aspects of service innovation, which were previously ignored due to the application of an assimilation view for innovation in service sectors. Also, recent studies show the integrative approach is found to be the most promising and comprehensive theoretical perspective that is employed to discuss innovation in service sectors. The relationship between innovation in services and economic performance were discussed using productivity and employment as two important indicators for economic performance.

This article has sought to provide an extensive and multifaceted review of the research on innovation in services over the last two decades. Its aim is to generate more achievable policy implications for how innovation in the service sector should be discussed in an integrative approach in order to reveal the vital role that innovation in services might play in modern economies. This literature review opens further discussion about new issues in innovation in services, such as innovation networks in services – mainly public-private innovation networks, social innovation, and entrepreneurship in the service sector.

About the Author

Rabeh Morrar is an Assistant Professor of Innovation Economics at An-Najah National University in Nablus, Palestine. Rabeh's doctoral dissertation from Lille 1 University in France focused on public-private innovation networks in the service sector, and his current research is focused on innovation in the service sector, R&D management, and technology management. Rabeh is also CEO of BEST, a small business in Palestine that provides innovation solutions and training.

References

Barras, R. 1986. Towards a Theory of Innovation in Services. *Research Policy*, 15(4): 161–173.
http://dx.doi.org/10.1016/0048-7333(86)90012-0

Biege, S., Lay, G., Zanker, C., & Schmall, T. 2013. Challenges of Measuring Service Productivity in Innovative, Knowledge-Intensive Business Services. *The Service Industries Journal*, 33(3-4): 378–391.
http://dx.doi.org/10.1080/02642069.2013.747514

Bitran, G. & Pedrosa, L. 1998. A Structured Product Development Perspective for Service Operations. *European Management Journal*, 16(2): 169–189.
http://dx.doi.org/10.1016/S0263-2373(97)00086-8

Castellacci, F. 2006. *Innovation and the International Competitiveness of Manufacturing and Service Industries.* Brussels: DIME Network of Excellence.

De Brentani, U. 2001. Innovative Versus Incremental New Business Services: Different Keys for Achieving Success. *Journal of Product Innovation Management*, 18(3): 169–187. http://dx.doi.org/10.1111/1540-5885.1830169

Djellal, F. & Gallouj, F. 2009. *Measuring and Improving Productivity in Services: Issues, Strategies and Challenges.* Cheltenham, UK: Edward Elgar Publishing.

Djellal, F. & Gallouj, F. 2010a. The Innovation Gap and the Performance Gap in the Service Economies: A Problem for Public Policy. In F. Gallouj & F. Djellal (Eds.), *The Handbook of Innovation and Services*: 653–676. Cheltenham, UK: Edward Elgar Publishing.

Djellal, F. & Gallouj, F. 2010b. Services, Innovation and Performance: General Presentation. *Journal of Innovation Economics & Management*, 5(1): 5–5. http://dx.doi.org/10.3917/jie.005.0005

DTI. 2007. Innovation in Services. Occasional Paper No. 9. London: Department of Trade and Industry.

Edquist, C. 2012. *Systems of Innovation: Technologies, Institutions and Organizations.* London: Routledge.

Evangelista, R. 2000. Sectoral Patterns of Technological Change in Services. *Economics of Innovation and New Technology*, 9(3): 183–222. http://dx.doi.org/10.1080/10438590000000008

Fisk, R. P., Brown, S. W., & Bitner, M. J. 1993. Tracking the Evolution of the Services Marketing Literature. *Journal of Retailing*, 69(1): 61–103. http://dx.doi/org/10.1016/S0022-4359(05)80004-1

Freeman, C. P. & Soete, L. 1987. *Technical Change and Full Employment.* New York: Blackwell Publishers.

Fuchs, V. R. 1968. *The Service Economy.* New York: Columbia University Press.

Gadrey, J. 2000. The Characterization of Goods and Services: An Alternative Approach. *Review of Income and Wealth*, 46(3): 369–387. http://dx.doi.org/10.1111/j.1475-4991.2000.tb00848.x

Gadrey, J. & Gallouj, F. 1998. The Provider-Customer Interface in Business and Professional Services. *The Service Industries Journal*, 18(2): 01–15. http://dx.doi.org/10.1080/02642069800000016

Gallouj, F. 1994. *Économie de l'innovation dans les services.* Paris: L'Harmattan.

Gallouj, F. 1998. Innovating in Reverse: Services and the Reverse Product Cycle. *European Journal of Innovation Management*, 1(3): 123–138. http://dx.doi.org/10.1108/14601069810230207

Gallouj, F. 2002. *Innovation in the Service Economy: The New Wealth of Nations.* Cheltenham, UK: Edward Elgar Publishing.

Gallouj, F. & Savona, M. 2009. Innovation in Services: A Review of the Debate and a Research Agenda. *Journal of Evolutionary Economics*, 19(2): 149–172. http://dx.doi.org/10.1007/s00191-008-0126-4

Gallouj, F. & Weinstein, O. 1997. Innovation in Services. *Research Policy*, 26(4–5): 537–556. http://dx.doi.org/10.1016/S0048-7333(97)00030-9

Gallouj, F. & Windrum, P. 2009. Services and Services Innovation. *Journal of Evolutionary Economics*, 19(2): 141–148. http://dx.doi.org/10.1007/s00191-008-0123-7

Gebauer, H. 2008. Identifying Service Strategies in Product Manufacturing Companies by Exploring Environment–Strategy Configurations. *Industrial Marketing Management*, 37(3): 278–291. http://dx.doi.org/10.1016/j.indmarman.2007.05.018

Grönroos, C. 2006. Adopting a Service Logic for Marketing. *Marketing Theory*, 6(3): 317–333. http://dx.doi.org/0.1177/1470593106066794

Hicks, J. R. 1987. *Capital and Time: A Neo-Austrian Theory.* Oxford University Press.

Hill, T. P. 1977. On Goods and Services. *Review of Income and Wealth*, 23(4): 315–338. http://dx.doi.org/10.1111/j.1475-4991.1977.tb00021.x

Hipp, C., Tether, B. S., & Miles, I. 2000. The Incidence and Effects of Innovation in Services: Evidence from Germany. International *Journal of Innovation Management*, 4(4): 417–453. http://dx.doi.org/10.1142/S1363919600000226

Howells, J. 2006. Intermediation and the Role of Intermediaries in Innovation. *Research Policy*, 35(5): 715–728. http://dx.doi.org/10.1016/j.respol.2006.03.005

Johnston, R. & Jones, P. 2004. Service Productivity: Towards Understanding the Relationship between Operational and Customer Productivity. *International Journal of Productivity and Performance Management*, 53(3): 201–213. http://dx.doi.org/10.1108/17410400410523756

Kline, S. J. & Rosenberg, N. 1986. An Overview of Innovation. In R. Landau & N. Rosenberg (Eds.), *The Positive Sum Strategy: Harnessing Technology for Economic Growth*: 275–305. Washington, D.C.: National Academy Press.

Lancaster, K. J. 1966. A New Approach to Consumer Theory. *Journal of Political Economy*, 74(2): 132–157. http://www.jstor.org/stable/1828835

Lundvall, B.-Å. 1992. *National Systems of Innovation: Towards a Theory of Innovation and Interactive learning.* London: Pinter Publishers.

Lusch, R. F. & Vargo, S. L. 2014. *Service-Dominant Logic: Premises, Perspectives, Possibilities.* Cambridge University Press.

Manley, K. 2007. The Systems Approach to Innovation Studies. *Australasian Journal of Information Systems*, 9(2): 91–102. http://dx.doi.org/10.3127/ajis.v9i2.196

Mccabe, D. 2000. The Swings and Roundabouts of Innovating for Quality in UK Financial Services. *The Service Industries Journal*, 20(4): 01–20. http://dx.doi.org/10.1080/02642060000000043

Melvin, J. R. 1995. History and Measurement in the Service Sector: A Review. *Review of Income and Wealth*, 41(4): 481–494. http://dx.doi.org/10.1111/j.1475-4991.1995.tb00140.x

Miozzo, M. & Soete, L. 2001. Internationalization of Services - A Technological Perspective. *Technological Forecasting and Social Change*, 67(2): 159–185. http://dx.doi.org/10.1016/S0040-1625(00)00091-3

Nelson, R. 1993. *National Innovation Systems: A Comparative Analysis.* Oxford University Press.

OECD. 2005. *Growth in Services: Fostering Employment, Productivity and Innovation*. Paris: Organisation for Economic Co-operation and Development.

Pasinetti, L. L. 1983. *Structural Change and Economic Growth: A Theoretical Essay on the Dynamics of the Wealth of Nations*. Cambridge University Press.

Quinn, J. B., Doorley, T. L., & Paquette, P. C. 1990. Technology in Services: Rethinking Strategic Focus. *MIT Sloan Management Review*, 1990(Winter).

Riedl, C., Böhmann, T., Rosemann, M., & Krcmar, H. 2008. Quality Aspects in Service Ecosystems: Areas for Exploitation and Exploration. *Proceedings of the 10th International Conference on Electronic Commerce*: 19.1–19.7. New York: Association for Computing Machinery (ACM).
http://dx.doi.org/10.1145/1409540.1409566

Salter, A. & Tether, B. S. 2006. Innovation in Services: Through the Looking Glass of Innovation Studies. Background paper for the AIM Grand Challenge on Service Science, Oxford.

Saviotti, P. P. & Metcalfe, J. S. 1984. A Theoretical Approach to the Construction of Technological Output Indicators. *Research Policy*, 13(3): 141–151.
http://dx.doi.org/10.1016/0048-7333(84)90022-2

Say, J. B. 1855. *A Treatise on Political Economy; Or the Production, Distribution, and Consumption of Wealth*. Philadelphia: Lippincott, Grambo & Co.

Singelmann, J. 1978. The Sectoral Transformation of the Labor Force in Seven Industrialized Countries, 1920-1970. *American Journal of Sociology*, 83(5): 1224–1234.
http://www.jstor.org/stable/2778192

Sirilli, G. & Evangelista, R. 1998. Technological Innovation in Services and Manufacturing: Results from Italian Surveys. *Research Policy*, 27(9): 881–899.
http://dx.doi.org/10.1016/S0048-7333(98)00084-5

Smith, A. & Skinner, A. 1982. *The Wealth of Nations: Books I-III*. London; New York: Penguin Classics.

Soete, L. & Miozzo, M. 1989. *Trade and Development in Services: A Technological Perspective*. Maastricht, The Netherlands: Maastricht Economic Research Institute on Innovation and Technology.

Stanback, T. M. J. 1979. *Understanding the Service Economy*. Johns Hopkins University Press.

Suchitra, P. 2013. Building Multi-Skills Based Talent Management. *IOSR Journal of Business and Management*, 15(2): 1–3.
http://dx.doi.org/10.9790/487X-1520103

Sundbo, J. & Gallouj, F. 1999. *Innovation in Services in Seven European Countries: The Result of Work Package 3-4 of the SI4S Project*. Roskilde, Denmark: Forskningsrapport / Center for Servicestudier, Roskilde Universitetscenter.

Tether, B. S. 2005. Do Services Innovate (Differently)? Insights from the European Innobarometer Survey. *Industry & Innovation*, 12(2): 153–184.
http://dx.doi.org/10.1080/13662710500087891

Tidd, J. 2006. *Innovation Models*. London: Imperial College London.

Ulaga, W. & Reinartz, W. J. 2011. Hybrid Offerings: How Manufacturing Firms Combine Goods and Services Successfully. *Journal of Marketing*, 75(6): 5–23.
http://dx.doi.org/10.1509/jm.09.0395

Utterback, J. M. & Abernathy, W. J. 1975. A Dynamic Model of Process and Product Innovation. *Omega*, 3(6): 639–656. http://dx.doi.org/10.1016/0305-0483(75)90068-7

Van der Aa, W., & Elfring, T. 2002. Realizing Innovation in Services. *Scandinavian Journal of Management*, 18(2): 155–171.
http://dx.doi.org/10.1016/S0956-5221(00)00040-3

Vargo, S. L. & Lusch, R. F. 2004. Evolving to a New Dominant Logic for Marketing. *Journal of Marketing*, 68(1): 1–17.
http://www.jstor.org/stable/30161971

Vivarelli, M. 2007. Innovation and Employment: A Survey. Discussion Paper No. 2621:22. Institute for the Study of Labor.

Vivarelli, M. & Pianta, M. 2000. *The Employment Impact of Innovation: Evidence and Policy*. London: Routledge.

Windrum, P. & García-Goñi, M. 2008. A Neo-Schumpeterian Model of Health Services Innovation. *Research Policy*, 37(4): 649–672.
http://dx.doi.org/10.1016/j.respol.2007.12.011

Keywords: innovation, service innovation, assimilation approach, demarcation approach, synthesis approach, economic performance

5

Risk Management in Crowdsourcing-Based Business Ecosystems

Suchita Nirosh Kannangara and Peter Uguccioni

❝ Risk comes from not knowing what you're doing. ❞

Warren Buffet
Business magnate, investor, and philanthropist

The benefits of crowdsourcing are enabled by open environments where multiple external stakeholders contribute to a firm's outcomes. However, crowdsourcing typically has been examined as a general process and not from the specific perspective of a mechanism for driving value creation and capture within a business ecosystem. In this conceptual article, we highlight this research gap by examining crowdsourcing from a business ecosystem perspective and by identifying the inherent business risks in crowdsourcing-based business ecosystems. We apply the concept of ecosystem health to the crowdsourcing context, in terms of how firms create and capture value, and we examine the methods by which these firms can maximize health by mitigating risk in crowdsourcing-based business ecosystems.

Introduction

Crowdsourcing has emerged as a new approach to innovation that leverages the potential of the "collective brain" to broaden the scope of open R&D (Traitler et al., 2011; tinyurl.com/lej7dkm). As originally defined, it is "the act of a company or institution taking a function once performed by employees and outsourcing it to an undefined (and generally large) network of people in the form of an open call" (Howe, 2006a; tinyurl.com/yfwtk2d). In order to build a foundation to both create and capture value equitably from a crowd, companies need to understand the elements of crowdsourcing and define their business models accordingly.

For firms engaging in crowdsourcing, the benefits are enabled by open environments where multiple external stakeholders contribute to the firm's outcomes. Thus, a firm is able to capture value through ideas and innovations contributed from outside the firm. For firms that are looking at producing innovative products at low cost, crowdsourcing is "the new pool of cheap labor" (Howe, 2006b; tinyurl.com/lxbf7).

However, despite the potential benefits, firms may be hesitant to use crowdsourcing because a dependency on external knowledge can also be a significant source of risk (Feller et al., 2012; tinyurl.com/l8oxsle). In this conceptual article, we examine how this risk may be managed by taking a business ecosystem perspective. In particular, we explore the concept of ecosystem health (cf. Iansiti and Levien, 2002; tinyurl.com/o7s4ok9) as a mechanism for risk management.

The article is organized as follows. First, we briefly summarize literature that describes business ecosystems. Next, we map the business ecosystem concept against the practice of crowdsourcing to develop the concept of a crowdsourcing-based business ecosystem. We then examine the approaches that can help management teams mitigate risk and maintain the health of such ecosystems using crowdsourcing. Finally, we offer conclusions and identify avenues for future research.

Through this article, managers, innovators, and entrepreneurs will be better able to comprehend how to shape their crowdsourcing environment by reducing risk. Researchers will be able to identify future research areas and build effective crowdsourcing models to improve the quality of risk management.

Business Ecosystems

Ever since the term "business ecosystem" was introduced by Moore (1993; tinyurl.com/cygzy6o), the topic has gained important recognition in business model discourse (for example, see Moore, 2005: tinyurl.com/5j7jux and many articles in this publication). There are various definitions of the term, but practitioners generally agree that a business ecosystem features companies interacting both cooperatively and competitively around a common platform to meet market requirements (Muegge, 2011; timreview.ca/article/495). Muegge defines a business ecosystem as a "field of economic actors whose individual business activities, anchored around a platform, share in some large measure the outcome of the whole ecosystem".

The major difference between business ecosystems and business networks is the variety of actors (Heikkilä and Kuivaniemi, 2012; timreview.ca/article/564). Typically, business networks are groups of firms working together to address market needs, whereas business ecosystems include not only partners but also actors such as complementors, competitors, customers, etc. (Heikkilä and Kuivaniemi, 2012: timreview.ca/article/564; Bloom and Dees, 2008: tinyurl.com/mkq33km). For example, in some cases, creating a business ecosystem can be a means for a company to access specific knowledge or capabilities that it does not itself possess or wish to develop, but are possessed by a competitor (Heikkilä and Kuivaniemi, 2012; timreview.ca/article/564).

Firms create business ecosystems to coordinate innovation with different contributors and partners within different market segments (Chesbrough, 2006; tinyurl.com/d5aaxah). Not every firm has all the resources, competencies, and knowledge to output complete solutions for customer needs (Traitler et al., 2011; tinyurl.com/mkejq69). Therefore, to solve a customer's problem, a firm may require the participation of a few other firms with knowledge and expertise in their own innovation domains. The organizational and governance structures of a business ecosystem helps these companies work together and manage their "distributed creativity" (Moore, 2005; tinyurl.com/5j7jux).

Business ecosystems can enable value-creating actors to respond rapidly and effectively to market changes by capturing value (Adegbesan, 2009; tinyurl.com/kgks23r).

However, different roles played by different ecosystem actors will be needed for the ecosystem to function effectively. The keystone organization orchestrates the business ecosystem and holds a leadership role in managing its activities (Iansiti and Levien, 2004a; tinyurl.com/7t4xgvn). The keystone organization also provides the platform: the technological building block for innovation and operations (Iansiti and Levien, 2004b; tinyurl.com/nmfpyms). Other participants include niche players, who are the focused actors in a business ecosystem. They provide rapid innovation in the niche areas of their expertise and contribute to the overall value proposition of the ecosystem (Iansiti and Levien, 2004a; tinyurl.com/7t4xgvn).

So how does a keystone create a productive and sustainable business ecosystem? A keystone should not only implement strategies to pursue their own goals but also strategies to maintain the overall health of the ecosystem. Iansiti and Levien (2002; tinyurl.com/o7s4ok9) introduced health as an overall performance indicator of business ecosystems; they focus on robustness, productivity, and niche creation as the determinants of overall business ecosystem health. Robustness is the ability of an ecosystem to face and survive disruptions. In order to provide durable benefits for its actors, an ecosystem should encourage endurance to survive changes in the market using a stable platform. Ecosystem robustness enhances the ability to enjoy relative predictability of the outcomes in the innovation process. Productivity is the efficiency of the ecosystem in generating new innovation (Iansiti and Levien, 2002; tinyurl.com/o7s4ok9). Ecosystem actors must benefit from their affiliation to the ecosystem and capture value. Thus, productivity is considered a determinant of ecosystem health because it reflects the importance of converting inputs from ecosystem actors into valuable outputs. Niche creation encourages diversity within ecosystems; an ecosystem must have meaningful diversity to foster new valuable innovation. Stagnant ecosystems that do not create valuable innovation will urge actors to find niches in alternative ecosystems.

Promoting Health in Crowdsourcing-Based Business Ecosystems

As in business ecosystems, a variety of actors make a crowdsourcing process successful. The aggregation of a crowd and other types of actors, such as solver brokerages (i.e., intermediary who facilitate innovation exchanges between organizations and crowds) and material suppliers, work together to execute the crowdsourcing process. The presence of a platform is also a key ingredient in the crowdsourcing process (Vukovic, 2009; tinyurl.com/qzc4d83). Thus, we can conceive most instances of crowdsourcing as a particular type of business ecosystem that uses a crowdsourcing process to drive collaborative innovation between different actors using a common platform.

The success of any business ecosystem depends on the collective health of the actors that influence innovation (Iansiti and Levien, 2004a; tinyurl.com/7t4xgvn). Thus, in viewing the crowdsourcing process from a business ecosystem perspective, we expect the benefits of a crowdsourcing process to contribute to the health of an ecosystem through the actions of its constituent actors. In Table 1, we map Iansiti and Levien's (2002; tinyurl.com/o7s4ok9) determinants of ecosystem health to the benefits of the crowdsourcing process in a crowdsourcing-based business ecosystem. These relationships highlight how crowdsourcing contributes to ecosystem health, but also help identify where risks might arise in the ecosystem.

Just like any other business ecosystem, crowdsourcing-based ecosystems have business risks. Table 1 helps us understand how the benefits of crowdsourcing contribute to ecosystem health. Efforts must be made to capture these benefits by reducing any ecosystem risks, thereby maintaining good health in crowdsourcing ecosystems. Some of these risks may be common to all business ecosystems, but others may be unique to crowdsourcing-based business ecosystems generally or specific instances of such ecosystems. Control measures are required to manage these risks while capturing the benefits of crowdsourcing in the ecosystem.

Managing Risk in Crowdsourcing-Based Business Ecosystems

Smith (2013; timreview.ca/article/685) analyzed the business risks that need to be considered by firms when entering or participating in a business ecosystem, and he recommended a risk management strategy to be used in such cases, depending on the type of ecosystem being considered. Here, we extend this risk management perspective by recommending an approach aimed at managing the risks of participation in a crowdsourcing-based business ecosystem.

Our recommended strategy is inspired by business management research, which quantifies risk as the product of probability and impact of risk. Thus, a risk can be mitigated by reducing the probability that it will occur or reducing its impact, or both. We adopted Iansiti and Levien's (2004a; tinyurl.com/7t4xgvn) health determinants and factors as measurements that demonstrate the impact of events that affect an ecosystem. We define probability aspects of risk management by considering how crowdsourcing affects the likelihood of each of the risk elements that apply to the ecosystem and how these risks can be managed to gain benefits of crowdsourcing to maintain ecosystem health.

From the crowdsourcing and business ecosystem literature, we identified eight risk categories:

1. Relationship complexity
(Purdy et al., 2012; tinyurl.com/bs9n5h2)

2. Control/effectiveness
(Koenig, 2012; tinyurl.com/cck69qa)

3. Coopetition
(Koenig, 2012; tinyurl.com/cck69qa)

4. Keystone/actor interdependence
(Koenig, 2012; tinyurl.com/cck69qa;
Adner, 2012: tinyurl.com/lf7yxcs)

5. Replication of business model
(Koenig, 2012; tinyurl.com/cck69qa)

6. Loss of know-how
(Elmquist et al., 2009; tinyurl.com/ndatchc)

7. Loss of certainty in results
(Felstiner, 2010: tinyurl.com/myh2t76;
Trompette et al., 2008: tinyurl.com/8q3uvs7)

8. Intellectual property risks
(Felstiner, 2010; tinyurl.com/myh2t76)

In the subsections that follow, we describe each of these categories of risk from the perspective of crowdsourcing-based business ecosystems. Then, in Table 2, we show how crowdsourcing affects the probability of each type of risk and which of Iansiti and Levien's (2004a; tinyurl.com/7t4xgvn) health metrics are most directly impacted. We also discuss and list crowdsourcing management strategies that may reduce the probability or impact of each type of risk.

Table 1. Benefits of crowdsourcing to ecosystem health

Ecosystem Health Determinant	Factor	Benefits of Crowdsourcing to Ecosystem Health
Niche creation	Variety	Participants come from different backgrounds and occupy different niches in the crowd. The range of new ideas from these diverse sources provide the ecosystem multiple opportunities to create and capture value.
	Value creation	Ideas generated by the crowd may allow ecosystem actors to brainstorm on new innovative areas.
Productivity	Total factor productivity	Ecosystem actors need to assure that the productivity of their crowd participants creates more additional value for the ecosystem than the capital employed in the innovation process.
	Productivity improvements	Motivation and incentives for the crowd will enable them the ability to contribute ideas/solutions with much interest. The crowdsourcing process is low cost, thus it will reduce the R&D expenditure in the ecosystem.
	Delivery of innovations	Governance models and crowd incentives and motivation ensures that the crowd will deliver new ideas and viable solutions. The delivery of new ideas provides ecosystem actors to start R&D and implement them into products.
Robustness	Survival Rates	This attribute measures how long actors stay with the ecosystem. Incentives for the crowd is a good retention mechanism to keep the crowd in the ecosystem.
	Persistence of structure	The relationship among crowd members and the focal firm must be persistent. Incentives and motivations for the crowd helps to retain the crowd for future innovation processes. Retaining the crowd helps to continuously generate novel ideas and continue the innovation process. Retaining the crowd ensures the ecosystem structure is not changed by recruiting other crowds to the ecosystem.
	Predictability	The crowdsourcing platform enables the interaction between the crowd and the keystone. The platform does not change even though the crowd may change. The core of the ecosystem is not affected by a change in ecosystem actors.
	Limited obsolescence	Most of the installed base or investment in technology or components used in the crowdsourcing platform finds continued use after dramatic changes to the platform such as different crowds joining the platform.
	Continuity	The crowd will continuously generate new ideas and innovations for the firm as the platform continuously provides incentives for the crowd. These incentives promote crowd retention for future innovation activities, which provides further continuity.

1. Relationship complexity

Purdy and colleagues (2012; tinyurl.com/bs9n5h2) described relationship complexity risk in terms of the complexity and entropy in managing relationships between actors within the ecosystem and the keystone. In a crowdsourcing context, the increased number of participants and diversity within the crowd can increase the probability of risk in managing relationships with the crowd. Incentives offered to the crowd by the keystone can contribute goodwill to the relationship and build trust. Firms can also have internal champions within the crowd to run the course of the innovation process by guiding the crowd. This role will help the crowd to have a better understanding of the requirements needed by the other actors of the ecosystem.

2. Control/effectiveness

Control risk refers to the effectiveness of the control measures, whether centrally located or distributed throughout the ecosystem (Koenig, 2012; tinyurl.com/cck69qa). Control of a crowd in any measure can seem counter-intuitive; so much of crowdsourcing research focuses on freeing participants from control and allowing broader participation that governing bodies may have historically screened out (Nambisan, 2009; tinyurl.com/pfmymbk). Effective crowd monitoring and effective solution evaluation can include control measures provided they do not act as crowd inhibitors.

3. Coopetition

Coopetition, as described by Koenig (2012; tinyurl.com/cck69qa), refers to the effects or impact of co-innovating with competitors within an ecosystem. Crowdsourcing within ecosystems focuses on innovation around "challenges" that may introduce competitive risk. Using common/shared incentives to recruit and retain membership is another method found in crowdsourcing literature to manage competitive instincts. Strong enforcement of crowd charter rules and agreements can reduce the negative impacts of competitors getting to know internal knowledge shared within an ecosystem.

4. Keystone/actor interdependence

Keystone/actor interdependence was highlighted by Adner (2006; tinyurl.com/bpj4syf) as a risk due to the uncertainties that can occur while coordinating with actors (Smith, 2013; timreview.ca/article/685). This means some actors may need to wait until other actors succeed in their contribution. The innovation's success depends not only on a firm's successful completion of its contribution but on the successful development of other actors' contributions as well. In crowdsourcing, the keystone relies on the crowd as a supplier of ideas or solutions. The crowd has less at stake relative to the keystone. They might not show interest in contributing or cheat in the process of gaining incentives from the platform (Hirth et al., 2011; tinyurl.com/l32exln). This risk can cause project delays and disrupt the innovation process of the whole ecosystem. Focused and measured "challenges", cheat-detection mechanisms, and recruiting methods that carefully manage incentives and motivations within the crowd can reduce the probability of this type of risk, and can reduce the impact of its consequences.

5. Replication of business model

Within local markets, there can be a risk of replicating business models (Koenig, 2012; tinyurl.com/cck69qa), and this risk is exacerbated by the presence of crowds within an ecosystem. With many diverse members, crowds may gain access to business model data or related insights through the crowdsourcing tasks. Careful and measured "challenges" that do not reveal business model sensitivities can reduce the probability of copycats emerging. Charter enforcement can also manage the impact by invoking enforcement rules against its own members.

6. Loss of know-how

Loss of know-how can also be a risk introduced by the presence of crowds within an ecosystem. The keystone's knowledge and internal resources are fundamental to an innovation process. When the crowd is integrated to the innovation process, they may acquire some of the a keystone's know-how. The risk of integrating the crowd is that crowd members could use a firm's know-how for their own purposes or even sell it to competitors (Elmquist et al., 2009; tinyurl.com/ndatchc). Crowd monitoring and evaluation mechanisms and strict quality assurance of solutions ensure that positive crowdsourcing outcomes are integrated back into the ecosystem.

7. Loss of certainty in results

Loss of certainty of results is always a possibility when the crowd does not feel the responsibility and accountability for solving tasks. Even the most committed crowd worker will have less at stake than a formal employee (Felstiner, 2010; tinyurl.com/myh2t76). By putting higher-qualification restrictions to govern the crowd or by using multiple crowd actors to work on a single task increases the probability of success through the innovation process.

Table 2. Crowdsourcing strategies to reduce risks in crowdsourcing-based business ecosystems

Risk Category	How Crowdsourcing Affects Probability	Most Direct Health Determinant Impacted	Crowdsourcing Strategy to Reduce Risk
Relationship complexity	Can introduce more complexity and more uncertainty	• Productivity • Robustness • Niche creation	• Internal champions to guide the crowd • Incentives for crowd • Crowd governance
Control/ effectiveness	Control is less attractive in crowds	• Productivity • Robustness	• Crowd monitoring • Solution evaluations
Coopetition	Larger mix and diversity of participants	• Niche creation	• Common/shared incentive • Charter enforcement • Focused challenge
Keystone/actor interdependence	Crowdsourcing requires proxy, but not internal control	• Productivity • Robustness	• Focused challenge • Cheat detection • Common/shared incentive
Replication of business model	Larger number and diversity of participants	• Niche creation	• Charter enforcement • Focused challenge
Loss of know-how	Crowd actors will gain access to internal knowledge of firms in the ecosystem	• Niche creation	• Monitoring and evaluation mechanisms. • Crowd monitoring
Loss of certainty in results	The crowd actor has less at stake for not contributing to the innovation process	• Productivity • Robustness	• Higher qualification restrictions to govern the crowd • Multiple actors working on a single task
Intellectual property risks	Crowd actors have access to intellectual property when solving a task	• Niche creation	• Nondisclosure policies and crowdsourcing rules

8. Intellectual property risks

Keystones may encounter serious intellectual property risks by assigning tasks or problem-solving challenges to an anonymous crowd. Crowd actors may have access to intellectual property within an ecosystem by completing even small tasks (Trompette et al., 2008: tinyurl.com/8q3uvs7; Felstiner, 2010: tinyurl.com/myh2t76). The platform may impose nondisclosure policies or set rules to protect proprietary material as part of an agreement when enlisting a crowd.

Conclusion

In this conceptual article we applied the perspective of business ecosystems to the process of crowdsourcing to conceptualize crowdsourcing-based business ecosystems. We described crowdsourcing and what roles actors can typically play in a crowdsourcing-based business ecosystem if they are recruited and managed by an ecosystem keystone. We reviewed the attributes a strong business ecosystem and the factors that determine its health through the participation and interaction of its actors (Iansiti and Levien, 2002; tinyurl.com/o7s4ok9). These factors were used to define the impact used by risk management strategies. This article also builds on the work of Smith (2013; timreview.ca/article/685), who offered risk management strategies for entry into business ecosystems. Our risk management approach helps mitigate the risks introduced by crowdsourcing activities within a business ecosystem.

Firms should consider crowdsourcing-based business ecosystems for the purposes of low-cost R&D, to generate and gather novel ideas, and to understand the latent needs of customers. To further help these firms identify and manage the risks of such an approach, future empirical research should explore and test the concepts and strategies identified in this article. Further research could examine how managing horizontal relationships in crowdsourcing-based ecosystem can enhance a firm's ability grow value in a business.

About the Authors

Nirosh Kannangara is a graduate student in the Technology Innovation Management (TIM) program at Carleton University in Ottawa, Canada. He holds a BEng in Communications Engineering, also from Carleton University. Nirosh has more than two years of experience designing software in the optical transport communication industry and currently works as a Photonics Software Engineer at Ciena Corporation.

Peter Uguccioni is a graduate student in the Technology Innovation Management (TIM) program at Carleton University in Ottawa, Canada. He holds a bachelor's degree in Computer Science from the University of Ottawa. Peter has more than 20 years of experience in software development and as a manager of technology innovation at a variety of firms in Ottawa.

Keywords: crowdsourcing, business ecosystems, risk management, business ecosystem health

6

Disruptive Innovation vs Disruptive Technology: The Disruptive Potential of the Value Propositions of 3D Printing Technology Startups

Finn Hahn, Søren Jensen, and Stoyan Tanev

" The distinctions we use to build a language and "
discuss strategy are as commonsense as left/right
and up/down, but they rise from the specifics of the
business context rather than everyday life.

J.-C. Spender
Engineer, professor, and author

This article describes an empirical study focusing on the classification of existing business opportunities in the 3D printing technology sector. The authors address three research questions. First, how do technology startups integrate new 3D printing technologies into specific market offers? Second, which value propositions are most attractive in terms of interest from the public and investors? Third, how does the degree of disruptiveness of value propositions relate to the degree of interest from the public and investors? The most notable finding is the link between the business traction of 3D printing technology startups and the degree of disruptiveness of their value propositions. Thus, the article provides empirical support for the conceptualization of the degree of disruptiveness of the value proposition as a metric for the evaluation of the business potential of new technology startups.

Introduction

3D printing is a term used to describe the production of tangible products by means of digitally controlled machine tools. The novelty of this manufacturing approach consists of the selective addition of materials layer-upon-layer, rather than through machining from solid material objects, moulding, or casting. There is clearly articulated perception by both scholars and practitioners that 3D printing technologies have the potential to change the traditional manufacturing paradigm as well as to enable the emergence of new innovation practices based on mass customization, user design, and distributed product innovation. As a result, 3D printing is considered to be a truly disruptive technology. At the same time, however, it is an emerging technology that is exploited today by only a small number of early global adopters (McKinsey & Company, 2013). It appears to be significantly over-hyped, which could potentially demotivate the variety of potential adopters who could influence the dynamics of its technology adoption life cycle.

The existing literature focusing on 3D printing is very scarce and appears to suffer from a "double disease". First, it appears dominated by consultancy reports and reviews by practitioners, which lack the methodological depth and the predictive power of serious research studies. Such publications contribute to the hype without offering much analytical substance. Second, it is dominated by technical publications, which, although highly valuable, focus on the engineering aspects of the technologies and much less on the specific ways they are expected to disrupt the existing manufacturing and innovation practices. In addition, there seems to be confusion in the use of the terms "disruptive technology" and "disruptive innovation" (Christensen, 2006; Schmidt et al., 2008; Hang et al., 2011), which does not really help in examining the market opportunities associated with specific 3D printing technologies. All this suggests the need for more systematic studies focusing on the potential business and investment opportunities associated with the emergence of 3D printing technologies.

The present article addresses the lack of literature on 3D printing innovation by offering the results of an empirical study focusing on the classification of emerging business opportunities in the 3D printing technology sector. It starts with a brief description of the technology sector and continues with the description of the methodology. One of the key research steps includes the evaluation of the disruptiveness of the different types of value propositions with respect to existing ways of user involvement in design, manufacturing, and product customization. The evaluation focuses on how the market offers address the needs of new market segments in a convenient and affordable way as well as on the way they address overshot customers in existing markets that are currently overlooked by incumbent firms. The summary of results helps in comparing the degree of disruptiveness of the value propositions to the degree of public and investor interest. The article ends with a brief conclusion which emphasizes some the key findings and helps in conceptualizing the degree of disruptiveness of the value propositions as a metric for the evaluation of the business potential of new technology startups.

The 3D Printing Technology Sector

The 3D printing sector has enjoyed sustained double-digit growth in recent years, and it is realistic to forecast the sector to be worth more than $7.5 billion USD by 2020 (McKinsey & Company, 2013). There are clearly opportunities for the adoption of this technology in key sectors such as aerospace, medical devices and implants, power generation, automotive manufacturing, and the creative industries. Many companies have already assessed the technology or have begun using it on a small scale. In addition, 3D printing technologies could reduce the use of materials, energy, and water by eliminating waste together with all additional harmful process enablers, thus having a positive impact on sustainability (Cozmei & Caloian, 2012). Due to their digital nature, 3D printing technologies are progressively being integrated with the Internet, which enables consumers to engage directly in the design process, and allows for true customer co-creation and personalization. The adoption of 3D printing is expected to stimulate the emergence of alternative business models and supply-chain management approaches by mitigating the need for expensive tooling, freeing up working capital within the supply chain, and reducing business risk in new product development and innovation. There is a growing perception among both innovation scholars and business experts that 3D printing technologies will generate a new wave of technology adoption that could

be associated with the emergence of multiple business opportunities for both technology entrepreneurs and existing firms. There is, however, little research on the specific ways 3D printing technologies are integrated into specific market offers as well as the potential business models that could help in delivering the corresponding value propositions.

Cozmei and Caloian (2012) have summarized the benefits of 3D printing technologies by pointing out that they are particularly relevant where:

• the production volumes are low, which is typical of companies engaging in small batch production

• the geometries of the parts and their assembly are complex

• the design complexity and capability should be maximized with no cost penalty

• there is a need for shorter lead times

• there is a need to personalize products and there is an opportunity to differentiate by offering unique personalized products

• the fixed-cost tooling cannot easily be amortised into the price of the individual parts

• the customer base is widely distributed and target customers or suppliers have ethical or environmental concerns

• the materials that are used are expensive and difficult to process by conventional means

Despite all the benefits, the adoption of 3D printing technologies is associated with several technological issues, including the lack of a supportive framework, comprehensive underfunding, and the absence of proper industry standards (Royal Academy of Engineering, 2013). A recent roundtable forum hosted by the Royal Academy of Engineering in the United Kingdom enumerated several key problems:

1. *Materials:* There is a great demand for better materials to be used in 3D printing processes. Although new metal alloys are already addressing some key manufacturing needs, polymers require greater research and development. In addition, whereas metals are often recyclable, polymers have a much lower degree of recyclability.

2. *Software:* Existing computer-aided design (CAD) systems are not at all suited for exploring the design freedom of 3D printing processes. The organic shapes required for biomimetics, for example, cannot easily be replicated using existing CAD systems, which are better suited to designs with many straight lines or circles. More importantly, CAD interfaces do not tend to be user friendly. Thus, the software problem is major issue for the adoption of 3D printing technologies, because the true potential of the new manufacturing paradigm can be actualized only if it reaches the non-expert designer.

3. *Data management:* Issues associated with data management are related to the need for substantial memory storage capacity, and not the manufacturing technology itself. In this sense, "rather than advancements in the machines themselves, software developments are what will 'drive the industry forward'" (Royal Academy of Engineering, 2013). It might be worth looking for insights from the development of the electronic design automation (EDA) industry, which could be quite useful in predicting some of the future trends in the evolution of 3D printing software design tools (MacMillen et al., 2000).

4. *Sustainability:* Although low-volume production offers opportunities for customization and reduction of materials, its benefits for sustainability are not always obvious. Although manufacturers are driven by efficiency goals that lower their carbon emission rates and energy consumption, homemakers can hardly be expected to care that much about wasted materials and energy. In this sense, the democratization of 3D printing design and innovation may introduce uncontrollable sustainability issues.

5. *Affordability:* There are significant financial overheads for running machines and buying feedstock for the 3D printing manufacturing process. Materials for 3D printing are significantly more expensive than traditional injection moulding materials.

6. *Production speed:* Although low-volume production using 3D printing technologies is faster than conventional manufacturing, higher-volume production is considerably slower. British experts believe that there will be a need for a new generation of machines in order for 3D printing to be able to compete and eventually replace injection moulding and casting machines (Royal Academy of Engineering, 2013).

7. *Reliability and reproducibility:* It is difficult for 3D printing technologies to compete with traditional techniques in terms of reliability and reproducibility. Traditional manufacturing methods aim for a rejection rate of just a few parts per million, which cannot be achieved with current 3D printing technology (Royal Academy of Engineering, 2013).

8. *Intellectual property rights:* Compared to traditional manufacturing, there is a much greater potential for users to infringe copyrights using 3D printing technologies, especially in combination with 3D scanning technology. Insights into this key issue may be gleaned from the experiences and business practices within the open source software domain, which contributed to the rethinking of earlier ways of managing intellectual property rights (Cohendet & Pénin, 2011).

9. *Industry standards:* There is a need for a set of standards that would provide the necessary assurance to businesses and manufacturers that 3D printing processes, materials, and technologies are safe and reliable. The challenge here would be to quickly introduce key formal standards to the sector, while leaving room for open innovation.

10. *Funding:* Government programs to encourage companies to enter the sector and university research focusing on increasing the awareness of potential benefits and business opportunities associated with the adoption of 3D printing technologies could help drive the adoption of the new technology.

Research Methodology

The objective of this research is to empirically examine emerging 3D printing business opportunities by studying technology startups in this sector. To meet this objective, we have addressed three research questions:

1. How do technology startups integrate new 3D printing technologies into specific market offers?

2. Which value propositions are most attractive in terms of interest from the public and investors?

3. How does the degree of disruptiveness of value propositions relate to the degree of interest from the public and investors?

For the sake of this research, we conceptualize a value proposition by means of three components: i) the specific market offer; ii) the target customer; and iii) the job that the target customer is trying to do by using the market offer (Johnson et al., 2008).

Information about the value propositions was complemented by the specific profit formula and the key human and technology resources used by the startups to develop their market offers. The focus on technology startups (i.e., technology companies incorporated within 3 years from the start of the study) allows the development of insights about emerging business opportunities that are currently explored by entrepreneurs across the world. Finally, the research aims to conceptualize the degree of disruptiveness as part of the evaluation criteria of emerging business opportunities by both entrepreneurs and investors.

Research design
The research study adopts a combination of qualitative and quantitative approaches. It is based on a research sample of 79 3D printing startups (up to three years old) that were labelled as such on the AngelList startup platform (https://angel.co/3d-printing). The AngelList platform was chosen as a source for data collection because it provides publicly available online information about:

1. The classification of the startups in terms of their main technology orientation.

2. The composition of their executive management team.

3. The websites of the firms with all the additional information about their mission, products, hiring priorities (job announcements), etc.

4. Their investors, and the type and amount of the investments.

5. The number of people interested in following their progress (i.e., their online "followers").

6. The ranking of the firms on the basis of a proprietary composite metric corresponding to their business traction (signal).

We examined the information about each of the 79 startups included in the sample by focusing on: the description of the firm, including its location, year of incorporation, mission statement, etc.; the market of-

fer; the target customer; whether the startup offers a product or a service; the number of investors and the total amount of investments attracted by the firm; the public interest in the firm expressed as the number of followers on the AngelList platform; the signal value as a measure of the business traction of the firm, as estimated by the AngelList experts. The market offer of each of the value propositions was analyzed along several constitutive dimensions by examining: whether the offer is hardware or software; whether it integrates the 3D printing technology (and how); whether there are any online tools available to support its use; and whether there are any open source hardware or software products that could complement its value in use. The examination of the market offer, the target customers, and the "job to be done" by the target customers resulted in a classification of the value propositions of all the firms included in the sample and a comparative analysis of the different types of value propositions in terms of their business traction (signal), investments, number of followers and degree of disruptiveness.

In addition to analyzing the startups using the metrics from the AngelList platform, we evaluated the disruptiveness of the value propositions by using the Disrupt-o-Meter tool suggested by Anthony and colleagues (2008). The tool was designed to evaluate the degree of disruptiveness of company offers to particular customer target segments with respect to existing solutions (including the lack of solutions associated with non-consumption). We used the tool to evaluate the seven value propositions by considering their specific market offers against nine different criteria (Table 1). Each of the nine criteria is evaluated by choosing between one of three options corresponding to 0, 5, or 10 points. At the end, all points are summed to provide the value of the Disrupt-O-Meter up to a maximum of 90 points: the higher the value, the more disruptive the value proposition.

Classification of the Value Propositions

This section provides an overview of the results from the analysis of the data collected from the AngelList startup platform. The value propositions of the 79 startups were categorized in seven types with respect to their specific market offers (Table 2).

Type A: Access to online printing networks offered by firms that do not own the printers
The customer value of the access to such networks is two-fold. First, it offers a relatively easy and affordable option for people or organizations interested in print-

Table 1. Evaluation criteria included in the Disrupt-O-Meter (Anthony et al., 2008)

	Evaluation Criteria	0 points	5 points	10 points
1	**First-year target**	Mass market	Large market segment	Niche market
2	**Customers' opinion about the job to be done**	Needs to be done better	Needs to be done less expensively	Needs to be more easily
3	**Customers' view on offer**	Perfect	Good	Good enough
4	**Customers' view on price**	High	Medium	Low
5	**Business model**	What has been always done	What has been always done but with a few tweaks	Radically different
6	**Channel to market**	Existing	At least 50% new	Entirely new channel
7	**Competitors' urgency to do something**	Willing to act as soon as possible	Willing to watch for any new developments very carefully	Do not care
8	**Expected first-year revenue**	Large	Average	Small
9	**Required investment over next 12 months**	Above average	Average	Below average

Table 2. Classification of the value propositions of the startups with respect to their market offers

Type	Market Offer Description	Number of firms
A	Access to online printing networks allowing both printing services and offering the use of privately owned printers at a cost as part of the network resources (i.e., the firms managing the networks do not own the printers).	14
B	Online printing services offered through a platform enabling the access to a network of 3D printers. The firms managing the networks own the printers.	12
C	Design tools and software applications for 3D modelling.	4
D	3D model-generation products such as scanners or special cameras.	4
E	Commercial 3D printers that anyone can afford to purchase.	15
F	Online 3D printing services with a focus on a particular application such for printing action figures or toys.	5
G	Specialized applications of 3D printing (usually business-to-business).	4
Other	Individual market offers that are different from the ones given above.	21

ing services. The online network platform takes care of everything around the job. Second, it offers an option for people or organizations owning 3D printers to integrate their printers as part of the network resources and make revenue through the printing services by sharing that revenue with the network administrators. The access to such networks can be an affordable entrance point for local "maker movements" or just an opportunity to meet other people sharing the same professional interests. The customer has the option of using print service anonymously. Once printed, the object is shipped by mail and the payment can be handled through the company's website.

Type B: Online printing services through a platform enabling the access to a network of 3D printers

Besides getting the desired object printed, the platform makes it easier for customers to either become designers themselves or to access the innovative designs of others. Some of the companies managing such platforms offer tools for collaborative work around the design of the objects, thereby ensuring a growing library of models for the customers and the possibility to be part of the design process.

Type C: Tools and software applications for 3D modelling used in the 3D printing process

The software tools allow customers to easily create and modify 3D objects and models. In this way, users with no prior CAD knowledge are able to model 3D objects in a convenient and simple way. These tools can be seen as complementary products to the 3D printing machines, because they enable home users to create their own input models for their 3D printers.

Type D: 3D model-generation products such as scanners or special cameras

These companies enable customers to convert their own existing 2D pictures into working 3D scans. In this way, customers can create content for their own 3D printers or share models on the Internet. Further, this technology converts an existing printer into a 3D "copy machine" because it easily allows people to digitize real-world models. These tools can be also seen as complementary products to the 3D printing machines, because they enable home users to capture their own input models for their 3D printers.

Type E: Commercial 3D printers that anyone can afford to purchase

The direct value for the customers is to be able to print 3D models at home. Some of the companies are further engaged in delivering less expensive materials for the printing process. One company (Honeycomb Technologies) enables doctors to print customized exoskeletons to support the healing of fractured bones, as an alternative to plaster or fibreglass casts. Further, these printers can significantly lower the barriers to manufacturing. For a few hundred dollars, customers can assemble a small factory that can make fully customized plastic parts for products or they can use printing networks or services.

Type F: Online 3D printing services with a focus on a particular application such as for printing action figures or toys

The value for the customers is grounded in the opportunities for customization. The high degree of potential customization makes the offer highly valuable for every single customer.

Type G: Special applications of 3D printing (usually business-to-business)

Customers benefit from access to state-of-the-art advances in 3D printing technologies and processes, which enable them to do things they were not able to do before (e.g., mass customization). They are also able to enhance existing processes to work faster or better, for example, through enhanced processes for medical doctors or the use of new resins or other materials.

Comparative Analysis of the Different Types of Value Propositions

The value propositions associated with the seven market offers A to G (Table 2) correspond to 73% of the firms. The value propositions of the rest of the (or other) firms were based on unique specialized market offers that did not fall into the seven categories given above and were not included in the analysis. Figure 1 shows that the three highest ranking value propositions in terms of business traction are not the ones focusing on the production of 3D printers, but are those offering design tools and software applications for 3D modelling (market offer type C), 3D model-generation products such as scanners or special cameras (market offer type D), and online 3D printing services with a focus on a particular application such as action figures or toys (market offer type F).

A report by McKinsey & Company (2013) suggests a similar conclusion: "The success of 3D printing also depends on improvements in products such as design software, 3D scanners, and supporting software applications and tools. Commercial 3D scanners are an important enabling technology." Companies selling affordable 3D printers (market offer type E) are fourth in the list in terms of their business traction (Figure 1). At the same time, these companies rank highest in terms of the amount of investments and the number of followers interested in knowing about their future progress (Figures 2 and 3).

The three value propositions that rank highest in terms of number of investors in the corresponding companies are selling commercial 3D printers that anyone can afford to purchase (Figure 2, market offer type E), online 3D printing services with a focus on a particular application such as action figures or toys (market offer type F), and companies developing and offering design tools and software applications for 3D modelling (market offer type C). These findings suggest that investors tend to prefer more tangible products that are in the very core of the technology sector.

The three highest ranking value propositions in terms of number of followers of the corresponding companies are selling commercial 3D printers that anyone can afford to purchase (market offer type E), online 3D printing services with a focus on a particular application such as action figures or toys (market offer type F), and companies with 3D model-generation products such as scanners or special cameras (market offer type D). The comparison between Figures 2 and 3 suggests that followers are attracted to the companies with the highest degree of external investments.

Table 3 provides a quantitative representation of the comparison of the different value propositions in terms of their degree of disruptiveness. It is based on the criteria described in Table 1.

Figure 4 provides a visual representation of the results from the application of the Disrupt-O-Meter tool. The ranking is based on the data presented in Table 3. The Disrupt-o-Meter analysis shows that the offers associ-

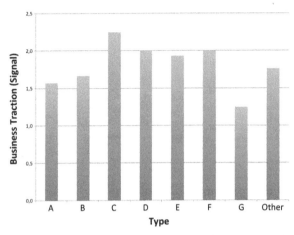

Figure 1. Ranking of the 3D printing value propositions in terms of their business traction

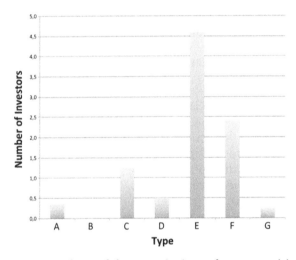

Figure 2. Ranking of the 3D printing value propositions in terms of number of investors

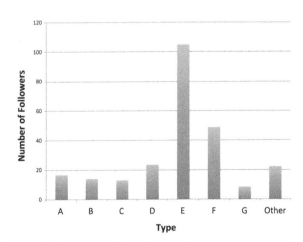

Figure 3. Ranking of the 3D printing value propositions in terms of number of followers

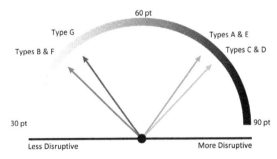

Figure 4. A visual representation of the ranking of the value propositions in terms of degree of disruptiveness

Table 3. Evaluation of the disruptiveness of the different types of market offers on the basis of the Disrupt-O-Meter tool (Anthony et al., 2008)

	Disruption Criteria	Type A	Type B	Type C	Type D	Type E	Type F	Type G
1	First-year target	10	5	10	10	10	10	10
2	Customers' opinion about job to be done	10	10	10	10	10	0	10
3	Customers' opinion about the offer	5	5	10	10	5	0	5
4	Customers' opinion about the price	5	0	10	10	10	0	0
5	Business model	10	5	5	5	5	5	5
6	Channel to market	10	5	5	10	10	5	5
7	Competitors' urgency to act	5	5	10	5	5	10	5
8	First-year revenue	10	5	10	10	10	10	5
9	Investment over next 12 months	10	5	10	10	10	5	5
	Total points	**75**	**45**	**80**	**80**	**75**	**45**	**50**

ated with model generation (market offer type C) and scanning software applications (market offer type D) are the most disruptive. The next two groups in terms of disruptiveness are the offers associated with online printing networks (market offer type A) and the 3D printers themselves (market offer type E). These results provide an opportunity to compare the disruptiveness of the value propositions to their business traction and the number of external investors.

The comparisons in Figures 5 and 6 show that the ranking of the value propositions in terms of business traction (signal quality) corresponds to the ranking in terms of the degree of disruptiveness but does not correspond to the one based on the number of external investors. This finding has two implications: i) the degree of disruptiveness could be used as a valuable metric in the evaluation of business traction and ii) investors do not seem to consider the degree of disruptiveness when rationalizing their investment decisions.

Conclusion

This article summarized the results of an empirical study focusing on identifying some of the emerging business opportunities in the 3D printing technology sector. The business opportunities was examined by studying the value propositions of startups operating in

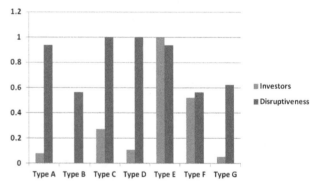

Figure 5. Comparing the disruptiveness of the value propositions to number of investors (normalized units)

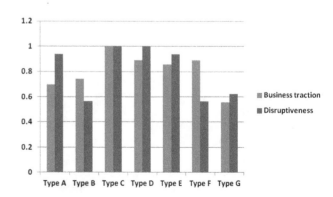

Figure 6. Comparing the disruptiveness of the value propositions to their business traction (normalized units)

this technology sector. The assumption is that the value propositions of most recent startups are an indicator of the type of emerging opportunities in a specific sector. The most notable finding is the link between the business traction of 3D printing technology startups and the degree of disruptiveness of their value propositions. Therefore, the main contribution of this study is the empirical support for the conceptualization of the degree of disruptiveness of the value proposition as a metric for the evaluation of the business potential of new technology startups.

The article also contributes to the research stream focusing on 3D printing by discussing emerging business opportunities and suggesting a method for their evaluation. The methodology could be successfully applied to other emerging technologies. The results of the study will be relevant for both academic researchers and stakeholders in the public and private sectors; it may help them evaluate the competitive position of specific value propositions based on 3D printing technologies. It may also be relevant to potential investors who could use the research insights in rationalizing their investment decisions.

Acknowledgements

An earlier version of this paper was presented at the first ISPIM Americas Innovation Forum in Montreal, Canada, on October 5–8, 2014. The International Society for Professional Innovation Management (ISPIM; ispim.org) is a network of researchers, industrialists, consultants, and public bodies who share an interest in innovation management.

About the Authors

Finn Hahn is a Product Development Engineer at Egatec A/S in Odense, Denmark. He holds an MSc (Eng) degree in Product Development & Innovation from the University of Southern Denmark and a BEng in Interaction Design. His special interest is in shaping technology in a way that technology products and systems become more meaningful to people. Finn is also working with entrepreneurship and business-development strategies where he is trying to incorporate the insights gained in the area of interaction design.

Søren Jensen is an Associate Professor in the Faculty of Engineering at the University of Southern Denmark. Previously, he worked in a seed-financing company analyzing technology business ideas. As investment analyst, his special interests lay within intellectual property and technology assessment. He now teaches intellectual property and entrepreneurial business understanding. Søren is also Head of the PDI MSC engineering program, an interdisciplinary engineering program training students to act on the border between technical and business understanding.

Stoyan Tanev is an Associate Professor in the Department of Technology and Innovation at the University of Southern Denmark, Odense, as well as Adjunct Professor in the Department of Systems and Computer Engineering at Carleton University in Ottawa, Canada, where he was previously a faculty member in the Technology Innovation Management Program. He has a MSc and a PhD in Physics jointly from the University Pierre and Marie Curie in Paris, France, and the University of Sofia, Bulgaria. He also holds a PhD in Theology from the University of Sofia, Bulgaria, an MEng in Technology Innovation Management from Carleton University in Ottawa, Canada, and an MA from the University of Sherbrooke, Canada. He has multidisciplinary research interests with a focus on the fields of technology entrepreneurship and innovation management, born-global technology startups, business model design, and value co-creation. Dr. Tanev is a Senior IEEE member, and he is a member of the editorial boards of the *Technology Innovation Management Review* and the *International Journal of Actor-Network Theory and Technological Innovation.*

References

Anthony, S., Johnson, M., Sinfield, J., & Altman, E. 2008. *The Innovator's Guide to Growth: Outting Disruptive Innovation at Work.* Boston, MA: Harvard Business Press.

Christensen, C. 2006. The Ongoing Process of Building a Theory of Disruption. *Journal of Product Innovation Management,* 23(1): 39–55.
http://dx.doi.org/10.1111/j.1540-5885.2005.00180.x

Cohendet, P., & Pénin, J. 2011. Patents to Exclude vs. Include: Rethinking the Management of Intellectual Property Rights in a Knowledge-Based Economy. *Technology Innovation Management Review,* 1(3): 12–17.

Cozmei, C., & Caloian, F. 2012. Additive Manufacturing Flickering at the Beginning of Existence. *Procedia Economics and Finance,* 3: 457–462.
http://dx.doi.org/10.1016/S2212-5671(12)00180-3

Hang, C. C., Chen, J., & Yu, D. 2011. An Assessment Framework for Disruptive Innovation. *Foresight,* 13(5): 4–13.
http://dx.doi.org/10.1108/14636681111170185

Johnson, M., Christensen, C., & Kagermann, H. 2008. Reinventing Your Business Model. *Harvard Business Review,* 86(12): 50–59.

MacMillen, D., Butts, M., Camposano, R., Hill, D., & Williams, T. 2000. An Industrial View of Electronic Design Automation. *IEEE Transactions on Computer Aided Design of Integrated Circuits and Systems,* 19(12): 1428–1448.
http://dx.doi.org/10.1109/43.898825

McKinsey & Company. 2013. *Disruptive Technologies: Advances That Will Transform Life, Business, and the Global Economy.* McKinsey Global Institute. Accessed December 1, 2014:
http://www.mckinsey.com/insights/business_technology/disruptive_technologies

Royal Academy of Engineering. 2013. *Additive Manufacturing: Opportunities and Constraints.* London: Royal Academy of Engineering.

Schmidt, G., & Druehl, C. 2008. When Is a Disruptive Innovation Disruptive? *Journal of Product Innovation Management,* 25: 347–369.
http://dx.doi.org/10.1111/j.1540-5885.2008.00306.x

Keywords: 3D printing technology, additive manufacturing, disruptive innovation, value proposition

7

Personal Health Systems Technologies: Critical Issues in Service Innovation and Diffusion

Doris Schartinger, Ian Miles, Ozcan Saritas, Effie Amanatidou,

Susanne Giesecke, Barbara Heller-Schuh,

Laura Pompo-Juarez, and Günter Schreier

" If I could time travel into the future, my first port of call "
would be the point where medical technology is at its best.
Because, like most people on this planet, I have this aversion
to dying.

Neal Asher
Science fiction novelist

Personal health system (PHS) technologies can enhance public and private health service delivery and provide new business opportunities in Europe and around the world. Although much PHS technology has already been developed and could potentially provide virtually everyone with access to personalized healthcare, research driven primarily by a technology push may fail, because it fails to situate PHS within the wider health and social care service systems. In this article, we explore the scattered PHS research and innovation landscape, as well its relevant markets, using several types of analyses: bibliometrics, patent analysis, social network analysis, stakeholder workshops, and interviews. Our analyses aim to identify critical issues in the development and implementation of service systems around PHS technologies.

Introduction

Healthcare systems face well-known challenges: rising costs, ageing populations, increasing demand, and shortage of health care professionals, among others. Personal health systems (PHS) assist in the provision of continuous, quality-controlled, and personalized health services to empowered individuals. PHS involve a variety of patient groups, clinical specialties, technology fields, and health services. Hence, the development of PHS requires and can mobilize the emergence of novel cross-disciplinary and cross-sectoral innovation partnerships. For the purposes of this article, we build on earlier definitions (Codagnone, 2009) of PHS, which we define as consisting of:

1. Ambient, wearable, or in-body devices that acquire, monitor, and communicate physiological and other health-related data

2. Intelligent processing of the acquired information (i.e., data analytics), and coupling it with expert biomedical knowledge and, in some cases, knowledge of social circumstances and living conditions

3. Action based on the processing of acquired information, either applied to the individuals being monitored, or to health practice more generally, concerning information provision or more active engagement in anything from disease and disability prevention (e.g., through diet and lifestyle management) to diagnosis, treatment, and rehabilitation

We need deeper understanding of mismatches between the potential of, and need for, PHS, and current policy and innovation initiatives and framework conditions, for example, in terms of future technological opportunities and societal demands. To date, research in the area of PHS has often given little account of special patterns of innovation in the PHS sector (Cunningham et al., 2005). Knowledge and experience about implementing relevant research results into concrete policy and strategy development in health (particularly at the European level) remains in its infancy.

The main question of this article is why PHS technologies do not diffuse readily despite the advantages they offer to a variety of actors in the health and social care system.

This article is structured as follows. In the next section, we introduce the conceptual approach of this research by examining the concept of "service systems" and describe the shift to PHS as a system transition. Next, we discuss the various methods of investigation we applied to answer our research question, and then we present the results of our analyses. Finally, we discuss the implications of the results and present our conclusions.

Conceptual Approach: Service Systems

Services are often thought of as essentially person-to-person interactions, where the service "product" is co-produced in the course of a service relationship. But, we have become familiar with technology-to-person services, where instead of directly interacting with a member of staff of a service organization, the client interacts with technology – often through online and mobile communications, and sometimes through devices based at the premises of service organizations. The service is created within a "service system", involving the customer/client and the devices (and software) they are using, the service organization they reach through these interfaces, the personnel of this organization – some of whom they may interact with (front-office staff) and others who provide unseen support services (back-office staff) – and the technologies these organizations use, some for information processing and communication, some for surgery and other medical interventions, physical transport, and so on.

The concept of service systems is one that has evolved quite rapidly, with some specialist versions (often coming from the information systems community) being rather elaborate and restrictive. One well-known definition introduces the notion of POTI, or "people, organizations, technologies, and shared information", in which service systems are seen as "dynamic configurations of resources [POTI] that can create and deliver value to customers, providers, and other stakeholders" (IfM and IBM, 2008). Maglio (2010) sees these four key building blocks of service systems as varying on two dimensions:

i) physical / non-physical and ii) possessing / not possessing rights. This view characterizes the various four resources of service systems as follows:

1. People (physical, with rights)

2. Organizations (non-physical, with rights)

3. Technologies (physical, without rights)

4. Information (non-physical, without rights)

Various authors, such as Karni and Kaner (2006), stress that, in service systems, as compared to many other sociotechnical systems, customers/clients are much more important parts of the "P" component – their participation and inputs are vital in service design and provision. They may also place limits upon what the (formal) service provider can do, and set standards for what should be achieved. In health and social care systems, the customers/clients can include not only the recipients of care, but also other stakeholders (such as family members), any of whom may make their own demands upon, and inputs into, the service.

People – whether consumers or service suppliers – are complex agents, with highly diverse cognitive frameworks, values and attitudes, physical and emotional needs, and so on. Service systems are thus complex to model and manage – but they may also be resilient and innovative. People can be empowered to act in non-mechanical ways, responding to unexpected circumstances and collaborating to solve problems. They can be linked together in new ways through new information technologies.

Now, what is the service that we are discussing in this study? Many levels of granularity could be considered: which level is chosen for analysis depends on the practical purposes at hand. For some purposes, the issue may be the immediate response to a particular event (e.g., the administration of a drug); for other purposes it may be the set of interactions immediately surrounding this specific service activity (e.g., a visit by the consumer to a clinic or other appointment or a visit by a health and social care professional to the person's house); or the broader treatment of the consumer in question over a series of interactions (i.e., "touchpoints") with the service organization across their "service pathway" or "service journey"; or the overall service to the community that is provided by a particular health and social organization (which may be a constellation of many of the specific services discussed above).

System innovation and transitions

Rotmans (2006) has described system innovations as "organization-transcending innovations that drastically alter the relationship between the companies, organizations, and individuals involved in the system". Such ambitious innovations are required to address many of society's grand challenges, including those associated with active independent living and the introduction of PHS. System innovation often implies to the need for "transition management" (Schot & Geels, 2008), which enables breaking out of various locked-in heritages and organizational routines. There are costs as well as benefits in such changes, and protracted processes of learning and negotiation are liable to be involved.

The transitions approach argues for the need to take the interests and perspectives of numerous stakeholders into account. For example, hospitals are an important part of the health and social care chain, but hospital management may not benefit from the reduction of inpatient stays associated with the use of PHS. The approach suggests experimenting with and developing of strategic niche markets; determining "boundary objects" through which stakeholders can gain their own appreciation of the innovation; and developing transition pathways through which the new service system can be constructed.

The shift to PHS may be understood as a system transition in the sorts of terms established in transition management accounts and drawing on ideas from the approaches developed in "social construction of technology" and similar approaches to innovation studies. As an example, Broch (2011) provides a multilevel analysis of innovation around care services for the elderly.

Methodology

Figure 1 gives an overview of the different types of analysis that were applied in our research project. The first approach was to obtain a comprehensive overview of the various types of PHS projects through web-based research. Apart from purely technical research projects, PHS projects exist at different levels of aggregation and analysis:

1. **Meta-level PHS projects:** These are mainly research projects that have made considerable efforts in defining and demarcating the PHS area. They are academic projects that follow an analytical approach in their occupation with the field. They are mostly publicly financed and well documented.

2. **Meso-level PHS projects:** These projects combine an analytical approach with a strong applications focus. Typically, the project partners involved are from research and consulting organizations. Also, academic organizations are typically found on one side, and on the other side, the partners are based on various case studies distributed over Europe where actors from the private, public, and third sectors are involved in implementing local personal health systems. These projects are well-documented, especially on the single-case level.

3. **Micro-level PHS projects:** These are national/regional local bottom-up projects, primarily focused on application – they are PHS cases according to the definition applied in this article. Project partners develop out of their ecosystems and receive financing at some points in time. Typically, projects and follow-ups develop over at least one decade; it is often difficult to demarcate the start and end of these undertakings. A wide variety of these projects exist on the national and local levels. They are not well documented – in most cases there is not even a project website.

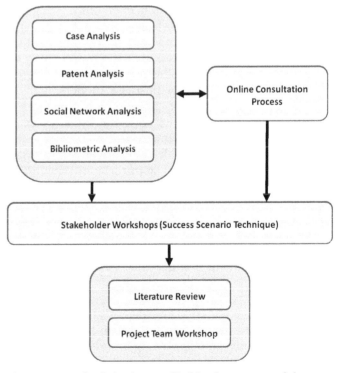

Figure 1. Methodologies applied in the course of the project

At the outset, we conducted several small analyses to provide a first overview of the PHS area:

- A bibliometric analysis was used to explore the present state and future trends on the PHS topic.

- A small study analyzed the patents in the PHS field, using information obtained from the Derwent Innovation Index and the "Patent Citation Index".

- Social network analysis (SNA) tools and concepts were used to visualize R&D collaboration networks and central actors in the area of PHS on the European level, to move the focus beyond the individual social actors and toward the broader interaction contexts within which the actors are embedded.

The project website (phsforesight.eu) was deployed to establish an online platform for launching a structured and systematic online consultation process, with multiple phases for generating and clustering visions concerning breakthrough innovations and societal demands.

Two stakeholder workshops were organized in order to explore pathways for desirable future developments, and to use scenario analysis to deepen our understanding of how PHS might be configured and applied to specific health/wellbeing conditions over the coming decades up to a time horizon of 2030. In particular, we sought to deal with the challenging questions of system organization: what sorts of business model might be pursued and what is the organizational ecology of service provision? The scenarios were not intended to be predictions of what will happen, but to provide some idea of the range of plausible developments that might characterize the PHS field. The purpose of scenarios is to provide us with insight into the circumstances under which different developments might unfold, and the relations between different issues. Reality is liable to be a complicated and diverse mixture of different elements of these scenarios, varying over time, place, organization, and even medical conditions. The scenario workshop process involved alternating between plenary and break-out group discussions. The workshop, bringing together individuals with knowledge and expertise of the operation of health pathways, or of the potential of new PHS systems, and combining different perspectives (from academia, policy, industry, and society) discussed ways in which these pathways and systems might evolve over the next decade and beyond. Stakeholders invited to the workshops were identified via different channels: stakeholders registered via the PHS project website

were asked to pass the word and invited their colleagues and networks to engage. Furthermore, outreach activities were established through social networks, printed leaflets, and targeted promotion (by way of emailing to the stakeholders of initiatives and through the website visibility with banners and hyperlinks). Coordinators or leading members of other projects in the PHS field were emailed. For the workshops, we took care of a roughly equal distribution of stakeholders with a research, business, policy, and third-sector background. For more information on the workshops, please see the report by Amanatidou and colleagues (2014).

Results from all previous analyses, the online consultation process, and the stakeholder workshops were then again cross-checked with existing literature and discussed and rounded up in a project team workshop.

Results

The various strands of analysis identified a number of critical issues and related governance deficits:

1. **Social acceptance of PHS:** issues that enhance the positive appraisal, and finally use, in stakeholder groups of PHS (e.g., patients, informal carers, medical professionals)

2. **Service systems of PHS:** issues such as systemic failures or lock-ins, including networks that are too weak (e.g., barrier to knowledge transfer, missing mutual understanding of actors' perspectives and roles) or too strong (e.g., causing incumbent actors to be dominant)

3. **Markets for PHS:** supply-side and demand-side issues; issues of interfaces between supply and demand; business models; and market opportunities

4. **Research and technological development of PHS:** covers research for technological solutions (i.e., pre-commercial), for standardization, but also for indicators about success of PHS

5. **Framework conditions of PHS:** cover institutional change, including the creation of new organizations/institutions, assigning new missions to existing institutions, regulation, and legislation

These critical issues can be the basis for possible policy designs to facilitate the adoption and diffusion of PHS technologies and services. We discuss each issue in greater detail in the subsections that follow.

1. Social acceptance

Stakeholders with whom the PHS project engaged in interviews and discussions, as well as the literature reviewed, see individualization in healthcare and growing affinity for technology as drivers for PHS diffusion. The global dissemination of sophisticated technologies and mobile phones and consequently the use of these devices (e.g., Internet access, smartphones, and application development) is a strong trend that is reinforced as the senior part of the population becomes increasingly familiar with advanced ICT, having used it already in their professional and private lives (The Capital Region of Denmark & Health Care Innovation Centre, 2011). Technology affinity contends with technology skepticism: elderly individuals show hesitancy as to new technologies, frequently commenting, for example, that they are unable to use touchscreens. There is suspicion that technical devices may fail, through operating errors or technical deficiencies.

Social acceptance of technology includes also acceptance on behalf of professionals. Innovation-mindedness on a lower management level, and a positive attitude of care professionals, can be of vital importance for eHealth innovations. If there is a general fear of operating errors or hard-to-control alarms, this will slow down adoption rates of PHS service systems (Gkaitatzi et al., 2010; van der Plas & van Lieshout, 2012). These attitudes depend on several factors, including: levels of digital literacy in society; alleviation of public and professional concerns about confidentiality of health-related data; approaches to pricing of and payment for PHS use; and strategies concerning the "imposition" of PHS or changes in – or even the withdrawal of – the traditional services they may replace.

Social insurance funds have a culture of financing health services once the damage is done – providing healthcare services to prevent further damages is increasingly the role that is expected from them, but has not always been. Implementation of PHS may entail that actors in health and social care have to leave their predefined and expected roles; this is always likely to cause resistance. Physicians may be reluctant to engage in further services and training in order to empower patients and treat them as equals, as experts themselves; this reluctance may prevent PHS implementation and use. Patients are often expected to show more commitment, participation, and self-management, abandoning the traditional doctor–patient hierarchy: not all may be keen on this change of role. A further obstacle is medical professionals' primary mono-disease orientation.

A point of general concern in the workshops organized during the PHS foresight project was the issue of equity and equality of access to PHS. The equal distribution principle applied in hospitals (i.e., that all people should receive equal attention and treatment) may be harder to apply when healthcare is "brought out into society". More advantaged social groups will probably be able to afford more sophisticated services that can the less advantaged, but there is also the possibility of PHS directly contributing to social inclusion, for example by reaching out to remote geographical locations that have been less well served by centrally managed public health systems (Amanatidou et al., 2014).

Social acceptance of PHS is crucial for their widespread implementation and use. Discussions and analyses during the PHS workshops and interviews suggest that social acceptance relates to: digital literacy of the population as a whole; concerns about confidentiality; and issues around the pricing of and payment for PHS use. What is often neglected in discussions about social acceptance are fears that the introduction of new services relating to PHS technologies may be accompanied by a premature withdrawal of traditional services, or that access to other services (e.g., insurance) may be made conditional on the use of PHS.

2. Service systems of PHS

A wider systems approach takes into account the need to design complex architectures relating together people (e.g., recipients of care, care-givers, and others), organizational structures and processes (e.g., that determine divisions of labour and responsibilities and flow of resources) and technologies – especially the information technologies, but also other devices and software related to health and social care – and information.

One notion that has increasingly attracted attention in this context is the notion of ecosystems. Ecosystems consist of different stakeholders, each with its own goals, perspectives, and challenges. Stakeholders here include part of the science and technology system (e.g., firms, technology developers, the scientific community), the health and social care delivery system (e.g., public and private practitioners and managers, and also patients and their organizations and relatives). All of these stakeholders are heavily influenced by regulators and the institutional framework in general.

In order to introduce innovative ideas in healthcare successfully, it is often vital to take account of the ecosystem. Integrated service solutions require aligning various actors in the ecosystem, and are hinged to the healthcare reimbursement and financing models, regardless of the differences in institutional set-ups of public health care in EU countries. Basically, there are two models of reimbursement in public health care: fee for service (e.g., reimbursement based on diagnosis-related group, or DRG, which is typical for hospitals), and fee per capita (e.g., number of patients treated, regardless of measures taken, which is typical for general practitioners). Both models for reimbursement applied in public health and social care systems can be problematic for the implementation of PHS and integrated service solutions for health and social care in general. Keeping patients out of hospital – through successful implementation of PHS – reduces the fee for services that hospitals receive, and hence reduces their incentives to adopt PHS. On the contrary, general practitioners who receive fees per capita may be unwilling to accept extra (and maybe unpaid) work that is associated with the additional PHS services (Abadie et al., 2011). These funding silos in residential and hospital care pose substantial difficulties to the introduction of PHS services, which often aim at linking the two or avoiding one for the other. Reductions in inpatient services can lower the burden on health and social care expenses, and technologically advanced outpatient services can help healthcare providers to deliver better and more individualized service. This situation suggests alternative funding mechanisms, additional fees (for PHS services), or other types of remuneration and financing. These new approaches are only likely to develop in the medium and long term.

But, this discussion also highlights some of the problems that a transition between service systems can involve. As already noted, the challenge of system innovation typically requires more than just excellent technological solutions, but also a multi-stakeholder process of service system design. Another major problem in health and social care is the division in many countries between healthcare and homecare practice and funding, which has severe consequences for the widespread introduction and adoption of PHS.

3. Markets for PHS

Reliable data on the markets for PHS are rare, despite the variety of reports by market research companies and consultancy firms that promote optimistic views of the markets, or particular market segments, of PHS (e.g., Baum & Abadie, 2013; Datamonitor, 2007; Frost & Sullivan, 2010; Khandelwal, 2010; Ludwig, 2009; Taga et al., 2011). Such reports tend to use a technology-driven market segmentation, and often are unclear as to their methodology and definitions of what units are actually counted in sales figures. Some of the reports note that ehealthcare investment has generally been proxied by ICT investment rather than healthcare investment (Baum & Abadie, 2013). In general, the perception of PHS markets by these market reports is skewed by a supply-side view.

There is an inherent difficulty in surveying the supply-side of the PHS market, as it is likely that supply is also characterized by individuals or very small companies. The advent of smartphones has significantly lowered the market-entry barriers for new producers, who can now rely on an existing platform and program an "app" at nearly marginal price (Baum & Abadie, 2013). The mHealth supply is dominated by individuals or small companies, with 30% of mobile app developer companies being individuals and 34.3% being small companies (defined as having 2–9 employees) (IDC, cited in European Commission, 2014).

In contrast, existing surveys of the PHS supply side suggest that most suppliers are large and medium-sized firms (e.g., Baum & Abadie, 2013). This finding points to the difficulties of identifying small-scale operations (e.g., individual programmers) and young firms, which can be assumed to also populate the supply-side of the PHS markets, especially in the mHealth and fitness realms.

Still, in terms of markets share it seems likely that most markets are dominated by large incumbents (Baum & Abadie, 2013). Purchasing decisions of public healthcare organizations may be powerful factors of success. Such customers typically have long innovation and adoption cycles of five to 10 years. Firms need certain characteristics to cope with such lengthy adoption processes, which often involve much adaption to customer needs. Furthermore, public healthcare providers need reliable partners over years or decades, which make them more likely to ally with incumbent supply firms with established track records and relationships.

Furthermore, the present research project suggests that that the optimistic market projections from market research and consultancy firms may fail to take into account the demand side and more general systems features. A wider systems approach led to the following considerations concerning the demand for PHS:

1. It seems to be a characteristic of demand in PHS markets that clients are on the one hand users and may on the other hand be patients, in which case the cli-

ent may be a different kind of person/organization. This relationship depends of course on the type of PHS service solution, and accordingly, the literature on PHS markets is torn between the focus on users (i.e., an ICT focus) and on patients (i.e., a health focus). The question arises as to whether demand for PHS will rise substantially on the basis of out-of-pocket money from users/patients, on the basis of private insurances who acquire additional services for their clients, or from financing or spending decisions from public health care bodies (see also Abadie et al., 2011).

2. Another, issue impacting on demand in the PHS area is lack of confidence in individual applications. If many applications exist, which one should the user/patient as an individual trust? And does the physician trust the same one? How then, does a general need for change and efficacy in healthcare translate into demand for single PHS products and services?

3. Finally, this translation may be difficult, because it often involves systemic innovation which, as noted above, needs a multi-stakeholder process and thus takes time. Furthermore, PHS solutions are often related to age-based conditions, and demand for age-based innovations shows distinct features depending on the obviousness of the *age-specialization of the product or service* (Levsen & Herstatt, 2014). Products or services with a moderate to high age specialization face distinct challenges. First, that users are hard to reach when their autonomy has been substantially impaired, and their search for information and ability to make purchasing decisions are limited. Distribution via regular consumer channels may be significantly restricted, which results in costly and difficult sales processes. Second, if others, such as informal carers, take over the purchasing decision, these products and services bear the risk of non-acceptance by the targeted users. Third, if users do not suffer from significantly reduced mobility or cognitive abilities, products with moderate to high age specialization bear the risk of stigmatization, or of being non-prestigious at the least.

Stakeholders in the PHS area expect that new business models have to develop in order to gain value from PHS technologies (Amanatidou et al., 2014) – the logic being that valuable market opportunities for PHS solutions pass because of ill-defined value propositions for stakeholders. This shortcoming poses the question of why new business models in the PHS area do not develop readily. What prevents profit-seeking individuals or or-

ganizations from defining new value propositions and exploiting technological opportunities if they seem obvious?

The few studies of business models in health technologies indicate that the definition of value propositions may indeed be fraught with difficulties. Other than studies of the pharmaceutical industry and its alliances with biotech spin-offs, there is little examination of how business models and health technology co-evolve. One of the few exceptions is Lehoux, Daudelin, Williams-Jones, Denis, and Longo (2014), who stress that business model innovation may take time because a number of interacting factors are relevant: the development of a business model results from a "sequential adaptation to new information and possibilities" and articulates an innovation's value proposition and its market segment, the value chain, the revenue model, the value network, and the competitive strategy (Chesbrough & Rosenbloom, 2002: cited in Lehoux et al., 2014). It starts with a selection of one value proposition (out of several that are latent in the new technology). The definition of the market segment to which the (health) technology will offer value also has important consequences. There is an uneven distribution of benefits resulting from the new technology, and of ability and willingness to pay for these, from patients and their relatives, informal carers, physicians, nurses, health care managers, governments, employers, and third-party payers. Managing the value chain for creating and distributing the value(s) offered involves tradeoffs and affect different stakeholder interests (Lehoux et al., 2014). Hence, the development of a business model faces significant uncertainties regarding the innovation, its market, and its supplier (uncertainty being higher for a newly founded firms – especially those emerging from non-business spheres, but even firms emerging from the industrial sphere may face uncertainties reflecting the industry's dominant logic) (Sabatier et al., 2012).

Thus, the establishment of a business model may well involve successive synergistic readjustments – or even drastic reconfigurations of the original business model (Lehoux et al., 2014).

PHS technologies and services are associated with positive externalities – benefits accruing to others than those who pay the price. In case of PHS, many different stakeholders may experience benefits from the introduction of PHS, as suggested above, but which are priced depends on the business model. Economic theory sees this as one type of market failure that justifies government action. If left to private producers, the product or service in focus is supplied insufficiently, which may slow the growth of PHS markets. Private firms expect investment by public actors, who face financial restrictions, and would have to engage in a process of system innovation in order to implement PHS service systems efficiently. The public actors expect investment by private firms. These mutual expectations may result in underinvestment on both sides.

4. Research and technological development of PHS

In the PHS workshops, the main role of public policy, in order to ensure quality of services and allow interoperability, was seen to be certification and standardization of hardware, software, devices, and systems. Processes for health and social care often engage many system players, in several different organizations: one way of dealing with the interfaces that arise in such contexts is promoting interoperability (i.e. the capability of systems to exchange data in a plug-and-play like fashion). Interoperability is generally thought to have at least three distinct levels:

1. Syntactic interoperability (e.g., Bluetooth, USB)

2. Semantic interoperability (e.g., IEEE X73, HL7 CDA)

3. Pragmatic interoperability

Most standards widely in use today are concerned primarily with the syntactic layer: they deal with data communication protocols and message composition. Standards for the semantic layer, which are concerned with the "meaning" of the data, are much harder to use and less mature today. Such standards are essential for enabling systems to understand each other. For example, decision support on a multi-modal data basis, taking into account information from clinical documents and data provided by patients directly via PHS, requires that these data can be meaningfully together.

Finally, to achieve pragmatic interoperability means being able to orchestrate different healthcare providers (and their ICT infrastructures) into a continuous caring process, spanning the borders of healthcare organizations – or even, considering cross-border healthcare, whole healthcare systems.

Standards alone are often not enough to achieve higher levels of interoperability: this requires initiatives that guide the utilization of standards in the context of well-defined use cases. Major interoperability initiatives in

the field of healthcare are the "Integrating the Healthcare Enterprise" (IHE) and the "Continua Health Alliance" (CHA) initiatives. IHE is an initiative by healthcare professionals and industry to improve the way in which healthcare IT systems share information. IHE promotes the coordinated use of established standards to address specific clinical need in support of optimal patient care. CHA's mission is to "establish an ecosystem of interoperable personal connected health systems that empower individuals and organizations to better manage their health and wellness" (Carroll et al., 2007). Neither organization creates standards itself, instead promoting clearly defined use cases in which existing standards are deployed.

Whereas IHE is primarily healthcare system focused and becomes relevant mostly in the last step while sending healthcare related data to EHR systems, CHA focuses on systems and devices close to the patient. CHA's mission is broader; it includes not only telehealth in terms of remote monitoring of vital signs but also systems more dedicated to wellness and fitness, as well as those supporting elderly people in terms of independent living (e.g., ambient assisted living) and those being cared for at home (e.g., telecare). As such, CHA is of prime importance to the PHS domain. IHE, however, is also essential in cases where PHS systems are to be linked to healthcare professionals and are not confined just to the patients themselves, informal care or consumer-oriented systems (i.e., "gadgets").

Market-entry barriers are a major concern for competition policy. Organizations promoting standards thus should construct open alliances that provide access to various types of firms and organizations in partnership; otherwise, market entry may be restricted.

Finally, research on PHS is not only necessary for technologies and standards, but also to analyze the benefits of PHS applications. This is the basis for comparing PHS applications and also for communicating success. The empirical investigation of efficacy and effectiveness of PHS implementation in turn is the basis for the wider diffusion of these technologies and development of new services around these technological solutions. However, further research on criteria for success and indicators is needed in order to compare either different service solutions or before-and-after situations.

Questions guiding this kind of research are likely to be:

• What are criteria for the successful implementation of PHS in new services?

- How did PHS solutions impact health and wellbeing in society?

- Who benefits and how can this benefit be measured best?

5. Framework conditions

During the PHS workshops and interviews, it was often suggested that healthcare services will not be solely provided by traditional caregivers such as nurses or physicians. Many other qualifications will continue to emerge in health and social care. Policy makers need better evidence to assess these developments and take decisions to maintain a critical supply of the service workforce (see also MovingLife, 2012). New technologies require technically skilled experts able to implement, run, and maintain the systems and to train and support users (i.e., patients, nurses, doctors, relatives) for daily usage of such systems. By the same token, many caregivers who originally are not affiliated with modern technologies are facing new challenges when needing to adapt to their daily use. Different patients might need different technologies, with (multiple?) devices in people's homes and, in many cases, it is actually the caregiver rather than the patient using them. All players in the health sector will need to think how these additional skills can be achieved by the caregivers – and how they will be reimbursed.

How healthcare organizations deal with their accumulated digital information (i.e., big data) is crucial for the uptake of health ICT. Sharing sensitive patient data in a large, heterogeneous environment complemented by the use of web-based applications raises a number of privacy and security concerns. Case study evidence by OECD (2010) suggests that appropriate privacy protections must be integrated in the design of new health ICT systems from the beginning – they proved difficult to be introduced ex-post (OECD, 2010).

According to EHTEL (2008) the implementation of incident-reporting procedures – similar to those employed by the pharmaceutical industry – would also be welcome. Associated with such incident reporting should be ways of checking that eHealth information systems have been properly implemented and audit trails managed; this should be the subject of constant monitoring for incorrect operation or abuse. Despite standards for medical products on the basis of the Medical Device Directive (MDD; tinyurl.com/d7o56wj), there are apparently gaps with respect to service packages based on PHS technologies.

Discussion and Conclusion

The concept of PHS is often collapsed into the specific information systems that are constructed to support new health and social care services, or even into the specific devices that are employed within these information systems, such as wearable sensors to monitor health conditions or behaviour patterns. This article has argued the importance of a wider systems view, one that situates PHS within health and social care service systems. Such a wider approach takes into account the need to design complex architectures relating together people (i.e., recipients of care, caregivers, and others), organizational structures and processes, with their divisions of labour and responsibilities, flows of resources, etc., and technologies (especially information technologies, but also other devices and software related to health and social care). It also highlights some of the problems that a transition between service systems can involve – the challenge of system innovation. This challenge typically requires more than just excellent technological solutions, but also a multi-stakeholder process of service system design.

It is widely, and plausibly, argued that PHS can contribute to improved health outcomes *and* increase the efficiency of health services. In principle, there should be very substantial contributions, though early demonstrator studies are at best equivocal in displaying major gains and, in particular, cost-savings. This ambiguity reflects the fact that we are dealing with "wicked problems" involving numerous stakeholders and numerous specialized types of expertise – and indeed, a multiplicity of specific problems aggregated together under the health and social care rubric, and often intertwined in the circumstances of specific individuals and communities. PHS are emerging at a time when complex restructuring of health systems – and even of the notion of health itself – is being prompted by demographic, technological, and social changes. PHS will be part of this restructuring, and the extent to which the potential gains of PHS are achieved will be affected by the form it takes. Substantial challenges are involved in shaping this restructuring so that it can rapidly capitalize on the potential of PHS, while supporting equity, patient empowerment, and movement towards more healthy lifestyles.

Numerous stakeholders will be involved in this process, which involves building what participants described as "a PHS innovation ecosystem". It will be important to recognize the very real interests of different stakeholders – for avoiding deterioration in health outcomes; for maintaining and extending the equity and social inclusion elements of health systems; for stimulating the development of innovative and effective health interventions and medical technologies; for maintaining professional competences and social status; for rewarding entrepreneurial behaviour; and for protecting and for using personal data. At present, the emergence and potential of PHS has not been widely debated beyond expert communities. Much wider processes of consultation, dialogue, and vision creation will be required to ensure that interests can be articulated – and where necessary challenged – in a transparent manner.

Meeting these challenges will require experimentation, dialogue, and monitoring of change. This study indicated some of the major aspects of change that will need to be addressed. They range from the creation of new business models and partnerships between organizations of different kinds, through stimulating the acquisition of new skills and the emergence of new professions in health (and related) workforces, to putting regulatory frameworks into place that can allow for informed acceptance of evidence-based solutions. In all of these aspects of change, public attitudes will need to be taken into account, because citizens are crucial stakeholders in these processes. These processes will need to be the focus of much greater effort in the near future.

The present study is, hopefully, one step in the direction of adopting a holistic and combined approach in understanding PHS and establishing and sharing visions of the desirable futures that can be achieved with the use of PHS, and the problems that may be encountered and the ways in which these may be addressed, in the course of shaping these desirable futures.

Acknowledgements

The research leading to these results has received funding from the European Union's Seventh Framework Programme (FP7 2007-2013) under the project "Personal Health Systems Foresight" (Grant agreement no. 305801).

An earlier version of this article was presented at the 2014 Annual Conference of the European Association for Research on Services (RESER), which was held from September 11th to 13th in Helsinki, Finland. RESER is a network of research groups and individuals active in services research and policy formulation.

References

Abadie, F., Codagnone, C., van Lieshout, M., Pascu, C., Baum, P., Hokkainen, A., Valverde, J. A., & Maghiros, I. 2011. *Strategic Intelligence Monitor on Personal Health Systems (SIMPHS): Market Structure and Innovation Dynamics*. Joint Research Centre Scientific and Technical Reports. Brussels: European Commission. http://is.jrc.ec.europa.eu/pages/TFS/SIMPHS1

Amanatidou, E., Miles, I., Saritas, Ö., Schartinger, D., Giesecke, S., & Pombo-Juárez, L. 2014. *Personal Health Systems: A Success Scenario*. Personal Health Systems Foresight.

Baum, P., & Abadie, F. 2013. Market Developments – Remote Patient Monitoring and Treatment, Telecare, Fitness/Wellness and mHealth. In F. Abadie, M. Lluch, F. Villanueva Lupianez, I. Maghiros, E. Villabla Mora, & M. B. Zamora Talaya (Eds.), *Strategic Intelligence Monitor on Personal Health Systems*. Brussels: European Commission. http://is.jrc.ec.europa.eu/pages/TFS/SIMPHS2deliverables.html

Chesbrough, H., & Rosenbloom, R. S. 2002. The Role of the Business Model in Capturing Value from Innovation: Evidence from Xerox Corporation's Technology Spin-Off Companies. *Industrial and Corporate Change*, 11(3): 529–555. http://dx.doi.org/10.1093/icc/11.3.529

Codagnone, C. 2009. *Reconstructing the Whole: Present and Future of Personal Health Systems*. Brussels: PHS2020, 7th Framework Programme, European Commission.

Cunningham, P., C., G.-P., Green, L., Miles, I., Rigby, J., & Uyarra, E. 2005. In Sickness, in Health and in Innovation: NHS DIRECT – A Health Sector Innovation Study. *Administration*, 53(3): 42–65.

Datamonitor. 2007. *Telehealth Spending in Europe through 2012*. London: Informa.

European Commission. 2014. *Green Paper on mobile Health (mHealth)*. Brussels: European Commission.

Frost & Sullivan. 2010. *European Remote Patient Monitoring Market*. Mountain View, CA: Frost & Sullivan.

Gkaitatzi, O., Bekiaris, E., Mourouzis, A., Lekka, E., Karavidopoulou, Y., Villagra, F., Schaller, P., & Sörgel, P. 2010. *Definition of REMOTE User Requirements and Use Cases. Deliverable D1.1 for Project ICT-Based Solutions for Prevention and Management of Chronic Conditions of Elderly People*. REMOTE Project Report AAL-2008-1-147.

IfM and IBM. 2008. *Succeeding through Service Innovation: A Service Perspective for Education, Research, Business and Government*. Cambridge, UK: University of Cambridge Institute for Manufacturing.

Karni, R., & Kaner, M. 2006. *An Engineering Tool for the Conceptual Design of Service Systems, Advances in Service Innovations*. New York: Springer.

Khandelwal, N. 2010. *The World Market for Telehealth – A Short and Long-term Analysis*. Wellingborough, UK: InMedica.

Lehoux, P., Daudelin, G., Williams-Jones, B., Denis, J. L., & Longo, C. 2014. How Do Business Model and Health Technology Design Influence Each Other? Insights from a Longitudinal Case Study of Three Academic Spin-Offs. *Research Policy*, 43(6): 1025–1038. http://dx.doi.org/10.1016/j.respol.2014.02.001

Levsen, N., & Herstatt, C. 2014. *Lead Markets in Age-Based Innovations. Technology and Innovation Management Working Paper 80.* Hamburg University of Technology.

Ludwig, S. 2009. *The Fitness Market.* Düssseldorf, Germany: Deloitte.

Maglio, P. P. 2010. Challenges in Service Science. Presentation at Cambridge Service Alliance Conference on Challenges in Services, based on work reported more fully in P. P. Maglio, C. A. Kieliszewski, & J. C. Spohrer (Eds). *The Handbook of Service Science.* New York: Springer.

MovingLife. 2012. MObile eHealth for theVINdication of Global LIFEstyle Change and Disease Management Solutions. D2.1State of Play in Mobile Healthcare. Accessed February 1, 2015: http://moving-life.eu/

OECD. 2010. Improving Health Sector Efficiency. The Role of Information and Communication Technologies. *OECD Health Policy Studies.* Accessed February 1, 2015: http://www.oecd.org/els/health-systems/improvinghealthsectorefficiency.htm

Rotmans, J. 2006. *Societal Innovation: Between Dream and Reality Lies Complexity.* Rotterdam: Erasmus University.

Sabatier, V., Craig-Kennard, A., & Mangematin, V. 2012. When Technological Discontinuities and Disruptive Business Models Challenge Dominant Industry Logics: Insights from the Drugs Industry. *Technological Forecasting and Social Change,* 79(5): 949–962.
http://dx.doi.org/10.1016/j.techfore.2011.12.007

Schot, J., & Geels, F. W. 2008. Strategic Niche Management and Sustainable Innovation Journeys: Theory, Findings, Research Agenda, and Policy. *Technology Analysis and Strategic Management,* 20(5): 537–554.

Taga, K., Bohlin, N., Brennan, J. W., & Kuruvilla, T. 2011. *Capturing Value in the mHealth Oasis.* Boston: Arthur D. Little, Telecom and Media Viewpoint.

The Capital Region of Denmark & Health Care Innovation Centre. 2011. Discussion Paper for the mHealth Wworkshop on December 5th 2011: Theoretical Framework of Understanding. *MOVING LIFE Project.* Accessed February 1, 2015: http://www.moving-life.eu/viewpage.php?page_id=5

van der Plas, A., & van Lieshout, M. 2012. Strategic Intelligence Monitor on Personal Health Systems Phase 2 (SIMPHS 2) Country Study The Netherlands. In F. Abadie, M. Lluch, F. Lupiañez, I. Maghiros, E. Villalba, & B. Zamora (Eds.), *JRC Scientific and Technical Reports.* Brussels: European Commission. http://is.jrc.ec.europa.eu/pages/TFS/SIMPHS2

Keywords: personal health systems, service innovation, foresight studies, ehealth, mhealth, healthcare, health and social care, stakeholders, innovation ecosystem, service systems, system design, technology adoption

About the Authors

Doris Schartinger is a Scientist at the Austrian Institute of Technology (AIT) in Vienna, Austria. She studied Economics, and her primary focus of research is technological change and economic development. She covered many aspects of innovation processes and diffusion in private manufacturing firms, public organizations, public-private networks, and service innovation. Her recent projects concentrated on innovation in the healthcare service system and intellectual property rights as indicators for innovation. She has been involved in a number of contract research projects for different clients and is experienced in co-ordinating and managing such projects.

Ian Miles is Professor of Technological Innovation and Social Change in the Manchester Institute of Innovation Research at Manchester Business School, United Kingdom. He is also Head of the Laboratory for the Economics of Innovation at the Higher School of Economics in Moscow, Russia. In addition to research on service innovation and knowledge-intensive business services, his work – funded by a wide range of bodies – has encompassed foresight studies, information technology innovation, and social indicators. He makes numerous presentations to academic, industry, and policy groups; he has over 20 edited or authored books, and over 250 journal articles and book chapters.

Ozcan Saritas has been employed by the Manchester Institute of Innovation Research (UNIMAN) at Manchester Business School, United Kingdom, where he works on innovation studies and foresight, and where he is also Editor of the journal *Foresight*. He has numerous publications in the areas if foresight and roadmapping, has been lead researcher on several major projects, and is actively engaged in executive education.

Efthymia (Effie) Amanatidou is a Research Associate at the Manchester Institute of Innovation Research at Manchester Business School, United Kingdom. She has more than 15 years of experience in research and innovation policy analysis including in particular foresight studies and evaluation/impact assessment of research policies and programmes. During this time, she has closely collaborated with a number of European Commission and Members States' policy makers, distinguished researchers, and corporate managers. Effie has been invited to several conferences as a speaker and has published in a number of scientific journals.

Susanne Giesecke is a Senior Scientist at the Austrian Institute of Technology (AIT) in Vienna, Austria. She studied Political Science and North American Studies in Berlin, Germany, and in Wisconsin, USA. She has been engaged in several research projects and foresight exercises as well as foresight networks discussing emerging technologies such as biotechnology, convergence of technologies, quantum cryptography, and ICT security issues. At AIT, she was responsible for the FP7 project FORESEC: Europe's evolving security, and she also designed the evaluation for the Austrian security research programme.

Barbara Heller-Schuh is a Scientist at the Austrian Institute of Technology (AIT) in Vienna, Austria. She studied History, German Language, Literature studies, and Knowledge Management in Graz/Krems, Austria, and Göttingen, Germany. Her main research interests cover RTI policy, social networks. as well as governance and funding systems for universities. She has been involved in several research projects dealing with the exploration of collaborative R&D projects to analyze network structure and dynamics on different policy levels. Furthermore, she is responsible for the maintenance of the EUPRO database, a comprehensive database containing standardized information about all accessible projects and their participants of the EU-Framework Programmes.

Laura Pombo Juárez is Senior Researcher and President of Impetu Solutions. Before founding Impetu Solutions, she worked in ICT companies including InterSystems, Telefónica, Sun Microsystems, Afianza, Autoedición y Publicidad, and Sadiel. She has a long track record in ICT applications in the healthcare sector and auditing and security issues, especially in connection with the management of national and international R&D projects. She holds an MSci Eng degree in Computer Science from Antonio Nebrija University in Madrid, Spain, and an Executive MBA from IE Business School, also in Madrid.

Günter Schreier is the Thematic Coordinator of the Austrian Institute of Technology's "Predictive Health Information Systems" research program, and he an Associate Professor for Biomedical Informatics at Graz University of Technology in Austria. His research interests are in eHealth/mHealth and predictive modelling in healthcare. He is the head of the working group "Medical Informatics and eHealth" for the Austrian Computer Society, a member of the board of the Austrian Society of Biomedical Engineering, and the Founder and President of the annual conference on "Medical Informatics meets eHealth" in Vienna, Austria.

8

Optimizing Innovation with the Lean and Digitize Innovation Process
Bernardo Nicoletti

" It must be remembered that there is nothing more difficult " to plan, more doubtful of success, nor more dangerous to management than the creation of a new system. For the initiator has the enmity of all who would profit by the preservation of the old institution and merely the lukewarm defense in those who gain by the new ones.

Nicolo Machiavelli (1469–1527)
Philosopher and playwright

Actionable knowledge to improve innovation and bring value to the customers and organizations is essential in today's economy. In the past, there have attempts to apply Lean Thinking and Six Sigma to the innovation processes, with mixed results. The aim of this article is discuss how to improve innovation processes using the Lean and Digitize Innovation process, which integrates digitization into the Lean Six Sigma method. Through the redesign of innovation processes and their automation, the process aims to add value to customers, improve effectiveness, eliminate waste, minimize operating costs, and reduce time-to-market. This new method is characterized by seven stages, or "the 7 Ds" (define, discover, design, develop, digitize, deploy, and diffusion), with 29 steps. This article describes the Lean and Digitize Innovation process and presents cases where the approach has been successful in helping innovation processes from start to end: from the definition of the value for the customers up to the implementation of a prototype and engineering of the delivery processes.

Introduction

Innovation is crucial to the success of any business. Far too many organizations spend the bulk of their efforts on improving production, finance, and marketing and not enough efforts on improving innovation. Innovation is becoming increasingly more important as the demands of the global economy increase. Organizations need to be agile, current, and smart in order to face the challenges of the changing global economy (Oza & Abrahamsson, 2009; Wilson & Doz, 2011).

Lean Innovation represents the systematic interpretation of Lean Thinking principles relative to innovation in its different forms. There are few systematic implementations of Lean Thinking in innovation management, contrary to what has happened in the production world (Liker, 2003; Schuh et al., 2009). High uncertainties of processes, novelty, and complexity indicate special requirements for the implementation of Lean

Thinking in innovation processes. They require holistic rethinking for the implementation of Lean Thinking.

This article focuses on the lean processes, describes their phases, and shows how to use and benefit from the combination of Lean Six Sigma with digitization towards a powerful lean innovation method for improving processes. The method aims to add value to customers, improve effectiveness, eliminate waste, minimize operating costs, and reduce time-to-market through the redesign of the innovation processes and their automation. This approach is increasingly necessary for global success and is an important pre-requisite for success in the lean application of innovation processes.

The Lean and Digitize Innovation process represents the systematic interpretation of Lean Thinking principles regarding to the different types of innovation and development, while also taking into account the possibilities of automation.

Review of Literature on Improving Innovation Processes

First, we examine the literature that examines issues connected with the implementation of Lean Innovation. Lean management and innovation are two driving forces of today's business success. However, with fundamentally different concepts, some aspects of lean management may negatively affect an organization's ability to be successful with certain types of innovations.

Subramanyam, Srinivasan, and Prabaharan (2011) applied Lean and Six Sigma to new product development activities. To make the system effective and deliver the design at the shortest time to market with good quality, it is necessary to optimize material cost and design time. Subramanyam and colleagues dealt with an approach associated with the optimization of the above-mentioned problems with the strategy of Six Sigma.

Shuh, Lenders, and Hieber (2009) introduced Lean Innovation and described the core findings of their survey on Lean Innovation at the Laboratory for Machine Tools and Production Engineering WZL at RWTH Aachen University. Their paper focused on the value system, described its elements, and showed how to use and benefit from the value system towards powerful Lean Innovation. The value system is one core element of Lean Innovation, which is the basis for the value stream design in innovation and development projects. The value system defines, structures, and prioritizes "values" adaptively for one specific innovation project. All relevant stakeholders in the innovation process, such as external and internal customers, define the values considering the organization's strategy and culture. This activity represents the basis for a consequent value-oriented alignment of projects and processes in innovation.

Hoppmann and colleagues (2011) studied the implementation of Lean Product Development . They surveyed 113 product development departments of international organizations. Based on the insights gained from the testing of the hypotheses and the available empirical data, they defined a Lean Innovation Roadmap. They used a novel, two-step methodology called Adjusted Past Implementation. The resulting roadmap for implementing Lean Product Development consists of four major phases and shows the introduction of the eleven Lean Product Development components in the form of eleven overlapping implementation streams. For each of the components, Hoppmann and colleagues defined four detailed characteristics and depicted the time for implementing these characteristics on the roadmap, giving an idea of when to introduce the elements of Lean Product Development relative to each other. For organizations intending to implement a Lean Product Development system, the Lean Innovation Roadmap can serve as a guideline for learning and continuously improving their organizations.

Gerhard and colleagues (2012) investigated the impact of lean principles in innovation-intense organizations, that is, companies of the automotive and machinery industries as well as in research facilities. They suggested that the implementation of lean principles creates positive effects in technology development, for instance, in reducing the development time and increasing the development efficiency. They found that out of the existing lean principles, the two principles of "avoidance of waste" and "flow", have the highest influence on the improvement of development activities

Browning and Sanders (2012) pointed out that, when operations are novel and complex – as in product development, research, information technology, and many other kinds of projects – cutting out the waste turns out to be much more challenging. To understand the impact of lean in an environment characterized by extreme novelty and complexity, these authors drew on their experiences with a number of processes, and in particular Lockheed Martin's lean implementation for the F-22 fighter aircraft. Their find¬ings lead to a path that executives and managers can follow to become lean without compromising innova¬tion.

Chen and Taylor (2009) presented five propositions based on a comparison between the lean culture, lean design, lean supply chain management, and lean human resource management with the characteristics and contributing factors of different types of innovations. These authors discussed different strategies for an organization to achieve the balance and maintain lean and innovation at the same time. They analyzed advantages, disadvantages, and suitable situations for each strategy.

Nepal (2011) extended the new product development literature by presenting a case study of a Lean Product Development transformation framework implemented at a manufacturing firm in the United States. In a departure from typical Lean Product Development methods, they integrated the design structure matrix and the cause and effect matrix into the lean transformation framework. In this way, they allowed analysis of the underlying complexity of a product development system, and thus facilitating determination of the root causes of wasteful reworks. They discussed several strategies to transform the current product development process into a lean process. In order to support the recommended changes in the new product development processes, they recommended a two-phase improvement plan, a new organizational structure roadmap, and a human resources plan. The results of the Lean Product Development show a 32% reduction in product development cycle time due to the proposed new product development process. Nepal's paper also details the lessons learned and the implications for engineering managers based on the case study presented.

For organizations to survive and thrive in today's environment, a key strategy is to leverage innovation capability through an effective process of converting unmet customer needs into successful innovations, thereby creating value for customers, the organizations, and other stakeholders. Welo, Olsen, and Gudem (2012) demonstrated how Lean Thinking could become a precompetitive factor in product innovation through its focus on customer value. The goal of this paper was to determine the applicability of user-centered methodologies in generating inputs that ultimately lead to differentiated innovations. Welo and colleagues presented an office chair case study that implied that, although user-focus is necessary, it will not inevitably lead to novel products, because users are engrossed with past and present.

Lean Thinking can even be used to drive general innovation in organizations (Byrne et al., 2007; Hoerl & Gerdner, 2010). Lean Thinking frees up an organization's resources – people, space, time, and money – such that more resources can be allocated to innovation projects. Another consequence of the application of lean is the support for a fundamental culture shift. Morale will go up when people in an organization start dealing with the complexity in the business. Lean Thinking eliminates or streamlines the processes and products that waste time, that frustrate customers, and that do not add value, thus freeing up the time for people to start thinking about what should come next (Cross, 2012, 2013).

Lean transformation and innovation have both been touted as strategies that are essential to the long-term survival of organizations. The question of whether the two approaches can be used simultaneously remains unanswered. Srinivasan (2010) attempted to derive a theory of lean systems of innovation that combines the notions of lean enterprise trans¬formation with that of innovation. The descriptive understanding of Rockwell Collins, as developed in their paper, draws on publicly available material to support the identification of the key elements of a strategic system of innovation. Srinivasan's analysis highlights the successful use of technology scanning, internal R&D, and open innovation within the innovation system at Rockwell Collins. Furthermore, the existence of a shared value proposition, a strong organizational culture that recognized and rewarded innovation, and the requisite organizational infrastructure serve as key enablers to designing a strategic system of innovation that is reflective of lean enterprise thinking.

Fichman, Dos Santos, and Zheng (2014) adopted a particularly broad conceptualization of digital innovation that allows for a variety of teaching styles and topical emphases for the information system core class. This conceptualization includes three types of innovation (i.e., process, product, and business model innovation), and four stages for the overall innovation process (i.e., discovery, development, diffusion, and impact). Based on this conceptualization, these authors examined the implications of adopting digital innovation as a fundamental and powerful concept in teaching organizations

None of the papers examined in this literature review analyzed the actual process of Lean Innovation projects in depth. Thus, the purpose of this article is to introduce the Lean and Digitize Innovation Process.

Innovation Processes

Innovation can be in the product or the process (Tushman & Nadler, 1986). Innovation can also be relative to organization or to business models (Nicoletti, 2013). Breuer (2013) reports some successful examples of Lean Innovation in venturing (see also Euchner, 2013). Innovation can be classified based on the whether it is incremental or radical (Ettlie et al., 1984), or modular or architectural (Henderson & Clark, 1990). At the heart of the innovation work is the ability to connect the strategy and tactics associated with developing a system of innovation from a macro-per¬spective, with the mechanics of effectively transitioning ideas into products, processes, organization, or business models.

Freeman and Perez (1988) define innovation as the introduction of new and improved ways of doing things at work. In an economic sense, an innovation is accomplished with the first commercial transaction involving a new or improved product, process, or organization of business model. Thus, innovation is restricted to intentional attempts to bring about benefits from changes. These might include economic benefits, personal growth, increased satisfaction, improved group coherence, better organizational communication, as well as productivity and economic measures that are usually taken into consideration. The innovations of technology firms often include technological changes such as new products, production processes, the introduction of advanced manufacturing technology, as well as the introduction of new information and communication technologies (ICT).

Many models have been developed for acquiring a better understanding of the innovation process. These models have ranged from simple "pipeline" or "black box" models to complicated models. Some of them focus on consumer product innovation; others are concerned with industrial innovation. Although numerous models have been developed to describe the innovation process, no model appears to be capable of being used as a generalized model of innovation (Koskinen & Vanharanta, 2002).

Based on observations in the Toyota Production System, Mehri (2006) illustrated some of the negative effects of the lean design process on product innovation. In particular, he underlined that the original Lean Thinking method, rather than allowing open innovation, requires engineers to follow strict flows of design. Due to a product design approach that is heavily based on benchmarking and standardization, internal innovations seem to be impossible. The Lean and Digitized Innovation process allows organizations to overcome this challenge.

Research Methodology

Essential for Lean Innovation is the definition of value for the innovation itself. Therefore, the starting point of Lean and Digitize Innovation is a systematic method to define and handle target values and requirements regarding the innovation as an enabler for a lean development process – the value system. The value system represents a framework for mapping value in a holistic, hierarchical, dynamic, and transparent way (Schuh et al., 2008).

The value system defines, structures, and prioritizes "values" adaptively for one specific innovation project. All relevant stakeholders in the innovation processes, such as external and internal customers, define the values, while considering the organization strategy and

culture. It represents the basis for a consequent value-oriented alignment of innovation projects and processes. According to Gudem and colleagues (2013), maximizing customer value is a core principle in innovation, but the value definitions used tend to be based on logical reasoning rather than real-life observations. These authors, based on empirical insights concerning different stakeholders' perceptions of customer value, suggested a redefinition of the functional product value calculation in Lean Product Development. Their method integrates emotional customer value into the traditional model, which is based on minimizing operating costs and reducing time-to-market.

Lean management and innovation are two driving forces of business success. However, with fundamentally different concepts, some aspects of lean management may negatively affect an organization's capability to be successful with certain types of innovations. This article develops a process to minimize such impacts. It is based on combining Lean Six Sigma principles and tools with automation of the innovation processes. In addition, the article discuss different example where this process was successful.

Value system practices focus on market orientation of products and services. Products and services heavily rely on the supply chain process to contribute to the value system. Globalization, competition, and high cost of production influence the value system imperatives. Organizations involved in the value system are challenged with the creation of innovation. ICT can support the improvements in the performance of innovation in many organizations. There are efforts to use ICT as a tool to innovate processes, products, and services for establishing improved management practices to harness better returns on investment and customer satisfaction

Results and Discussion

Several stages compose the Lean and Digitize (short for Lean Six Sigma and Digitize) Innovation process. To be successful, Lean and Digitize Innovation must adopt a process that this article describes as "the 7 Ds: define, discover, design, develop, digitize, deploy, and diffusion. It is essential to apply this methodology and its tools in strong partnership between the sectors of the organization involved, including quality and support departments (such as ICT, finance, or operations) (Nicoletti, 2012). Stakeholders from all parties need to align in setting up and staffing the improvement project team. Perhaps more importantly, the organizations must treat the initial application of the Lean and Digitize Innovation process as the beginning of an iterative cycle that generates continuous improvement and leads to a change in the culture of the organizations towards Lean thinking (Womack & Jones, 2003). A "problem" or "challenge" should not trigger process-improvement efforts. It should be a substantial part of the organizational culture.

It is important to blend process improvement and ICT technology. Based on research and experience, one can profitably use the Lean and Digitize Innovation process. In reference to Lean Innovation, Lean and Digitize Innovation can be summarized as follows. It can be divided into seven stages and 29 steps, as described below and illustrated in Figure 1. At the end of each stage are "toll gates", where the project needs to be checked by the innovation steering committee.

Stage 1: Define
In this stage, the environment is defined to set the ground for the innovation.

1. Context: identify the needs or the requests of the customers, shareholders, and employees, as well as the challenge of competitors and the degree of respect for compliance (e.g., legislation and regulations)

2. Culture: detect the culture of the organization, of the community, and of the nation in which the organization is located

3. Vision: tackle the problems of effectiveness, efficiency, economy, and quality of innovation

4. Strategy: define the possible content of innovation

5. Kick-off: launch the project during a special meeting and notify all the stakeholders

6. Governance: define how to manage the project and set up the team

7. Voice of the Customer: listen to the Voice of the Customers (VoC) associated with the potential innovation and verify it

Stage 2: Discover
In this stage, new ideas are discovered for potential development into a process, product, organization, or business model innovation.

8. Invention: the creation of something new through a organization's own creative process

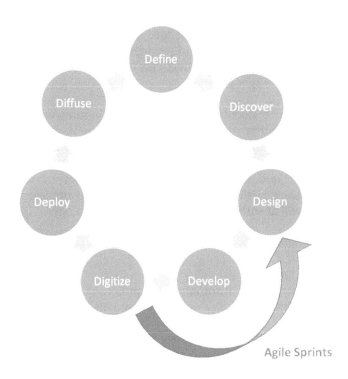

Figure 1. The Lean and Digitize Innovation process and its seven stages, or "the 7 Ds"

9. Selection: finding and evaluating an innovation to potentially develop or adopt

10. Metrics: translate the innovation and the VoC into Critical-to-Quality (CtQ) factors

11. As-Is: map the existing situation in terms of products, processes, organization, or business models

Stage 3: Design
In this stage, the framework and the sequence of activities are defined.

12. Lean: define how to innovate with the support of the team in workshops and meetings

13. Kaizen Plan: define the improvement intervention plan

14. Architecture Design: define the rules, policies, and process structure of the potential innovation

Stage 4: Develop
In this stage, an idea is developed into a usable innovation.

15. Build: construct the chosen solutions

16. Packaging: surround the core technology with complementary products and services that together form a solution that can be effectively used for a given purpose by a target adopter

17. Configure: decide which technology features will be used, whether they will be used as is or with adaptations, how the technology will be integrated with other technologies the organization already has in place, how related organizational elements (e.g., structures, processes) will be changed, and how the organization will absorb and make use of the technology

18. Change management: manage the changes

Stage 5: Digitize
In this stage, the automation is applied at the highest possible level.

19. Implementation: implement the digitized application

20. Test: unit tests, system tests, integration tests, and user acceptance tests should all be conducted

Stage 6: Deploy
In this stage, the innovation is implemented and the ancillary activities are performed.

21. Deploy: implement the chosen solution

22. Document: issue the documents related to the innovation

23. Verify: control the improvements

24. Internal and External Benefits: assess the benefits, both external (i.e., take notice of customers, shareholders, and employees satisfaction) and internal (i.e., assess the profitability, market share, and internal improvements related to the new process)

25. Lessons Learned: learn from the initiative

26. Celebration: acknowledge the team's work

Stage 7: Diffusion
In this stage, it is necessary to assemble and arrange the resources necessary to i) persuade and enable a population of organizations or individuals to adopt and use the innovation and ii) to diffuse or spread it across a population of potential users.

27. Assimilation: when individuals and other units absorb the innovation into their daily routines and the work life of the firm

28. Appropriation: involves such tasks as managing intellectual property and the ecosystem of complementary products and services so that profits are protected from suppliers, customers, and imitators

29. Transformation: the technology and organization to take advantage of the new opportunities brought about by the innovation; transformations can also happen at the market and societal levels

Stages 3, 4, and 5 should be done with an Agile approach, doing several cycles, or "springs" in the Agile terminology. An Agile approach is a development method based on iterative and incremental development, where requirements and solutions evolve through collaboration between self-organizing, cross-functional teams (Socha et al., 2013). It promotes adaptive planning, evolutionary development and delivery, and a time-boxed iterative approach, and it encourages rapid and flexible responses to change. It is a conceptual framework promoting tight interactions throughout the development cycle.

Margaria and Steffen (2010) stressed the simplicity of the Agile approach. Its importance in introducing innovation in software development has been stressed (Aaen, 2008). Brown and Levison (2011) also highlighted how Agile can foster innovation. A similar concept was introduced for instructional systems development (Groves et al., 2012).

The Agile Manifesto is based on twelve principles (Beck et al., 2001). They can be customized in connection with Lean and Digitize Innovation:

1. Customer and organization satisfaction should be pursued by rapid delivery of useful innovation

2. Requirement changes should be welcomed, even late in the innovation process

3. Incremental working innovations should be delivered frequently (e.g., every few weeks rather than months)

4. Incremental working innovations are the principal measure of progress

5. Development should be sustainable; the team must be able to maintain a constant pace

6. There should be close, daily cooperation between business people and the innovation team

7. In-person conversation is the best form of communication (co-location but also virtual teams)

8. Projects should be built around motivated individuals, who should be trusted

9. Continuous attention should be paid to technical excellence and good design

10. Simplicity – the art of maximizing the amount of work not done – is essential

11. Teams should be self-organizing

12. Adaptation to the changing environment is encouraged

Tools

Many tools can be used in conjunction with the process described. They can come from the tools used in Lean, Six Sigma, Agile management, and digitization. This article will not consider the latter ones, because since they are extensive and well covered in many publications. The following discussion does not consider all the possible tools that can be used but only the most appropriate.

One of the best tools for process design is Quality Function Deployment (QFD), commonly known as the House of Quality. It identifies the potential customer value of the innovation based on the customer's (be they internal or external) needs and an innovation's (normally a product) quality characteristics. The analysis through QFD is used to determine when a new innovation is useful, so excess resources are not consumed for innovation that may not be beneficial.

Another useful tool is TRIZ (a Russian acronym for Theory of Inventive Problem Solving). The requirements for innovation can be defined by introducing the TRIZ problem-solving approach in finding innovative solutions to technical problems, especially in product development processes. TRIZ is implemented to define the solutions necessary to improve these processes. The use of TRIZ is beneficial with the lean practice because it efficiently utilizes resources in the system to eliminate waste.

Yamashima, Ishida, and Mizuyama (2005) describe a new method, named the Innovative Product Development Process (IPDP). It systematically integrates QFD with TRIZ and enables the effective and systematic creation of technical innovation for new products. In IPDP, the target products' functions and mechanisms are deployed in parallel into hierarchical structures, and the mechanism that most requires technical innovation is specified from an analysis of customers' needs by calculating a mechanism weight. Then, the technical problems to be solved are defined by considering the relationship between the specified mechanism and corresponding functions or quality characteristics. The application of TRIZ helps in developing the "technical" innovation. The technical innovation of a washing machine proved the effectiveness of IPDP.

Another important tool is prototyping, which is both a culture and a language (Kelley, 2001). Just about anything can be prototyped – a new product or service, a process, even an organization or a business model. What counts is moving the ball forward, achieving some part of a goal.

In the case of product innovations, Digital Mock Up (DMU) is a concept that allows the description of a product, usually in 3D, for its entire life cycle (Subramanyam et al., 2011). The product design, manufacturing, and support engineers work together to create and manage the DMU. One of the objectives is to have important knowledge of the innovation to replace any physical prototypes with virtual ones, using 3D computer graphics techniques. As an extension, it is frequently referred to as Digital Prototyping or Virtual Prototyping. The benefits of DMU are:

1. Reduced time-to-market by identifying potential issues earlier in the design process

2. Reduced product development costs by minimizing the number of physical prototypes that need to be built

3. Increased product quality by allowing a greater number of design alternatives to be investigated before a final one is chosen

There are several practices connected with the Agile approach, such as extreme programming from software engineering, which enables the team to work together to determine goals and shared objectives; the rational unified process from both systems and software engineering because of its iterative development methodology; the focus on eliminating waste from lean manufacturing; and the daily scrum update meetings from product development. These processes enable the innovation team to adapt to changing requirements, reduce the project risk, increase the visibility of team progress, involve stakeholders and learners from the beginning of projects, and speed up the creation of value that the team makes to the business.

Innovation in organizations is important. A key to effective and efficient innovation is the ability to commercialize new products quickly and economically while leveraging the advantages of global outsourcing. The growing role of global outsourcing in innovation represents a paradigm shift that has had a large impact on innovation and commercialization, as noted by Marion and Friar (2012). They explored the use of outside innovation and commercialization resources, from contract employees to short-run manufacturers. They then synthesized their research into four areas where innovation operators could most effectively leverage outsourcing throughout the innovation continuum. Opportunities include developing strong strategic partnerships with outside vendors, using rapid prototyping resources to support agile development, using short-run manufacturers to test products and markets before building to volume, and using expert contractors to reduce fixed personnel costs.

These tools and approaches are helpful for a lean environment because they promote effective and efficient innovation.

Business Cases

The best examples of the Lean and Digitize Innovation process have been tested and implemented in General Electric (Nicoletti, 2006). General Electric teaches innovation operators to use Lean and Digitize Innovation to respect all their processes using a few of the lesser-known lean tools (Immelt, 2012; Prokesch, 2009):

• 7-ways

• Pugh matrix

• Mock-up

• Kaizen

• 5 Why's

• Right-size machine prototyping

Business success starts with understanding the challenges the customers need to solve. It requires reams of information for answers. However, as data sources proliferate, organizations risk being overwhelmed. The Lean and Digitize Innovation process has proved particularly beneficial in these cases.

Veolia Water – the water division of Veolia Environnement, a French company that is the global leader in environmental businesses that include water, waste, and energy – use sifts through masses of information for business intelligence (Laîné, 2014). Starting in 2007, Veolia Water implemented a program to identify and manage strategic knowledge for competitive intelligence and patent services that help the organization anticipate technological developments and environmental threats and sort information from specialized sources – including databases, websites, and institutional sources and compile targeted information for its experts to analyze.

Not all of an organization's knowledge resides in databases. Each employee's knowledge is even richer, but more distributed or isolated by function. Social innovation technology inspired by Facebook but tuned for business can use employee knowledge regardless of location or role.

When automotive parts supplier Visteon assembled a cross-functional global team to develop a new concept for an automotive component, it used cloud-based social innovation applications that, in a lean and digitized way, facilitate collaboration, idea sharing, and progress tracking (Laîné, 2014).

Misra and Choudhary (2010) presented the efforts of a rug company in the direction of an innovation cycle management to ensure a development-oriented value chain. They developed a framework to examine initially the ICT intervention scenario and then how ICT can mediate in certain areas in the value chain.

Conclusions and Further Research

This article presents a Lean and Digitized Innovation process that has proved very successful in a certain number of business cases. The Lean and Digitize Innovation process is based on the application of several stages described as "the 7 Ds": define, discover, design, develop, digitize, deploy, and diffusion). These seven stages are further divided into 29 steps. The process is based on Lean Six Sigma principles but optimizes the use of ICT systems and agile methodologies to tackle the novelty and complexities in innovation processes.

Improving the innovation process is the competitive advantage in innovation-intense industries, as required by today challenging times. The combination of lean and digital technologies helps in making organizations faster and more efficient than competitors, thus creating the basis for competitiveness and future success. In this context, the transfer and application of lean principles and digitization is an appropriate approach to face these challenges.

The Lean and Digitize Innovation process presented in this article has proved successful in a certain number of business cases in manufacturing companies. It would be interesting to consider its extension to service industries, where the digitized components become much more important. Campanerut and Nicoletti (2010) started some work in this direction for the Design for Six Sigma (DFSS), but additional work is necessary.

The Lean and Digitize Innovation process has demonstrated benefits in cases involving product innovation. It seems particularly important to extend its applications to innovation in processes, organizations, and business models. This extension might require modifications to make it successful.

About the Author

Bernardo Nicolletti is a Lecturer at the Master in Procurement Management at the Università di Tor Vergata in Rome, Italy. He serves as a Director in Transigma, a strategy consultancy company specialized in process improvements and digitization in financial services with assignments in Europe, USA, and the Middle East. Bernardo has worked with General Electric Capital as Program Manager of a Common Systems and later as Group Chief Technology Officer of GE Money and Acting CIO. He has also been CIO Latin America for AIG UPC. He is a frequent speaker at international conferences and author of books, papers, and blog posts (lean digitize.com), through which he describes his approaches to synthesizing Lean Six Sigma and automation.

Keywords: lean innovation, agile innovation, lean six sigma, lean and digitize, innovation management, re-engineering

Acknowledgements

An earlier version of this article was presented at the 2014 International Conference on Engineering, Technology, and Innovation (ICE), which was held from June 23rd to 25th in Bergamo, Italy. The ICE conference discusses systems engineering as a socio-technical task, with a focus on design of products and services, and the entrepreneurial innovation process for its adoption in society and the economy.

References

Aaen, I. 2008. Essence: Facilitating Agile Innovation. In *Agile Processes in Software Engineering and Extreme Programming*, 1–10. Berlin, Germany: Springer.

Beck, K. et al. 2001. *Principles behind the Agile Manifesto*. Manifesto for Agile Software Development. Accessed March 1, 2015:
http://agilemanifesto.org/principles.html

Breuer, H. 2013. Lean Venturing: Learning to Create New Business through Exploration, Elaboration, Evaluation, Experimentation, and Evolution. *International Journal of Innovation Management*, 17(3): 1–22.
http://dx.doi.org/10.1142/S1363919613400136

Brown, R., & Levison, M. 2011. *Creativity for Agile Teams*. Accessed March 1, 2015:
http://agilecrossing.com/wp-content/uploads/2011/11/Handout-Agile2011.pdf

Browning, T. R., & Sanders, N. R. 2012. Can Innovation Be Lean? *California Management Review*, 54(4): 5–19.
http://dx.doi.org/10.1525/cmr.2012.54.4.5

Byrne, G., Lubowe, D., & Blitz, A. 2007. Using a Lean Six Sigma Approach to Drive Innovation. *Strategy & Leadership*, 35(2): 5–10.
http://dx.doi.org/10.1108/10878570710734480

Campanerut, M., & Nicoletti, B. 2010. Best Practices for DFSS in the Development of New Services: Evidence from a Multiple Case Study. *The Journal of American Business Review*, 16(1): 1–8.

Chen, H., & Taylor, R. 2009. Exploring the Impact of Lean Management on Innovation Capability. In *Proceedings of the 2009 International Conference on Management of Engineering & Technology*, 826–834.

Cross, B. 2012. *Lean Innovation: Understanding What's Next in Today's Economy*. Boca Raton, FL: CRC Press.

Cross, B. 2013. Lean Innovation – Getting to 'Next'. *Ivey Business Journal*, 77(3): 23–27.

Ettlie, J. E., W. P. Bridges, & O'Keefe, R. D. 1984. Organization Strategy and Structural Differences for Radical versus Incremental Innovation. *Management Science*, 30: 682–695.
http://dx.doi.org/10.1287/mnsc.30.6.682

Euchner, J. 2013. What Large Companies Can Learn from Start-Ups. *Research Technology Management Journal*, 56(4): 12–16.

Fichman, R. G., Dos Santos, B. L., & Zheng Z. 2014. Digital Innovation as a Fundamental and Powerful Concept in the Information Systems Curriculum. *MIS Quarterly*, 38(2): 329–353.

Freeman, C., & Perez, C. 1988. Structural Crises of Adjustment, Business Cycles and Investment Behavior. In G. Dosi, C. Freeman, R. Nelson, G. Silverberg, & L. Soete (Eds.), *Technical Change and Economic Theory*, 38–66. London, UK: Pinter Publishers.

Gerhard, D., Engel, S., Schneiner, C., & Voigt, K. I. 2012. The Application of Lean Principles and its Effects in Technology Development. *International Journal of Technology Management*, 57(1/2/3): 92–109.
http://dx.doi.org/10.1504/IJTM.2012.043953

Groves, A., Rickelman C., Cassarino, C., & Hall, M. J. 2012. Are You Ready for Agile Learning Design? *TD Magazine*, 66(3): 46–50.

Gudem, M., Steinert, M., Welo, T., & Leifer, L. 2013. Redefining Customer Value in Lean Product Development Design Projects. *Journal of Engineering, Design and Technology*, 11(1): 71–89.
http://dx.doi.org/10.1108/17260531311309143

Henderson, R. M., & Clark, K. B. 1990. Architectural Innovation: The Reconfiguration of Existing Product Technologies and the Failure of Established Firms. *Administrative Science Quarterly*, 35(1): 9–30.
http://www.jstor.org/stable/2393549

Hoerl, R. W., & Gerdner, M. M. 2010. Lean Six Sigma, Creativity, and Innovation. International *Journal of Lean Six Sigma*, 1(1): 30–38.
http://dx.doi.org/10.1108/20401461011033149

Hoppmann, J., Rebentisch, E., Dombrowski, U., & Zahn, T. 2011. A Framework for Organizing Lean Product Development. *Engineering Management Journal*, 23(1): 3–15.

Immelt, J. R. 2012. The CEO of General Electric on Sparking an American Manufacturing Renewal. *Harvard Business Review*, 90(3): 43–46.

Kelley, T. 2001. Prototyping is the Shorthand of Innovation. *Design Management Journal (Former Series)*, 12(3): 35–42.
http://dx.doi.org/10.1111/j.1948-7169.2001.tb00551.x

Koskinen, K. U., & Vanharanta, H. 2002. The Role of Tacit Knowledge in Innovation Processes of Small Technology Companies. *International Journal of Production Economics*, 80(1): 57–64.
http://dx.doi.org/10.1016/S0925-5273(02)00243-8

Laîné, D. 2014. Working Smarter. *Compass Magazine*, January 2014. Accessed March 1, 2015:
http://compassmag.3ds.com/3/Cover-Story/WORKING-SMARTER

Liker, J. K. 2003. *The Toyota Way*. New York, NY: McGraw-Hill USA.

Margaria, T., & Steffen, B. 2010. Simplicity as a Driver for Agile Innovation. *Computer*, 43(6): 90–92.
http://doi.ieeecomputersociety.org/10.1109/MC.2010.177

Marion, T. J., & Friar, J. H. 2012. Managing Global Outsourcing to Enhance Lean Innovation. *Research Technology Management*, 55(5): 44–50.
http://dx.doi.org/10.5437/08956308X5505053

Mehri, D. 2006. The Darker Side of Lean: An Insider's Perspective on the Realities of the Toyota Production System. *Academy of Management Perspectives*, 20(2): 21–42.
http://dx.doi.org/10.5465/AMP.2006.20591003

Misra, H., & Choudhary, K. 2010. Opportunities and Challenges for ICT Mediated Innovations in Development Oriented Value Chain: The Case of Jaipur Rugs Company. *Vilakshan: The XIMB Journal of Management*, 7(2): 21–48.

Nepal, B. P., Yadav, O. P., & Solanki, R. 2011. Improving the NPD Process by Applying Lean Principles: A Case Study. *Engineering Management Journal*, 23(1): 52–68.

Nicoletti, B. 2006. Nuovo Pignone, l'Arte di Fondere Lean Management e Six Sigma, *Computerworld Italia*, 6 (Dec): 1–2.

Nicoletti, B. 2013. Innovazione: Una Ricetta per la Crescita. *Strategie & Procurement*, Luglio: 18-19.

Nicoletti, B. 2012. *The Methodology of Lean and Digitize*. Farnham, UK: Gower Press.

Oza, N., & Abrahamsson, P. 2009. *Building Blocks of Agile Innovation*. Charleston, SC: Book Surge Publishing.

Prokesch, S. 2009. How GE Teaches Teams to Lead Change. *Harvard Business Review*, 87(1): 99–106.

Schuh, G., Lenders, M., & Hieber, S. 2011. Lean Innovation: Introducing Value Systems to Product Development. *International Journal of Innovation & Technology Management*, 8(1): 41–54.
http://dx.doi.org/10.1109/PICMET.2008.4599723

Schuh, G. Lenders, M. & Hieber, S. 2008. Lean Innovation: Introducing Value Systems to Product Development. In *Proceedings of the 2008 International Conference on Management of Engineering & Technology*, 27-31.

Stevens, G. A., & Swogger, K. 2009. Creating a Winning R&D Culture II. *Research Technology Management*, 52(2): 22–28.

Socha, D., Folsom, T. C., & Justice, J. 2013. Applying Agile Software Principles and Practices for Fast Automotive Development. In *Proceedings of the FISITA 2012 World Automotive Congress*, 1033–1045.

Srinivasan, J. 2010. Creating a Lean System of Innovation: The Case of Rockwell Collins. *International Journal of Innovation Management*, 14(3): 379–397.
http://dx.doi.org/10.1142/S1363919610002696

Subramaniyam, P., Srinivasan, K., & Prabaharan, M. 2011. An Innovative Lean Six Sigma Approach for Engineering Design. *International Journal of Innovation, Management and Technology*, 2(2): 166–170.

Tushman, M. L., & Nadler, D. A. 1986. Communication and Technical Roles in R&D Laboratories: An Information Processing Approach. *Management of Research and Innovation*, 15: 91–111.

Welo, T., Olsen, T. O., & Gudem, M. 2012. Enhancing Product Innovation through a Customer-Centered, Lean Framework. *International Journal of Innovation & Technology Management*, 9(6): 1–28.
http://dx.doi.org/10.1142/S0219877012500411

Wilson, K., & Doz, Y. L. 2011. Agile Innovation: A Footprint Balancing Distance and Immersion. *California Management Review*, 53(2): 6–26.

Womack, J. P., & Jones, D. T. 2003. *Banish Waste and Create Wealth in Your Corporation*. New York, NY: Free Press.

Yamashina, H., Ishida, K., & Mizuyama, H. 2005. An Innovative Product Development Process for Resolving Fundamental Conflicts. *Journal of the Japan Society for Precision Engineering*, 71(2): 216–222.

9

Integrating Design for All in Living Labs

Madeleine Gray, Mikaël Mangyoku, Artur Serra,

Laia Sánchez, and Francesc Aragall

*" Design as a driver of user-centred innovation contributes "
to getting good ideas to market. It enhances agile and
focused product and service development ... It facilitates
the development of better, transparent and more
effective public services and contributes to social
innovation, thereby raising the quality of life for all
citizens of Europe. And for complex societal problems,
design offers people-centred approaches that can achieve
better solutions.*

Design for Growth and Prosperity (2012)

The European Union has identified innovation as a key driver behind business competitiveness and responsive governance. However, innovation in and of itself may not be sufficient
to help businesses bring new products to market and to help governments shape public services that meet the real needs of citizens. The Integrating Design for All in Living Labs
(IDeALL) project sought to identify and test methodologies for designing with users in real-
life settings. The results of the experiments showed how different methodologies can be applied in different contexts, helping to provide solutions to societal issues and to create
products and services that genuinely meet user requirements. In this article, we describe
the methodologies used in the IDeALL project and provide examples of the project's experiments and case studies across four main areas: i) services; ii) health and social care; iii) information and communication technology; and iv) urban design.

Introduction

Innovation is often promoted as essential to the
prosperity and indeed survival of European economies
in global markets, as exemplified at a policy level by the
European Commission's Innovation Union programme (tinyurl.com/2dxextn). With the rise of emerging
economies, the Commission warns that its member
countries may face chronic decline unless they can differentiate themselves through advances brought about
by innovation. Yet, even though it may be tempting to
view innovation as a magic solution, innovation in and
of itself may not have a universally beneficial impact,
as Rufo Quintavalle (2014) argues in his article titled
"Food Doesn't Grow in Silicon Valleys".

On the macro-level, funding for research and development in Europe has not necessarily translated into innovation uptake in Europe (Curley & Salemin, 2013).
On the micro-level, even in purely market terms, innov-

ation is no guarantee of the success of a product or service, as Mulder (2012) has shown in this publication.
Indeed, Gournville (2005) finds that, although "Innovation is crucial to the long-term success of many firms",
"highly innovative products... fail at a greater rate than
less innovative products", a phenomenon which he attributes to the need for a fundamental behaviour
change that the adoption of such products requires.

Accordingly, we ask:

• How can companies lead the innovation charge while
  mitigating the risks of launching new products?

• How can public services evolve in such a way that
  they empower citizens without leaving any one group
  behind?

• How can design be a factor of change while leading
  innovation to the market?

In this article, we describe the Integrating Design for All in Living Labs (IDeALL; ami-communities.eu/wiki/IDeALL) project, which aims to answer these questions. First, we describe how the European Union has begun to consider the discipline of design as a driver of innovation, and then we briefly explain two of the main themes of the project: design for all and living labs. Next, we explain the rationale behind the project and give examples of the methodologies collated and compared according to the different criteria used to classify them. We then provide examples and findings of some of the project's experiments and case studies across four main areas: i) services; ii) health and social care; iii) information and communication technology (ICT); and iv) urban design. Finally, we suggest further possible applications of these methodologies by other businesses and public-sector bodies.

Design as a Driver of Innovation

The European Commission has begun to address these questions at policy level in a number of ways, including a focus on non-technological innovation such as design. In 2011, it established a Design Leadership Board (i3s.ec.europa.eu/commitment/25.html), whose report *Design for Growth and Prosperity* (Thomson & Koskinen, 2012) includes recommendations aimed at enhancing design's "long-term contribution to smart, sustainable, and inclusive growth through increased competitiveness and the pursuit of a better quality of life". The report presents design as a driver of innovation, defining it as "an activity of people-centred innovation by which desirable and usable products are defined and delivered". By bringing the end user closer to the innovation process, the report argues, the risk of launching new products and services may be reduced.

Design for all, also known as universal design in North America, is a branch of design that takes human diversity into account so that anyone, no matter what their personal characteristics and including future generations, can access goods, services, and environments and hence can participate fully in society (Aragall and Montaña, 2012). Although technology brings new possibilities, it can be a barrier as well as a facilitator (Steinfeld and Maisel, 2012); design for all seeks to ensure that technological innovation is tied to social progress, as suggested by design-for-all professional Rafael Montes in an interview cited in the Design for All Foundation Awards brochure (Design for All Foundation, 2013).

Design for all emphasizes the importance of involving users in the design process, because this means the end

result is more likely to meet their needs. This view has traditionally put the discipline at odds with the "lone genius" stereotype of the designer; however, as *Design for Growth and Prosperity* suggests, this model is becoming increasingly discredited, as "the complexities of innovation call for a truly multidisciplinary approach" that involves users at all stages. Although many designers adopt a design-for-all approach as a matter of principle, successes such as the OXO product range imply that it has a role in bringing successful innovations to market (Aragall and Montaña, 2012; Steinfeld and Maisel, 2012). Steinfeld and Maisel suggest that universal design can help companies bridge the gap between innovations brought about by research, such as the synthesis of a new material, to a successful product launch through a holistic development approach that focuses on the end user; this point is also illustrated in IDeALL experiment with the company Lékué, as discussed below.

The emergence of living labs has provided a mechanism for precisely this kind of multidisciplinary, co-creative approach, allowing companies to test products with users and public bodies to try new ways of providing services. Living labs allow design for all to make the logical step from user-centred design to user-driven design. Living labs generate not only new methodologies but also help to organize complex communities (e.g., including universities, local authorities, companies, and citizens) in co-designing solutions for complex problems. In that sense, living labs allow the design professionals to work with a co-design perspective, thereby enabling a more strategic approach that goes beyond the traditional client-by-client model. As Mulder (2012) and others suggest, by providing a real-life environment for the co-creation and evaluation of innovations, living labs allow complex problems to be identified and they enable the devlopment of solutions that will ultimately be more acceptable to a range of end users. Furthermore, thanks to new technologies and manufacturing methods, more channels for co-creation and evaluation have been made possible, as many commentators have noted, including the European Design Leadership Board in Design for Growth and Prosperity. However, the ability of living labs to facilitate user-driven design has not yet been fully embraced by small and medium-sized enterprises (SMEs), which make up 99% of businesses in the European Union (European Commission, 2013), or by public bodies who may be intrigued by Government 2.0 but are wary of the risks involved in changing their ways of operating.

Integrating Design for All in Living Labs

The Integrating Design for All in Living Labs (IDeALL) project was developed as a response to this challenge. One of six projects co-financed under the European Commission's Design-Driven Innovation programme (tinyurl.com/mpg3blx), it aimed to bring the design and living lab communities closer together and to identify within these communities the best ways to innovate with users in different contexts. Led by the Cité du design (citedudesign.com) in France, itself a design centre and living lab, the project consortium included design centres, living labs, educational institutions, and research centres, as well as the European Society of Concurrent Enterprising Network (esoce.net) and the European Network of Living Labs (openlivinglabs.eu). Among the living labs in the consortium and its supporting community were examples of the different types analysed by Leminen, Westerlund, and Nyström (2012) in this journal.

Responding to Vérilhac, Pallot, and Aragall's (2012) identification of "the lack of comparative studies on design methods involving users" as one of the barriers to "a more integrating approach of methods that could be used in a [living lab]", a comparative analysis of user-centred design methodologies was undertaken. The methodologies were compared using the following criteria:

1. The phase of the development process (research/ideation/prototyping/evaluation)

2. The duration of the methodology (short/medium/long)

3. The user level of involvement (low/medium/high)

This analysis showed how the methodologies might be useful in different contexts according to different requirements and restrictions, and methodologies can be searched by these criteria on the IDeALLwebsite (tinyurl.com/o6jeaxp). For example, a company wishing to develop a service might use the Service Innovation Corner methodology used by the University of Lapland or the Service Innovation and Design methodology from Laurea University of Applied Science. A company wishing to design and prototype a new product might use the Cité du design's *Laboratoire des Usages et Pratiques Innovants* (LUPI; Innovative Use and Practice Laboratory, tinyurl.com/qf5xgt7) methodology, whereas a company wishing to shift to a more user-centred business model overall might consider Francesc Aragall's HUMBLES method for user-centred business (Aragall & Montaña, 2012). In the subsections below, we describe some examples of these methodologies, which are summarized in Table 1.

Table 1. Summary of four example methodologies for user-centred design

Methodology	Phase	Duration	User Involvement
1. Service Prototyping	• Ideation • Prototyping • Evaluation	• Short	• High
2. 3H	• Research • Ideation • Prototyping • Evaluation	• Medium • Long	• High
3. LUPI	• Research • Ideation	• Short • Medium	• Medium
4. HUMBLES	• Research • Ideation • Prototyping • Evaluation	• Medium • Long	• Medium

1. Service prototyping (University of Lapland)
The Service Innovation Corner (SINCO; sinco.fi) is a service prototyping lab at the University of Lapland in Rovaniemi, Finland. The SINCO lab helps visualise and concretize abstract services and experiences by using service design tools and prototyping methods. Service prototypes consist of pictures or videos that are projected to screens and also sounds, lights, and props (Figure 1). Service prototyping can be used in all stages of the design process but is especially valuable in the ideation or conceptualisation phase. The basic idea of prototyping is to concretize unclear ideas and to provide information for planning and decision making.

The methodology has proven effective in the following case study:
• Developing a new experience for the Rajalla Pa
  Gransen shopping mall (youtube.com/watch?v=GJHO9oZM1F8)

Figure 1. Users participating in a service prototyping exercise at the SINCO

2. 3H: Head, Heart, Hands-on (Citilab)
The 3H (Head, Heart, Hands-on) methodology uses the human body metaphor to describe a step-by-step user-driven innovation process. It is an open living lab methodology that has been specifically developed for the European CIP iCity project.

The methodology goes through three major phases of activity:

1. *Head:* identifying and mapping the actors of the community innovation system to provide protocols and tools to collect and understand the needs and barriers to participate.

2. *Heart:* consolidating all the relationships necessary to establish trust and commitment between all the stakeholders.

3. *Hands-on:* engaging the participants in the co-creation and development activity in itself. The final part of this activity includes an evaluation activity based on a client-driven set of indicators.

The 3H methodology favours multi-disciplinary teams; it is not restricted to a particular type of user. However, 3H has been developed by Citilab and has been tested in their citizen engagement activity. This in-house methodology has been adapted to the iCity project in order to engage its stakeholders, and to foster the co-creation of services in the public interest.

The methodology has proven effective in the following case study:
• iCity (icityproject.com)

3. LUPI (Cité du design)
The LUPI (Innovative Use and Practices Laboratory) is a user-centred co-creation tool conceived in the Cité du design. Inspired by research methods from the Cité du design research department, the LUPI's added value is its flexibility (it has been applied in the private as well as local government sector) as well as its short duration (three to six months), which is in line with the temporality of small and medium-sized enterprises. A LUPI project always consists of three phases:

1. Framing the issue (1 day): Partners share their issues and clarify them collectively. Throughout the day, with the help of designers and the project coordinator, these ideas are refined and a particular investigation track is chosen. When the issue is clarified, a typology of users is also defined in order to prepare the next phase of the LUPI project.

2. On-site observations (3 ½ days): The second phase is more immersive. LUPI partners are trained by the designers to capture and synthetize "hidden insights" during user interviews.

3. Sharing (1 day): LUPI partners present the collected insights from the on-site observations and interviews. After the presentations, an ideation phase enables the new ideas to be mapped with the help of the designers. Particular attention is givento concepts with strong strategic elements that may lead to sustainable business models.

The most significant concepts generated from the last LUPI step are rendered in the form of a scenario title associated with a presentation pitch, which is illustrated by visual elements (e.g. sketches, videos, animations) (Figure 2). The storytelling medium is therefore the form of the final LUPI deliverable, which includes hypotheses assembled in a portfolio created by the designers (as a resource).

The methodology has proven effective in the following case studies:
• PLUG (*Plot de liaison à usage général*; tinyurl.com/orlrxr4)
• *Le "Robot lycéen"* (High school robot; tinyurl.com/ozqquqc)

4. HUMBLES (DfA Foundation)

HUMBLES was created by Francesc Aragall, President of the Design for All Foundation, who published the methodology in a book together with Jordi Montana from the ESADE Business Shool's Faculty of Business Administration in Barcelona, Spain (Aragall & Montana, 2012). The name of this human-centred methodology is derived from its seven iterative steps:

1. **H**ighlight Design for All opportunities
2. **U**ser identification
3. **M**onitor interaction
4. **B**reakthrough options
5. **L**ay out solutions
6. **E**fficient communication
7. **S**uccess evaluation

HUMBLES is adapted to the following typology of users: CEO, CFO, human resources, marketing, R&D, employees, customers, and consumers. Therefore, it is strongly adapted to the world of small and medium-sized enterprises. For gathering end-user insight, HUMBLES is quite effective on a quantitative level, because it is mainly based on surveys. On the downside, this method of collecting user insights limits the potential for qualitative insights.

The HUMBLES method is mainly focused on shaping the companies' strategies by human diversity and users expectations. The concrete tools to research the end users and to involve them in the design process vary for each business sector and company strategy. The methodology is particularly useful for changing companies' perception of the value of users as knowledge source.

The methodology has proven effective in the following case studies:
• Adopting Design for All at Lékué (tinyurl.com/qynuc8u)
• IDeALL platform (tinyurl.com/o57z9bo)

Figure 2. A visual element from a LUPI presentation pitch

Testing Methodologies in Real-Life Environments

With the aim of testing these methodologies and finding how they may be best suited to different contexts, experiments were carried out in the Rhône-Alpes region of France, Catalonia, Slovakia, Latvia, and Finland. Case studies showing additional applications of the methodologies were also collated on the IDeALL website (usercentredbusiness.com), allowing users to see examples of the methodogies in action, adapted to the requirements of the local context. The range of examples hints at the extent of the potential field of application for such approaches. A few examples, set out below, demonstrate how they can be used to address key social issues such as unemployment and skill mismatches, independent living for an ageing population, and the design of public spaces.

Service design

Service design is becoming an increasingly important sector, and good service design can result in increased customer loyalty. The two Finnish partners involved in the IDeALL project, Laurea University of Applied Sciences and the University of Lapland, are at the forefront of service design in Europe. Lapland's SINCO service-prototyping methodology is particularly useful for delivering mock-ups of services that immerse users in the experience before the service is fully designed. This methodology was used in an IDeALL experiment to explore ways to make a shopping centre more interactive and multisensory (Figure 3); the techniques included interviews, customer observation, surveys, and service prototyping. The shopping centre's manager

Figure 3. SINCO Living Lab methods in action at the Ragalla shopping centre

commented: "Young people who grow up here can be seen as long-term clients for us. They use certain services now, but if they stay in [the] …area as grown-ups, they can continue to be our clients for a very long time".

Laurea's approach to service design was demonstrated through case studies collected for the project. These case studies provide examples of co-designing services that might be complicated or involve ethical considerations, such as creating home safety devices to support independent living in the Guarantee project (guarantee-itea2.eu) or designing the HeartBug (superecg.com), a kit to self-test heart arrhythmia.

Health and social care
With rising levels of obesity and an ageing population, the health challenges faced by European countries are familiar to many industrialized nations. Technology may lead to the creation of increasingly sophisticated healthcare solutions, but focusing on the user is essential if they are to be genuinely responsive and personalized.

Several experiments were undertaken in the area of healthcare as part of the IDeALL project, and they show how businesses and public bodies can select methodologies to respond to users' healthcare needs. Examples include the development of a smart pill dispenser, supported by IDeALL partner Medic@lps, and innovative orthopaedic supports developed using LUPI methodology in an experiment led by the Cité du design. The HUMBLES method for user-centred business was ap-

plied in an experiment involving Lékué, a Catalan company with a strong focus on innovation, which helped them to shift their business aims from "being a market leader in the production of silicon-based products", to "producing utensils which would support people to cook well and follow a healthy diet".

Information and communication technology
Information and communication technology clearly plays a pivotal role in this new co-creative landscape, providing both the paradigms (e.g., open source) and the tools (e.g., user-generated content-sharing networks). IDeALL consortium member Artur Serra (2013) divides living labs in Europe along two main lines: "those who are focused principally on helping companies to connect with user requirements, facilitating processes by which these requirements can be incorporated into the design of products and services" and those that "concentrate on opening innovation systems to the society in general, which we would call citizen laboratories". Although some of the examples cited above fulfil the first category, he classifies his organization, IDeALL-partner Citilab in the second.

Several experiments and case studies selected by the IDeALL project show how new technologies can open new possibilities for all users, as shown in the example of Barcelona Laboratori (barcelonalab.cat), an IDeALL case study that seeks to make the whole city of Barcelona into a living lab. Serra describes Barcelona Laboratori and the different use cases developed by Citilab of Cornella de Llobregat for the IDeALL as a project "to build a second generation of citizen laboratories involving both the current official innovation system (universities, research centres, large businesses) and new, emerging stakeholder, such as entrepreneurs, urban innovation communities, (arduinos, *fablabbers*, social innovators), extending this innovation potential to as many citizens as possible … through schools, cultural centres, retirement homes, not-for-profit organizations and more'". This ethos is exemplified in the IDeALL experiment the iCity project (icityproject.com), which seeks to open up cities' information infrastructure to promote the co-creation of public services in areas such as mobility, environment, security, and health, by developers. This example has used the 3H engagement methodology designed by Citilab, which may be instructive for local governments wishing to introduce smart technology into their area. They can use this approach to ensure that new services are responsive to residents' needs and that big data is used in a way that benefits citizens.

At the local level, Citilab experiments have been directed towards equipping participants with the skills to adapt to a new digital economy and participate in the Internet of Things. *The Nuevos Artesanos* (New Artisans; nartesanos.citilab.eu) experiment, for example, was developed as a response to people with traditional craft skills finding themselves out of work. Combining programming and electronics workshops with a "do it yourself" ethos, participants were able to put their craft skills to use in the creation of smart items, documenting the process as they went along (Figure 4). Similarly, the *Inventa't la feina* (Invent your own job) experiment sought to find a solution to the situation in Mataró, which has some of the highest youth unemployment levels in Europe, by supporting young people to develop and assess their own business ideas.

In the Rhône-Alpes area, the *Agence Régionale du Développement et de l'Innovation* (ARDI; Regional Development and Innovation Agency) oversaw further experiments opening out technological innovation to a wide range of users. In the Webnapperon 2 (Web Doily 2; webnapperon.com) experiment by ERASME HOST, co-creation workshops (Figure 5) led to the "Web doily", which works with an RFID-equipped doily linked to a photo frame, allowing online content to be shared. It enables older users in particular to keep in touch with family and friends without needing computer skills. In another ARDI experiment, carried out by the *Laboratoire d'InfoRmatique en Image et Systèmes d'information* (Computing in Image and Information Systems Laboratory), users participated in workshops where they could take advantage of software and hardware capabilities offered by Arduino, Lego Mindstorms, and 3D printing to co-create a hub of connected smart items, leading to smart home automation that could improve quality of life.

Urban design

With an ever-increasing proportion of populations living in cities, coupled with changing conditions in industry and the pressures brought about by increasingly scarce resources, the need to create cities that are vibrant and sustainable, and that promote health and wellbeing is a key policy issue for many European nations. Accordingly, several IDeALL experiments have taken place in the urban sphere. In Saint-Étienne, several experiments used the LUPI methodology, where stakeholders such as local businesses were trained to work with users and the best qualified stakeholder was chosen to produce prototypes, such as the *Plot Urbain à Usage Général* (Urban Pillar for General Use) to develop street furniture.

Figure 4. Nuevos Artesanos at work during Citilab workshop session in 2014

Figure 5. Co-creation workshop during Web Doily 2 development

An experiment in Slovakia, a country where, according to the Slovak Design Centre, the concept of design for all was not well known, showed how users could co-create public spaces based on real needs. The original idea was to come up with designs for street furniture, but this evolved into a more fundamental question: what do people want in public spaces? The Slovak Design Centre involved the following in the project: the City of Bratislava, designers, architects, an art academy, a university of technology, cycling and accessibility associations, a bicycle manufacturer, and a street-furniture manufacturer. Using a range of user-centred methods to gather and prototype ideas in the actual setting (Figure 6), the experiment was widely publicized in the Slovak press. By helping the city council work towards its sustainable transport objectives, the experiment to redesign a street gained their support, while simultaneously introducing a new generation of students to the idea of user-driven, design-led innovation.

Conclusion

Although technological innovation is crucial to remaining competitive in international markets, the results will only be adopted if they are attractive to end users. The IDeALL project has helped to demonstrate the potential of combining methodologies from the design for all and living labs domains in order to achieve innovations accepted by users. It has shown that, through this collaboration, some changes have been recognized.

Design for all has to move from user-centred methodologies to *user-driven* methodologies, as living labs propose. Considering the user as co-designers is a perspective that has been a key element of living labs since the beginning of that movement. In addition, users should be understood from a dual perspective: they are consumers but also citizens. On the other

Figure 6. Street for All experiment organized by the Slovak Design Centre (Photo credit: Jan Mytny)

hand, living labs should recognize the need to include more professional design methodologies into their communities.

The IDeALL project has demonstrated that there is a wide range of user-centred design methodologies that can be adapted to different contexts and that can help provide solutions for societal issues, such as caring for an ageing population, obesity, and unemployment. Different methodologies will be of interest to different organizations: for example, businesses planning to deliver tailored services may wish to use service-design methodologies such as those used by the University of Lapland and Laurea University of Applied Sciences, whereas local governments may wish to consider methodologies such as LUPI to help co-design public spaces and at the same time support local businesses. Further experiments using these methodologies would help to determine different applications.

One of the most interesting results of the project has been the creation of a Master's course called "Smart Cities: Designing with Citizens" (tinyurl.com/oj25whv). Launched by the Design for All Foundation and BAU School of Design in Barcelona, this course aims to ensure that the smart cities of the future will be co-created with their citizens.

Finally, the project has also helped build a taxonomy of methodologies: a majority of the collated methods implicate the user at a high level at the ideation/conception phases, but gaps remain in the latter phases, such as prototyping.

The IDeALL consortium invites anyone interested in user-driven, design-led innovation to explore the user-centred business portal and provide feedback on how this can be improved to better meet their requirements: www.usercentredbusiness.com

About the Authors

Madeleine Gray is the former Communication Manager at the Design for All Foundation. She has worked in the area of universal design for several years, having previously worked as Head of Knowledge Development at the Centre for Accessible Environments where she was editor of the inclusive-design journal *Access by Design*. Based in Barcelona, the Foundation works to compile and disseminate information in the area of design for all, as well as to recognize examples of best practice through its annual awards scheme and Flag of Towns and Cities for All.

Mikaël Mangyoku is the Living Lab Project Manager for the Campus Manufacture Plaine Achille near the Cité du design and the European Project Manager for IDeALL. He has an Innovation Project Management and Industrial Design Master's degree from Strate College in Sèvres, France. He is both an engineer and a designer, and his research compares and analyses user-centred methodologies.

Artur Serra has been Deputy Director of the i2cat Foundation in Catalonia, Spain, since its creation in 2003. In 2006, he started from i2cat the project Anella Cultural (Cultural Ring), which connects the cultural community from five cities in Barcelona and Catalonia to a future Internet media infrastructure. He is a founding member of the European Network of Living Labs, and he organizes public-private-citizens partnerships fostering open innovation projects in Spain, such as Citilab.eu.

Laia Sánchez is responsible for the Social Media Lab at Citilab and is Assistant Professor of Comunication Sciences Faculty in the Universitat Autònoma de Barcelona.

Francesc Aragall is President of the Design for All Foundation in Barcelona, Spain, and Director of ProAsolutions, a consultancy company for urban and infrastructures design and strategic planning.

References

Aragall, F., & Montaña, J. 2012. Universal Design: *The HUMBLES Method for User-Centred Business.* Farnham, UK: Ashgate.

Curley, M., & Salemin, B. 2013. *Open Innovation 2.0: A New Paradigm.* EU Open Innovation Strategy and Policy Group (OISPG).

Design for All Foundation. 2013. International Awards 2013 (Brochure). http://designforall.org/new/doc/Folleto_Premios_DfAFd2013_EN.pdf

European Commission. 2013. Fact and Figures about the EU´s Small and Medium Enterprise (SME). May 1, 2014: http://ec.europa.eu/enterprise/policies/sme/facts-figures-analysis/index_en.htm

Gournville, J. T. 2005. The Curse of Innovation: Why Innovative New Products Fail. Marketing Science Insitute Working Paper Series, No. 05-117.

Leminen, S., Westerlund, M., & Nyström, A.-G. Living Labs as Open-Innovation Networks. *Technology Innovation Management Review,* 2(9): 6–11. http://timreview.ca/article/602

Mulder, I. 2012. Living Labbing the Rotterdam Way: Co-Creation as an Enabler for Urban Innovation. *Technology Innovation Management Review,* 2(9): 39–43. http://timreview.ca/article/607

Quintavalle, R. 2014. Food Doesn't Grow in Silicon Valleys. Stanford Social Innovation Review (Blog). May 1, 2014: http://www.ssireview.org/blog/entry/food_doesnt_grow_in_silicon_valleys

Serra, A. 2013. Tres problemas sobre los laboratorios ciudadanos. Una mirada desde Europa (Three Problems Concerning Living Labs: A European Point of View). *Revista Iberoamericana de Ciencia, Tecnología y Sociedad,* 8(23): 283-298.

Steinfeld, E. & Maisel, J. 2012. *Universal Design: Creating Inclusive Environments.* Hoboken, NJ: Wiley.

Thomson, M., & Koskinen, T. 2012. *Design for Growth and Prosperity:* Report and Recommendations of the European Design Leadership Board. Helsinki: DG Enterprise and Industry of the European Commission.

Vérilhac, I., Pallot, M., & Aragall, F. 2012. IDeALL: Exploring the Way to Integrate Design for All Within Living Labs. *Proceedings of the 18th International ICE Conference on Engineering, Technology and Innovation,* 1-8. http://dx.doi.org/10.1109/ICE.2012.6297699

Keywords: innovation, services, design, living labs, methodologies, design for all, health, social care, ICT, urban design, user-centred approaches, co-creation, service prototyping, 3H, LUPI, HUMBLES

10

Reviewing the Knowledge Systems of Innovation and the Associated Roles of Major Stakeholders in the Indian Context

Punit Saurabh, Prabha Bhola, and Kalyan Kumar Guin

" For good ideas and true innovation, you need human "
interaction, conflict, argument, debate.

Margaret Heffernan
Entrepreneur and author

In this article, we review various models of knowledge systems and discusses the relationships between various component stakeholders of innovation, namely higher-education institutions, industry, and government. The article uses India as a case study to examine new challenges and opportunities facing its innovation ecosystem. Within this context, we review existing models of knowledge systems through an innovative representation exemplifying the knowledge landscape and the model positioning. We argue for a reinforcing role of major stakeholders in the proliferation of innovation and entrepreneurship, and the need to promote healthy interactions between them.

Introduction

To address the challenge of creating jobs and wealth in modern economies, governments promote innovation because of its perceived contributions to the creation of jobs and wealth (Orhan & Scott, 2001). In particular, to fuel job creation, governments worldwide encourage students in higher-education institutions to consider entrepreneurship as an alternative to traditional employment. Indeed, there has been an increasing emphasis on entrepreneurship as a career option, especially during the recent global economic recession, which provided a boost to the types of course offerings in higher-education institutions and led to an upswing in student enrolment (Solomon, 2007). Recently, higher-education institutions have been offering an increasing number of courses related to entrepreneurship, especially in the United States during the difficult economic periods between 1996 and 1999 (Kuratko, 2005), when student attendance in entrepreneurial courses increased by 92% (Solomon, 2007).

Because of their role in entrepreneurship education, higher-education institutions can be viewed as societal innovation systems. Their task is not only to produce entrepreneurially oriented and competent individuals, but also to foster social mechanisms that underpin and facilitate the birth and growth of businesses and firms at a regional level (Laukkanen, 2000). Through regional innovation-based practices, higher-education institutions are increasingly acting as centers of growth and are poised to play a prominent role in economic development. This new, broader role has also opened up new challenges and opportunities for higher-education institutions, particularly in emerging countries (Gupta, 2005).

Lundvall and colleagues (2002) found that the efficiency of knowledge activities depends on the innovation system and its performance on several aspects of socio-economic and political institutions. They characterized knowledge systems and their relationship with economic development and innovation by interconnecting them with the introduction of knowledge into the economy and the society at large. Numerous researchers (e.g., Edquist et al., 2000; Parikh, 2001) also link knowledge systems to innovation. And, the link between entrepreneurial activity and economic growth has been made by several researchers (Caree & Thurik, 2002), who recognize the relevance of entrepreneurial activity and innovation in the economic development of a nation. Thus, there is a subtle linkage existing between innovation and knowledge systems. Others (e.g., Lundvall et al., 2002; Reynolds et al., 2002) have also referred to the interconnectivity of innovation and entrepreneurship, and the resultant role of other knowledge system stakeholders, specifically the role of higher-education institutions in economic growth.

In the present article, we use India as a case study to examine new challenges and opportunities facing its innovation ecosystem and the role played by higher-education institutions and other knowledge system stakeholders The Indian context is unique due to its demographic, geographic, and socio-economic positioning. India is the second most populous nation and has a fledgling economy with consumer appetite for all types of market-driven goods and services. It has vast diversities of religion, castes, and sects with a complex mix of problems echoing the severity of sub-Saharan African nations, which often lack the basic necessities of food, health, education, safe drinking water, etc. while in contrast matching the capabilities of developed nations with rapid strides in the field of high technology and software. Yet, the challenges are grave and look insurmountable unless serious remedial actions are initiated.

We provide background information about the Indian context in terms of barriers to innovation and identify a key collaboration gap in the innovation ecosystem: a lack of interaction between innovation stakeholders. As a potential means to fill this gap, we examine the role of knowledge systems by reviewing some of the models available in the literature. The article highlights the role of major stakeholders and points to the perceived gaps of the Indian innovation ecosystem and the role of knowledge systems in an Indian context. The knowledge system landscape indicates the positioning of the existing knowledge system models highlighted in the literature review. The ideal roles of major stakeholders in the innovation construct has been highlighted from an Indian perspective, which is pro-development and all-inclusive, but it is also relevant to other similarly placed economies.

Literature Review: Knowledge Systems

Parikh (2001) describes knowledge systems as consisting of four important knowledge processes: identification, preparation, documentation, and actualization. Primarily, the categorization of knowledge systems aims to support knowledge transformation suitable for its distribution and sharing among stakeholders. Scientific and technological developments have had con-

siderable impact on socio-economic processes of change of technological innovations (Leydesdorff & van den Besselaar, 1994). Correspondingly, socio-economic conditions also play an important role in research and development (R&D) based decision processes within the knowledge systems, especially in the industrial sector. Several conceptual models and approaches to linking innovation to important constituents of knowledge systems and the economy have evolved.

Pol and Carroll (2006) have argued in favour of knowledge system as a critical dimension of economic change with components of innovation, entrepreneurial activities, and market power playing an important role. Comparatively, Drucker (1985) considered innovation as "a specific instrument of the entrepreneur" and an "output of knowledge-based systems". For Lindley (2003), a knowledge system, much like a society, is "a process of structural change leading to the production diffusion and use of knowledge in the economy with a potential to play a major role in wealth creation". Twarog (2003) describes knowledge systems as entities comprised of research systems, higher-education institutions, industries and governments, policy making bodies, and R&D labs that integrate several factors of innovations and its respective aiding mechanisms.

Leydesdorff and Meyer (2006) refer to a knowledge-based innovation system as: "an outcome of interaction among different social coordination mechanisms like markets, knowledge production, and governance at interfaces". Edquist (1997) states that a knowledge system might remain active at different levels (e.g., industrial, local, regional, national, and international). According to Etzkowitz and Leydesdorff (2000), knowledge system models are indication of flux and the rearrangement and widening of the role of knowledge in society and the economy. Nine of these conceptual models and approaches to understanding innovation as an important constituent of knowledge systems and economies are summarized in Table 1.

Representing the Knowledge System Landscape

Notwithstanding the interface of innovation, a need was felt to represent the existing knowledge system models, leading to the conceptualization of the knowledge system landscape. The new construct adds another critical dimension, which provides a wide-angle view of several existing knowledge system processes, models, and stakeholders, in addition to their the sub-divisions and its areas of emphasis.

Table 1. Summary of key knowledge system models

Knowledge System Model	Description
National Innovation System (Lundvall, 1988; Nelson, 1993)	• focuses on flows of knowledge, flow of technology, and information among people, enterprises, and institutions
Post-Modern Research System (Rip & van der Meulen, 1996)	• consists of two systemic aspects of research systems: "steering" (i.e., the degree of sensitivity when implementing an objective) and "aggregating" (the organization of processes of agenda building within the system) • analyzes the infrastructure support, quality of support, and other aspects to determine the quality of research at an institution
Research System in Transition (Rip, 1990)	• refers to the role of R&D systems as the dynamics of change while laying out an agenda for future directions of science policy research
Mode I (Gibbons et al., 1994)	• refers primarily to basic university research organized in a disciplinary structure • describes a mode of knowledge production whose foundations rest on principles of scientific expertise, peer review, and non-interference • differentiates itself from scientific discovery of theoretical, experimental science by an internally-driven taxonomy of disciplines and by the autonomy of scientists and their host institutions (i.e., the higher-education institutions)
Mode II (Carayannis & Campbell, 2012)	• describes the new production of knowledge featuring production, trans-disciplinary work, high reflexivity, and ingenious methods of quality control • varies depending on the context, which could differ significantly due to variations in geographical, historical, social, and cultural settings
Mode III (Carayannis & Campbell, 2012)	• refers to open, adaptive, learning-driven knowledge at the foundational level and innovation, and refers it as "a multilayered, multimodal, multinodal, and multilateral system", encompassing mutually complementary and reinforcing innovation networks and knowledge clusters • comprises clusters of human and intellectual capital, outlined by social capital and underlined by financial capital
Triple Helix (Etzkowitz & Leydesdorff, 2000)	• refers to a spiral model of innovation that captures multiple reciprocal relationships at different points in the process of knowledge capitalization • denotes the university–industry–government relationship as one of relatively equal, yet interdependent and overlapping, institutional spheres
Quadruple Helix (Carayannis & Campbell, 2012)	• highlights the government, higher-education institutions, industry, and civil society as key actors promoting a democratic approach to innovation through which strategy development and decision-making are exposed from the feedback, leading to policies and practices responsible in a social context • offers a future-oriented outlook and vision, addressing the current challenges and introducing a problem-solving approach that emphasizes a sustainable development perspective that brings together innovation, entrepreneurship, and democracy
Quintuple Helix (Carayannis & Campbell, 2010)	• brings together different and complex perspectives to understand, manage, and govern Mode III as well as the Quadruple and Quintuple Helices • identifies open innovation diplomacy as a novel strategy • includes the "media-based and culture-based public" and "civil society"

The knowledge system landscape tries to accommodate various existing models that have not been explored in this way before. It also helps clarify the positioning of the existing models in the knowledge system. For example, there are several existing stakeholders of the knowledge systems, including higher-education institutions, industry, government, R&D labs, funding agencies, venture capitalists, and high-net-worth individuals (HNIs), and civil society. The representation helps clarify the perspectives, functioning, and proximities of differing models as well as their differentiators. In one case, researchers have been able to identify government, higher-education institutions, and industry as major stakeholders of the knowledge systems aptly defined in the Triple Helix model. Referring to this model, Leydesdorff and Meyer (2003) emphasize three different sub-dynamics of knowledge-based innovation systems: economic exchanges in the market, geographical disparities, and the organization of knowledge. Similarly, government, higher-education institutions, industry, and civil society are key actors promoting a democratic approach to innovation emphasized by the Quadruple Helix Model (Carayannis & Campbell, 2012). The knowledge system landscape provides a pictorial representation of the models and their positioning, as shown in Figure 1. It also helps elucidate the important role played by secondary and tertiary knowledge stakeholders, namely the R&D labs, government and private funding agencies, high-net-worth Individuals, social entrepreneurs, nongovernmental organizations (NGOs), and several other crucial stakeholders .

The knowledge system landscape integrates several other associated modules, namely the Post-Modern Research System, Modes I, II, and III, and the National Innovation System, which all have a healthy connectivity with the resources of higher-education institutions and the facilitations of government to aid, promote, and measure research and its outputs. Notably, research and innovation is considered as key to the growth of knowledge systems and hence finds mention in several models, such as the Post-Modern Research

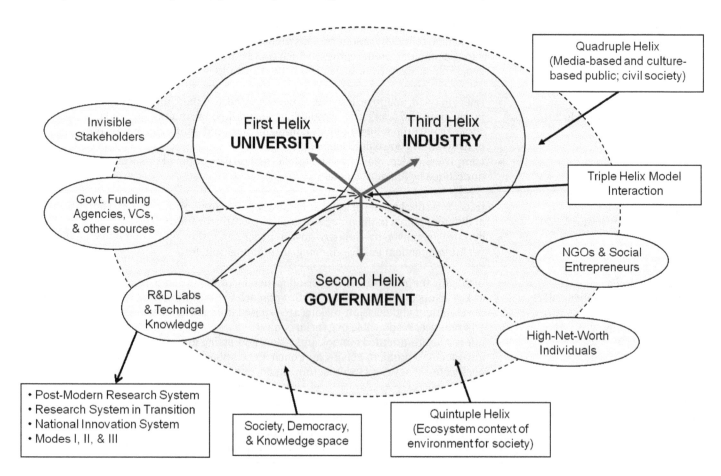

Figure 1. The knowledge system landscape

System, the National Innovation system, and the Research System in Transition. The knowledge system landscape provides adequate representation of the R&D labs, as referred to by Rip (1990), who highlighted the essential role of R&D systems in the Research Systems in Transition model in terms of dynamics of change and a step towards setting an agenda for science policy research. High reflexivity found favor from Nowotny and colleagues (2003) who, while explaining Mode I, note the key role of independence and autonomy provided to researchers at higher-education institutions and research labs in the growth of knowledge systems. The connectivity between the higher-education institutions and research labs is therefore adequately represented. Thus, the knowledge system landscape connects the independent and dependent stakeholders and provides a wider view of the context. In keeping with the construct, we now explore the issues faced by the innovation stakeholders in promoting innovation in an Indian context.

Barriers to Innovation in India within the Context of Knowledge Systems

In India, the growth and quality of innovation has been a subject of debate for some time (e.g., National Knowledge Commission, 2007). New product development through innovation has not happened at the desired pace in India due to myriad factors. These factors include the developing nature of the Indian economy (Sikka, 1997), an overdependence on the government, and inadequate contributions from higher-education institutions, and industry.

Open Innovation accounts for a fair share of the Government of India's initiatives to help create a global innovations and startups originating in India. However, most of the business incubators and innovation programs that have been set up by the Government of India have only been partially successful in promoting collaborations with industry and higher-education institutions. Lately, efforts have been made by successive governments to promote innovation in higher-education institutions with active industry participation, but they have so far met with little success because the role of industry is generally very restricted to core areas of interest. Industry support for "corporate social responsibility" for open innovations is also negligible due to the government's unfavourable taxation policies. Some of the major obstacles that are generally observed between the stakeholders of innovation in an Indian setting are:

- an absence of joint collaboration mechanisms between higher-education institutions and industries in the area of joint product development and research

- a lack of innovations emerging from higher-education institutions, and a failure to commercialize innovations that do emerge

- a failure of products developed by higher-education institutions to meet the expectations of industry

- the dearth of intellectual property sharing mechanisms between industry and higher-education institutions

- inadequate industry sponsorship for research in specific areas of industrial importance

- a deficiency of infrastructure available at higher-education institutions and in industry, which impairs the development of joint research platforms and mutually beneficial collaborative work

- insufficient orientation in innovation and entrepreneurship orientation provided by schools and higher-education institutions

- a scarcity of trained manpower to groom innovators and foster entrepreneurship, especially in technology parks, which are incubators that are generally based within higher-education institutions

- a want of support programs based in higher-education institutions and managed by their staff to help innovators carry out innovation/product commercialization and entrepreneurship

In several cases the role of a higher-education institution is partially or wholly visible, and hence their role in entrepreneurship comes into focus (Saurabh, 2014). From the above discussion, we conclude that there is a key collaboration gap due to a lack of interaction between the stakeholders of innovation and key players participating in the innovation ecosystem. So far, some of the issues identified above have been addressed by the major stakeholders of innovation, namely higher-education institutions, government, and industry. For example, the government has reformatted and re-conceptualized several innovation funding and support programs for product development and commercialization to support incubation of companies through marketing, intellectual property, and monetary support.

These efforts have not yet led to overall improvement, as can be observed by the failure of government programs to motivate entrepreneurs and innovators to come up with product- and service-based innovations and startups. A portion of the failures could be attributed to inadequate management practices as well as communication lapses between the innovators, government agencies, support agencies, etc.

Ideal Roles of Indian Innovation Stakeholders

Several knowledge system models consider higher-education institutions, government, and industry to be the significant stakeholders in innovation creation. In a developing nation such India, the onus for innovation promotion thus lies primarily with the government and the higher-education institutions, with private and public R&D labs and industry playing supporting roles. All three major stakeholders and their roles in creating an innovation ecosystem in India are discussed in the subsections that follow.

Higher-education institutions

Higher-education institutions assume greater responsibility than other stakeholders due to their tacit and close relationship with the government and other stakeholders. According to Mansfield and Lee (1996), the role of the university as a key contributor to wealth generation and economic development has increased in recent decades. In the Indian context, there is an increasing need for economic development through provision of better services and infrastructure support for hospitals, roads, electricity, housing, and transportation, etc., which require a highly trained workforce. All of these requirements can be effectively met with a judicious mix of good educational institutions acting as the baseline for knowledge creation at all levels from kindergarten to higher-education institutions. Sadly, there is a dearth of quality higher-education institutions in India to support the demands of the population. India's 2013 ranking in the Global Innovation Index (Dutta & Lanvin, 2013) for human capital and research stood at a dismal 105th position, which puts it on par with several lower, middle, and underdeveloped economies. The World Bank Institute's (2012) Knowledge for Development report, put India in the 120th position among 145 countries in their knowledge index ranking, which indicates the plight of education and knowledge in India. The need for improving the quality of higher-education institutions is urgently felt.

With growing economic challenges, higher-education institutions in India should no longer remain as factories for producing employees for companies, but should rather focus on nurturing job creators or entrepreneurs. Higher-education institutions should reinvent themselves as potential locations for initiating successful companies by projecting their proximity to industries and advanced research infrastructure. They should focus on innovative research utilizing the available resources, knowledge, and expertise available with faculty members and the student community to promote innovation and entrepreneurial activities within their campuses. Because the vibrant ecosystem around higher-education institutions is rich in technical resources, infrastructure, labour force, and other resources, it is seen as better suited for setting up high-tech industrial clusters, labs, and research centres. Etzkowitz and Leydesdorff (2000) highlight the increasing role of higher-education institutions leading to increased knowledge creation and contributions to economic development. Former Indian Prime Minister Manmohan Singh recently referred to the need for changing the culture in favour of promoting innovation at Indian higher-education and scientific institutions and called for a change in mindsets to promote an innovation culture by aligning with the expectations of the industrial and social sectors (Padma, 2010). He had also emphasized the need to improve the "outward orientation" of higher-education institutions by strengthening links with industry and creating international research partnerships.

Even though India is the second most populous nation in the world, its development in the field of Science and Technology is not visible in its Patent Cooperation Treaty (PCT) rankings in the Global Innovation Index (Dutta & Lanvin, 2013). For example, India ranked 55th and 54th respectively in domestic resident patent applications and PCT resident patent applications. In terms of the context of innovation in India, a lack of proper orientation during initiation days at education institutions for adopting innovative practices is also a valid reason for higher-education institutions in India not producing patents. Effective steps to generate scientific research outputs leading to patents should be implemented. The higher-education institutions should also generate quality research papers to improve its research and innovation culture at their institutions.

India's 99th place ranking in the Global Innovation Index (Dutta & Lanvin, 2013) for new businesses in the

15–64 age group shows the lack of initiative for starting businesses. Higher-education institutions in India do not prepare students for creative thinking, taking on risk, or starting businesses. Hence, entrepreneurial training for students in higher-education institutions should promote a risk-taking attitude, skill development and training, and a general motivation to become entrepreneurial. Higher-education institutions should also provide its student innovators and entrepreneurs with financial support, incubation, technical support, and R&D lab facilities. Furthermore, product innovation and commercialization support, and venture support in the form of grants or soft loans, will encourage students to take up entrepreneurial work. Higher-education institutions should develop technical expertise in administration and encourage students to take up innovative research while assisting students with their creative efforts. The quality of research must be outstanding to create valuable technology companies for which academic excellence should be promoted.

Government

Government supported R&D programs and measures help in escalating economic development. They have the mandate to carry on the activities relating to indigenous technology promotion, development utilization, and transfer. Government-supported R&D programs in India enable stakeholders to acquire a technology base towards producing quality goods of international standard (Sikka, 1997). In India, due to the absence of major industrial players, the support systems and infrastructure support needed for any plan of action or project, including policy decisions, are designed and supported by the government. It is the government that has to plan the development of industrial parks equipped with modern facilities to host hi-tech, environmentally-sensitive new businesses and industries in the priority sectors. Government plays an increasingly important role in providing a regulatory environment and encouraging innovation. The involvement of higher-education institutions is ever-increasing along with industry through consulting, contract research, and company formation from research based in higher-education institutions (Leydesdorff & Etzkowitz, 2001) in which role of government is considered central.

Government agencies should focus on actively fostering product- and service-based innovation with a view to developing indigenous capacity. These agencies should support the higher-education institutions to organize awareness programs, conferences, and events with the aim of promoting the processes that contribute to innovation while helping the institutions become self-reliant in all aspects. Encouragement through awards, titles, and monetary support should be provided to innovators and entrepreneurs because they act as motivating factors for both the recipients as well as others. Entrepreneurship and innovation support programs should be actively promoted using all recognized forms of media communication. Government funding bodies should monitor the their programs to ensure that funding is used effectively. Obstacles and regulations that hinder innovation and entrepreneurship activities should be abrogated.

To promote creative and entrepreneurial thinking among students and faculty members, government bodies can provide support and funding to set up entrepreneurship and innovation centres at higher-education institutions. Marketing support required by innovators who have developed technologies and wish to commercialize should be provided separately. Presently, there is no specific program from the Government of India to support new technologies with marketing and commercialization. The government's efforts should be directed to support commercialization of technologies developed in India. Apart from funding, the government should try to assist the entrepreneurs with demonstration opportunities leading to product orders with public sector companies. Also, technical support is a major constraint; innovators and entrepreneurs should be provided with dedicated resources, such as labs or centres where they can receive support without cost or at low cost.

Industry

Industry provides the necessary push to the advancement of innovations. In India, the role of industry in promoting and encouraging innovation has not been vigorous except for some "big names" such as Reliance Industries, Tata, Wipro, and Mahindra. Within Indian industry, R&D budgets are still lower than the global average.

A combination of differential components creates significant and durable business value for one or more well-defined product platforms or for cost-effective development of processes and products. Technology transfer and innovation platforms can support customers in building highly sophisticated structures needed for efficient R&D collaboration, licensing, and open innovation. Industry should be willing to provide access to research labs and infrastructure for employees willing to innovate or take up intrapreneurship activities. It should give freedom to its employees to experiment, think creatively, and implement innovative ideas along with their regular work.

The support expected from industry in promoting innovation is rarely provided to higher-education institutions because the level of interaction between industry and these institutions is low. Industry efforts should be geared towards building a strategic knowledge partner through engagement of higher-education institutions and other important stakeholders for joint product development, patent sharing, etc. while helping the higher-education institutions in creating a research base. Efforts are being made by industry organizations to promote innovation and research-related interactions through industry bodies such as the Federation of Indian chambers of Commerce and Industry (FICCI; http://ficci.com/) and the Confederation of Indian Industry (CII; http://cii.in), but these efforts are still in their early stages. An "advanced very large scale integration" (AVLSI) lab at the Indian Institute of Technology Kharagpur (http://conf05.iitkgp.ac.in/avlsi/) is an example of industry–university research collaboration with 15 industry partners and the university participating together in several research projects to generate viable research outputs for the researchers and joint intellectual property and patents for the industry partners.

Globalization has created immense opportunities to leverage high-end technology for developing countries, which can be aptly harnessed through industry collaborations. Industry must change its mindset in favour of innovation. Simultaneously, copyright violation, piracy, and patent infringement should be discouraged.

To promote vigorous collaboration between innovators and industry, industry should create refined products from the R&D developed by the innovators and provide mentorship in commercialization.. It should take bold steps and play a leading role in encouraging path-breaking, home-grown technologies by investing in future technologies such as brain–computer interfaces, autonomous cars, and robotics. This approach would considerably help entrepreneurs with the application of available technology with industry feedback and encourage further innovation.

Industry can help innovators and entrepreneurs with funding, mentoring, commercialization support, technical and lab support, customer feedback, refinement, and marketing support, in part through links to higher-education institutions. Industries should look at providing technical and financial support to innovative students and even hiring key students or researchers with relevant ideas or domain expertise.

Conclusion

On the basis of a new representation of the landscape of various knowledge system models, this article has argued that the promotion of innovation is dependent on the roles of various important stakeholders in the knowledge system, which has been highlighted using the Indian context. With the increasing need for innovation and the new knowledge that is integrated within it, the knowledge system has also become more relevant in the current context. Due to the changing role of knowledge systems, the historical proximities and constituents of the various models and subsystems emphasize different aspects and highlight the importance of understanding the roles played by key stakeholders. Only by promoting healthy interactions between government, industry, and higher-education institutions can innovation and entrepreneurship proliferate to the benefit of the Indian innovation ecosystem.

About the Authors

Punit Saurabh recently completed his PhD in the domain of innovation and entrepreneurship development from the Indian Institute of Technology Kharagpur, India. He has hands-on experience in managing government innovation and entrepreneurship funding programs and is also involved with the academic aspects of entrepreneurship.

Prabha Bhola is an Assistant Professor in the Rajendra Mishra School of Engineering Entrepreneurship at the Indian Institute of Technology Kharagpur, India, where she also received her PhD in Poverty Economics. She has wide range of teaching experience at different institutions.

Kalyan Kumar Guin is Dean and Professor at the Vinod Gupta School of Management, Indian Institute of Technology Kharagpur, India. He is an alumnus of IIT Kharagpur and Banaras Hindu University in Varanasi, India, and he is a Fellow of the Indian Institute of Management Bangalore. His teaching interests cover marketing and operations management, and he has a special interest in quantitative modelling of strategic issues in management.

References

Carree, M., & Thurik, A. R. 2002. The Impact of Entrepreneurship on Economic Growth. In Z. J. Acs & D. B. Audretsch, *International Handbook of Entrepreneurship Research:* 437-471. Boston/Dordrecht: Kluwer Academic Publishers. http://dx.doi.org/10.1007/0-387-24519-7_17

Carayannis, E. G. & Campbell, D. F. J. 2010. Triple Helix, Quadruple Helix and Quintuple Helix and How Do Knowledge, Innovation and the Environment Relate To Each Other? A Proposed Framework for a Trans-disciplinary Analysis of Sustainable Development and Social Ecology. *International Journal of Social Ecology and Sustainable Development,* 1(1): 41–69. http://dx.doi.org/10.4018/jsesd.2010010105

Carayannis, E. G., & Campbell, D. F. J. 2012. *Mode 3 Knowledge Production in Quadruple Helix Innovation Systems.* Springer Briefs in Business 7. New York: Springer. http://dx.doi.org/10.1007/978-1-4614-2062-0_1

Drucker, P. F. 1985. *Innovation and Entrepreneurship: Practice and Principles.* New York: Harper Business.

Dutta, S., & Lanvin, B. (Eds.). 2013. *The Global Innovation Index 2013: The Local Dynamics of Innovation.* Geneva, Ithaca, and Fontainebleau: Cornell University, INSEAD, and WIPO. http://www.wipo.int/freepublications/en/economics/gii/gii_2013.pdf

Edquist, C. (Ed.). 1997. *Systems of Innovations: Technologies, Institutions, and Organizations.* London: Pinter.

Edquist, C., & Riddell, C. W. 2000. The Role of Knowledge and Innovation for Economic Growth and Employment in the Information and Communication Technology (ICT) Era. In K. Rubenson & H. G. Schuetze (Eds.). *Transition to the Knowledge Society: Policies and Strategies for Individual Participation and Learning:* 29. Vancouver, Canada: Institute for European Studies, University of British Columbia.

Etzkowitz, H., & Leydesdorff, L. 2000. The Dynamics of Innovation: From National Systems and "Mode 2" to a Triple Helix of University–Industry–Government Relations. *Research Policy,* 29(2): 109–123. http://dx.doi.org/10.1016/S0048-7333(99)00055-4

Gibbons, M., Limoges, C., Nowotny, H., Schwartzman, S., Scott, P., & Trow, M. 1994. *The New Production of Knowledge: The Dynamics of Science and Research in Contemporary Societies.* Thousand Oaks, CA: Sage Publications.

Gupta, A. 2005. *International Trends in Private Higher Education and the Indian Scenario.* Research and Occasional Paper Series, CSHE 11.05. University of California, Berkeley: Center for Studies in Higher Education. http://escholarship.org/uc/item/4ch9m7j0

Kuratko, F. D. 2005. The Emergence of Entrepreneurship Education: Development, Trends, and Challenges. *Entrepreneurship Theory and Practice,* 29(5): 577-97. http://dx.doi.org/10.1111/j.1540-6520.2005.00099.x

Laukkanen, M. 2000. Exploring Alternative Approaches in High-Level Entrepreneurship Education: Creating Micro-Mechanisms for Endogenous Regional Growth. *Entrepreneurship and Regional Development,* 12(1): 25-47. http://dx.doi.org/10.1080/089856200283072

Leydesdorff, L., & van den Besselaar, P. (Eds.). 1994. *Evolutionary Economics and Chaos Theory: New Directions in Technology Studies.* London and New York: Pinter.

Leydesdorff, L,. & Etzkowitz, H. 2001. The Transformation of University-Industry-Government Relations. *Electronic Journal of Sociology,* 5(4).

Leydesdorff, L., & Meyer, M. 2003. The Triple Helix of University-Industry Government Relations: Introduction to the Topical Issue. *Scientometrics,* 58(2): 191-203. http://dx.doi.org/10.1007/s11192-007-0200-y

Leydesdorff, L., & Meyer, M. 2006. Triple Helix Indicators of Knowledge-Based Innovation Systems: Introduction to the Special Issue. *Research Policy,* 35(10): 1441-1449.

Lindley, R.M. 2003. *Knowledge-Based Economies: The European Employment Debate in a New Context.* Coventry, UK: Warwick Institute for Employment Research, University of Warwick.

Lundvall, B.- Å. 1988. Innovation as an Interactive Process: From User–Producer Interaction to the National System of Innovation. In G. Dosi (Ed.). *Technical Change and Economic Theory:* 349. London: Pinter.

Lundvall, B.- Å., Johnson, B., Andersen, E. S., & Dalum, B. 2002. National Systems of Production, Innovation and Competence Building. *Research Policy,* 31(2): 213–231. http://dx.doi.org/10.1016/S0048-7333(01)00137-8

Mansfield, E., & Lee, J.-Y. 1996. The Modern University: Contributor to Industrial Innovation and Recipient of Industrial R&D Support. *Research Policy,* 25(7): 1047-58. http://dx.doi.org/10.1016/S0048-7333(96)00893-1

National Knowledge Commission. 2007. *Innovation in India.* Government of India: National Knowledge Commission.

http://www.knowledgecommission.gov.in/downloads/documents/NKC_Innovation.pdf

Nelson, R. R. (Ed.) 1993. *National Innovation Systems: A Comparative Analysis.* New York: Oxford University Press.

Nowotny, H., Scott, P., & Gibbons, M. 2003. Introduction: 'Mode 2' Revisited: The New Production of Knowledge. *Minerva,* 41(3): 179-194. http://dx.doi.org/10.1023/A:1025505528250

Orhan, M., & Scott, D. 2001. Why Women Enter into Entrepreneurship: An Explanatory Model. *Women in Management Review,* 16(5): 232–247. http://dx.doi.org/10.1108/09649420110395719

Padma, T. V. 2010. Indian Prime Minister Calls for 'Innovation Ecosystem'. *SciDev.Net.* August 1, 2014: http://www.scidev.net/en/news/indian-prime-minister-calls-for-innovation-ecosystem--1.html

Parikh, M. 2001. Knowledge Management Framework for High-Tech Research and Development. *Engineering Management Journal,* 13(3): 27-34.

Pol, E. P., & Carroll, P. 2006. *An Introduction to Economics with Emphasis on Innovation.* Innovation Planet.

Reynolds, P. D., Bygrave, W. D., Autio, E., Cox, L. W., & Hay, M. 2002. *Global Entrepreneurship Monitor 2002 Executive Report.* Wellesley, MA/London: Babson College/London Business School.

Rip, A. 1990. An Exercise in Foresight: The Research System in Transition – To What? In S. E. Cozzens, P. Healey, A. Rip, & J. Ziman (Eds.). The Research System in Transition, 387-401. The Netherlands: Kluwer Academic Publishers. http://dx.doi.org/10.1007/978-94-009-2091-0_29

Rip, A., & van der Meulen, B. J. R. 1996. The Post-Modern Research System. *Science and Public Policy*, 23(6): 343-352. http://dx.doi.org/10.1093/spp/23.6.343

Saurabh, P. 2014. *Education-Enterprise Model for Innovation Based Entrepreneurship Development at Higher Education Institutions in India*. Doctoral Thesis, Indian Institute of Technology-Kharagpur.

Sikka, P. 1997. Financing the Development of Indigenous Technology in India. *Current Science*, 73(5): 406-408.

Solomon, G. 2007. An Examination of Entrepreneurship Education in the United States. *Journal of Small Business and Enterprise Development*, 14(2): 168-82. http://dx.doi.org/10.1108/14626000710746637

Twarog, S. 2003. *Preserving, Protecting and Promoting Traditional Knowledge: National Actions and International Dimensions*. Selected Papers on Trade and Development Research Issues for Asian Countries.

World Bank Institute. 2012. *Measuring Knowledge in the World's Economies: Knowledge Assessment Methodology and Knowledge Economy Index*. Washington, DC: World Bank Institute Knowledge for Development Program.

Keywords: knowledge systems, innovation ecosystem, innovation system, government, industry, higher-education institutions, university, entrepreneurship, stakeholders, models

11

The Role of Managers as Agents in Successful Service Innovations: Evidence from India

Shiv S. Tripathi

" One person should not give orders to another person, but both "
should agree to take their orders from the situation. If orders
are simply part of the situation, the question of someone
giving and someone receiving does not come up.

Mary Parker Follett (1868–1933)
Management theorist and consultant

The article is based on a three-year study of 70 business executives belonging to 20 large organizations operating in India to identify the kind of interventions used by agents (managers) to make service innovations successful. For the purpose of analysis, the subject organizations were classified into highly successful, successful, and unsuccessful organizations on the basis of their growth rate, and their practices were analyzed to identify the role of agents in those processes or related decisions. The article also compares the practices followed by organizations based in India with global organizations operating in India to understand the contextual issues of service innovations.

Introduction

According to Gallouj (2002), services have three distinct features: i) they are processes, ii) they are interactive, and iii) there can be extremely diverse. This complex nature of services sets them apart from products (i.e., goods), whose development is relatively linear and independent. When a service-based organization chooses the path of innovation, it needs to be careful, because the development of successful service innovations requires more careful thought than the development of products. A company can offer an innovative service only when there is a management resolve and the service has a high probability of success in the market (Van de Ven, 1986). The reason is that service innovations are often a result of the demand of market or the clients (Barras, 1986; Pavitt, 1984), co-production (den Hertog, 2000), or close co-operation of the supplier and the client (Tether & Hipp, 2002). Therefore, unlike product innovations, whose acceptance or rejection by the market or the clients is visible almost immediately after the launch, services take a relatively longer time to gain acceptance. Industry-wise, there is also a marked distinction between manufacturing/product-based firms and service-based firms: the latter focus more on organizational innovations as compared to the product or process innovations of the former (Chamberlin et al., 2010). Thus, service innovations have organization-wide effects, whereas product innovations might affect only one line of business or product.

Another difficulty is that the immediate advantage of a service innovation may not be as objectively visible as a product; hence, service-innovation ideas may face increased scrutiny prior to implementation (de Jong et al., 2003). However, once a service innovation is implemented, and the feedback is positive, gaining commercial advantage can be relatively easier.

Thus, if a service-based organization wants to innovate, the agents (managers) have an important role to play in seeing that the service innovation overcomes every hurdle, because it is an organization wide effort that makes a service innovation successful. However, a key question remains as to whether the support provided by these agents really does make service innovations successful or whether these agents knowingly or unknowingly act as an impediment to successful service innovations.

To help answer this question we look to agency theory. A typical agency relationship is the one where one party (i.e., the principal) delegates work to another (i.e., the agent) who performs that work (Jensen & Meckling, 1976). Agency theory is concerned with solving two problems that might occur in agency relationships. The first problem occurs when the desires and goals of the principal and agent are in conflict with each other and it is difficult for the principal to verify what the agent is actually doing. The second problem occurs when the principals and agents have different attitudes towards risk. The present article focuses on the second issue, where the daily demands of their work cause the agents (managers) to become risk averse and thus curb the real spirit and potential of innovation present in the organization, which often brings them into conflict with the principal (Eisenhardt, 1989). Due to this risk aversion, an agent might apply their discretion in matters related to inputs, processes, and outputs of innovation and will not involve or pay attention to the frontline co-workers (Edgett & Parkinson, 1994, Easingwood, 1986), which might give birth to a "routines" that curb the development of a radically innovative service.

Thus, large organizations are faced with a dilemma as to whether to support innovations or focus on the sustainability of the organization. The solution lies in combining both efforts. The first part of the dilemma is the agency conflict: agents at all levels may not be ready to take risks that the principals might want them to take. The second part of the dilemma is the difficulty in making the organization sustainable, which is a challenge faced not only by startups but also large and established organizations, who may struggle to achieve for sustainable growth (McGrath, 2013). The present research is limited to large organizations only and explores the process of service innovations in large private sector organizations operating in India, including global organizations operating in India.

This article also examines the leadership view of an organization, which suggests that, even if an organization has the requisite resources and dynamic capabilities, it is the leadership that steers the innovative new service towards success (Chandy & Tellis, 2000; Si & Wei, 2012). It has been reaffirmed by researchers that visionary leadership is a necessary ingredient for innovation (Anderson & West, 1998; Thamhain, 2003; Tidd & Bessant, 2009) and therefore, the amount of time spent by senior executives on activities related to innovation is also important. Therefore, this article critically examines the role of executives as agents in successful service innovations.

Research Methodology

The current study is based on 70 in-depth interviews, lasting between 40 minutes and 1 hour and 45 minutes, with experienced executives from 20 organizations either based in India (8 organizations) or operating in India (12 global organizations). Each of these organizations were large (cf. OECD, 2005); each had a turnover of at least $200 million USD and was listed in one or more of the following stock exchanges: New York Stock Exchange, London Stock Exchange, Nasdaq, Bombay Stock Exchange, or the National Stock Exchange (of India).

Only service innovations developed by these subject organizations in the previous two years were considered. These service innovations included incremental or radical innovations but excluded routine process improvements. The idea was to select those service innovations that had a positive impact on revenue growth of the organization.

The organizations were categorized into highly successful, successful, and unsuccessful organizations based on three years of compounded annual growth rate (CAGR) of their net profit after tax. Organizations having a growth rate over 20% were classified as highly successful, those with growth rates between zero and 20% were classified as successful, and those having a negative growth rate were classified as unsuccessful.

Out of 22 items included in the discussion guide for the interviews (Tripathi et al., 2013), 19 analytical items were identified as themes that were discussed in detail with the respondents. The other three items were dropped because they were direct questions. In the following section, the practices followed by each category of organization are listed. A parallel comparison between organizations based in India and their global counterparts operating in India is also made, and discussion of the overall role played by the agents in these organizations is provided. The responses against each type of organization are the actual direct responses of the respondents analyzed through grounded theory methodology following Strauss and Corbin (1998).

Summary of Key Findings

For each of the 19 themes, this section summarizes the typical response from the interview subjects based on the success level of their organization. Also, for each theme, the role of agents in organizations based in India is compared against global organizations based in India.

Theme 1: Number of innovators in the organization

- *Highly successful organizations:* innovators include top management and the majority of managers, but innovation is encouraged throughout the organization

- *Successful organizations:* top 5–10% of employees; primarily, senior management is the driver; a few other managers also drive innovation

- *Unsuccessful organizations:* only the top management drives innovation; others are not encouraged

- *Role of agents:* only the top management controls the innovation front; employees down the line are not empowered to innovate. In contrast to organizations based in India, the process is more democratized with their global counterparts, where it is not limited to the top management, and employees down the line are encouraged to innovate in services.

Theme 2: Incentives for innovation

- *Highly successful organizations:* primarily non-monetary incentives, such as awards, recognition, job advancements in India or abroad, or implementation of ideas

- *Successful organizations:* no incentives unless there are patents; primarily rewards and recognition for patents

- *Unsuccessful organizations:* monetary incentives such as one-time rewards, gifts (e.g., iPads), or a lump sum . The belief is that monetary incentive is better because, when there is a lot of scope for innovation, the organization cannot recognize everyone.

- *Role of agents:* for companies based in India, the rewards and recognition systems are typically driven by agents and are often discretionary (and biased). The opposite is true with most of their global counterparts who rely on an open reward system with minimum intervention, often as part of a process of innovation that includes a reward system.

Theme 3: Frequency of change of mission statement

- *Highly successful organizations:* as per the demand of the market or business environment; to stay ahead in the market; as per changing market dynamics

- *Successful organizations:* changed rarely or not changed unless there is a restructuring

- *Unsuccessful organizations:* changed rarely or not changed unless there is a restructuring or crisis

- *Role of agents:* the agents in Indian organizations are not bothered about the internal communication of the change in mission statement because they do not feel it is important. In contrast, their global counterparts are relatively active in communicating any change in the mission statements to employees down the line, because they believe it enables better control and synchronization across all subsidiaries, and maintaining good communication and transparency.

Theme 4: Time to market

- *Highly successful organizations:* instantaneous to maximum of six months in the case of small improvements; in case of a major capital expenditure project, it may take up to one year

- *Successful organizations:* the majority of successful organizations require two to six months for small ideas/projects to reach the market; for large ones, up to one year

- *Unsuccessful organizations:* for small improvements the time to market is two to six months; for large ones, it takes two to five years

- *Role of agents:* if the idea provides a promising business opportunity or competitive advantage, agents in both types of organization take an active interest so that the service is launched in the market. Therefore, both the India-based organizations and their global counterparts are similar in this regard.

Theme 5: Number of ideas pursued by the company in a year

- *Highly successful organizations:* 10 to 15 ideas per year

- *Successful organizations:* two to five ideas in a year; the limitation is the capacity to execute, not the lack of ideas

- *Unsuccessful organizations:* none, one, or two ideas; respondents had no idea what was happening in other departments; execution is a problem

- *Role of agents:* distinctively, the agents in Indian organizations promote two to five ideas per year, out of which they expect one or two ideas to succeed. Their global counterparts allow all potential ideas to pass through the stage gates of innovation. However, agents in Indian organizations try to dictate the selection of final ideas, which results in execution problems at a later stage.

Theme 6: Time required in funding innovation

- *Highly successful organizations:* funding is immediate or within six months; whatever time taken (if any) is for the feasibility study

- *Successful organizations:* two to six months in most cases where the scale of implementation is small and one to three years where the scale of implementation is large

- *Unsuccessful organizations:* if the service is successful, there is no problem: adequate funds are available. However, the time depends on the amount of funds required and, at times, it is expedited if the person is a veteran in the company. Thus, employees with less experience find it difficult to negotiate for funds even if their ideas are commercially the best.

- *Role of agents:* although agents in both types of organizations show equal eagerness to fund potential innovations, in Indian organizations, the vision of agents is sometimes coloured by the experience and stature of the person floating the idea, and tend to neglect the ideas of a relatively new employee, at times even at the cost of merit.

Theme 7: Number of services the company is planning to launch in the next year

- *Highly successful organizations:* 20 to 30 service ideas are floated, but ultimately, only one or two merit a feasibility study

- *Successful organizations:* 20 to 100 ideas are floated; 20 to 100 merit a feasibility study

- *Unsuccessful organizations:* 10 to 15 ideas are floated; one merits a feasibility study

- *Role of agents:* both Indian and global organizations promote the ideation of new services; however, when comes to finalizing a new service for the client, the Indian organizations are at times biased towards the past successes and are not willing to accept radical departures from the past. Therefore, the agents in Indian organizations start looking at the background of an innovator as compared to the merit of an idea.

Theme 8: Number of intrapreneurs

- *Highly successful organizations:* at most, 5% of employees might have directly contributed; otherwise they all contribute because it is presumed to be a part of their job.

- *Successful organizations:* around 10 people at the top (i.e., a specific number that can be counted), but others are not empowered to be intrapreneurs

- *Unsuccessful organizations:* maximum 1–3% people at the top

- *Role of agents:* In Indian organizations, intrapreneurs by and large belong to the top management only. In global organizations, an employee even at a junior level has the opportunity to spearhead the service innovation if their idea is accepted.

Theme 9: Number of employees becoming entrepreneurs after leaving the company

- *Highly successful organizations:* one to ten employees (i.e., a specific number that can be counted)

- *Successful organizations:* very few or none; most employees who leave the company join another company

- *Unsuccessful organizations:* very few people leave the organization to become entrepreneurs, they leave to join a better company

- *Role of agents:* due to a limited scope of corporate entrepreneurship owing to agents and at times due to the nature of business, a number of employees leave Indian organizations to start their own business or to take up greater responsibilities in other organizations. However, their global counterparts do not typically leave organizations to start a new business; rather they switch organizations to take up greater responsibilities elsewhere.

Theme 10: Percentage of people trained in innovation

- *Highly successful organizations:* around 30–40% employees are trained in innovation

- *Successful organizations:* around 10-30%; for most of employees, there is no training on innovation per se

- *Unsuccessful organizations:* 1 to 2% of top management people are trained in innovation. Others are provided with routine training on services because they are not empowered to innovate.

- *Role of agents:* in Indian organizations, innovation training is typically initiated and given only to the agents (especially the top management); others are provided with the routine training only. However, their global counterparts provide training in innovation not only to the agents but also to key employees, irrespective of their level in the management hierarchy.

Theme 11: Number of people agreeing that there is a focus on strategic innovation

- *Highly successful organizations:* around 75% of employees would agree, but employees are unhappy when they lose out to competition

- *Successful organizations:* 10–30%

- *Unsuccessful organizations:* 60–80%

- *Role of agents:* here, the agents play a positive role in motivating the actors sufficiently so that they believe that the organization is innovating strategically innovations even if it is not actually able to do so. Personal interaction plays a major role in the Indian organizations, whereas in the global counterparts, all service innovations are promoted internally as well as externally so that everybody comes to know about a particular service.

Theme 12: Existence of a process to generate new business ideas within the company or outside the company

- *Highly successful organizations:* in a majority of cases, processes for both directions exist

- *Successful organizations:* idea generation is primarily "in-house"; there is an absence of process in some cases

- *Unsuccessful organizations:* idea generation is primarily "in-house"; implementation is a problem.

- *Role of agents:* the agents in this case act as gatekeepers who may "kill" the idea at one stage or another if they do not believe in it. All organizations based in India lacked a formal process to generate new business ideas either in-house or from outside the organization. Their global counterparts operating in India had

processes in place and thus avoided the interference of agents.

Theme 13: Availability of funds for innovation

- *Highly successful organizations:* plenty of funds are available, but there is a lack of good ideas

- *Successful organizations:* sufficient funds are available; outside collaboration is not required for financing; for high-risk projects, collaboration diversifies the risk

- *Unsuccessful organizations:* enough funds are available, but formal processes for innovation and fund allocation are lacking

- *Role of agents:* the agents controlled the sources and allocation of funds, and at times promoted mediocrity by allocating the funds to a favourite and not to the person having the best service innovation. In the global organizations, although the agents controlled the allocation of funds, they could not be biased because there were processes in place where only the winning ideas for service innovation would receive funding.

Theme 14: Responsiveness of top management

- *Highly successful organizations:* top management takes responsibility and is cooperative; it is a part of company culture

- *Successful organizations:* in most cases, top management takes responsibility or provide support

- *Unsuccessful organizations:* in many cases, top management will not take responsibility unless they are liable to take the blame for failure; there is also difficulty in implementing innovations

- *Role of agents:* in the majority of the above themes, there were thorough interventions by agents in Indian organizations; as a consequence, they took the responsibility for failures of innovative services provided unless there was an opportunity to place blame on others. In their global counterparts, because independence was given to the person whose idea of service innovation was implemented, the person heading the project directly held the responsibility for its success or failure, and the agents had no intervening role.

Theme 15: To launch a new service or revive an existing one

- *Highly successful organizations:* consider launching a new service almost every time

- *Successful organizations:* launch and revival in the ratio of 60:40; would launch new services if able to do so

- *Unsuccessful organizations:* launch new services in most cases

- *Role of agents:* the agents in almost all Indian organizations promoted the revival of existing services as the first option and launching new services as the second; they had limited willingness to take risks. Even when there was a requirement to launch new products, the agents used it as a last resort and therefore "killed" the launch of a new service at the right time in the market. Their global counterparts took calculated risks, although they preferred to launch new service as compared to reviving the old services. However, exceptions to these typical scenarios were found in both types of organizations.

Theme 16: The number of services being deliberately developed since last year

- *Highly successful organizations:* on their own, one to two services; as per the client's demand - 15 to 20; patents were being filed as required by the companies

- *Successful organizations:* in a majority of cases, two to five; patents were being filed as required by the companies

- *Unsuccessful organizations:* deliberately, one to two services; activities in the rest of the organization were not known

- *Role of agents:* the agents of Indian organizations promoted the development of one to two services only, whereas their global counterparts promoted substantially more due to the fact that the new service innovations were directive-driven in the Indian organizations as compared to proactive developments by the global organizations.

Theme 17: Perception of employees about their company innovating to stay ahead in the market

- *Highly successful organizations:* positive; employees perceive that their organization is better able to read

industry trends than others

- *Successful organizations:* in a majority of cases, the perception is that their organization is innovating or at least attempting to innovate

- *Unsuccessful organizations:* the perception is that their organization innovates as the market dynamics requires and to stay visible in the market

- *Role of agents:* the agents of both types of organizations were able to create an environment in which the employees thought that their company innovates to stay ahead in the market. This perception was a result of mentoring provided by the agents in Indian organizations and empowerment provided by the agents in the global organizations.

Theme 18: On innovating as required by the client or on its own

- *Highly successful organizations:* in a majority of cases, both drivers of innovation exist

- *Successful organizations:* both drivers of innovation exist, but in a majority of cases, it depends on market need or when the clients demand particular solutions.

- *Unsuccessful organizations:* mostly as required by the market

- *Role of agents:* the agents of most of the Indian organizations promoted the maintenance of status quo and were reluctant to support service innovations on their own unless the technology itself evolved or it was demanded by the client. In contrast, their global counterparts were more involved in supporting the development of service innovations proactively so that they can offer them to their clients before any competing organization does.

Theme 19: The success rate of innovative services launched by the company

- *Highly successful organizations:* 30–50% in most cases

- *Successful organizations:* 30–40% in most cases

- *Unsuccessful organizations:* around 20%

- *Role of agents:* the success rate of service innovations in Indian organizations was similar to their global counterparts due to the quantity of new ideas for service innovations supported by the agents. Although the Indian organizations followed fewer ideas and experienced fewer failures, the global organizations followed more ideas and achieved more successes.

Discussion and Conclusion

The findings suggest that, in Indian organizations, there is a substantial intervention by agents across most of the themes as compared to their global counterparts operating in India. In most cases, the intervention of agents is negative: for example, innovators are limited to a number of agents; awards/rewards for innovation are at the discretion of agents; agents do not feel the need to convey major changes in the direction of company to people down the line; there is a lack of a formal process for fund allocation to innovation projects; agents avoid accepting fresh ideas by relatively inexperienced people; they keep intrapreneurship opportunities to themselves; a formal process for idea generation is absent, giving agents discretionary powers; there is virtually no innovation training except to agents at a certain level; agents are risk averse in terms of launching new services; and there is a lack of interest in proactive service innovation among agents. Since there is a high degree of negative intervention of agents in the service innovation process, it becomes supervisor-driven and not self-driven, and that is why organizations in India tend to follow a kind of "directed innovation". In certain cases, where the agent (or manager) provides mentorship personally to staff at lower levels, it is a positive intervention provided they empower those employees to take decisions on their own.

To understand the cause of these often negative interventions of agents one needs to first understand that India follows a management system that is neither too individualistic, like the United States, nor it is purely collectivist, like Japan; rather, it is somewhere in between. This "in between" position gives substantial discretionary powers to the agents in Indian organizations who generally have an option to go towards any of these two extremes at their discretion. Second, because most of the sectors in the Indian economy have yet not become hypercompetitive as there is still a scope for growth, such negative interventions of agents might affect the innovations but it does not affect the growth or sustainability of the organizations, which can still flourish. However, such interventions will become a deterrent to growth the moment a particular sector becomes completely saturated. In that situation, innovation would be the only route to survival. Yet, in order

to create a culture of innovation, there should be processes in place to avoid any bias; this culture would enable an organization to bring out the true potential of its employees.

However, if we compare Indian organizations with their global counterparts operating in India, the element of discretion of agents at various stages of service innovation is limited or absent. The first reason is that most of the organizations whose employees were interviewed had well-defined processes, for example, for idea generation or allocation of funds, and thus minimized the role of agents in positively or negatively affecting the process. Second, the parent organizations of these companies reside in countries where the local market was saturated, and that is why they saw the solution to growth through innovation in a structured manner. There is a very little discretion available to the agents, and their approach is more objective. Third, the large size of these global organizations makes them more likely to have systems and processes in place and reduces the influence of local contextual factors in different parts of the world.

Based on the above discussion there, the following recommendations are provided for organizations wishing to pursue service innovations in India. Although they are targeted at Indian companies, they may also be relevant to global organizations with operations in India:

1. **Have clear processes for innovation:** To minimize the discretion of agents and ensure that there is objective assessment, companies should try to have clear systems and processes for the various components and phases of innovation including incentives, idea generation idea evaluation, and funding. Let the system of processes take over the task of producing successful service innovations and not the agents.

2. **Empower employees and support them in risk-taking:** The agents can mentor the people down the line yet provide them independence and empowerment so that they not only believe that their organization is innovative but also they can see it in action. In this process of empowerment, the employees should not feel alienated.

3. **Get off the fail-safe track:** Indian companies can break free from the fail-safe types of services or the fail-safe image of the agents by inviting fresh ideas and giving them an honest evaluation. In some cases, the same fail-safe idea or service may be selected.

But, the difference would be that it would be a deliberate and open selection based purely on merit within a culture where everyone feels involved in the process.

Due to the complex nature of services, service innovation require clear cut processes, close co-operation, and interaction between various functional areas and stakeholders so that they have a feeling of ownership in the organization. Agents should always keep the communication channels open to all levels to encourage transparency and feedback in the system, because even a seemingly small issue may curb the success of a service. Agents can always provide positive interventions in the process of service innovations by being approachable; welcoming ideas from any level in the organization; creating and supporting the system to take care of all processes; and acting as a mentor and not as an actor in the process of building successful service innovations.

About the Author

Shiv S. Tripathi is an Assistant Professor in the area of Strategic Management at the Management Development Institute in Gurgaon, India. He holds a PhD degree from Vinod Gupta School of Management at the Indian Institute of Technology Kharagpur. He has published papers in the area of product and service innovations, growth strategies, and innovations in large organizations. He has presented papers at national and international conferences organized by the Indian Institutes of Management, Indian School of Business, and Strategic Management Society, USA. His current research interests include service innovations, open innovations, ambidexterity, and innovation in large organizations.

References

Anderson, N., & West, M. A. 1998. Measuring Climate for Work Group Innovation: Development and Validation of Team Climate Inventory. *Journal of Organizational Behavior*, 19: 235-258. http://dx.doi.org/10.1002/(SICI)1099-1379(199805)19:3<235::AID-JOB837>3.0.CO;2-C

Barras, R. 1986. Towards a Theory on Innovations in Services. *Research Policy*, 15(4): 161-173. http://dx.doi.org/10.1016/0048-7333(86)90012-0

Chamberlin, T., Doutriaux, J., & Hector, J. 2010. Business Success Factors and Innovation in Canadian Service Sectors: An Initial Investigation of Inter-Sectoral Differences. *The Service Industries Journal*, 30(2): 225-246. http://dx.doi.org/10.1080/02642060802120174

Chandy, R., & Tellis, G. J. 2000. *Leader's Curse: Incumbency, Size & Radical Innovation*. Marketing Science Institute Report No. 00-100. Cambridge, MA: Marketing Science Institute.

den Hertog, P. 2000. Knowledge-Intensive Business Services as Co-Producers of Innovation. *International Journal of Innovation Management*, 4(4): 491-528. http://dx.doi.org/10.1142/S136391960000024X

Easingwood, C. J. 1986. New Product Development for Service Companies. *Journal of Product Innovation Management*, 3(4): 264-175. http://dx.doi.org/10.1111/1540-5885.340264

Edgett, S., & Parkinson, S. 1994. The Development of New Financial Services: Identifying Determinants of Success and Failure. *International Journal of Service Industry Management*, 5(4): 24-38. http://dx.doi.org/10.1108/09564239410068689

Eisenhardt, K. M. 1989. Agency Theory: An Assessment and Review. *Academy of Management Review*, 14(1): 57-74. http://dx.doi.org/10.5465/AMR.1989.4279003

Gallouj, F. 2002. *Innovation in the Service Economy: The New Wealth of Nations*. Cheltenham, UK: Edward Elgar.

Jensen, M. C., & Meckling, W. H. 1976. Theory of the Firm: Managerial Behavior, Agency Costs, and Ownership Structure. *Journal of Financial Economics*, 3(4): 305-360. http://dx.doi.org/10.2139/ssrn.94043

de Jong, J. P. J., Bruins, A., Dolfsma, W., & Meijaard, J. 2003. *Innovation in Service Firms Explored: What, How and Why?* The Netherlands: EIM Business and Policy Research.

McGrath, R. G. 2013. *The End of Competitive Advantage*. Boston: Harvard Business School Press.

OECD. 2005. *OECD SME and Entrepreneurship Outlook*. Paris: Organisation for Economic Co-operation and Development (OECD).

Pavitt, K. 1984. Sectoral Patterns of Technical Change: Towards a Taxonomy and a Theory. *Research Policy*, 13(6): 343-373. http://dx.doi.org/10.1016/0048-7333(84)90018-0

Si, S., & Wei, F. 2012. Transformational and Transactional Leaderships, Empowerment Climate and Innovation Performance: A Multilevel Analysis in the Chinese Context. *European Journal of Work and Organizational Psychology*, 21(2): 299-320. http://dx.doi.org/10.1080/1359432X.2011.570445

Strauss, A., & Corbin J. 1998. *Basics of Qualitative Research: Techniques and Procedures for Developing Grounded Theory* (2nd Ed.). Thousand Oaks, CA: Sage Publications.

Tether, B. S., & Hipp, C. 2002. Knowledge Intensive, Technical and Other Services: Patterns of Competitiveness and Innovation Compared. *Technology Analysis and Strategic Management*, 14(2): 163-182. http://dx.doi.org/10.1080/09537320220133848

Thamhain, H. J. 2003. Managing Innovative R&D teams. R&D Management, 33(3): 297-311. http://dx.doi.org/10.1111/1467-9310.00299

Tidd, J., & Bessant, J. 2009. *Managing Innovation: Integrating Technological, Market and Organizational Change* (4th Ed.). West Sussex, England: John Wiley & Sons.

Tripathi, S. S., Guin, K. K., & De, S. K. 2013. Product and Service Innovations in Large Organizations Operating in India: A Systems Approach. *IUP Journal of Business Strategy,* 10(3): 32-52.

Van de Ven, A. H. 1986. Central Problems in the Management of Innovation. *Management Science,* 32(5): 590-607. http://dx.doi.org/10.1287/mnsc.32.5.590

Wren, D. A., & Greenwood, R. G. 1998. *Management Innovators: The People and Ideas That Have Shaped the Modern Business.* New York: Oxford University Press.

Keywords: service innovation, agents, managers, India, global organizations, entrepreneurship, intrapreneurship

12

Generative Innovation Practices, Customer Creativity, and the Adoption of New Technology Products

Stoyan Tanev and Marianne Harbo Frederiksen

> *It is absurd to claim that our customers are missing!* So say surprised skeptics seeing our claim of missing customers. What if our problem with value is rooted in a misconception of our customers, the people we are creating value for?
>
> Peter J. Denning & Robert P. Dunham
> "The Missing Customer" (2003; tinyurl.com/kl7y2wp)

We offer a critical reflection on one of the key reasons for the startlingly low success rate of innovation initiatives worldwide – the fact that the interactive environment surrounding the customer is a critical part of the adoption process; it can and should be designed in a way that enables customer creativity, and thus adoption. In this article, we embrace a definition of innovation as "the adoption of a new practice by a community" where the innovator is the one who does not only sense and move into new opportunities but also mobilizes all the necessary resources needed by customers to adopt a new practice. The emphasis on adoption merges together innovation and entrepreneurship by shifting the focus from the inventor and the designer, through the entrepreneur, to the ultimate recipient of the innovative outcomes. Looking at customers as co-creators is critically important for technological product adoption; missing the chance to enable their creativity is equivalent to missing the opportunity of seeing them for who they really are. The result is a distorted vision that is ultimately rooted in the misconception of the dynamics of customer value. We particularly emphasize two points: i) the increasing degree of complexity of everyday technological products requires a higher degree of creativity by customers to adopt; and ii) customer creativity is not only a function of user-technology interaction, it is a function of the various actors in the interactive environment surrounding the customer such as other customers, other technologies, local distributors, customer/technical support providers, and competitors.

Introduction

According to a 2005 *Business Week* article, the success rate of innovation initiatives in terms of meeting their financial objectives is less than 4%, with the innovation success rates within specific industries ranging from a mere 1% in the toy industry to only 7.5% in the pharmaceutical industry (Nussbaum, 2005; tinyurl.com/krb6oyv). In a more recent study, Strategyn (2010; tinyurl.com/olgqvtp) used 12 different sources to evaluate the success rate of traditional innovation methods. The study reports success rates between 1% and 86%, with an average success rate of 17%. After removing the low and high outliers from the analysis, the average rate goes down to 8.5% – exactly half of the initially reported 17%. A most recent study by Accenture (2013; tinyurl.com/n7hdyb4) found that 93% of executives regard their company's long-term success to be dependent on its ability to innovate; but, at the same time, less than one out of five (18%) believe that their strategic investments in innovation are paying off. According to the study, such a poor track record discourages companies from taking the risk of initiating more radical innovation projects. There is no doubt that the specific success rates reported by the different studies depend on the methodology, the purpose of the study, and the particular context of their key messages. However, they seem to consistently indicate that, at the beginning of the 21st century, human involvement in dedicated innovation activities has not been as successful as we have been expecting it to be. Many companies are simply struggling with it – a fact that has been borne out in numerous other studies as well as in the marketplace, where new product introductions quite often fail to meet expectations even as others soar beyond expectations. What is the reason for such discouraging performance? Should we just lower our expectations by admitting that innovation is a risky game and silently agree to waste more than 80% of our investments? Or, should we try to locate the roots of the cause and work towards improving the success rate? What can innovators and entrepreneurs do to improve it?

In this article, we argue that one of the reasons for such failure could be associated with narrow or fluffy definitions of innovation that are impossible to translate into actionable insights. The problem with inadequate definitions is that: i) they misinterpret the job of the innovator and the entrepreneur; and ii) they misplace the focus of company efforts into activities that do not enable potential customers to become actual customers thus making the companies "miss the customer." We start by considering innovation as "the adoption of a new practice by a community", which emphasizes the critical roles of both innovators/entrepreneurs and customers as the two active poles of the dynamic adoption process. The entrepreneurial aspects are addressed by describing a generative approach to managing innovation, including several personal practices focusing on adoption. The customer aspects are addressed by conceptualizing customer creativity as an important factor in the adoption process. The article concludes by emphasizing the relevance of the topic with respect to the ever-increasing complexity of everyday technological products and summarizing the key insights of the analysis.

Innovation as the Adoption of a New Practice by a Community

The particular working definition of innovation appears to be of critical importance for companies. Baregheh, Rowley, and Sambrook (2009; tinyurl.com/ko9r7h4) emphasize the fundamental difficulties in defining innovation by referring to its multidisciplinary nature. They have analyzed 60 definitions from eight fields including: business and management; economics; organization studies; innovation and entrepreneurship; technology, science and engineering; knowledge management; and marketing. Building on these diverse definitions, they propose a general and integrative definition that could be applied to the majority of contexts: "Innovation is the multi-stage process whereby organizations transform ideas into new/improved products, services, or processes, in order to advance, compete, and differentiate themselves successfully in their marketplace."

In this article, we embrace a definition suggested by Denning and Dunham (2010; innovators-way.com) who stress that successful innovation cannot be completed until the community of the intended users has actually adopted a new practice. For them, innovation is "the adoption of a new practice by a community". With such a definition, the focus of innovation shifts from invention to adoption practices and emphasizes the fact that there are millions of inventions that have never found their way to the marketplace. Interestingly, Accenture's (2013; tinyurl.com/n7hdyb4) study mentioned earlier found that one of the key reasons for the low efficiency of companies' innovation activities is the so-called "invention trap" – the "overreliance on the invention process itself to produce success and relative lack of systematic, enterprise-wide processes capable of commercializing inventions into products or services at scale, bringing them to market in a sufficiently timely fashion and reaping the expected returns."

The key benefit of the definition provided by Denning and Dunham is that it decouples the practices of invention from the practice of innovation which focuses on enabling adoption. This decoupling has two main effects. First, it merges together innovation and entrepreneurship, because they both could now be considered as managing and implementing change as part of the adoption of new practices. Second, it opens the opportunity to account for the value co-creation role of customers during the adoption process – a point that needs to be strongly emphasized. The two effects should be considered in a self-consistent manner because they are dialectally interrelated.

A Generative Approach to Managing Innovation as Adoption

Denning and Dunham (2010; innovators-way.com) have developed a generative approach to managing innovation, which consists of eight practices within three categories: i) *the work of invention*, including the practices of sensing and envisioning; ii) *the work of adoption*, including the practices of offering, adopting, and sustaining; and iii) *the three practices providing the environment for all the other practices*, including executing, leading, and embodying. One of the key messages of this classification is that the major work of innovation is not related to invention but rather to the personal practices of innovators and entrepreneurs aiming at getting others to adopt a new practice enabled by a new product, process, or service. *Offering* is the first such practice including the presentation of a proposed new practice and its benefits to the community and its leaders so that they commit to considering it. *Adopting* is getting the community members to commit to adopting the practice for the first time, while reserving the option of dropping it if not satisfied after a trial period. *Sustaining* consists of getting the community members to commit to the practice for an extended period, integrating it into their other practices, standards, incentives, and processes, and making it productive for its useful life.

Denning and Dunham (2010; innovators-way.com) identify the following key activities associated with the offering practice:

- drawing listeners into a discussion about the ways of producing the new outcome

- modifying the proposal to fit listeners' concerns

- establishing trust in your expertise to fulfill the offer

They identify the following key activities associated with the adopting practice:

- achieving initial commitment to the new practice

- continuously demonstrating the value of the new practice

- showing how to manage risks and deal with resistance

- aligning action plans for coherence with existing practices, concerns, and interests

- addressing different community member adoption rates

- recruiting allies

- developing marketing strategies for the different groups in the community

- continuously look for ways to overcome resistance

And finally, they identify the following key activities associated with the sustaining practice:

- achieving commitment to stick with new practice

- developing supporting mechanisms, tools, and infrastructure

- integrating the new practice with the surrounding environment, standards, and incentive systems

- continuously assessing for negative consequences

- carefully abandoning bad or obsolete innovations

Denning and Dunham point out that the key activities associated with the three adoption practices should be considered at the personal level as conversational or rather discursive expressions of human behaviour. According to such a discursive perspective, the personality of the innovator or the entrepreneur should be considered in terms of the specific personal practices and their outcomes – "the streams of human actions and interactions, which can be understood in terms of their meanings for the actors and interactors and the norms and the traditions that are generally accepted by the people involved and which shape their actions" (Harré and Moghaddam, 2012; tinyurl.com/mq42vad).

It is true that conversation is very useful, but it is not the only model for analyzing such streams of action. However, it allows for treating all that people do collectively and individually, as well as privately and publicly, as if it were a kind of conversation or discourse – in other words, as consisting of meaningful exchanges constrained by a specific normative framework (Harré and Moghaddam, 2012; tinyurl.com/mq42vad). The entrepreneurial discursive skills and dispositions are a subset of human personal knowledge that most people possess to a certain extent but might not have been able to express, grow, or master. This realization has great implications for the study of entrepreneurship and innovation because it points out that the role of the learning process is to help all interested in entrepreneurship to discover the depths of their entrepreneurial self and nurture it in a consistent way.

Customer Creativity as a Key Factor in Technology Adoption

Denning and Dunham's approach has a great value in articulating the job of both innovators and entrepreneurs in terms of the specific practices that could be learned and perfected. Their approach, however, does not seem to sufficiently emphasize another important aspect – the fact that customers' activities are an equally important component of the adoption equation. We believe that the second major reason for the failure of the majority of innovation initiatives in the technology domain is the lack of proper understanding of the creativity needed by the ultimate users who are struggling to adopt the newly developed products. Our emphasis on customer creativity in the adoption of new products does not intend to undermine the efforts of designers, innovators, or entrepreneurs; it is just an attempt to locate another major source of the problem and suggest a way out of it. The solution includes the repositioning of the creativity concept within the context of customers' adoption efforts.

The widely acknowledged definition of creativity refers to the novelty, usefulness, and appropriateness of a new product (Duxbury, 2012; timreview.ca/article/594). However, this definition misses the important element of appropriation, which can be seen as a result of the creative efforts of the ultimate recipients of the new product. The increasing complexity of new technological products enlarges the difference between the total value built in as part of the design, development, and manufacturing process and the customer's perspective of that value. The difference allows us to emphasize two points. First, potential customers make purchase and adoption decisions on the basis of the relative benefit $\Delta 1$, which is the difference between the total value (reflecting the entrepreneurial perspective) and the value of whatever their currently existing solution is (Figure 1). Second, the estimation of the relative benefit $\Delta 1$ is based on the assumption that customers know in advance what the total value of a product is. It assumes that the total value is an objectively existing property that could be easily appreciated by potential customers. This last assumption is not true, especially in the case of more complex technology-based products. What customers really know is the perceived value of the product and, unfortunately, this perceived value could be lower than the value of their existing solution, leading to a negative relative benefit $\Delta 2$. In such situations, customers have two options: either neglect the new product or make the effort to further appreciate the total value of the new product.

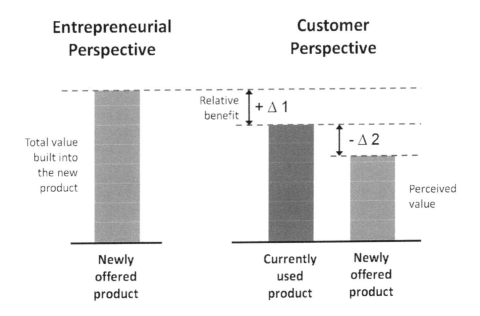

Figure 1. Visualization of the difference between the total value of a new product and its perceived customer value. Modified from Adner (2012; thewidelensbook.com).

The reason for us to focus in greater detail on the difference between the total and the perceived value of a new product is to emphasize that: i) an adoption decision does not happen before there is a positive difference between the perceived value of a newly offered product and the value of the existing solution used by the potential adopters of the new product, and ii) this process takes time and effort on the side of the potential customers. In this sense, the perception that will make a specific potential customer buy and adopt is to a great extent the result of this customer's own activities and creative efforts – in other words, it should be conceptualized as customer creativity.

Product attributes are manifested within the context of specific circumstances. For example, two different customers may associate an original technological product with completely different perceptions depending on the degree of their actual involvement and creative efforts in actively appreciating its use value. One could actually speak of this association as a process of "product co-creation" given that the evolution of the perception of a particular product makes sense only within the specific context of a particular customer. In other words, every customer co-creates the product for him or herself using accessible resources. In this sense, customer creativity is always co-creativity; it is dialogical and relational. The dialogue and the relations go far beyond the activities emerging within the context of the dyad formed by the user and the technology to include all possible insights from a variety of actors in the interactive environment surrounding the customer, such as other customers, other technologies, local distributors, customer/technical support providers, and competitors. This realization suggests that activity-based approaches such as actor-network theory (Latour, 2005; tinyurl.com/m99un78) and activity theory (Kaptelinin and Nardi, 2006; tinyurl.com/m4qp8s3) could be highly appropriate in studying the dynamics and the outcomes of product adoption.

The Increasing Complexity of Everyday Technological Products

The discussion of customer creativity suggested here is justified by the realization that there is an increased degree of complexity in most of the technological products used in everyday human lives. The higher degree of complexity generates both societal and personal pressures that are in the process of changing many aspects of the human condition. Scale is one of the critical concepts that could help in understanding how societal pressures are resulting in a significantly increased degree of technological complexity. It refers to the unprecedented increase of human population, the increasing intensity of the globalization processes, and the increasing relevance of technology in everyday human life. The increasing scale of society is forcing a shift from trust and trustworthiness based on personal relationships to impersonal trust, predictability, and compliance in both people and systems, which leads to different societal pressures from a number of different directions (Schneider, 2012; tinyurl.com/mcj8xwf):

1. Having more people in society changes the effectiveness of different reputational pressures driven by the necessity for the majority of people to follow dominant group norms due to fear from bad reputation.

2. There is a visible tendency for an increased degree of complexity of everyday technological products, given that having more people in society means more interactions among people. More interactions among people cause both the emergence of new societal dilemmas and interdependencies among them. The interdependency of newly emerging dilemmas requires new and more complex social management systems that need to rely on technology even more. Uncertainty is a key component of new technology development and more technology means that the new systems may have more flaws as well as a higher risk of failing in surprising and unexpected ways, which additionally complicates the entire socio-technological environment.

3. There is a growing variety of new technological systems. As more and different technology permeates human lives and society in general, there will be new areas of concern that will need to be addressed, new societal dilemmas, and newly emerging technological challenges. In this context, the concept of scale in society becomes even more important because more aspects of our society are going to be controlled not by people but by technologically automated systems. Unfortunately, the ongoing automation of social systems is paralleled by a process of depersonalization of the interaction between people, which additionally increases social pressures due to the inability to efficiently clarify problems associated with communication ambiguities.

4. Globalization has brought the opportunity for people to move much greater distances across national borders, across nations, and across continents. Greater

distances create the potential for more people, with weaker social ties, to be involved in mutual accidental interactions, which may weaken their moral and reputational pressures and diminish the strength of their home-based institutional pressures. This situation creates a necessity for more control and more monitoring, not only of people, but also of unprecedented amounts of goods and services, which additionally enhances the need for more complex technological solutions based on wireless, sensing, information and communication technologies.

Conclusion

In this article, we embraced a definition of innovation as "the adoption of a new practice by a community" where the innovator is the one who mobilizes all the necessary resources to enable customers to adopt the new practice. One of the benefits of such a definition is that it merges together innovation and entrepreneurship and shifts the focus from the inventor and the designer to the entrepreneur and the ultimate adopters of the innovative outcomes. The entrepreneurial aspects of technology adoption were discussed by summarizing the generative practices adoption framework suggested by Denning and Dunham (2010; innovators-way.com). We have, however, also emphasized the relevance of customers' creative efforts and activities as a key factor in the adoption process and suggested conceptualizing these efforts as part of customer creativity. The point of this emphasis is to underline the fact that customer creativity is another key prerequisite for the success of innovation initiatives. Failing to integrate the mastership of the personal innovation practices to the design and development of a commercialization environment that enables the co-creativity of customers will always result in missing the customers as the ultimate destination of the firm's offerings.

About the Authors

Stoyan Tanev is an Associate Professor in the Department of Technology and Innovation and member of the Centre for Integrative Innovation Management at the University of Southern Denmark, Odense, Denmark, as well as Adjunct Professor in the Department of Systems and Computer Engineering at Carleton University in Ottawa, Canada, where he was previously a faculty member in the Technology Innovation Management Program. He has a MSc and a PhD in Physics jointly from the University Pierre and Marie Curie, Paris, France and the University of Sofia, Bulgaria, a PhD in Theology from the University of Sofia, Bulgaria, an MEng in Technology Management from Carleton University, Canada, and an MA from the University of Sherbrooke, Canada. He has multidisciplinary research interests with a focus on the fields of technology innovation management, born global technology startup business model development and value co-creation. Dr. Tanev is Senior IEEE member and member of the Review Board of the *Technology Innovation Management Review*.

Marianne Harbo Frederiksen is an Associate Professor in the Department of Technology and Innovation and a member of the Centre for Integrative Innovation Management at the University of Southern Denmark. Currently, she is also a PhD student focusing on creative processes and outcomes in connection with new product development and adoption and therefore the linkages between creativity and innovation. She has an MSc in Architecture from the Aarhus School of Architecture, Denmark, with a specialization within industrial design and product development. She has been co-owner of a design company and has worked in and together with several industries as a designer and R&D Manager as well as an adviser in public-private research projects focusing on user experience, experience designing, and other aspects of product development.

Keywords: entrepreneurship, innovation, technology adoption, customer creativity, co-creation, customer value

13

Conceptualizing Innovation in Born-Global Firms

Erik Zijdemans and Stoyan Tanev

" It has been said that arguing against globalization is like "
arguing against the laws of gravity.

Kofi Annan
Diplomat and Nobel Laureate

This article summarizes the insights from a systematic study of the research literature focusing on the innovation aspects of born global firms – ventures that were launched to exploit a global niche from the earliest days of their operations. The authors provide a snapshot of opinions on the different aspects of innovation in the way they were conceptualized in the academic literature. The insights are based on a selection of 32 peer-reviewed journal articles addressing the different challenges associated with early internationalization and innovation in such ventures. The article emphasizes that the early internationalization of new ventures should be considered as an innovation process in itself and that innovation and internationalization have a positive effect on each other. In addition, it points out the role of knowledge acquisition and networking capabilities as key innovation enablers and refers to the emergence of the lean startup perspective on the innovation processes in born global firms. The suggested insights will be relevant to researchers and practitioners interested in the relationship between early internationalization and innovation in international new ventures and lean global startups.

Introduction

According to Knight and Cavusgil (2004), the early internationalization of a firm and its potential success in a foreign market are functions of its internal capabilities. The superior ability of certain firms to sustain innovation leads to new knowledge creation, which enables the development of organizational capabilities that result in superior performance, particularly in highly competitive environments. On the other hand, innovation results from various sources, such as internal R&D and imitation of the innovations of other firms. R&D in particular supports the opening of new markets and the re-invention of firm's operations in a way that enables the firm to better serve those new markets. The innovativeness of such firms includes the masterful leveraging of knowledge and organizational capabilities despite scarce financial, human, and tangible resources. Knight and Cavusgil (2004) provide evidence that born-global firms are inherently entrepreneurial and innovative firms, displaying a specific pattern of knowledge and capability management that engenders early internationalization and sustainable, superior performance in foreign markets.

In what follows, we will focus on the different aspects of innovation in the way it was conceptualized within the context of international new ventures and born-global firms. We used the Web of Knowledge academic research database to identify 32 peer-reviewed journal articles in the fields of business and management that discuss the challenges associated with early internationalization and innovation in such firms. The articles were selected by looking simultaneously for two keywords: "born-global firm" and "innovation". The underlying assumption is that the distinctive characteristics of such firms affect the way innovation is being conceptualized within their specific context. We start with the realization that the act of internationalization, and especially early internationalization, is an innovative act in itself. The next point focuses on the interrelation between internationalization and other types of innovation where particular attention is paid to the innovativeness of firms as a prerequisite for their commitment to a born-global way of internationalization. The next step in the discussion emphasizes the importance of two key innovation resources for born-global firms: knowledge and networking capabilities. Finally, we refer to the lean startup approach as one of the ways that could accelerate the early internationalization of startups.

Internationalization as an Innovative Act

While a large number of researchers have shown interest in the innovativeness of born-global firms or international new ventures, Jones and Coviello (2005) suggest that even the establishment of an existing business mode in a country new to the firm is a clear evidence for the existence of special innovative capabilities. Born-global firms are particularly innovative in this regard (Knight & Cavusgil, 2004). The early internationalization is stimulated by a strong innovation culture and interest to pursue international markets.

According to Afuah (2003), an innovation could be classified as incremental or radical depending on the extent to which it impacts a firm's capabilities. This is usually referred to as the organizational view of classifying innovations. In this view, an innovation is said to be radical if the knowledge required to exploit it is very different from knowledge that is available within the firm. In incremental innovations the knowledge required to develop a product builds on existing knowledge. Jones and Coviello (2005) suggest that internationalization as an innovative process can be also characterized as either radical or incremental depending on the geographic and cultural proximity to the domestic market. Internationalization as an incremental innovation is defined as the expansion to neighbouring countries or markets with only slight differences, which is in line with the traditional Uppsala model (Johanson & Vahlne, 1977), where firms acquire market knowledge of the domestic market before gradually moving to foreign markets that are culturally or geographically close. Internationalization as a radical innovation is defined as expansion to markets that are significantly different from the domestic market in regards to cultural and geographic qualities. According to this analogy, the internationalization of born-global firms is a radical innovation.

Innovation as a Result or as a Stimulus of Internationalization

Although numerous researchers suggest a close relationship between innovativeness and internationalization, a debate exists as to which is the cause and which is the effect. For example, Ramos Acedo, and Gonzalez (2011) suggest that the tendency to export is positively influenced by technical innovation. This is also acknowledged by Baronchelli and Cassia (2014), who describe that investments in product innovation accelerate the internationalization process of born-global firms. According to them, born-global firms have a higher level of innovativeness and innovation skills that they use to compete successfully, which in turn allows them to be more successful in penetrating new markets. The result is higher foreign sales relative to total revenues when the company commercializes an innovative product abroad. Knight and Cavusgil (2004) and Ramos and colleagues (2011) agree that innovative firms internationalize more rapidly as compared to other companies. In other words, the innovation culture of an organization and its proclivity to pursue international markets influence its internationalization speed.

On the other hand, there are scholars who view a firm's innovativeness as one of the outcomes of early internationalization. In other words, innovativeness, knowledge, and capabilities that increase the new venture's probability for growth and for success in foreign markets are gained through the process of internationalization. Hessels and Van Stel (2011) suggest that exporting new ventures develop completely new human capital and innovation management skills through the export activities themselves. Therefore, exporting new ventures will have a better chance of pursuing new market opportunities and commercializing new ideas. Such firms will be even more conducive to innovation as compared to the majority of domestically operating new ventures.

It seems that the polarity of the two different streams might be smoothed out if one goes beyond the classical way of seeing entrepreneurship as a rational, strategic process where opportunities are discovered through a well-planned search process. Many researchers started seeing entrepreneurship as a process of effectuation instead (Sarasvathy, 2001). Effectuation means that entrepreneurs start with a generalized idea and then attempt to work towards that idea using the resources they have at their immediate disposal. The strategy of a new firm is not clearly envisioned at the beginning, and the entrepreneurs and firms that use an effectuation processes can to a large extent remain flexible, take advantage of new ideas and opportunities as they arise, and constantly be learning (Perry et al., 2012). Under such circumstances, we can see the processes of innovation and internationalization as closely interlinked, and the search for an explicit causal relationship becomes irrelevant.

The Role of Innovation in the Emergence of a Born-Global Firm

Innovation plays a significant role in the emergence of the born-global firm. Laanti and colleagues (2007) even suggest that the main innovation is often developed prior to the establishment of such companies and is the reason why they were established in the first place. After the foundation of the company, innovation will keep playing a central role, regardless of the nature of the industry in which the firm competes. The presence of born-global firms in different industry sectors, high tech, low tech, or non tech, suggests that they must be innovative in all areas of value creation, both technological and non-technological (Weerawardena et al., 2007).

The early internationalization of born-global firms affects their innovativeness in terms of the emergence and implementation of their specific marketing strategies (Hallback & Gabrielsson, 2013). It is crucial that the firm is able to innovate, adapt, or reinvent its marketing strategies to suit the local markets, so that they can compete against incumbents in multiple foreign countries. According to Kocak and Cavusgil (2009), the firm's competitive advantage in the foreign market is maintained with the use of specific isolation mechanisms. An isolation mechanism is a way for a firm to isolate itself from competitors on one or more levels. One of the ways to build an isolation mechanism is innovation. In turn, knowledge acquisition and networking capabilities are essential in acquiring competitive advantage through innovation.

Knowledge as a Key Innovation Resource

Both Tolstoy (2009) and Prashantham and Young (2011) agree that innovative behaviour is driven by knowledge combination, an approach that is supported by entrepreneurship theory and practice. Entrepreneurship theory builds on the idea that different individuals know different things, which makes the combination of knowledge essential for opening up new opportunities. Especially the combination of market knowledge and technological knowledge is important to firms in achieving innovation and competitive advantage (Prashantham & Young, 2011). Therefore, top management has a key role in providing opportunities for employees from different functions and different departments (and sometimes even from other companies) to share and combine knowledge, for example through the reinforcement of organizational cohesiveness and collective goals.

The knowledge-based view regards knowledge as the most important resource and firms as superior to individuals in creating knowledge (Tolstoy, 2009). Knowledge creation can be either gradual or radical depending on its degree of impact on a firm's capabilities. Presutti, Boari, and Fratocchi (2007) suggest that the knowledge acquired from foreign business relationships positively influences foreign development of high-tech startups. The knowledge acquired through the network ties emerging between a globally present high-tech startup and its primary foreign customers can be exploited for both economic and innovative outcomes. In this way, knowledge acquisition from foreign customers is an important mechanism for the innovative effort of high-tech startups aiming to engage in collaborative R&D activities abroad.

The Innovative Role of Networking Capabilities

It was already pointed out that the acquisition and management of knowledge is frequently identified as an important antecedent of innovation. On the other hand, knowledge-development capabilities are directly related to the capacity of the firm to apprehend and use the relation among different informational factors to achieve their intended goals (Autio et al., 2000). According to Mort and Weerawardena (2006), the innovativeness of born-global firms is, among other things, expressed in their ability to develop networking capabilities in order to overcome their scarce tangible resources. One could argue, therefore, that the innovative behaviour of international entrepreneurial firms is stimulated by the degree of their engagement in networks (Tolstoy, 2009). There is a dialectical relation between networks and innovation, where network structure is shaped by innovations while the network structure contributes to firms' ability to innovate (Tolstoy, 2010).

Scholars agree that the emergence of born-global firms is not limited to the technology domain. Technology-driven born globals, however, manifest a stronger tendency towards the formation of open innovation networks. Blomqvist and colleagues (2008) explain that fast technological change and the need to innovate under limited resources and time pressure shape the type and the nature of the international networks born-global firms form or access. Under these circumstances, networks with hierarchies are not efficient enough, which often forces the firms to engage in open innovation initiatives and networked R&D activities catering to more flexibility, fast access to information, and high responsiveness. Capron and Mitchell (2010) elaborate on the logic of collaborating with other firms to acquire new resources and capabilities on the level of, for example, R&D. They argue that, once a firm decides to go for an external collaboration, the selection of the specific cooperation format should depend on the nature of the resource gap and that the choice should be made between a purchasing contract, alliance, or acquisition depending on the relevance of the resources, agreement on resource's value, and the desired closeness to the resource provider.

The Lean Startup Approach to the Management of Innovation

The lean startup approach (Blank, 2013) emphasizes the need for quick and responsive product development with a focus on customer feedback. The promoters of this approach propose the deployment of a minimum viable product to the market as early as possible in order to minimize the exposure of the startup to uncertainty (Moogk, 2012). The adoption of this approach is quite natural for the uncertain environment of technology-driven born-global firms. In fact, it was already suggested that one should introduce the concept of lean global startup as a way of emphasizing the impossibility for new technology startups to deal separately with business development, innovation, and early internationalization (Lemminger et al., 2014). In other words, for a newly established technology firm, the task of being global and innovative at the same time should be seen as one process.

The lean startup approach correlates with other frameworks emphasizing the emergent nature of the business environment of technology-based startups. For example, Onetti and colleagues (2012) introduced a business model framework for technology startups by emphasizing the link between entrepreneurship, innovation, and internationalization. The framework defines the business model as the way a company structures its own activities in determining the focus, the locus, and the modus of its business, whereby the "focus" of the business refers to the activities providing the basis for the articulation of a specific value proposition (i.e., the set of activities on which the company's efforts are concentrated); the "locus" refers to the location or locations across which the firms resources or value-adding activities are spread (i.e., local vs. foreign-based activities, inward-outward relationships with space, entry modes, local embeddedness, etc.); and the "modus" refers to the specific business approach with regards to the internal organization and the network design (i.e.,

insourcing and outsourcing of activities along social and inter-organizational ties, inward-outward relationships with other players, strategic alliances, etc.). This business model framework is probably the only one to accommodate the global allocation of resources and the emergence of global technology markets as an explicit part of the business model. Onetti's approach also emphasizes that the value proposition and the revenue model should be considered independently of the specific business activities because the value proposition and the revenue model belong predominantly to the strategic rather than to the operational level. Such focus on the relative independence of the value proposition could be considered as correlative to the focus on the emergent aspects of the business model in the lean startup approach where the emphasis is on the specific business activities helping the emergence of a specific value proposition and not on the business operationalization of a predefined value proposition.

After taking into account Onetti's approach to business model development of technology startups, one could argue that, in addition to the focus on the development of a minimum viable product, firms should focus on the clear articulation of the locus, focus, and modus of their businesses. The development of the minimum viable product and the modus of the startup could be regarded as key drivers of early internationalization when they push startups to find sourcing partners internationally for the required components, processes, or services that are not within the focus of the startup itself. Born-global firms make continuous innovation possible by linking these external value-creating actors to the internal processes of the firm in innovative ways (Bailetti, 2012). The adoption of the lean approach by technology startups influences the way the company manages its innovation processes (Tanev, 2012). The lean startup approach (Blank, 2013) significantly shortens the technology development cycle and time to market as well as lowers the risk of getting the product wrong. At the same time, it should be pointed out that companies should manage the competitive risks that could be associated with going to market with a product that is only "half-baked".

Conclusion

The main goal of this article was to elaborate on the understanding of innovation in born-global firms in the way it is was articulated in academic research journals. The literature on born-global firms is consistent in its conclusion that studying the sources of innovativeness of these companies is very important for other firms willing to engage into a "born-global journey". Although the topic of innovativeness has been touched on by many different authors in the literature focusing on born-global firms, it has not been addressed in an explicit and contextual way. This article offers a first step in this direction in the anticipation of future studies that could offer a more comprehensive analytical approach.

About the Authors

Erik Alexander Zijdemans is a Master's degree candidate in Product Development and Innovation with a focus on Global Supply Chain Development at the University of Southern Denmark in Odense. Additionally, he holds a BEng in Business Engineering from Hogeschool Utrecht, The Netherlands. He has over two years of working experience in project management and employee safety management. Currently, he is conducting his research at Carleton University in Ottawa, Canada, focusing on the role of business development agencies in the support of early globalization in technology startups.

Stoyan Tanev is an Associate Professor in the Department of Technology and Innovation and member of the Centre for Integrative Innovation Management at the University of Southern Denmark, Odense, Denmark, as well as Adjunct Professor in the Department of Systems and Computer Engineering at Carleton University in Ottawa, Canada, where he was previously a faculty member in the Technology Innovation Management Program. He has a MSc and a PhD in Physics jointly from the University Pierre and Marie Curie, Paris, France and the University of Sofia, Bulgaria, a PhD in Theology from the University of Sofia, Bulgaria, an MEng in Technology Innovation Management from Carleton University, Canada, and an MA from the University of Sherbrooke, Canada. He has multidisciplinary research interests with a focus on the fields of technology innovation management, global technology entrepreneurship, business model design and value co-creation. Dr. Tanev is Senior IEEE member, and he is a member of the editorial boards of the *Technology Innovation Management Review* and the *International Journal of Actor-Network Theory and Technological Innovation*.

References

Afuah, A. 2003. *Innovation Management: Strategies, Implementation and Profits.* Oxford: Oxford University Press.

Autio, E., Sapienza, H. J., & Almeida, J. G. 2000. Effects of Age at Entry, Knowledge Intensity, and Imitability on International Growth. *Academy of Management Journal,* 43(5): 909-924.
http://dx.doi.org/10.2307/1556419

Bailetti, T. 2012. What Technology Startups Must Get Right to Globalize Early and Rapidly. *Technology Innovation Management Review,* 2(10): 5-16.
http://timreview.ca/article/614

Baronchelli, G., & Cassia, F. 2014. Exploring the Antecedents of Born-Global Companies' International Development. *International Entrepreneurship and Management Journal,* 10(1): 67-79.
http://dx.doi.org/10.1007/s11365-011-0197-9

Blank, S. 2013. Why the Lean Start-up Changes Everything. *Harvard Business Review,* 91(5): 63-72.

Blomqvist, K., Hurmelinna-Laukkanen, P., Nummela, N., & Saarenketo, S. 2008. The Role of Trust and Contracts in the Internationalization of Technology-Intensive Born Globals. *Journal of Engineering and Technology Management,* 25(1-2): 123-135.
http://dx.doi.org/10.1016/j.jengtecman.2008.01.006

Capron, L., & Mitchell, W. 2010. Finding the Right Path. *Harvard Business Review,* 88(7-8): 102-107.

Dimitratos, P., Voudouris, I., Plakoyiannaki, E., & Nakos, G. 2012. International Entrepreneurial Culture: Toward a Comprehensive Opportunity-Based Operationalization of International Entrepreneurship. *International Business Review,* 21(4): 708-721.
http://dx.doi.org/10.1016/j.ibusrev.2011.08.001

Hallback, J., & Gabrielsson, P. 2013. Entrepreneurial Marketing Strategies During the Growth of International New Ventures Originating in Small and Open Economies. *International Business Review,* 22(6): 1008-1020.
http://dx.doi.org/10.1016/j.ibusrev.2013.02.006

Hessels, J., & van Stel, A. 2011. Entrepreneurship, Export Orientation, and Economic Growth. *Small Business Economics,* 37(2): 255-268.
http://dx.doi.org/10.1007/s11187-009-9233-3

Johanson, J., & Vahlne, J.-E. 1990. The Mechanism of Internationalisation. *International Marketing Review,* 7(4): 11-24.
http://dx.doi.org/10.1108/02651339010137414

Jones, M. V., & Coviello, N. E. 2005. Internationalisation: Conceptualising an Entrepreneurial Process of Behaviour in Time. *Journal of International Business Studies,* 36(3): 284-303.
http://dx.doi.org/10.1057/palgrave.jibs.8400138

Knight, G. A., & Cavusgil, S. T. 2004. Innovation, Organizational capabilities, and the Born-Global Firm. *Journal of International Business Studies,* 35(2): 124-141.
http://dx.doi.org/10.1057/palgrave.jibs.8400071

Kocak, A., & Abimbola, T. 2009. The Effects of Entrepreneurial Marketing on Born Global Performance. *International Marketing Review,* 26(4-5): 439-452.
http://dx.doi.org/10.1108/02651330910971977

Laanti, R., Gabrielsson, M., & Gabrielsson, P. 2007. The Globalization Strategies of Business-to-Business Born Global Firms in the Wireless Technology Industry. *Industrial Marketing Management*, 36(8): 1104-1117.
http://dx.doi.org/10.1016/j.indmarman.2006.10.003

Lemminger, R. S. L., Zijdemans, E., Rasmussen, E., & Tanev, S. 2014. Lean and Global Technology Start-ups: Linking the Two Research Streams. Paper to be presented at the ISPIM Americas Innovation Forum 2014, Montreal, Canada.

Moogk, D. R. 2012. Minimum Viable Product and the Importance of Experimentation in Technology Startups. *Technology Innovation Management Review*, 2(3): 23-26.
http://timreview.ca/article/535

Mort, G. S., & Weerawardena, J. 2006. Networking Capability and International Entrepreneurship: How Networks Function in Australian Born Global Firms. *International Marketing Review*, 23(5): 549-572.
http://dx.doi.org/10.1108/0265133061703445

Onetti, A., Zucchella, A., Jones, M. V., & McDougall-Covin, P. P. 2012. Internationalization, Innovation and Entrepreneurship: Business Models for New Technology-Based Firms. *Journal of Management & Governance*, 16(3): 337-368.
http://dx.doi.org/10.1007/s10997-010-9154-1

Perry, J. T., Chandler, G. N., & Markova, G. 2012. Entrepreneurial Effectuation: A Review and Suggestions for Future Research. Entrepreneurship Theory and Practice, 36(4): 837-861.
http://dx.doi.org/10.1111/j.1540-6520.2010.00435.x

Prashantham, S., & Young, S. 2011. Post-Entry Speed of International New Ventures. *Entrepreneurship Theory and Practice*, 35(2): 275-292.
http://dx.doi.org/10.1111/j.1540-6520.2009.00360.x

Presutti, M., Boari, C., & Fratocchi, L. 2007. Knowledge Acquisition and the Foreign Development of High-Tech Start-ups: A Social Capital Approach. *International Business Review*, 16(1): 23-46.
http://dx.doi.org/10.1016/j.ibusrev.2006.12.004

Ramos, E., Acedo, F. J., & Gonzalez, M. R. 2011. Internationalisation Speed and Technological Patterns: A Panel Data Study on Spanish SMEs. *Technovation*, 31(10-11): 560-572.
http://dx.doi.org/10.1016/j.technovation.2011.06.008

Sarasvathy, S. D. 2001. Causation and Effectuation: Toward a Theoretical Shift from Economic Inevitability to Entrepreneurial Contingency. *Academy of Management Review*, 26(2): 243-263.
http://dx.doi.org/10.2307/259121

Tanev, S. 2012. Global from the Start: The Characteristics of Born-Global Firms in the Technology Sector. *Technology Innovation Management Review*, 2(3): 5-8.
http://timreview.ca/article/532

Tolstoy, D. 2009. Knowledge Combination and Knowledge Creation in a Foreign-Market Network. *Journal of Small Business Management*, 47(2): 202-220.
http://dx.doi.org/10.1111/j.1540-627X.2009.00268.x

Tolstoy, D., & Agndal, H. 2010. Network Resource Combinations in the International Venturing of Small Biotech Firms. *Technovation*, 30(1): 24-36.
http://dx.doi.org/10.1016/j.technovation.2009.06.004

Weerawardena, J., Mort, G. S., Liesch, P. W., & Knight, G. 2007. Conceptualizing Accelerated Internationalization in the Born Global Firm: A Dynamic Capabilities Perspective. *Journal of World Business*, 42(3): 294-306.
http://dx.doi.org/10.1016/j.jwb.2007.04.004

Zhou, L. X., & Wu, A. Q. 2014. Earliness of Internationalization and Performance Outcomes: Exploring the Moderating Effects of Venture Age and International Commitment. *Journal of World Business*, 49(1): 132-142.
http://dx.doi.org/10.1016/j.jwb.2013.10.001

Keywords: innovation management, early internationalization, born global, lean startup approach, business model

14

Enhancing Innovation through Virtual Proximity
Tom Coughlan

" No distance of a place or lapse of time can lessen the "
friendship of those who are thoroughly persuaded of
each other's worth.

Robert Southey (1774–1843)
Poet, scholar, and historian

Historically, innovation strategists have focused on leveraging local resources and the development of local clusters, which have relied heavily on personal contact. It was assumed that serendipity would occur through casual contact and that this contact would result in rapid sharing of ideas. Many studies have supported this concept; however, the pace of innovation has changed and the most successful organizations promote not only physical proximity but also virtual proximity to resources. Virtual proximity refers to the level of emotional closeness between individuals, as developed through the use of information and communications technologies. This article argues that organizations can and should look to develop local virtual relationships supported by physical proximity: the mix of both virtual proximity and physical proximity can increase an organization's innovation capability.

Introduction

Ever since Samuel Morse tapped out "What hath God wrought?" on his telegraph to send the first electronic message (Howe, 2007; tinyurl.com/m8n724a), and with the release of every information communications technology since, there have been pundits who have proclaimed the "death of distance"(e.g., Bowersox and Calantone, 1998: tinyurl.com/m5rkxx2; Cairncross, 1997: tinyurl.com/m7sqhsc; Evans and Harrigan, 2005: tinyurl.com/ld2xjnu). But, to paraphrase another nineteenth century luminary, Mark Twain (tinyurl.com/57mptu), the reports of its death have been greatly exaggerated. Distance is still alive and well and creating havoc for those of us who practice or study innovation.

Even though we can tap out a text, send an email, make a phone call, or share in a video conference, part of the message is lost if we are not sharing the same physical location with the people on our innovation team. Just moving the location of a key person or resource a few metres can dramatically drop the level of interaction and therefore amount of innovation an organization will produce (Allen, 2007; tinyurl.com/lshbss7). But, the sharing of information is not just about physical distance – it is about a shared connection. To truly under-

stand these connections, and in turn how innovation happens, it is important to understand the concepts of proximity, effective communication, information architecture, and some of the properties of the media used for intra-organizational communications.

Managers, entrepreneurs, researchers, and innovators of all types need to find new ways of leveraging both their existing resources and discovering new potential innovation resources. Innovation is often a function of recombining ideas and resources that often already exist or building on the ideas of others – who may exist both inside and outside your organization (Kelley, 2005; tinyurl.com/l44ooal). Many studies have supported the notion that casual, serendipitous contact facilitates idea sharing (Bindroo et al., 2012: tinyurl.com/mmh5t58; Hauser et al., 2007: tinyurl.com/qdk4dhf; Huggins and Izushi, 2011: tinyurl.com/plnnt9a; Knoben and Oerlemans, 2006: tinyurl.com/kn3svq9; Porter, 1990: tinyurl.com/khf32f4); but, unfortunately, given the pace of modern lifestyles, our ability to travel, and the required commitments of many of our potential collaborators, it is often difficult if not impossible to be in the same place at the same time. However, some level of proximity is necessary in order for ideas to collide and serendipity to occur. Therefore, we need to develop a new virtual type of proximity that allows our collaborators to be aware of the new ideas or potential resources – and this awareness could lead to the development of a feeling of presence and possibly engagement, which increases the likelihood of innovation.

This article focuses on virtual proximity as a means of enhancing innovation. To understand the problems that make virtual proximity an important part of an innovation strategy, it is critical to understand some of the key principles surrounding it; therefore, this article will be structured as follows. First, the different types of proximity and their roles are identified. Next, the key elements of effective communications and media use are examined, and the key factors surrounding regional clusters and their effect on innovation are outlined. Then, some of the misconceptions surrounding virtual proximity are dispelled. Finally, a foundation for a solid virtual proximity strategy is provided, along with some simple and actionable recommendations for managers.

Proximity

Proximity to resources, and the clustering of resources by specific industries within a geographic region, has long been considered an important factor in the promotion of both the volume and the quality of innovation (Doloreux, 2004: tinyurl.com/k7botqn; Porter, 2001: tinyurl.com/kp2l8o8). The belief is that close geographic proximity to key resources would reduce friction and speed access to those resources and therefore increase innovation. Some researchers have gone as far as to suggest that tacit knowledge is an essential ingredient of innovation, and that tacit knowledge can only be transferred in close physical proximity. The true value of clustering emerges when proximity of both key resources and tacit knowledge fosters the spillover of knowledge within and across industries (Greunz, 2003: tinyurl.com/pefatjs; Knoben and Oerlemans, 2006: tinyurl.com/kn3svq9).

This perspective, however, begs the questions: what is proximity? The definition of proximity dramatically changed when Wilfred Beckerman (1956; tinyurl.com/lyjhhyx) introduced the term *psychic distance*. Beckerman's contention was that distance is not an absolute. The distance between two individuals is a function of the disparity of their cultures, not the physical distance between them. The concept of psychic distance has been expanded by a number of researchers, leading to the development of additional concepts such as:

- *cultural proximity:* how similar the cultures of network participants are on a national level (Hofstede, 2009: tinyurl.com/5p6sme; Knoben and Oerlemans, 2006: tinyurl.com/kn3svq9; Sousa and Bradley, 2006: tinyurl.com/n2na6by)

- *cognitive distance:* the level of diversity in the skills, knowledge, and cognitive frame (Wuyts et al., 2005; tinyurl.com/khvb7ca)

- *organizational proximity:* the distance felt by members of the same large or multi-site organization (Knoben and Oerlemans, 2006: tinyurl.com/kn3svq9)

- *technology proximity:* the level of overlap between the firms' technology or patent portfolio

- *vision proximity:* the similarity in vision (Cantu, 2010; tinyurl.com/prlxkb4)

- *virtual proximity:* the level of emotional closeness developed through the use of information and communications technologies (Coughlan, 2010; tinyurl.com/olqrel7)

These descriptions of proximity are not mutually exclusive, it is often unclear where they begin and end, and there are gradient scales to each and every one. For example, even geographic proximity, one of the most straightforward of the proximity metrics, can be measured in either physical distance or travel time. Some researchers have gone as far as to develop meta indexes that attempt to combine several of these elements into a single measure of proximity (Amin and Cohendet, 2005: tinyurl.com/k6ebtry; Coughlan, 2010: tinyurl.com/olqrel7). So, defining how close you are to a resource can be more difficult than what might be originally assumed.

Communications

The principles of proximity, culture, and cognition have a dramatic effect on the encoding, transmission, decoding, and processing of an idea from one individual to another. However, when understanding the strategy of communication, it is just as important to understand the "what and why" (i.e., the architecture) of the communications. Allen (2007; tinyurl.com/lshbss7) suggested that relationships within the organization affect the success of the communications, and that there are three types of communications, each of which is affected by its own proximity or relationship dynamics:

1. Type I: simple communications required to coordinate group or team projects.

2. Type II: the sharing of codified knowledge.

3. Type III: the transfer of tacit knowledge, which is the most important type of knowledge for innovation and the one most affected by distance.

Allen's study also found that, unsurprisingly, people who work in close physical proximity to each other will typically communicate more often than those who do not. However, what was surprising is that, when this relationship is plotted on a curve, little to no drop in the level of communications can be seen beyond 50 metres. Allen posited that visual clues to a person's existence are important in prompting communications.

Media

In order for innovation teams to properly communicate key ideas, their choice of communication media is often extremely important. Each medium has inherent properties and limitations; as we increase the distance between team members – and reduce the time they are physically co-present – the importance of this choice increases. Media richness theory (Lengel and Daft, 1988; tinyurl.com/ogd2k2v) posits that performance of communications improves with the richness of the communications media. For example, phone conversations are richer than text messages, and videoconferences are richer than phone calls. In addition, as the equivocality of the task increases, so should the richness of the media used (Lengel and Daft, 1988; tinyurl.com/ogd2k2v). After decades of study what has been discovered is that real communications often transcends the media (Dennis and Kinney, 1998; tinyurl.com/kw6qf8y): our successful use of media is often dependent on our familiarity with that media and our familiarity with the recipient of the message. Another key finding is that the less natural we feel in using a media, the more cognitive resources we will need to expend (Dennis et al., 2008; tinyurl.com/mk9w6c7). However, with time and effort, our familiarity with a specific medium improves and the cognitive effort declines (Dennis et al., 2008; tinyurl.com/mk9w6c7).

Anatomy of Clusters

According to Porter (1998; tinyurl.com/38rnvv6), clusters are "geographic concentrations of interconnected companies and institutions in a particular field." Porter's work has often been cited as seminal in terms of outlining the concepts of clusters and why cluster provide

a competitive advantage in efficiency and innovation. Porter points out that clusters often provides a company with access to employees, suppliers, specialized information, and key services that are difficult and more expensive to obtain outside the cluster. The clusters that have historically worked best have clear industry foci and many inter-organizational relationships, allowing that the advantages become specialized to a specific industry or the needs of a particular type of customer (Porter, 1998; tinyurl.com/38rnvv6). But, can we supplement the advantages that geographic proximity delivers through access to non-local resources? Would some other form of proximity, such as virtual proximity or cultural proximity, provide an even greater competitive advantage? For example, in comparing California's Silicon Valley to the Route 128 Corridor in Massachusetts, there is a cultural difference in how innovation has historically been handled. Although both regions are focused on the technology Industry, Silicon Valley has been much more open to inter-organizational relationships and sharing; resulting in a far more dramatic regional growth (Saxenian, 1994; tinyurl.com/m3xzkjq). Knoben (2008; tinyurl.com/l44ooal) demonstrated that it is not just about the density of firms or the size of the population; the success of innovation is dependent on the membership of the internal team as well as the connections and relationships developed outside the firm. The makeup of the regional economy has a strong influence on local success: "...simply bringing firms together, for example by building science parks, is unlikely to effectively stimulate the innovativeness of firms and might even hamper it" (Knoben, 2008; tinyurl.com/l44ooal). The cluster of firms must have a culture and a resource profile that not only allows but also encourages each firm to interact (Ben Letaifa and Rabeau, 2013; tinyurl.com/pjx9yj3). Virtual proximity might help fill a gap in a team's talent profile with a person or firm that has a better cultural fit than a local resource.

Studies by the author in the New York metropolitan area, have shown that firms that have a portfolio of inter-organizational relationships, which include both local and non-local linkages, are typically more innovative (Coughlan, 2010; tinyurl.com/olqrel7). In addition, top performers have inter-organizational relationship portfolios that are very broad in terms of the types of firms and industries included (Coughlan, 2010: tinyurl.com/olqrel7; Knoben, 2008: tinyurl.com/l44ooal). However, it is possible for a portfolio to be too broad. It is important that cognitive distance "be restricted for the sake of coordination" (Wuyts et al., 2005; tinyurl.com/khvb7ca). Diversity in thought is critical in innovation, but in this case you can have too much of a good thing. If a plot were developed to show innovation initiative over a scale of novelty and understandability an inverse U-shaped curve would develop. Too little diversity limits the available intellectual capital and too much diversity makes it difficult for team members to cognitively process the available information. So, organizations should be looking for a balance.

Virtual Proximity

Given this environment, virtual proximity can be a useful model if properly applied. However, there are a number of misconceptions or misunderstandings of how or when it should be leveraged – or even what it is.

Virtual proximity is about leveraging information and communications technologies to build and maintain relationships – the emphasis being on the relationship and not the technology. Simply having or using technology does not necessarily equate to an improvement in virtual proximity. Here, it might be important to think about the factors that nullified media richness theory, such as the familiarity with specific media tools and how cognitive ease improve with use (Dennis and Kinney, 1998; tinyurl.com/kw6qf8y). It is in the use of the technology and the integration into our work processes that we experience the advantages of virtual proximity. Once the use of a tool becomes familiar and easy to use, we can free up cognitive resources to work on innovation.

However, if the use of virtual proximity tools feels unnatural, too much of the cognitive effort will be devoted to the use of the tool and not into the content needed to develop the relationship or reorganizing of ideas and resources to develop new innovations. Although we can learn to use the tools and platforms, thereby reducing allocation of cognitive effort to the technology, we may struggle to keep up with the growth and change in these technologies and platforms. We want the latest technology, but we also want familiarity and efficacy.

It is tempting to assume that virtual proximity is primarily used to engage resources or individuals that exist outside the local region, and that it is not required for local relationships. However, this assumption is false. Allen (2007; tinyurl.com/lshbss7) points out that the probability of using a resource drops for every metre of separation up to 50 metres. Thus, the notion of "non local" starts at 50 metres. He also suggests that often we need visual clues to remind us that the resource is there. Increasing the number of visual clues or contacts should help in reminding the network of the existence of a resource, and increase the probability of it being integrated into the innovation process.

Virtual proximity is multidimensional. Measuring virtual proximity requires the development of a matrix, which includes a variety of different electronic media, the level of use, the proficiency, and the impact of the use. In some way, it is similar to the concept of the Klout score (klout.com), which measures the influence of a given user across social media. However, there is no claim that a virtual proximity measure is an absolute measure. It is intended to be a model for thinking, just as one would use the product lifecycle in marketing or Tuckman's stages of group development in management (tinyurl.com/2bpowb4). As with these models, there are generalities that do apply. For example, a high degree of virtual proximity does generally result in higher level of innovation and higher levels of disruptive or intersectional innovation (Coughlan, 2010; tinyurl.com/olqrel7).

Virtual proximity is similar to the notion of mental processing of social presence on the Internet, which has been described by Ning Shen and Khalifa (2008; tinyurl.com/lgl4by2) as:

> "...the moment-by-moment awareness of the co-presence of another sentient being accompanied by a sense of engagement with the other... as a global, moment-by-moment sense of the other, social presence is an outcome of cognitive stimulations (i.e., inferences) of the other's cognitive, emotional, and behavioral dispositions".

Whereas social presence emphasizes the real-time awareness of a resource's presence, virtual proximity emphasizes the ongoing awareness of a resource's existence. The key difference is that virtual proximity does not require engagement until the point it is integrated into the innovation process. In a sense, virtual proximity is more an awareness of the resource and the ability to readily engage the resource.

Virtual proximity is also different from the other forms of proximity outlined earlier in this article. However, it can act as a catalyst to improve other types of proximity such as psychic distance, cultural proximity, cognitive distance, and organizational proximity - all of which are broader concepts and span both the virtual and terrestrial worlds.

Conclusions

Virtual proximity is not a choice – just as your reputation is not a choice. It exists in relative terms to the environment in which you live and operate. Individually or as an organization, we have a level of virtual proximity with every team member, supplier, partner, or collaborator that we currently have or could potentially have. However, just as your reputation can be managed and improved with time, vigilance, and effort, so can your virtual proximity. Managers should realize that the majority of telecommunications traffic is local – whether it be phone calls, text messages, tweets, emails, Facebook posts, Linkedin requests, Vines, or what whatever means of virtual communications your organization or network participates in. Virtual proximity is a local phenomenon.

In addition, the engagement levels of resources drop significantly in a matter of a few metres and the old adage "out of sight, out of mind" is constantly eroding our ability to stay aware of the resources and maintain our relationships. Virtual technologies are powerful tools that allow us to maintain our relations whether they are within our own organizations, across the street, or on the other side of the world.

Therefore, managers looking to capitalize on their innovation opportunities should have a proximity strategy. At a minimum, this strategy should include the following:

1. *Visual clues*: if at all possible, visual clues should be incorporated for key resources. Examples include making sure that photographs in social media profiles are up to date and that regular posts remind key resources of your existence. Simple tools that show presence are also important. Instant messaging tools such as Google Hangouts or Microsoft Lync could remind potential collaborators of each other's existence.

2. *Combined proximities*: as stated earlier, the effect that diversity has on innovation can be plotted as an inverse U-shaped curve. So, we need to find resources that have some minimal level of proximity on multiple scales of proximity (i.e., cultural, cognitive, organizational, technological, or vision), and we should engage resource outside the firm to help bolster the diversity of thought.

3. *Common tools*: it is important to develop familiarity with tools that enable virtual proximity. Virtual proximity can be developed using tools as simple as SMS or as complex as telepresence conference rooms; however, it is important that the users feel comfortable with whatever tools are chosen. Some of these tools will require training and all will require practice to use them properly without excessive cognitive effort. So, there must be some agreement, whether overt or implied, as to which tools will be used and why.

4. *Regular integration of new tools*: new tools are constantly being introduced in this area; however, managers must be careful in how they are integrated. New tools may have a technical advantage but the advantage might be negated but the additional overhead that it takes to be competent with a new tool. The introduction of too many new tools, or tools that feel unnatural to the users, could actually be a detriment to the process. Conversely, not introducing new capabilities that would improve the communications process and improve the level of virtual proximity could have the same effect.

5. *Roll out of new tools with closely knit teams*: given that familiarity with both the tools and the participants is important in reducing the cognitive overhead, when possible, new tools should be first introduced to participants who are familiar with each other. This approach will reduce the cognitive overhead and allow faster integration of the tool into the innovation process with the least disruption.

6. *Experimentation*: virtual proximity is a broad principle with few hard edges. It is likely that many of the key variables that surround virtual proximity will change over time and so will the specifics of virtual proximity. However, it is likely that the innovators will need to find power tools to maintain a broad set of relationships and expand their reach working with new collaborators and resources. In this sense, virtual proximity will likely increase in importance over time, and it will be necessary to develop new skills and techniques and capabilities in this area as our existing tools and techniques complete their lifecycle.

About the Author

Tom Coughlan, DBA, is the Associate Dean of the School of Business at Mercy College in Dobbs Ferry, New York. He is also is an adjunct faculty in the graduate programs of the University of Phoenix, the Manhattan Institute of Management, the University of Bridgeport, and the Weller International Business School in Paris. His fields of practice include management, marketing, and e-business with a particular emphasis on the development of virtual proximity to increase levels of applied innovation within and across organizations. In addition to his academic activities, Dr. Coughlan has over 30 years of field experience as an entrepreneur, consultant, and marketing/management professional.

Keywords: virtual proximity, innovation, communication, distance, clusters, tools

15

Radical Versus Incremental Innovation: The Importance of Key Competences in Service Firms

Marit Engen and Inger Elisabeth Holen

" A manager is responsible for the application and " performance of knowledge.

Peter Drucker (1909–2005)
Author and Management Consultant

Today, innovation often takes place using open practices and relies on many sources for knowledge and information. The purpose of this article is to study how different knowledge-based antecedents influence the ability of service organizations to innovate. Using data about the Norwegian service sector from the 2010 Community Innovation Survey, we examined how three types of competence, namely R&D activities, employee-based activities, and customer-related activities, influence the propensity of firms to introduce radical or incremental innovations. The results show that R&D-based competence is important for service firms when pursuing radical innovations, whereas employee-based activities such as idea collaboration are only found to influence incremental innovations. The use of customer information was found to be an important driver for both radical and incremental innovations. The findings points to managerial challenges in creating and balancing the types of competence needed, depending on type of innovation targeted by an organization.

Introduction

Studies of service innovation have increased along with the growth of the service sector, and they have emerged from being marginal and neglected to achieve recognition as an important field to study (Miles, 2000). Until recently, this research field has to a great extent been divided between two contrasting approaches: demarcation and assimilation (Coombs & Miles, 2000). The demarcation approach assumes that services as different from goods, and it is in need of its own theoretical framework to fully understand the concept and process of innovation in services. The assimilation approach, on the other hand, sees innovation (whether it is goods or services) within the same framework of understanding (Coombs & Miles, 2000; Drejer, 2004). However, these two traditions are the subject of ongoing debate, and a third perspective – the synthesis approach – has been suggested in the literature. The purpose of the synthesis approach is to create both a theoretical and an empirical approach to innov-

ation that is able to capture all economic activities – both services and industrial activities – without favouring one over the other (Drejer, 2004). Therefore, the synthesis approach focuses on the need to study service innovation from a perspective that include the central aspects of service production at the same time, not just reflecting the manufacturing-service dichotomy (Drejer, 2004; Ordanini & Parasuraman, 2011). The perspective assumes similar underlying mechanism of innovation, though acknowledging that the importance of the dimensions may vary depending on context, both between and within the sectors (Nijssen et al., 2006). Given that the study of service innovation is still considered to be in a relatively early stage of development (Drejer, 2004), this article aims to gain more knowledge on innovation activities within the service sector. However, the study will be based on a model that is in line with Drejer (2004) and includes elements that are assumed to be of relevance regardless of industries, and thus aims to contribute to the synthesis approach.

According to Hult, Hurley, and Knight (2004), a firm's capacity to innovate is among the most important factors that impact its performance. Yet, little is known about the drivers of innovativeness in general (Hult et al., 2004), and empirical findings are both limited and inconclusive regarding the antecedents to innovation in services in particular (e.g., Ordanini & Parasuraman, 2011). In this article, a framework that includes antecedents to innovation and how they influence the capacities of service firms to innovate is proposed and tested. More precisely, building on the existing literature, we have identified three forms of competence (e.g., knowledge and skills) that are related to innovation activities of firms: i) R&D-based competence; ii) employee-based competence; and iii) customer-based competence. Furthermore, we distinguish between innovations based on their degree of novelty, and we examine how the different competences influence the propensity of service firms to introduce innovations that can be considered as being either radical or incremental.

The article makes two main contributions. First, the study suggests that different types of competence have varying influence over the ability of firms to introduce radical versus incremental innovations. Thus, managing the innovation process requires knowledge about how to balance the competences and exploit them differently depending on the innovation objective. Second, the findings indicate that R&D activities, although often described as being more relevant to innovation in manufacturing, are an important determinant to radical innovation in service firms.

The article is structured as follows. First, we introduce the theoretical background for the framework developed for the study. Second, we present the model and the research hypotheses, followed by the research method. Finally, we report and discuss the results, including their implications for management.

Theoretical Background

All definitions of innovation include the development and implementation of something new (de Jong & Vermeulen, 2003). An ongoing debate in the literature is the question of the degree of novelty and how "novel: should be understood. The concepts of radical (or discontinuous) innovation and incremental innovation can be seen as representing opposite ends of a novelty spectrum (de Brentani, 2001). Radical change was defined by Tushman and Romanelli (1985) as "processes of reorientation wherein patterns of consistency are fundamentally reordered." Although there are other definitions of the concept, the common feature is the effect of the change on the resources or technology in the organization. Incremental innovation, representing the other end of the spectrum, is characterized as a change that implies small adaptions to the status quo (Tushman & Romanelli, 1985), and it is often described as a step-by-step process.

Innovations in services are commonly characterized as being incremental (Sundbo & Gallouj, 2000). The innovations are often connected to the service process, and the development of the ideas is thus partly intertwined with the organizational structures and processes in the company. However, although the innovation is characterized as evolutionary in nature, the sum of the changes may well require major reallocation of resources or technology, and consequently be towards the radical end of the novelty spectrum. Hence, there is a need to separate how ideas and innovations emerge from their actual outcomes (e.g., Toivonen & Tuominen, 2009), recognizing that diverse innovation processes may lead to the implementation of ideas ranging from incremental to radical changes. The line of separation between when an innovation is categorized as incremental versus radical can be unclear. However, incremental innovations are typically represented by, for example, minor adaptions to the existing service concept or service delivery process, whereas radical innovations often imply changes that have a significant impact on a market, for example, changing the structure of the market or creating a new market.

Antecedents to innovation

Innovations depend on multiple factors that influence the process from idea generation through development to implementation. Sundbo and Gallouj (2000) describe it as an interactive process, depending on both external and internal factors. According to these authors, innovation in service firms is primarily driven by internal forces, which are defined as: i) the management and strategy of the firm; ii) employees at all levels of the firm; and iii) R&D departments – with the first two seen as the main factors. The external forces are divided into trajectories and actors. The former refers to ideas and logic that are diffused through social systems, whereas the latter corresponds to key market actors such as customers, suppliers, and competitors, with customers usually being identified as the most crucial.

The two internal factors – i) employees and management and ii) strategy – are emphasized as the most important in the innovation process (Sundbo & Gallouj, 2000). Managers need to be able to balance and lead the process while ensuring that the innovations fit within the chosen strategy. The importance of incorporating employees' knowledge in service innovation is also consistent with the literature (de Brentani, 2001; Ordanini & Parasuraman, 2011). Employees gain valuable knowledge from the interaction with customers through their mutual participation in the service delivery process.

Along with the internal drivers, innovation processes are said to depend on external knowledge, in particular customer-related knowledge. The customers play an active part in the service delivery process, and the value of gaining customer knowledge is well established in the literature, both for the general performance of organizations and for innovations in particular (Matthing et al., 2004; Slater & Narver, 2000). In recent literature, customers have been defined as co-creators of value (e.g., Vargo & Lusch, 2008), and a current research topic is how customers can play a more active part in the innovation processes of firms (e.g., Edvardsson et al., 2010).

Research Framework and Hypotheses

Based on the background above, we developed a research framework that incorporates three types of competence that are described in the literature as highly relevant antecedents to innovation. These antecedents are presumed to affect the ability of service firms to introduce innovations along the spectrum of novelty. Notwithstanding the continuous nature of this spectrum, following Mention (2011), we classified novelty into one of two categories: *radical innovations*, which have a high degree of novelty, and *incremental innovations*, which have a low degree of novelty. The framework is illustrated in Figure 1, and the rationale and hypotheses for the model are addressed next.

R&D-based competence
According to Sundbo and Gallouj (2000), a model describing a typical pattern for innovation in services is relying on employees acting as corporate entrepreneurs influenced by management to regulate and control this internal entrepreneurial process. In their model, traditional R&D departments play less important roles as drivers of innovation. However, their study also showed that the pattern of innovation in services varies within the sector, depending on the line of business. Although R&D-based knowledge is generally more relevant to manufacturing (e.g., Tether, 2005), recent studies found that R&D investments and activities are also important in service firms (Leiponen, 2012; Trigo, 2013). In view of the somewhat inconsistent findings regarding R&D, R&D-based knowledge and its potential influence on innovation are considered worthy of further investigation. Hence, we have included the investigation of this aspect as part of this study. Because R&D departments are rarely found in service firms (Sundbo & Gallouj, 2000), we divided R&D-related knowledge according to wheth-

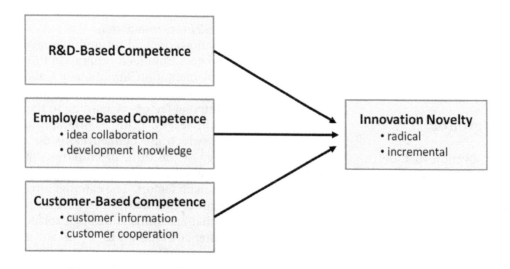

Figure 1. Research framework of determinants of innovation and novelty

er it originated from an in-house department or was externally acquired. In line with the study of Nijssen, Hillebrand, Vermeulen, and Kemp (2006), who found that R&D strength influenced the degree of novelty of new services, we defined the following hypothesis:

Hypothesis 1a: *Internal R&D-based competence is positively related to firms introducing radical innovations.*

Hypothesis 1b: *External-R&D based competence is positively related to firms introducing radical innovations.*

Employee-based competence

Several studies have found that the involvement of employees in the innovation processes is important for successful innovation (de Brentani, 2001; Ordanini & Parasuraman, 2011; Sundbo, 2008). The employees interact with customers and so are in positions to learn from customers. Thus, they may come up with new ideas, and employees' creative ideas are known to be important in organizational innovation (Zhou & Woodman, 2003). However, employees' knowledge and ideas need to be transferred within the organization if they are to be adopted by management, so interaction between individuals is thought to be important for successful innovation. Hence, management would be wise to facilitate a work environment for employees to interact and collaborate (e.g., Shalley & Gilson, 2004). According to Gwinner, Bitner, Brown, and Kumar (2005), employees can continuously adapt and customize the services provided, thereby creating innovations through evolutionary change. Ordanini and Parasuraman (2011) also found employee collaboration to contribute to innovation radicalness, hence:

Hypothesis 2a: *Employee idea collaboration is positively related to firms introducing radical innovations.*

Hypothesis 2b: *Employee idea collaboration is positively related to firms introducing incremental innovations.*

The innovation process is knowledge intensive, and the need for skilled employees is not limited to the R&D function (Leiponen, 2005). The innovation process in service organizations is often characterized as being a broad process, wherein many individuals and departments of the organization are involved. The employees may need to acquire new knowledge in order to participate in the development and implementation of the ideas. Thus, management needs to ensure that the em-

ployees have the skills necessary to fulfil these tasks. The concept of development knowledge is applied in the study by referring to the competence building of employees related to the innovation activities of the firm. Hence;

Hypothesis 3a: *Development-based knowledge is positively related to firms introducing radical innovations.*

Hypothesis 3b: *Development-based knowledge is positively related to firms introducing incremental innovations.*

Customer-based competence

Customer-related knowledge plays an important role in the innovation processes of firms. However, it has also been argued that firms should, to some extent, view customers as partners in the innovation process (Alam & Perry, 2002; Edvardsson et al., 2010). Consequently, customer-based competence can be divided according to how the knowledge is created, either by gaining information from the customers or by collaborating with them.

Although customers are conceptualized as significant for innovation, previous studies have yielded inconclusive results about the effects of their contributions. Ordanini and Parasuraman (2011) found that collaboration with customers enhanced the capacity of firms to generate new ideas, but did not affect the degree of radicalness of the innovations. On the other hand, Mention (2011) found a positive relationship between using customer-based information and novelty of innovations but no effect from co-operating with the customers on novelty. In view of this uncertainty, we formulated the following hypotheses:

Hypothesis 4a: *Use of customer-based information is positively related to firms introducing radical innovations.*

Hypothesis 4b: *Use of customer-based information is positively related to firms introducing incremental innovations.*

Hypothesis 5a: *Customer-based co-operation is positively related to firms introducing radical innovations.*

Hypothesis 5b: *Customer-based co-operation is positively related to firms introducing incremental innovations.*

Method

The study is based on data from the 2010 Community Innovation Survey (CIS, 2010), which was conducted in Norway for the years 2008 to 2010. The data were collected by Statistics Norway. The CIS originated in the early 1990s as an initiative of the Organisation for Economic Co-operation and Development (OECD; oecd.org), and it resulted in the development of an innovation manual that became known as the Oslo Manual (OECD, 2005). The statistical unit in the CIS survey is the firm or enterprise.

The study was based on cross-sectional data. The original sample included 3330 Norwegian service firms. However, organizations with fewer than 10 employees answered a less extensive questionnaire, which was not adequate for our purposes, and so have been omitted. Thus the results will be biased towards the larger firms. The final sample consisted of 2636 firms.

The data were analyzed using a multinomial regression (see Appendix 1). The dependent variable in our study is innovation novelty (see Figure 1). This variable is defined as having three possible outcomes: i) radical innovation, ii) incremental innovation, or iii) no innovation. By including the firms that reported not having introduced any innovations during the timespan of the survey, we are able to study the differences not just from incremental to radical, but also what distinguishes firms engaging in innovation from those who do not.

The independent variables were defined as R&D-based competence, employee-based competence, and customer-based competence. For details concerning model variables, descriptive statistics and results, see Appendix 1.

Results

Each of the three types of competence was used by the firms in the group reporting no innovations at all in the period, but to a lesser extent for all types than firms in the other two categories. The results also showed that firms introducing radical innovations used customer information as a source to a greater extent than the incremental innovators. Likewise, cooperation with customers was far more common in firms engaged in radical innovation than among the incremental innovators and non-innovators.

Out of the ten hypotheses, eight were confirmed. The regression results (see Appendix 1) show that R&D-based competence, both internal and external, increased the probability of a service firm introducing novel innovations, thereby confirming Hypotheses 1a and 1b. Hypotheses 2a and 2b reflected the view that idea collaboration would influence innovations at both extremes of the innovation novelty spectrum. However, only incremental innovation was found to benefit from idea collaboration among employees, thus, Hypothesis 2a is not supported. Hypotheses 3a and 3b, which relate to how employees throughout the organization need knowledge to contribute to the development and implementation of innovations, were shown to influence both incremental and radical innovations, thus confirming both hypotheses. Regarding customer competence, Hypotheses 4a and 4b were fully supported. The use of customer-based information increased the probability of introducing both incremental and radical innovations. Cooperation with customers only seems to influence firms introducing radical innovation, thus supporting Hypothesis 5a; however, the hypothesized relationship to incremental innovation was not significant.

The model controlled for firm size (i.e., number of employees) and export orientation. The coefficients for firm size were not significant, whereas export orientation reduced the probability of not implementing innovations at all.

Discussion and Conclusions

This study has focused on how antecedents to innovation, here identified as R&D, employee and, customer-based competence, influence the capacities of service firms to innovate, including both ends of the novelty continuum: radical versus incremental innovation. The study does not address whether the innovation activities and the extent of innovativeness, as is measured here, are based on a firm's strategic decision. That is, a firm might strategically decide not to use resources to engage in innovation whether radical or incremental. This study merely discusses the type of competences that influence innovation and novelty, and not the possible reasons why firms choose not to innovate.

Our findings contribute to our understanding of innovation in services in several ways. First, our findings raise some questions about the assumption that innovations in service firms rarely depend on R&D (e.g., Sundbo & Gallouj, 2000). The findings indicate that R&D-related knowledge is an important driving force for service organizations when developing radical changes, thus confirming recent research on service firms' reliance on

R&D knowledge (Leiponen, 2012). The results contribute to the synthesis approach in innovation literature, which upholds the need for studying service innovation from a perspective that includes elements assumed to be of relevance regardless of industry (e.g., Drejer, 2004).

Second, the results confirm the general notion in the service innovation literature that skilled employees make important contributions to the innovation capacity of organizations. However, the findings also add to the ambiguity regarding the effects of employees collaborating on innovation. Collaboration was expected to influence both the extent and novelty of innovations, but was found to be significant only for incremental innovation. It may be that the measure of collaboration in idea generation we used in this study is more reflective of exploitation of knowledge and therefore leads to incremental changes, rather than reflecting increased knowledge that can contribute to radical change.

Finally, the findings confirm the importance of using customer information when innovating. In line with previous studies (e.g., Evangelista, 2006) customer-related information was found to influence both radical and incremental innovation. However, collaboration with customers was found to effect only radical change. It may be that incremental innovation is largely driven by internal processes and knowledge held by employees.

In summary, the results indicate that there are differences in how various kinds of competence influence the ability of firms to introduce radical versus incremental innovations. R&D-based knowledge appears to be more important when pursuing changes with a high degree of novelty, whereas employee-related competences, as in idea collaboration, play a larger role in incremental changes. The findings all points to managerial challenges in creating and balancing the competences needed.

Managerial implications

From a practical perspective, the results obtained imply that the processes leading to radical versus incremental innovations rely on different kinds of competence. To align with a chosen strategy for innovation, managers need to understand what knowledge to invest in and what ways of generating ideas to pursue. The results suggest that R&D-based knowledge is not as relevant for developing incremental innovation, as it is when developing and implementing radical changes, here defined as new to the market for services. Furthermore, the results suggest that the R&D-based knowledge does not need to originate from a firm's own departments, because such knowledge can also be externally acquired. Consequently, managers of service firms should consider how a more systematic approach to the R&D-based knowledge may benefit their innovation efforts if radical changes are the goal.

The results also point to the role of employees in the innovation processes. Ensuring that employees throughout the organization have the knowledge necessary to contribute to the innovation process and to implement the change is related to both ends of the novelty scale. Given that innovations in services often extend across departments, it is important that management invest in the employees' knowledge in general, to broaden the knowledge base within firm.

Finally, the results confirm the importance of the ability of firms to continuously collect and use information from customers in order to contribute to, and facilitate, the innovation effort. New services must be developed in response to customers' needs if they are to succeed, and it is important that managers have systems in place to continuously collect market information and disseminate it within the organization as part of knowledge sharing. Moreover, managers should also find ways to engage in collaborating activities with customers when pursuing radical innovations. It seems that customers may be able not only to evaluate present service offers, but they can also contribute with more radical ideas for new services. Thus, creating ways to cooperate better with customers may be essential to the capacity of the firm to innovate.

To conclude, innovations in service firms will benefit from the use of knowledge from a diversity of sources, internally and externally, making it important for managers to have a strategy that balances the type of competences, as well as the ability to exploit them in pursuit of different innovation objectives.

About the Authors

Marit Engen is an Assistant Professor at Lillehammer University College, Norway, where she is also a PhD student at The Centre for Innovation in Services. Her research project focuses on the management of employee-driven service innovation with a particular focus on idea creation in frontline employees and how ideas from the front end are absorbed into the innovation processes in service organizations. She holds an MSc in Marketing from Buskerud and Vestfold University College, Norway, with a specialization in knowledge management. She has worked as an advisor in the tourism sector for several years and has broad experience from projects in both the private and public sectors.

Inger Elisabeth Holen is a PhD student in the field of public and private service innovation at the Centre of Innovation in Services at Lillehammer University College, Norway. Her research has a special focus on linkages between innovation activity and business performance in service firms, but also on how public policy can stimulate innovation. She holds an MSc in Business and Economics from the BI Norwegian Business School in Oslo, Norway. She is also a co-owner of a milk-producing farm and has experience from agriculture and business consulting, and she has worked with a variety of entrepreneurs as well as established companies.

References

Alam, I. & Perry, C. 2002. A Customer-Oriented New Service Development Process. *Journal of Services Marketing*, 16(6): 515-534.
http://dx.doi.org/10.1108/08876040210443391

Coombs, R. & Miles, I. 2000. Innovation, Measurement and Services: The New Problematique. In M. J. S. & I. Miles (Eds.), *Innovation Systems in the Service Economy*: 83-102. Boston: Kluwer.

CIS. 2010. Community Information Survey. European Commission Eurostat. April 1, 2014:
http://epp.eurostat.ec.europa.eu/portal/page/portal/microdata/cis

de Brentani, U. 2001. Innovative Versus Incremental New Business Services: Different Keys for Achieving Success. *Journal of Product Innovation Management*, 18: 169-187.
http://dx.doi.org/10.1111/1540-5885.1830169

de Jong, J. P. J. & Vermeulen, P. A. M. 2003. Organizing Successful New Service Development: A Literature Review. *Management Decision*, 41(9): 844.
http://dx.doi.org/10.1108/00251740310491706

Drejer, I. 2004. Identifying Innovation in Surveys of Services: A Schumpeterian Perspective. *Research Policy*, 33(3): 551-562.
http://dx.doi.org/10.1016/j.respol.2003.07.004

Edvardsson, B., Gustafsson, A., Kristensson, P., & Witell, L. 2010. Customer Integration in Service Innovation. In F. Gallouj & F. Djellal (Eds.), *The Handbook of Innovation and Services: a Multi-Disciplinary Perspective*. Cheltenham: Edward Elgar.

Evangelista, R. 2006. Innovation in the European Service Industries. *Science & Public Policy*, 33(9): 653-668.

Gwinner, K. P., Bitner, M. J., Brown, S. W., & Kumar, A. 2005. Service Customization Through Employee Adaptiveness. *Journal of Service Research*, 8(2): 131-148.
http://dx.doi.org/10.1177/1094670505279699

Hult, G. T. M., Hurley, R. F., & Knight, G. A. 2004. Innovativeness: Its Antecedents and Impact on Business Performance. *Industrial Marketing Management*, 33(5): 429-438.
http://dx.doi.org/10.1016/j.indmarman.2003.08.015

Leiponen, A. 2005. Skills and Innovation. International *Journal of Industrial Organization*, 23(5–6): 303-323.
http://dx.doi.org/10.1016/j.ijindorg.2005.03.005

Leiponen, A. 2012. The Benefits of R&D and Breadth in Innovation Strategies: A Comparison of Finnish Service and Manufacturing Firms. *Industrial and Corporate Change*, 21(5): 1255-1281.
http://dx.doi.org/10.1093/icc/dts022

Long, S. J. & Freese, J. 2006. Regression Models for Categorical Dependent Variables Using Stata. Texas: Stata Press.

Matthing, J., Sandén, B., & Edvardsson, B. 2004. New Service Development Learning from and with Customers. *International Journal of Service Industry Management*, 15(5): 479-498.
http://dx.doi.org/10.1108/09564230410564948

Mention, A.-L. 2011. Co-operation and Co-opetition as Open Innovation Practices in the Service Sector: Which Influence on Innovation Novelty? *Technovation*, 31(1): 44-53.
http://dx.doi.org/10.1016/j.technovation.2010.08.002

Miles, I. 2000. Services Innovation: Coming of Age in the Knowledge-Based Economy. *International Journal of Innovation Management*, 4(4): 371-389.
http://dx.doi.org/10.1142/s1363919600000202

Nijssen, E. J., Hillebrand, B., Vermeulen, P. A. M., & Kemp, R. G. M. 2006. Exploring Product and Service Innovation Similarities and Differences. *International Journal of Research in Marketing*, 23(3): 241-251.
http://dx.doi.org/10.1016/j.ijresmar.2006.02.001

OECD. 2005. *Oslo Manual: Guidelines for Collecting and Interpreting Innovation Data*, third ed. Paris: OECD.

Ordanini, A. & Parasuraman, A. 2011. Service Innovation Viewed Through a Service-Dominant Logic Lens: A Conceptual Framework and Empirical Analysis. *Journal of Service Research*, 14(1): 3-23.
http://dx.doi.org/10.1177/1094670510385332

Schumpeter, J. A. 1934. *The Theory of Economic Development*. *Cambridge*, MA: Harvard University Press.

Shalley, C. E. & Gilson, L. L. 2004. What Leaders Need to Know: A Review of Social and Contextual Factors That Can Foster or Hinder Creativity. *The Leadership Quarterly*, 15(1): 33-53.
http://dx.doi.org/10.1016/j.leaqua.2003.12.004

Slater, S. F. & Narver, J. C. 2000. The Positive Effect of a Market Orientation on Business Profitability: A Balanced Replication. *Journal of Business Research*, 48(1): 69-73. http://dx.doi.org/10.1016/S0148-2963(98)00077-0

Sundbo, J. 2008. Innovation and Involvement in Services. In L. Fuglsang (Ed.), *Innovation and the Creative Prosess. Towards Innovation with Care.* Cheltenham, UK: Edward Elgar.

Sundbo, J. & Gallouj, F. 2000. Innovation as a Loosely Coupled System in Services. *International Journal of Services Technology and Management*, 1(1): 15-36.

Tether, B. S. 2005. Do Services Innovate (Differently)? Insights from the European Innobarometer Survey. *Industry & Innovation*, 12: 153-184. http://dx.doi.org/10.1080/02642060902749492

Toivonen, M. & Tuominen, T. 2009. Emergence of Innovations in Services. *The Service Industries Journal*, 29(7): 887 - 902. http://dx.doi.org/10.1080/02642060902749492

Trigo, A. 2013. The Nature of Innovation in R&D- and Non-R&D-Intensive Service Firms: Evidence from Firm-Level Latent Class Analysis. *Industry and Innovation*, 20(1): 48-68. http://dx.doi.org/10.1080/13662716.2013.761380

Tushman, M. L. & Romanelli, E. 1985. Organizational Evolution: A Metamorphosis Model of Convergence and Reorientation. In L. L. Cummings & M. B. Staw (Eds.), *Research in Organizational Behavior*, 7: 171-222). Greenwich, CT: JAI press.

Vargo, L. S. & Lusch, F. R. 2008. Service-Dominant Logic: Continuing the Evolution. *Journal of the Academy of Marketing Science*, 36: 1-10. http://dx.doi.org/10.1007/s11747-007-0069-6

Zhou, J. & Woodman, R. W. 2003. Managers' Recognition of Employees' Creative Ideas: A Social-Cognitive Model. In V. L. Shavinina (Ed.), *The International Handbook on Innovation.* Oxford: Elsevier.

Appendix 1: About the Research

The categories of innovation in the CIS survey were based on Schumpeter's (1934) original categories of product, process, organizational, and marketing innovation. The different categories were coded as binary (yes/no). The survey did not use the notions of radical or incremental innovation. The questions were framed to discover whether the product or process innovations were new to the market or new to the firm. According to de Brentani (2001), the degree of novelty can be defined using these two categories, where "new to the market" describes a higher degree of innovativeness compared to "new to the firm". Hence, we defined the group of radical innovators to consist of the firms that had introduced a product or service new to the market or a process innovation new to the market in the period from 2008 to 2010, whereas the group of incremental innovators consists of the firms that had introduced products, services, or processes, or that had been engaged in organizational or market innovation only new to the firm, in the same period. A similar categorization of innovation novelty has been used on CIS data by other researchers (e.g., Mention, 2011). The last group of non-innovators consists of the firms that had reported no innovation at all in the three-year period.

A description of the dependent and independents variables and how they are modelled is shown in Table 1.

Both internal R&D and external R&D were included as separate, binary variables in the model as measures of R&D-based competence.

Employee-based competence was evaluated with two measures. First, development-based knowledge was handled with a binary variable reflecting whether or not the firm had engaged in competence building for the purpose of developing or implementing new or enhanced products or processes. Second, we modelled employee collaboration via two binary variables, one capturing the firm's successful use of idea-brainstorming groups, and the other measuring the use of interdisciplinary work groups intended to stimulate new ideas.

Customer-based competence was modelled with a variable for the use of information and cooperation. The original survey scale on information use ranged from 0 for no use to 3 for great importance. To avoid an interval scale interpretation of an ordinal scale, the scale was reduced to a binary scale for the analysis with the value 1 for high or medium importance and 0 for low importance or no use. The customer-based cooperation was also measured using a binary scale.

In addition to the variables directly connected to the firm's innovation activities, two control variables were included: i) firm size, in terms of the number of employees, and ii) export orientation.

Model specification

Even though the outcomes of our dependent variable, innovation novelty, could be seen as ordered in degree of newness, the "distances" between the categories are not likely to be equal. Thus, the assumption of parallel regressions could be violated, so that ordinal regression will not be the appropriate choice (e.g., Long & Freese,

2006). The Wald-test gives a p-value of 0,000 as evidence for rejecting the null hypothesis that the coefficients are equal across the categories of innovators. A second alternative is estimation of binary logistic regressions for all comparisons among the alternatives of the dependent variable, but a problem of doing so is that each binary logit is based on a different sample. Although our main interest is in the differences between service firms engaged in incremental and radical innovation respectively, we also want to compare the innovative firms with the firms that have not introduced innovations at all. Hence, we used multinomial logit regression to estimate the model, specifying firms engaged in incremental innovation as the base category.

Table 2 presents descriptive statistics for our model variables. The sample distribution on the dependent variable is 19.5% of the service firms introducing radical innovations and 22.2% using incremental innovations, which leaves 58.3% of the firms with no innovations at all between the years 2008 and 2010.

Regression results
The parameter estimates of the multinomial regression model are presented in Table 3. The overall accuracy of the model is relatively good (pseudo R^2 = 0.3433). Because incremental innovation is defined as the base category, the reported coefficients in Table 3 for radical innovation and no innovation are both estimated in comparison to incremental innovations. The discussion of the results below Table 3 is however presented in line with the hypotheses, referring to expected outcome on radical and incremental innovation.

Table 1. Description of the variables included in the model

Variable Type	Description	Range
Dependent	*Innovation novelty* (0= no innovation, 1=incremental innovation only, 2= radical innovation)	0–2
Independent	*R&D-based competence*	
	Internal R&D (1 if used internal R&D, 0 otherwise)	0–1
	External R&D (1 if used externally acquired R&D, 0 otherwise)	0–1
	Employee-based competence	
	Idea collaboration (1 if used brainstorming/interdisciplinary work groups, 0 otherwise)	0–1
	Development knowledge (1 if used internal competence building, 0 otherwise)	0–1
	Customer-based competence	
	Customer-based information sources (1 if used, 0 otherwise)	0–1
	Customer-based co-operation (1 if used, 0 otherwise)	0–1
Control	Export orientation (1 if firm was exporting, 0 otherwise)	0–1
	Size (number of employees)	10–16700

Table 2. Descriptive statistics for model variables

Variable	No Innovation	Incremental Innovation	Radical Innovation
Number of firms	1537	586	513
% of firms in each group	58.3	22.2	19.5
R&D-based competence (% with use within each group)			
Internal R&D	5.7	29.0	76.4
External R&D	1.8	11.1	33.9
Employee-based competence			
Idea collaboration	24.2	68.3	82.5
Development knowledge	2.5	29.5	69.2
Customer-based competence			
Customer-based information sources	22.0	69.6	90.6
Customer-based cooperation	0.9	5.5	22.0
Control variables:			
Export orientation	28.7	43.1	58.1
Number of employees (mean/std.dev)	92/215.59	160/788.45	120/350.57

Table 3. Multinomial regression: type of innovation by independent variables

	Radical Innovation	No Innovation
R&D-based competence		
Internal R&D	1.335 (0.173)***	-0.248 (0.192)
External R&D	0.441 (0.185)*	-0.302 (0.283)
Employee-based competence		
Idea collaboration	-0.043 (0.174)	-1.176 (0.122)***
Development knowledge	0.806 (0.157)***	-1.735 (0.211)***
Customer-based competence		
Customer-based information sources	0.512 (0.204)*	-1.306 (0.125)***
Customer based cooperation	0.582 (0.231)*	0.234 (0.374)
Control variables		
Export orientation	-0.025 (0.146)	-0.270 (0.121)*
Number of employees	-0.000 (0.000)	-0.000 (0.000)
Constant	-1.747 (0.201)***	2.440 (0.104)***
Pseudo R^2	0.3433	
Number of observations	2636	

Note: Unstandardized multinomial regression coefficients, robust standard errors in parentheses.
Significant at * p<0.05, ** p<0.01, *** p< 0.001. Incremental innovation is the base category.

Keywords: innovation, services, competences, innovation novelty, community innovation survey

16

Using Trademarks to Measure Innovation in Knowledge-Intensive Business Services

Matthias Gotsch and Christiane Hipp

" *Branding the innovation can potentially help make the innovation visible, communicate its features, and provide credibility and substance to the perceived innovativeness of the organizational brand.* "

David Aaker
Author of *Innovation: Brand It or Lose It*

We present an empirical approach to measuring service innovation on the company level through the analysis of trademarks. Prior empirical investigations in several industries have shown that a trademark may be used as an innovation indicator. This article explores the use and relevance of trademarks by conducting a survey in the knowledge-intensive business services (KIBS) industries with 278 participating companies. Our survey results explain the use of trademarks as a way to protect innovation and intellectual property for KIBS. In sum, we show that trademarks can be described as adequate and useful indicators to measure new service innovations in the KIBS industries. Additionally, we show that trademarks have the potential to overcome weaknesses of traditional measurement concepts towards KIBS innovation and might make special surveys redundant in the future.

Introduction

Due to the lack of adequate innovation indicators, it is not trivial to measure the innovativeness of the services sector in general (Abreu et al., 2010), and of so-called knowledge-intensive business services (KIBS), which are profoundly related to information and knowledge, in particular (Miles, 2000; Toivonen & Tuominen, 2009). But for all stakeholders, such as entrepreneurs introducing new services, researchers focusing on innovation measurement, as well as policy makers considering support programs for service companies, it is important to have reliable indicators on a company level to applicably compare industries and regions regarding their recent intensity of service innovation.

Because service providers do not produce material goods, in the past they were often classified as non-innovative (Pires, et al., 2008). This view is mostly due to the unsuitability of many traditional innovation indicators, such as R&D expenditures. The indicator's high explanatory power for the manufacturing sector is not necessarily transferable to the services and KIBS sector (Abreu et al., 2010). Also, the non-patentability of many service innovations compromises the significance of patent indicators. Fundamentally, many of the innovation indicators used in the past could be questioned regarding their suitability for KIBS innovation.

Trademark analysis offers a possible solution to overcome the existing weaknesses of traditional innovation surveys and measurement concepts that were mainly developed for manufacturing industries (Hipp & Grupp 2005). Previous empirical investigations have shown that trademark analysis may be used as an alternative approach (e.g., Amara et al., 2008; Gotsch & Hipp, 2012; Mendonça, et al., 2004). The analysis of trademarks could contribute to an improved understanding of innovation in services that goes beyond traditional survey-based indicator concepts (Schmoch, 2003). By doing so, researchers as well as policy makers and entrepreneurs can learn about the possibilities and limitations of trademarks as a new innovation indicator in order to better describe, understand, and benchmark innovation activities in the KIBS industries.

Knowledge-Intensive Business Services and Innovation

KIBS are firms that provide knowledge-intensive services for other business firms. Since the mid-1990s, interest in KIBS in particular has grown, as reflected in a growing number of publications dealing with their special characteristics (Schricke et al., 2012). KIBS are service companies that provide knowledge inputs mainly to the business processes of other organisations. Examples of KIBS industries include computer services; research and development (R&D) services; legal, accountancy, and management services; architecture, engineering, and technical services; advertising; and market research (Miles, 2005).

KIBS combine knowledge from different sources (Hipp, 1999) and are increasingly considered to be major users, originators, and transfer agents of technological and non-technological innovations. They play a major role in creating, gathering, and diffusing organizational, institutional, and social knowledge in other economic sectors (Iden & Methlie, 2012). The KIBS sector has a role as a knowledge-producing, knowledge-using, and knowledge-transforming industrial sector (Schricke et al., 2012). For this reason, Czarnitzki and Spielkamp (2003) characterize KIBS as bridges for innovation.

However, just because KIBS play an important role in the innovation system of a region, country, industry, or value chain and are often considered as co-producers of innovation for their clients (Hauknes, 1998), this does not necessarily mean that KIBS are highly innovative on their own. Rather, it could be that some KIBS are much better at helping their clients to innovate than in managing their own innovation processes (Christensen & Baird, 1997), therefore it is also important to observe and measure innovation happening inside KIBS companies.

The Oslo Manual for the collection and interpretation of innovation data is a widely used reference for service innovation and classifies four innovation forms: product, process, marketing, and organizational innovation (OECD, 2005). Depending on their specific field of activity, innovation in KIBS may consist of new products and technologies (e. g., customization of software), new processes (e. g., new forms of delivering services), as well as new organizational types or marketing procedures (Schricke et al., 2012). Therefore, service innovation is indeed captured by the Oslo Manual to some extent, but compared to technologically oriented processes in the manufacturing sector, innovation in

KIBS is shaped by certain specificities (Tether & Hipp, 2002). For instance, the innovations often are of intangible nature and are characterized by a strong connectivity to customers as production and consumption take place simultaneously (Schricke et al., 2012). The nature of innovation within KIBS is mostly project based, ad hoc, and interactive (Toivonen, 2004). The high importance of human capital results from the fact that, according to Strambach (2008), knowledge is embodied in the people and embedded in networks, while R&D departments in the usual sense are very rare among KIBS (Kanerva et al., 2006).

Innovation Indicators

For entrepreneurs, managers, and policy makers, it is interesting to evaluate impact and leverage effects of KIBS industries and innovations. But how can we measure them in order to better understand, guide, and manage innovation activities? To measure something that cannot be recognized directly, one can use specific indicators, which provide at least an indication of reality (Gault, 2007). Indicators use empirically ascertainable variables to represent different latent quantities that are not directly measurable. Because their predictive power is limited, all indicators should be used restrictively and interpreted carefully (Kleinknecht et al., 2002). Nevertheless, the use of science, technology, and innovation indicators has greatly increased since the 1990s (Lepori et al., 2008), in part because of two interrelated events. First, access to digitized databases has made the collection and analysis of data easier. Second, there has been a corresponding interest in the use of indicators in politics, business, and society.

Indicator data can be collected in various ways, and so the choice of methodology is critical. The data for most indicators can be collected using either empirical surveys or publicly accessible databases. Indicators that can be determined only through empirical surveys are primarily related to internal company resources such as investment in human resources or turnover with new services.

Indicators commonly used in the manufacturing industries typically relate to R&D activities or patent counts (Pavitt, 1982). In the context of a linear innovation model, R&D was established as the source of innovation, and was supported by a relatively simply constructed measurement concept. The Frascati manual standardized and harmonized this R&D-based approach (OECD, 2002). Acs, Anselin, and Varga (2002) point out: "Measures of technological change have typically involved one of the three major aspects of the innovative process: (1) a measure of the inputs into the innovation process, such as R&D expenditures; (2) an intermediate output, such as the number of inventions which have been patented; or (3) a direct measure of innovative output."

Patents as indicators of intermediate output are still among the most commonly used innovation indicators (Smith, 2005). Because intellectual property rights, such as patents, are recorded in centralized databases, it is relatively easy to access related indicator data (Flor & Oltra, 2004). Although technological change is not exclusively based on R&D activities or patents, these input and output indicators are often used as single variables for measuring innovation activities, thereby allowing statistical bias to influence the analysis (Kleinknecht et al., 2002).

Innovation in KIBS, as defined in this article, is multidimensional. For example, service innovations often are not generated in special departments (Kanerva et al., 2006), but during daily work in cooperation with customers (Gallouj & Windrum, 2009) or in time-restricted project groups (Howells & Tether, 2004), and they are not necessarily connected to R&D investments. Therefore, a traditional R&D investment indicator is not applicable for KIBS innovation. Instead, human capital, team work, networking and cooperation, customer integration, and the specific role of information technology are important input factors for the success of a service innovation (Tether & Hipp, 2002).

Also, the innovation process in services does not necessarily aim to acquire or generate technical know-how. Therefore, patents have major weaknesses as indicators of service innovation (Coombs & Miles, 2000). Miles Andersen, Boden, and Howells (2000) point out that protection strategies used in the service sector differ from those of manufacturing companies. The authors argue that service companies have grown up without a formal protection culture, and, therefore, most innovations are not protected in the traditional sense. "Innovation studies have tended overwhelmingly to focus on the manufacturing sector. Similarly, research linking together innovation and the intellectual property rights system has been almost exclusively centered on patenting, with its emphasis on protecting physical artefacts centered on new products and processes" (Miles et al., 2000).

Summing up, because innovation in services can take multiple forms, it can be difficult to measure it using traditional input and throughput indicators (Camacho & Rodriguez, 2008). Coombs and Miles (2000) evaluate traditional indicators and measurement concepts as especially disadvantageous for the assessment of service innovation, especially in highly innovative KIBS. Abreu, Grinevich, Kitson, and Savona (2010) argue that "the complexity and variability of the innovation process means that new and different indicators will be appropriate in different sectors of the economy [...] though these may make it harder to compare sectors". In this context, Abreu, and colleagues (2010) develop four criteria to be considered as desirable for a new innovation indicator: accuracy, longevity, comparability, and ease of collection. In this article, we propose that these criteria can be met with an indicator based on intellectual property rights, namely trademark registrations. Trademarks are registered with publicly available databases of state authorities; therefore, they are saved over long periods and comply with international regulations (WIPO, 2006). In the following section, we will explore trademarks in detail to illustrate how they might be suitable innovation indicators for KIBS.

Trademarks as Innovation Indicators in Knowledge-Intensive Business Services

Intellectual property strategies for innovative service firms can be linked to the wider development of the strategic assets or core competencies of such firms (Prahalad & Hamel, 1990). One of the potential measures to protect intellectual property for service firms is the use of trademarks. A trademark is a legally protected symbol, which has two main functions. The first function is to clearly distinguish the products and services of one company from those of other firms (WIPO, 2006). We call this the distinction function of a trademark (Greenhalgh & Rogers, 2007), which is primarily used to inform and help potential customers. The second function is a protection function, which means that the trademark serves as a protection of intellectual property and gives monopoly rights by prohibiting other companies from operating with similar or identical trademarks in similar or identical markets (Millot, 2009).

The distinction function of a trademark can help to overcome difficulties resulting from the immateriality of services. Due to limited opportunities to assess information, customers often focus on key information and look for alternative assessment standards (Mangàni, 2006). In this case, a well known and trusted trademark can serve as an indicator of the expected overall quality performance of the service and, in this way, reduce the perceived risk of purchase and provide security (King, 1991). Aaker (2007) states that "branding the innovation can potentially help make the innovation visible, communicate its features, and provide credibility and substance to the perceived innovativeness of the organizational brand."

The protection function is more competition oriented and refers to the comparatively simple interchangeability of many services (Mangàni, 2006). Because of this ease of imitation, the need arises to differentiate the offered services. The use of trademarks does not provide full protection against imitation, because the trademark does not protect innovation or novelty in itself; nevertheless, it gives some monopoly rights (Davis, 2005). Moreover, a strong and well-known mark can discourage potential new competitors from entering the market (Aaker, 2007). The trademark increases the barrier to market entry, because high levels of investment would be needed to enter the market (Jensen & Webster, 2004).

The origin of trademark protection can be traced to the gild practices of the Middle Ages. According to Besen and Raskind (1991) "the initial purpose of trademark protection was to make it illegal to pass off the goods of another artisan as those of a guild member." Today, trademark protection also includes the possibility of achieving a mark for service activities. Mangàni (2006) identifies five reasons for the increasing economic importance of service trademarks: i) structural changes in developed economies, ii) market liberalization, iii) increased tradability of services, iv) decreased direct customer contacts, and v) increased quality competition.

A classification of the different forms of service trademarks is possible based on the service object that is primarily protected by the trademark (Flikkema et al., 2010). Common branding strategies apply for a single service (single brand), a bunch of similar services (family brand), all services of the company (umbrella brand), or the company itself (company brand). Registering a trademark gives the company a monopoly on its use, usually for a period of ten years. The registration of the mark can be renewed at any time, but its actual use in the marketplace must be shown (Blind et al., 2003). Trademarks can be registered at the national, regional, or international level. An example of a regional authority is the Office for Harmonization in the Internal Market (OHIM; oami.europa.eu), which grants community trademarks for protection in the member states of the European Union. Worldwide protection is available at the World Intellectual Property Organization

(WIPO; wipo.int), at least for signatory countries of the Madrid Protocol (tinyurl.com/66pm8af).

Dealing with the question of whether trademarking could signal innovative activity, prior investigations found a correlation between trademarks and productivity (Greenhalgh & Rogers, 2007) or stock market value (Sandner & Block, 2011), as well as between trademarks and innovation (e.g., Amara et al., 2008; Schmoch, 2003). In a next step, other researchers tried to use trademarks as an indicator of innovation (e.g., Gatrell & Ceh, 2003; Malmberg, 2005; Mendonca et al., 2004; Millot, 2009; Schmoch & Gauch, 2009). For instance, Päällysaho and Kuusisto (2008) found that companies introducing services generally use some kind of protection measure. Thereby, trademarks are primarily used to differentiate a firm's own services from potentially competing services. In particular, when patent protection is not possible, trademarks seem to have a positive impact on innovation success (Schmoch, 2003). Gotsch and Hipp (2012) already showed that international distribution markets, competitive market environments, and highly standardised services increase the number of trademark registrations. Therefore, KIBS with these characteristics are more likely to register trademarks than other companies.

However, there are also arguments against the suitability of trademarks as an innovation indicator. For instance, services that have only a low level of innovation could also be protected by trademarks (Davis, 2009), which may reduce the statistical value of a trademark indicator. Moreover, trademarks are only indirectly linked to innovation (Blind et al., 2003). Primary motives for trademark applications could be to increase the level of public awareness or to support competitive strategies of the company. There are also other formal and informal protective measures in addition to trademarks. According to the situation and the need for protection, different measures are appropriate. Amara, Landry, and Traoré (2008) classify protective measures depending on the tangible or intangible nature of the product and the implicit or codified form of connected knowledge. In this framework, patents are mainly important for material goods with codified knowledge. But, due to the immateriality of services and rather implicit form of knowledge used, trademarks are an essential protection mechanism for service innovations by KIBS.

To protect their innovations, service businesses have adopted a wide range of alternative practices for intellectual property management and protection, which are tailored to the specific needs of service innovations. Hipp and Bouncken (2009) describe strategic protection measures as essential tools for preventing misuse or imitation by competitors. These informal and strategic measures for intellectual property protection (e.g., secrecy, lead-time advantage, or complexity of design) are obviously not centrally registered like formal intellectual property rights (e.g., patents, trademarks, copyrights, or industrial designs). To understand how KIBS register trademarks, it is important to understand why business services use trademarks as a protection measure. Given that trademark registrations are supposed to be indicators of innovation, we aim to determine whether or not trademarks are used primarily to protect new products and services. Accordingly, we developed related hypotheses, which we tested by conducting a survey of KIBS, as described in the next section. The hypotheses were as follows:

Hypothesis 1: *KIBS use a bundle of formal and informal protection measures to guard their intellectual property.*

Hypothesis 2: *KIBS register trademarks primarily to protect new products and services.*

A Survey of Knowledge-Intensive Business Services

In our survey, the sample of KIBS includes companies based in Germany and listed in the MARKUS company database provided by Bureau van Dijk and the Credit Reform Association. The item definitions correspond to recommendations given in the Oslo Manual (OECD, 2005) concerning the measurement and interpretation of innovation survey data. A pretest with ten experts from appropriate firms enabled us to optimize the questionnaire. The main survey was carried out as an online survey with a sample of 6,176 KIBS. The return rate after follow-up was 278 KIBS (4.5%), which is in line with other similar Internet-based surveys conducted in Western countries. Below, we present the results of the hypotheses we tested using independent regression models of the survey data. Details of the research design and data handling can be found in Appendix 1.

The first hypothesis develops assumptions concerning the appropriate use of formal and informal protection measures to guard the intellectual property of KIBS. In order to test the hypothesis, we developed an empirical model with a dependent variable reflecting the innovation success of the firm. As a proxy variable of innovation success, we use the share of turnover achieved

with new services (i.e., market introduction during the last three years). The results regarding the usefulness of intellectual property protection measures is ambiguous. Although the use of trademarks and industrial design as intellectual property rights have positive and significant effects on innovation success, no such effect is found for either patents or copyrights. Given that patents and copyrights do not have a positive or significant effect on service innovation, and industrial design registrations cannot be evaluated in detail, as can trademark registrations, we can conclude that trademarks best fulfil the criteria of an innovation indicator compared to other protection measures used in the model.

None of the informal protection tools, which we believed to be very important, were statistically significant in our model; even lead-time advantage has a non-significant negative effect on innovation success. The use of informal protection measures may be important for the firm, but because there is no record or registration of their use, they cannot easily be used as an innovation indicator. Special surveys would be necessary to obtain the required information on informal protection measures. Because registered trademarks indeed may be an indicator of service innovation, it becomes even more important to understand the reasons for trademark registration and why business services use trademarks as protection measure. Therefore, we test the second hypothesis that deals with questions concerning the purposes for which firms register trademarks.

All participants of the KIBS survey were asked to give their reasons for registering trademarks and to rank the importance of those reasons on a scale of one to five. The results illustrate that the protection of new products and services is the most important motive for registering a new trademark. For greater precision, we estimated two regression models with the number of trademark registrations as dependent variable. Both models came to the same conclusion: the only variables with significant positive effects on trademark registration are those that protect new products and services. None of the other variables in the simplified models were significant. Therefore, we conclude that the primary reason for KIBS to register trademarks is to protect their newly introduced goods and services against imitation by their competitors.

Research Limitations and Future Research

Indicators provide only an indication of reality, not a direct and complete measure, and are likely to be imperfect. However, the use of patents as an innovation indicator in manufacturing industries is a conventional and very similar approach. In this context, an indicator based on intellectual property rights, such as trademark registrations, best fulfils the desirable criteria for an innovation indicator: accuracy, longevity, comparability, and ease of collection. But, even if the relationship between trademarks and KIBS innovation is made clear, larger problems remain.

Obviously, there are difficulties in the data consolidation, depending on the brand strategies selected by particular companies. Depending on whether a company is pursuing a single, family, or umbrella-brand strategy, one trademark application can represent just one or several innovations. Sectoral differences between KIBS industries and weaknesses in the international comparability also exist. Therefore, further research is needed for a full assessment of trademarks as an innovation indicator for KIBS.

Future research could also match trademark databases with corporate databases. The information contained in corporate databases (e.g., information on individual balance sheets, amount of intangible assets) could add a variety of new insights. An enhanced consideration of intangible assets, which give information regarding the monetary value of trademarks, can generate knowledge about the meaning and importance of individual trademarks and would increase the significance of the innovation indicator.

Research Contribution and Managerial Implications

The goal of this article was to show that trademarks are suitable as indicators of KIBS innovation because they provide information about innovation activities and innovation success. Given that there are few other adequate indicators for service innovation activities, the use of trademark registrations as an additional indicator is certainly promising.

First, our study shows that the interrelation between trademark registration and innovation success is positive and statistically significant in the KIBS sector. These findings are in line with Schmoch (2003) and Amara, Landry, and Traoré (2008), who also found a relation between trademarks and innovation for KIBS, and with Flikkema, de Man, and Wolters (2010) who investigated the entire services sector.

Second, we show that trademarks are usually registered by KIBS to protect new products and services. Other motives seem to be of secondary importance, hence there appears to be a connection between trademarks and new services. This finding corresponds to other research on this topic. For instance, Davis (2005) showed that, because of the ease of imitation of services, the need arises to protect services by registering trademarks, which provide at least some protection against imitation. In fact, a trademark does not protect innovation or novelty in itself, but according to Aaker (2007), a strong and well-known trademark can discourage potential new competitors by increasing the barrier to market entry.

According to Acs, Anselin, and Varga (2002) a huge disadvantage of survey-based innovation measures is the emerging cost to generate data and the danger of subjective answers. As a result, the development of appropriate, easy to use, and low-cost indicators to measure innovation in the KIBS sector is certainly useful. Trademarks are a promising alternative indicator to fill this existing gap, because trademark registrations are available in public databases. The great advantages of indicators that can be extracted from databases are the relatively low overhead costs and the comparability of results. The data relating to innovation indicator does not need to be collected discretely, but can be extracted at a suitable location (e.g., a trademark registration database). Thus, special surveys in KIBS industries could be redundant in the future.

Furthermore, KIBS practice can benefit from these results. Entrepreneurs and managers, as well as policy makers, can use trademarks as an innovation indicator in order to better describe, understand, and benchmark innovation activities in the KIBS sector. By doing so, they can identify the degree of innovation in particular industries and derive the degree of competitive rivalry among existing firms. Based on this information, entrepreneurs can decide to whether or not to enter or exit a specific market.

As survey results also have shown, it seems advisable for companies to protect all new service innovations with trademarks. Because a trademark can be registered in a straightforward manner and gives the trademark owner a monopoly on its use, trademark registration should be incorporated in every competition strategy, both for incumbent firms as well as startups. On the basis of these suggestions, entrepreneurs and managers can create better and more successful ventures. By doing so, the use of trademarks as an additional indicator could also contribute to an improved innovation model for business services.

About the Authors

Matthias Gotsch is a senior researcher in the Competence Center for Industrial and Service Innovations at the Fraunhofer Institute for Systems and Innovation Research ISI in Karlsruhe, Germany. He holds a PhD from Brandenburg Technical University of Cottbus for his research on innovation measurement in the knowledge-intensive services industry and a German university diploma in Industrial Engineering with the focus on industrial business, technology, and innovation management from the University of Erlangen-Nürnberg. He has expertise in service innovations, industrial services, and designing innovative service-based business models and has contributed several papers and articles to the field of service science.

Christiane Hipp is Dean and Professor for Organisation, Human Resource Management and General Management at the Technical University Cottbus, Germany. She received her diploma in Industrial Engineering in 1994 and her PhD in Economics in 1999. From 1995 until 1999. Christiane was a Research Associate at the Fraunhofer Institute for Systems and Innovation Research. She received her postdoctoral lecture qualification in 2005. Her areas of interest include demographical change, service innovation, innovation strategies, intellectual property, and innovation processes.

References

Aaker, D. 2007. Innovation: Brand It or Lose It. *California Management Review*, 50(1): 8–24.
http://dx.doi.org/10.2307/41166414

Abreu, M., Grinevich, V., Kitson, M., & Savona, M. 2010. Policies to Enhance the "Hidden Innvation" in Services: Evidence and Lessons from the UK. *The Service Industries Journal*, 30(1): 99–118.
http://dx.doi.org/10.1080/02642060802236160

Acs, Z. J., Anselin, L., & Varga, A. 2002. Patents and Innovation Counts as Measures of Regional Production of New Knowledge. *Research Policy*, 31(7): 1069–1085.
http://dx.doi.org/10.1016/S0048-7333(01)00184-6

Amara, N., Landry, R., & Traoré, N. 2008. Managing the Protection of Innovations in Knowledge-Intensive Business Services. *Research Policy*, 37(9): 1530–1547.
http://dx.doi.org/10.1016/j.respol.2008.07.001

Armstrong, J. S., & Overton, T. S. 1977. Estimating Nonresponse Bias in Mail Surveys. *Journal of Marketing Research*, 14(3): 396.
http://dx.doi.org/10.2307/3150783

Besen, S. M., & Raskind, L. J. 1991. An Introduction to the Law and Economics of Intellectual Property. *The Journal of Economic Perspectives*, 5(1): 3–27.
http://www.jstor.org/stable/1942699

Blind, K., Edler, J., Schmoch, U., Anderson, B., Howells, J., Miles, I., et al. 2003. *Patents in the Service Industries*. No. EC Contract No. ERBHPV2-CT-1999-06. Karlsruhe, Germany: Fraunhofer Institute Systems and Innovation Research.

Box, G. E. P., & Cox, D. R. 1964. An Analysis of Transformations. *Journal of the Royal Statistical Society. Series B (Methodological)*, 26(2): 211–252.

Camacho, J. A., & Rodriguez, M. 2008. Patterns of Innovation in the Service Sector: Some Insights from the Spanish Innovation Survey. *Economics of Innovation and New Technology*, 17(5): 459–471.
http://dx.doi.org/10.1080/10438590701362874

Christensen, C. M., & Baird, B. J. 1997. Cultivating Capabilities to Innovate: Booz.Allen & Hamilton. Harvard Business School Case No. 698-027. Boston: Harvard Business School.

Coombs, R., & Miles, I. 2000. Innovation, Measurement and Services: The New Problematique. In J. S. Metcalfe & I. Miles (Eds.), *Innovation Systems in the Service Economy*: 85–103. Berlin: Springer.

Czarnitzki, D., & Spielkamp, A. 2005. Business Services in Germany: Bridges for Innovation. *The Service Industries Journal*, 23(2): 1–31.

Davis, L. 2005. The Strategic Use of Trademarks. Presented at the 5th European Policy on Intellectual Property (EPIP) Conference, Copenhagen.

Davis, L. N. 2009. Leveraging Trademarks to Capture Innovation Returns. Presented at the Copenhagen Business School Summer Conference 2009, Copenhagen: Copenhagen Business School.

Flikkema, M. J., de Man, A. P., & Wolters, M. J. J. 2010. *New Trademark Registration as an Indicator of Innovation: Results of an Explorative Study of Benelux Trademark Data*. No. 0009. Amsterdam: Vrije Universiteit Amsterdam, Faculty of Economics and Business Administration.

Flor, M. L., & Oltra, M. J. 2004. Identification of Innovating Firms through Technological Innovation Indicators: An Application to the Spanish Ceramic Tile Industry. *Research Policy*, 33(2): 323–336.
http://dx.doi.org/10.1016/j.respol.2003.09.009

Gallouj, F., & Windrum, P. 2009. Services and Services Innovation. *Journal of Evolutionary Economics*, 19(2): 141–148.
http://dx.doi.org/10.1007/s00191-008-0123-7

Gatrell, J. D., & Ceh, S. L. B. 2003. Trademark Data as Economic Indicator: The United States, 1996-2000. *The Great Lakes Geographer*, 10(1): 46–56.

Gault, F. 2007. Introduction. In *Science, Technology and Innovation Indicators in a Changing World Responding to Policy Needs*. Paris: OECD Publishing.

Gotsch, M., & Hipp, C. 2012. Measurement of Innovation Activities in the Knowledge-Intensive Services Industry: A Trademark Approach. *The Service Industries Journal*, 32(13): 2167–2184.
http://dx.doi.org/10.1080/02642069.2011.574275

Greenhalgh, C., & Rogers, M. 2007. Trade Marks and Performance in UK Firms: Evidence of Schumpeterian Competition through Innovation. Working Paper, Oxford: Oxford Intellectual Property Research Centre.

Hauknes, J. 1998. *Services in Innovation – Innovation in Services.* STEP Report series No. 199813. The STEP Group, Studies in Technology, Innovation and Economic Policy.

Hipp, C. 1999. Knowledge-Intensive Business Services in the New Mode of Knowledge Production. *AI & Society*, 13(1-2): 88–106. http://dx.doi.org/10.1007/BF01205260

Hipp, C., & Bouncken, R. B. 2009. Intellectual Property Protection in Collaborative Innovation Activities within Services. *International Journal of Services Technology and Management*, 12(3): 273–296. http://dx.doi.org/10.1504/IJSTM.2009.025391

Hipp, C., & Grupp, H. 2005. Innovation in the Service Sector: The Demand for Service-Specific Innovation Measurement Concepts and Typologies. *Research Policy*, 34(4): 517–535. http://dx.doi.org/10.1016/j.respol.2005.03.002

Howells, J., & Tether, B. 2004. *Innovation in Services: Issues at Stake and Trends.* Brussels: Commission of the European Communities.

Iden, J., & Methlie, L. B. 2012. The Drivers of Services on Next-Generation Networks. *Telematics and Informatics*, 29(2): 137–155. http://dx.doi.org/10.1016/j.tele.2011.05.004

Jensen, P. H., & Webster, E. M. 2011. Patterns of Trademarking Activity in Australia. Working Paper No. 2/04. Melbourne: Melbourne Institute.

Kanerva, M., Hollanders, H., & Arundel, A. 2006. *Can We Measure and Compare Innovation in Services?* Brussels: European Commission.

King, S. 1991. Brand-Building in the 1990s. *Journal of Marketing Management*, 7(1): 3–13. http://dx.doi.org/10.1080/0267257X.1991.9964136

Kleinknecht, A., Van Montfort, K., & Brouwer, E. 2002. The Non-Trivial Choice between Innovation Indicators. *Economics of Innovation and New Technology*, 11(2): 109–121. http://dx.doi.org/10.1080/10438590210899

Lepori, B., Barré, R., & Filliatreau, G. 2008. New Perspectives and Challenges for the Design and Production of S&T Indicators. *Research Evaluation*, 17(1): 33–44. http://dx.doi.org/10.3152/095820208X291176

Malmberg, C. 2005. Trademarks Statistics as Innovation Indicator? - A Micro Study. Working Paper No. 2005/17. Lund, Sweden: Centre for Innovation, Research and Competence in the Learning Economy (CIRCLE), Lund University.

Mangàni, A. 2006. An Economic Analysis of Rise of Service Marks. *Journal of Intellectual Property Rights*, 11(4): 249–259.

Mendonça, S., Pereira, T. S., & Godinho, M. M. 2004. Trademarks as an Indicator of Innovation and Industrial Change. *Research Policy*, 33(9): 1385–1404. http://dx.doi.org/10.1016/j.respol.2004.09.005

Miles, I. 2000. Services Innovation: Coming of Age in the Knowledge-Based Economy. *International Journal of Innovation Management*, 04(04): 371–389. http://dx.doi.org/10.1142/S1363919600000202

Miles, I. 2005. Knowledge Intensive Business Services: Prospects and Policies. *foresight*, 7(6): 39–63. http://dx.doi.org/10.1108/14636680510630939

Miles, I., Andersen, B., Boden, M., & Howells, J. 2000. Service Production and Intellectual Property. *International Journal of Technology Management*, 20(1): 95–115.

Millot, V. 2009. *Trademarks as an Indicator of Product and Marketing Innovations.* No. 2009/6. Paris: OECD.

OECD. 2002. *Frascati Manual* (6th Edition). Paris: Organisation for Economic Co-operation and Development.

OECD. 2005. *Oslo Manual* (3rd Edition). Paris: Organisation for Economic Co-operation and Development.

Paallysaho, S., & Kuusisto, J. 2008. Intellectual Property Protection as a Key Driver of Service Innovation: An Analysis of Innovative KIBS Businesses in Finland and the UK. *International Journal of Services Technology and Management*, 9(3): 268–284. http://dx.doi.org/10.1504/IJSTM.2008.019707

Pavitt, K. 1982. R&D, Patenting and Innovative Activities: A Statistical Exploration. *Research Policy*, 11(1): 33–51. http://dx.doi.org/10.1016/0048-7333(82)90005-1

Pires, C. P., Sarkar, S., & Carvalho, L. 2008. Innovation in Services – How Different from Manufacturing? *The Service Industries Journal*, 28(10): 1339–1356. http://dx.doi.org/10.1080/02642060802317812

Prahalad, C. K., & Hamel, G. 1990. The Core Competence of the Corporation. *Harvard Business Review*, (May-June).

Rammer, C., & Weißenfeld, B. 2007. *Innovationsverhalten der Unternehmen in Deutschland 2006.* No. 04-2008. Mannheim: Zentrum für Europäische Wirtschaftsforschung (ZEW).

Sandner, P. G., & Block, J. 2011. The Market Value of R&D, Patents, and Trademarks. *Research Policy*, 40(7): 969–985. http://dx.doi.org/10.1016/j.respol.2011.04.004

Schmoch, U. 2003. Service Marks as Novel Innovation Indicator. *Research Evaluation*, 12(2): 149–156. http://dx.doi.org/10.3152/147154403781776708

Schmoch, U., & Gauch, S. 2009. Service Marks as Indicators for Innovation in Knowledge-Based Services. *Research Evaluation*, 18(4): 323–335. http://dx.doi.org/10.3152/095820209X451023

Schricke, E., Zenker, A., & Stahlecker, T. 2012. *Knowledge-Intensive (Business) Services in Europe.* No. EUR 25189: 52. Luxembourg: European Commission.

Smith, K. 2006. Measuring Innovation. In J. Fagerberg, D. C. Mowery, & R. R. Nelson (Eds.), *The Oxford Handbook of Innovation*: 148–179. Oxford: Oxford University Press.

Strambach, S. 2008. Knowledge-Intensive Business Services (KIBS) as Drivers of Multilevel Knowledge Dynamics. *International Journal of Services Technology and Management*, 10(2/3/4): 152. http://dx.doi.org/10.1504/IJSTM.2008.022117

Tether, B. S., & Hipp, C. 2002. Knowledge Intensive, Technical and Other Services: Patterns of Competitiveness and Innovation Compared. *Technology Analysis & Strategic Management*, 14(2): 163–182. http://dx.doi.org/10.1080/09537320220133848

Toivonen, M. 2004. Foresight in Services: Possibilities and Special Challenges. *The Service Industries Journal*, 24(1): 79–98. http://dx.doi.org/10.1080/02642060412331301142

Toivonen, M., & Tuominen, T. 2009. Emergence of Innovations in Services. *The Service Industries Journal*, 29(7): 887–902. http://dx.doi.org/10.1080/02642060902749492

Verbeek, M. 2008. *A Guide to Modern Econometrics.* John Wiley & Sons.

WIPO. 2006. *Making a Mark: An Introduction to Trademarks for Small and Medium-Sized Enterprises.* Geneva: World Intellectual Property Organization.

Wooldridge, J. 2008. *Introductory Econometrics: A Modern Approach.* Mason, OH: Cengage Learning.

Appendix 1. About the Research

Our online survey yielded 278 responses, which corresponds to a 4.5% response rate. In evaluating the representativeness of our survey, we conducted a unit-non-response analysis to assess whether there are differences between responding and non-responding firms. A standard method to estimate possible differences is a comparison of rapidly responding to late-responding companies, because the latter are most similar to the non-responding companies (Armstrong & Overton, 1977). If both groups show no statistically significant differences, it can be assumed that the survey is representative. In the present case, we used the amount of turnover and the number of employees to compare the two groups. In addition, we carried out a Kruskal-Wallis test to check whether samples differ in the expected value of an ordinal variable, in this case the sector membership of the enterprises. There were no statistically significant differences between the comparison values of the two groups regarding turnover of the companies, number of employees, or sector membership, so we conclude that the survey is representative.

In the case of item-non-response, a complete case analysis was used, which in the regression models consequently ignores the records where one or more of the characteristics is a missing value (Wooldridge, 2009). By doing so, for analysis purposes, only the respectively complete data sets are used.

Research design of first model
The model is partly based on an approach by Rammer (2007), who analyzed the importance of various protective measures, but did not make a distinction between services and KIBS. However, to achieve meaningful results in the very heterogeneous services sector, such a distinction appears essential. Therefore, the present model concentrates on KIBS and additionally accounts for different KIBS industries. We choose an ordinary least squares regression analysis to test the first hypothesis. Because the dependent variable does not have a

normal distribution, a Box-Cox transformation (Box & Cox, 1964) was carried out to stabilize the variance of the variable. Table 1 presents the summary statistics and description of the variables used in the model.

For the explanatory variables, we first constructed a dummy variable for each formal intellectual property right that reflects whether the firm uses the protection measure. Trademarks are considered as an additional protection tool, so other intellectual property rights are also taken into account in the model. As informal or strategic measures, we included secrecy, lead-time advantage, and complexity in design, all of which were operationalized as dummy variables that indicate the use of the specific strategic protection tool.

We also controlled for several factors that may influence our dependent variable. The degree of competitiveness is reflected by the number of competitors in Germany. Innovation input is expected to influence innovation output, so we include innovation input in the model, represented by the level of innovation expenditure in relation to the firm's turnover. Firm size is reflected by the number of employees in the KIBS firm. In addition to the explanatory variables, we created dummy variables for the different KIBS industries. To avoid a heteroscedasticity problem, we conduct a robust regression analysis, which is presented in Table 2.

We calculated the variance inflation factors (VIF) to test for multi-collinearity of the explanatory variables. All variables show uncritical values with a mean VIF of the explanatory variables of 1.33. However, a possible existence of endogeneity or simultaneity between dependent and explanatory variables cannot be completely excluded and has to be considered during data interpretation. Seeing the control variables in the model, all show expected signs, with the exception of the amount of competitors, which must be investigated in detail. For the number of competitors in Germany, we observe a very low effect. Within an alternative regression analysis with the exclusion of one extreme value of the variable, only the coefficient is significant because of this specific runaway. Therefore, we must be very careful in interpreting the coefficient for the number of competitors, but the model in general is not influenced.

Research design of second model
All participants of the KIBS survey were asked to give their reasons for registering trademarks and to rank the importance of those reasons on a scale from one to five. The results are shown in Figure 1.

Table 1. Descriptive statistics of variables used in the first model

Variable	Description	Mean	S.D.	Min.	Max.
Turnover with new services	*Percent of turnover achieved with services introduced in the last three years*	46.47	7.46	0	100
Use of trademarks	Firm uses trademarks as protection tool	0.45	0.50	0	1
Use of patents	Firm uses patents as protection tool	0.21	0.40	0	1
Use of copyrights	Firm uses copyrights as protection tool	0.28	0.45	0	1
Use of industrial designs	Firm uses industrial designs as protection tool	0.04	0.19	0	1
Use of secrecy	Secrecy is used for protection	0.35	0.48	0	1
Use of lead-time advantage	Lead-time advantage is used for protection	0.45	0.50	0	1
Use of complexity	Complexity is used for protection	0.35	0.48	0	1
Competitors in Germany	Number of competitors in Germany	1 196	8 992	1	10 000
Innovation expenditures	Total innovation expenditures/turnover	16.16	15.29	1	80
Number of employees	Number of persons employed in the firm	71.12	153.29	3	1 045

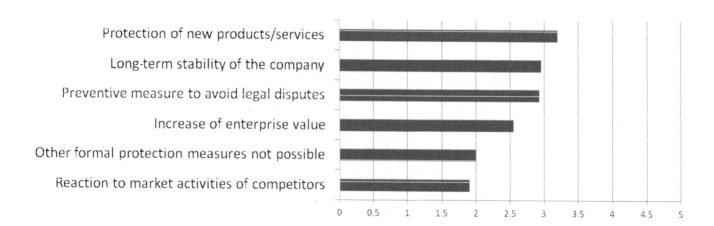

Figure 1. Importance of reasons for KIBS to register trademarks
Answers of responding firms considered in model 3 (n=96), response options ranked from low importance (0) to high importance (5)

Table 2. Results of the first model

Item	Turnover with new services
Use of trademarks	2.53*
Use of patents	-0.71
Use of copyright	-1.88
Use of industrial design	5.41**
Use of secrecy	0.90
Use of lead-time advantage	-0.80
Use of complexity	1.56
Competitors in Germany	0.000088***
Innovation expenditures	0.059
Number of employees	-0.011***
Publishing of books, periodicals, and other publishing activities	-5.07*
Software publishing	-0.055
Computer programming, consultancy, and related activities	-0.067
Data processing, hosting, and related activities; web portals	-5.55*
Architectural and engineering activities	-4.17**
Technical testing and analysis	0.38
Research and development on natural sciences and engineering	0.56
Research and development on social sciences and humanities	5.13*
Observations	130
R^2	0.267
F	6.41
Prob > F	0.00

OLS regression with KIBS Survey, showing coefficients.
Dependent variable is Box-Cox transformed. Sector "Others" serves as base.
Significance levels are denoted by: *** $p<0.01$, ** $p<0.05$, * $p<0.1$

To make more precise statements, we first estimated an ordered logistic regression model to examine the impact of a range of explanatory variables on a dependent variable that takes a finite set of ordered values. This process conforms to the first alternative to ordinal-scaled trademark registration with five response options as the dependent variable. In the second alternative, we use a continuous variable that reflects the number of trademark registrations of the firm. This process conforms to the numeric scaled trademark registration as the dependent variable. In this case, we chose a tobit regression analysis over the more common least squares method, because the dependent variable has a censored distribution with a lower threshold of zero percent trademark share on the protection measures. As explanatory variables, we limited the model to the response options presented in Figure 1 and company size, measured by number of employees. Of course, this limitation leads to a model that is not comprehensive, but it is effective to examine the motivations for trademark registrations. Table 3 shows the values of all used variables.

The r-squared values, which are the proportions of variability accounted for by the explanatory variables used in the statistical model, are very low in both alternatives. However, because there is no claim to be complete, according to Verbeek (2009) the comparatively low r-squared values can be ignored in this case. The second alternative also results in a comparatively low significance of the whole model (Prob>chi-square=0.12) due to the fact that our model is consciously and artificially limited to the given response options and therefore completely ignores other explanatory variables. The results of the regression models are presented in Table 4.

Table 3. Descriptive statistics of variables used in the second model

Variable	Mean	S.D.	Min.	Max.
(3a) Trademark registration (ordinal)	*2.28*	*1.21*	*1*	*5*
(3b) Trademark registration (numeric)	*13.96*	*109.00*	*0*	*1 100*
Protection of new products/services	3.25	1.66	1	5
Long-term stability of the company	2.96	1.57	1	5
Preventive measure to avoid legal disputes	2.93	1.58	1	5
Increase in enterprise value	2.59	1.45	1	5
Other formal protection measures not possible	2.02	1.38	1	5
Reaction to market activities of competitors	1.93	1.15	1	5
Number of employees	70.32	152.78	1	1 044

Table 4. Results of the second model

Reason for Trademark Registration	Trademark Registration (ordinal)	Trademark Registration (numeric)
Protection of new products/services	0.47**	29.51*
Long-term stability of the company	-0.11	-11.17
Preventive measure to avoid legal disputes	-0.23	19.35
Increase in enterprise value	0.28	2.41
Other formal protection measures not possible	-0.01	-11.34
Reaction to market activities of competitors	-0.28	-9.22
Number of employees	-0.0006	-0.032
Observations	96	96
Chi-squared	14	10.26
Pseudo R^2	0.052	0.012
Prob > chi-square	0.051	0.17
Uncensored Observations		61

Ordered logistic regression with KIBS Survey; Tobit regression with KIBS Survey, showing coefficients.
Significance levels are denoted by: *** $p<0.01$, ** $p<0.05$, * $p<0.1$

Keywords: knowledge-intensive business services, KIBS, trademarks, innovation, innovation indicator

17

Innovation Opportunities:
An Overview of Standards and Platforms in the Video Game Industry

Mikael Laakso and Linus Nyman

" Man will always use his most advanced technology "
to amuse himself.

David Crane
Co-founder, Activision

The video game industry offers insights into the significance of standards and platforms. Furthermore, it shows examples of how new entrants can offer innovative services, while reducing their own risk, through bridging the boundaries between standards. Through an exploration of both past and present, this article aims to serve as a primer for understanding, firstly, the technological standards and platforms of the video game industry, and secondly, the recent innovations within the video game industry that have enabled products to be made available across platforms.

Introduction

Over a billion people worldwide play video games (eMarketer, 2013). The revenues of the video game industry (including consoles, hardware and software, online, mobile, and PC games) for 2013 were estimated to total $93 billion USD (Gartner, 2013). This revenue is significantly larger than, for instance, the box office revenues of all films released worldwide ($35.9 billion [MPAA, 2013]) and global recorded music sales ($15 billion [IFPI, 2014]) for that same year combined.

What has led the industry to such success? Whereas the foundation of a successful game may be that it is "easy to learn and hard to master" (a phrase attributed to Atari founder Nolan Bushnell), the foundation of the success of the video game industry as a whole, we argue, is standardization – and the innovation that has been able to spring from and around its standards.

Standards have the capability to mitigate both technological and market fragmentation by reducing diversity in solutions where multiple solutions to a specific problem compete. Without the restrictive effect of standards, the potential for both innovation and commercialization is significantly hampered due to a lack of common ground to build upon. Furthermore, standards have served to level the playing field, lower barriers of entry, and allow actors both big and small to compete on more even terms.

The article is structured as follows. First, we offer a brief definition of standards and platforms and how they relate to the video game industry. Then we discuss the emergence of video game platforms and their standards. Finally, we discuss recent as well as upcoming changes and innovations in the video game industry – changes that go beyond improvements within a standard to products and services that span multiple standards.

Standards and Platforms

Technology standards come in many varieties and can emerge through different processes. Thus, succinctly defining the term "standard" poses a challenge. The following definition is used throughout this article:

> *"A standard is an approved specification of a limited set of solutions to actual or potential matching problems, prepared for the benefits of the party or parties involved, balancing their needs, and intended and expected to be used repeatedly or continuously, during a certain period, by a substantial number of the parties for whom they are meant."* (de Vries, 2005)

The spectrum of openness in standards is broad, with potential for complex implications for commercialization (West, 2003). Despite the benefits of technology standardization, the process of settling on a standard can be problematic: it is often, if not always, in tension with technology development. The video game industry has traditionally emphasized having the most advanced graphics and technically impressive presentation. By the time a standard becomes established and widely adopted, it may no longer reflect state-of-the-art hardware or software. Indeed, the video game industry is awash with examples of new innovations and new standards that render previously successful standards all but obsolete. Furthermore, the adoption of a standard – for example, the size of the install base for a specific video game system – influences the availability of software and other complementary products, such as accessories. This network effect creates an environment where a more long-term use of standards and systems is strengthened (Shankar & Bayus, 2003; Prieger & Hu, 2006).

In the video game industry, standards form a key ingredient of platforms (for discussion on the composition of platforms, see, for example: Eisenmann et al., 2008). Indeed, each gaming platform implements a myriad of standards, including those for electric current, connector types, etc. However, for content creators, three central types of standards apply to: i) hardware architectures, ii) operating systems, and iii) software development environments, including both compatibility and compliance guidelines to match the platform holder's requirements. Figure 1 depicts the layered relationships between each of these types of standards. As will be shown throughout the article, innovations in one of these layers affect the others.

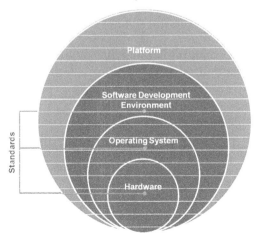

Figure 1. Layers of standards used to create video game platforms

Although standards create platforms, platforms create markets by establishing a common ground between developers and end users. Through platforms, developers know the specific features and functionality of the targeted software and hardware environment, while end users benefit by knowing that adopting a specific platform (e.g., buying a specific video game system) will enable them to access everything developed for it. The adopters of a specific platform define the maximum audience and the content market, while developers produce the content.

The Emergence of Video Game Platforms and Their Early Standards

In this section, we briefly cover the computer, video arcade, console, and mobile phone platforms, as well as the standards that they are built upon. Such an historical overview allows for viewing the bigger picture of the significance of both the initial lack of certain standards, as well as their later emergence. Additionally, how some platforms, regardless of standardization, have fallen out of public favour due to successful innovations in others.

Computer games
The earliest computer games of the 1940s and 1950s were housed within massive, custom-built contraptions intended to showcase what computers were capable of (e.g., Donovan, 2010). These computers could only run the one single (and simple) game for which they were built. However, as computers evolved, video games caught the public interest as a form of entertainment. An early favourite, *Spacewar!*, was released in 1962, making it one of the earliest digital computer games. Computers at the time were not only few and far between, they were also incompatible with other models of computers. Thus, although *Spacewar!* made famous the PDP-1 (tinyurl.com/mquub) computer for which it was written (for details, see the Computer History Museum: tinyurl.com/y9dgav2), it could not be run on other models of computer without rewriting the source code.

Increased standardization was stimulated during the early 1980s by the introduction of IBM-compatible computers, all of which could run MS-DOS. This standardization in turn greatly facilitated game development. As a platform, computers are the most flexible when it comes to choice, because there are multiple viable producers for each major platform standard (i.e., hardware, operating system, software development environment) and users can mix and match between them as they see fit.

Computers built around x86 processors are currently the dominant hardware architecture, with the main standards for operating systems being Windows, Mac OS, and Linux. For video gaming purposes, Windows remains dominant as the most popular operating system among game developers; however, Mac OS and Linux are seeing an increasing number of high-profile titles released for their platforms as well. Various software development environments are available for all three operating systems, which provide developers with tools to produce compatible software to run on top of the operating system.

Arcade games

In addition to its significance to computer gaming, *Spacewar!* also served as the inspiration for the first arcade game, Galaxy Game (tinyurl.com/mzw8qs4), released in 1971. At that time, arcade games were one-off unique creations: big black boxes designed to accept coins in exchange for the opportunity to play one specific game. Each new arcade game system could largely be designed from scratch, without much concern regarding uniformity in either hardware or software across the line of existing arcade games. The business model was similarly designed around delivering one-off, bite-sized experiences (i.e., insert coin, play the game) without requiring that the consumer buy or invest in the system outright, lessening the need to establish conformity among arcade systems.

Though it took longer than in other video game platforms, arcade games also saw the introduction of influential standards. The Japan Amusement Machinery Manufacturer's Association standard (JAMMA; tinyurl.com/cv88dpk), developed in 1985 by an industry consortium of arcade game developers, made it possible to create more modular hardware, with arcade games programmed on detachable game cartridges. These cartridges, hidden inside the arcade cabinet itself, enabled the arcade owner or operator to change a game while keeping the same arcade cabinet. The same hardware could thus be used to run different software, lowering manufacturing costs for the arcade boards and reducing the need for expensive logistics for switching cabinets around different locations. However, advances in both home computers as well as consoles would soon usher in the end of the golden age of the video arcade. Throughout the rest of the article, focus is placed on other platforms that still have a strong presence today.

Consoles

Video game consoles for home use made their debut in the late 1960s (*TIME*, 2014). The first devices came with only one, or sometimes a few, built-in games, without any possibility of running additional software code. As with arcade games, this one-off nature of the product lessened the need for any strict standards to be implemented, given that the systems were closed from further hardware or software expansions.

A significant development for home consoles came with the release of the first systems for which one could program games for later individual purchase. This advancement also introduced a new source of income and fundamentally different business model for platform holders. It was the Atari 2600 (tinyurl.com/odlwg), released in 1977, that popularized the use of game cartridges. During its heyday, another breakthrough happened in the dynamics of game development for game consoles: third-party development (Barton & Loguidice, 2008). In the past, it had mostly been console manufacturers that created and published games for their own platforms, but third-party development for the Atari 2600 thrived, despite initial legal efforts from Atari to thwart the sale of such games (e.g., Atari & Tengen vs. Nintendo, 1992). Though the relationship between platform holder and third-party developer can usually be assumed to be symbiotic, there have been multiple attempts by software developers to circumvent software licensing fees and potential authentication methods by reverse engineering compatible cartridges (see, for example: Linhoff, 2004).

Although the hardware and software standardization involved in cartridges allowed for compatibility within a console, there was also an effort at creating a cross-company platform standard for consoles. This effort came in the form of the short-lived 3DO project (tinyurl.com/on7gb2n), released in 1993. 3DO was a consortium owned by several manufacturers, allowing anyone within the consortium the right to manufacture a 3DO-compatible console as long as they paid a license fee. This approach can be compared to, for instance, VHS and DVD standards, where anyone could produce compatible hardware.

The major hardware release cycles in the video game industry are commonly referred to as generations, with the latest console releases (e.g., Xbox One: tinyurl.com/n72ba7c; PlayStation 4: tinyurl.com/nfs5yuq; and Wii U: tinyurl.com/8zgpyz3) being Generation 8. A shift from one generation to the next has often left software from previous generations incompatible with the new platform's hardware, meaning that the software library is often thin during the initial launch period. Backwards compatibility has been suggested to facilitate the success of the system (Kramer & de Vries, 2009). However, having to potentially design the new system around old standards for hardware architecture and media format might constrain the degree to which the system can introduce state-of-the-art features.

Mobile phones
Standards played a critical role in the evolution of mobile phones and the subsequent smartphones and tablets. Though appearing several decades later than consoles, mobile phones have in many respects echoed their evolution. Mobile phones, like consoles, initially came with a limited amount of built-in games and without any means of expansion. It was not until the first smartphones that it became possible for users to install additional software on handsets. However, actual widespread adoption of software expansion had to wait for several years due to technological fragmentation and a lack of viable methods for both distribution and payment. Before the App Store, Google Play, and Windows Phone store, the only way to install software on smartphones was to side-load the installation files by first downloading them from the web, potentially paying for them, and then executing the files through a file manager. By standardizing the means of acquiring games and apps, a new – and hugely profitable – market was created.

Mobile phones have evolved from dedicated appliances into small powerful computers. Currently, smartphones and tablets are almost exclusively built around architectures implementing ARM processors on the hardware level. On top of this common ground, differentiation is achieved through hardware configurations and operating systems (e.g., Apple's iOS, Google's Android, Microsoft's Windows Phone). Each of these platforms has their own development environments and storefronts for distributing software. Apple controls the entire stack: hardware, operating system, and software development environment. Microsoft and Android provide the operating system and software development environment; although they do not provide the hardware, they offer guidelines for hardware manufacturers to abide by for compatibility.

With the move to mobile devices (i.e., phones and tablets), many significant changes occurred in the gaming industry. One such change was improved access as games became more readily available on non-dedicated gaming devices. Many, including those that had not previously engaged with games, now carried with them a device on which they could play games. By way of example, in 2013 more than half of US mobile phone owners (125.9 million people) were estimated to have played games on their phone (eMarketer, 2013). The increase in gamers, as well as potential gamers, resulted in the rise in popularity of casual games (e.g., puzzle games and match-three games). Significant changes also occurred on the business model front. Though income initially was generated from selling the games, other business models soon emerged: generating income through ads, through offering in-app purchases, or a combination of the two.

Not surprisingly, developers large and small are responding to the increased demand for mobile games: over 220,000 games were released on Apple's iOS alone during the first four years since its launch, making games the largest category of application overall (Pocket Gamer, 2012). The most financially successful mobile games generate incomes in the millions of dollars per day (Strauss, 2013). However, the rise of the mobile gaming industry has been a significant generator of revenue for platform holders as well, as they take a cut of all sales.

Standardization patterns
As can be seen even from so brief an overview of the evolution of the video game industry, wherever a new form of video game was developed, standardization inevitably followed. Indeed, as games moved out of the arcades and into our living rooms, and more recently onto our mobile devices, the significance as well as proliferation of standards has grown considerably.

Although the triple layer of hardware, operating system, and software development framework is applicable across gaming platforms, there are differences in its implementation. Video arcades are perhaps most notable in this sense in that they did not commonly include an operating system. Modern consoles bundle the entire stack into one product, whereas computers and mobile phones (to varying degrees) allow for variability in the stack by either hardware manufacturers or users themselves.

Over time, development and standards have evolved to become more high-level. Where initially there was very little separating the programmer from the hardware, today development frameworks and other middleware facilitate development by providing toolsets that let programmers focus on creating content rather than having to learn and manage the intricacies of the hardware architecture. High-level development also facilitates porting, meaning releasing games across multiple platforms. A further significant development is that game developers have become more involved in the standardization process. Whereas the console or platform holder previously dictated standards, they now commonly evolve as more of a joint effort among several stakeholders.

Beyond Standards

While innovations such as the App Store and Google Play have made accessing mobile device software easier for consumers, other new entrants have sought to bridge both computer hardware and operating system platform divides. Good old Games (gog.com) offers old games rewritten to work across a broader spectrum of hardware and operating systems. Game publishers have similarly launched their own storefronts, or platforms, combining elements such as digital distribution, digital rights management (DRM), multiplayer, and social networking. The three main storefronts are: Electronic Arts' Origin (origin.com), Ubisoft's Uplay (uplay .ubi.com), and Valve's Steam (store.steampowered.com). These storefronts, commonly available for several different operating systems, provide online purchasing of, and subsequent access to, games by both the publishers themselves and by other developers. However, because these storefronts are not a platform defined at the hardware level, they do not guarantee that the customer's hardware is compatible with the game requirements. Steam is arguably the most successful such storefront, and has to a great extent managed to unify a fragmented computer market despite the diversity in hardware specifications and non-standardized DRM practices across publishers.

Browser-based games also span hardware and operating system divides, allowing access through any platform (not just computers) that offers access to a standard web browser, regardless of hardware or operating system. HTML5 has enabled advanced native web programming functionality, rendering the use of external browser plugins, such as Adobe Flash, optional. Similarly, massively multiplayer online games (MMOGs; tinyurl.com/fzbyv) commonly offer separate game clients for different operating systems, thus allowing common access to a game regardless of operating system.

Some of the most significant platform spanning has occurred in the area of software development environments. Traditionally, developers had to choose, before starting a project, for which platform they wanted to develop their game, and they were subsequently more or less locked in to that platform. Innovations in the industry have granted developers substantial freedom from such limitations. Game development tools such as the Unreal Engine (unrealengine.com) and Unity (unity3d.com) have enabled game developers to work largely independent of platform considerations. These tools make it possible to develop a game first, and then publish to one or multiple platforms upon completion.

In the not-so-distant future, gaming may become almost completely detached from platforms and hardware considerations due to platform spanning on the side of end users. Online video game streaming services, currently pioneered by Onlive (games.onlive.com) and Playstation Now (tinyurl.com/mbbqav5), work like Software as a Service (tinyurl.com/2j3d5z): the actual game being played runs on a remote server. The gamer's controller inputs (i.e., what they want to do in the game) are transmitted to the server, and the video and audio feed of the game (i.e., what then happens in the game) are transmitted back to the gamer's screen. This architecture results in minimal hardware requirements on the user's end, while the back-end at the service provider can be upgraded without the user making any new hardware purchases. However, low-latency, high-speed broadband access is essential for this approach to become commonplace, something that is currently not ubiquitous on a global scale.

During the last two decades, there has been a substantial performance gap between the technological capabilities of stationary versus mobile devices, a gap that has been closing as technology has evolved. Shigeru Miyamoto, the top game designer at Nintendo, recently stated that they are considering the unification of their home and portable console hardware architectures to facilitate more efficient game development (Kaiser, 2014). This unification would mark a historical change in their hardware and software development strategy, which has been split in two distinct components since the 1980s.

Conclusions

The early years of the video game industry were a time of almost exclusive in-house development, with little in the way of standards either within or across platforms. This early phase was followed by a gradual standardization, which opened up the gaming industry to third-party development. More recent innovations have enabled the spanning of platforms, making games more easily available across several platforms, as well as making it easier to develop games for multiple standards.

The lines between platforms are blurring and unification is happening on many fronts due to the proliferation and advancement of standards, some becoming so integrated that their implementation and use is transparent on the surface. This process is happening both on the side of game development as well as for players.

The gaming industry offers insights into the importance of standardization, but goes beyond that to show the opportunities that exist for those who manage to offer products or solutions either on a higher level of standard, or indeed that can span multiple standards or platforms.

Even an evolving industry can find itself become near-obsolete. Advances and innovations within video arcades were rendered all but irrelevant by advances and innovations in the home computer and console platforms. Now, some believe gaming computers and consoles may be going the way of the arcade due to advances in handheld devices, offering ease of access as well as promising to turn tablets into de-facto gaming computers for the home through streaming services.

As shown through the history of the video game industry, standards traditionally mitigate both technological and market fragmentation. Standards have been used to create technological platforms on to which content creation and commerce can be conducted. However, these platforms have mostly been isolated due to a lack of cross-compatibility, which segments the market for both software developers and end users. It is only recently that platform spanners have emerged for both software developers and end-users, creating bridges between platforms. The hierarchy for the chain of relationships is depicted in Figure 2.

Where an individual platform can be left abandoned by new technological advances being introduced and the market migrating to more modern options, innovative platform spanners do not rely on the success of any single platform. This flexibility benefits all major stakeholders in the videogames industry and facilitates a more inclusive market space where more content is made available on more devices than ever before.

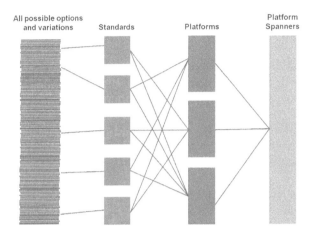

Figure 2. Innovative platform spanners unify standards and platforms with potential benefits to both developers and consumers

Recommended Reading

- *Replay: The History of Video Games*
  (Donovan, 2010; tinyurl.com/bwu4qyz)

- "For Amusement Only: The Life and Death of the American Arcade"
  (June, 2013; tinyurl.com/aawzxev)

- "Industry Life-Cycle Theory in the Cultural Domain: Dynamics of the Games Industry"
  (Peltoniemi, 2009; tinyurl.com/nx27wy9)

- "Structure and Competition in the US Home Video Game Industry"
  (Williams, 2002; tinyurl.com/lh223ys)

- "Entry into Platform-Based Markets"
  (Zhu & Iansiti, 2011; tinyurl.com/p5c22uu)

About the Authors

Mikael Laakso is a postdoctoral researcher at the Hanken School of Economics in Helsinki, Finland. He has published research on open access in scientific publishing and standardization of construction IT. Mikael has a Doctoral and Master's degree in Information Systems Science from the Hanken School of Economics.

Linus Nyman is a doctoral researcher at the Hanken School of Economics in Helsinki, Finland, where he has recently submitted his PhD on code forking in open source software. Linus has a Master's degree in Economics from the Hanken School of Economics.

References

Atari & Tengen vs. Nintendo, 1992. United States Court of Appeals for the Federal Circuit, 91-1293.

Barton, M., & Loguidice, B. 2008. A History of Gaming Platforms: Atari 2600 Video Computer System/VCS. *Gamasutra.* July 1, 2014: http://www.gamasutra.com/view/feature/131956/a_history_of_gaming_platforms_.php

Donovan, T. 2010. *Replay: The History of Video Games.* Hove, UK: Yellow Ant Media.

de Vries, H. 2005. IT Standards Typology. In: Jakobs K. (Ed.) *Advanced Topics in Information Technology Standards and Standardization Research,* 1:11-36. Hershey, PA: Idea Group Publishing.

Eisenmann, T. R., Parker, G., & Van Alstyne, M. W. 2008. Opening Platforms: How, When and Why? Harvard Business School Entrepreneurial Management Working Paper No. 09-030. Cambridge, MA: Harvard Business School. http://dx.doi.org/10.2139/ssrn.1264012

MPAA. 2013. Theatrical Market Statistics, 2013. *Motion Picture Association of America.* July 1, 2014: http://www.mpaa.org/wp-content/uploads/2014/03/MPAA-Theatrical-Market-Statistics-2013_032514-v2.pdf

eMarketer. 2013. Half of US Mobile Users to Play Games in 2013. *eMarketer.* July 1, 2014: http://www.emarketer.com/Article/Half-of-US-Mobile-Users-Play-Games-2013/1009928

Gartner. 2013. Gartner Says Worldwide Video Game Market to Total $93 Billion in 2013. Press Release: October 29, 2013. http://www.gartner.com/newsroom/id/2614915

IFPI. 2014. Key Statistics. *International Federation of the Phonographic Industry.* July 1, 2014: http://www.ifpi.org/global-statistics.php

Kaiser, T. 2014. Nintendo's Top Designer: We're Looking to Unify Mobile, Console Games. *DailyTech.* July 1, 2014: http://www.dailytech.com/Nintendos+Top+Designer+Were+Looking+to+Unify+Mobile+Console+Games/article36107c.htm

Linhoff, J. 2004. Video Games and Reverse Engineering: Before and After the Digital Millennium Copyright Act. *Journal on Telecommunications & High Technology Law,* 3: 209-237.

Kramer, J., & de Vries, H.J. 2009. Impact of Backwards Compatibility on Standard Dominance - The Case of Game Consoles. *Proceedings of the 2009 European Academy of Standardisation (EURAS) Conference:* 149-160.

Pocket Gamer. 2012. App Store Metrics, September 2012. *Pocket Gamer.* July 1, 2014: http://www.pocketgamer.biz/metrics/app-store/

Shankar, V., & Bayus, B. L. 2003. Network Effects and Competition: An Empirical Analysis of the Home Video Game Industry. *Strategic Management Journal,* 24(4), 375–384. http://dx.doi.org/10.1002/smj.296

Strauss, K. 2013. The $2.4 Million-Per-Day Company: Supercell. *Forbes.* July 1, 2014: http://www.forbes.com/sites/karstenstrauss/2013/04/18/the-2-4-million-per-day-company-supercell/

Spil Games. 2013. State of Online Gaming Report. *Spil Games.* July 1, 2014: http://www.spilgames.com/state-online-gaming-2013-2/

TIME. 2014. A History of Video Game Consoles. *TIME.* July 1, 2014: http://content.time.com/time/interactive/0,31813,2029221,00.html

Prieger, J. E., & Hu, W. M. 2006. An Empirical Analysis of Indirect Network Effects in the Home Video Game Market. Working Paper No. 06-25. New York: NET Institute. http://dx.doi.org/10.2139/ssrn.941223

West, J. 2003. How Open Is Open Enough? *Research Policy,* 32(7): 1259–1285. http://dx.doi.org/10.1016/S0048-7333(03)00052-0

Keywords: video game industry, standards, platforms, innovation, computer games, arcade games, console games, mobile games

18

A Citation-Based Patent Evaluation Framework to Reveal Hidden Value and Enable Strategic Business Decisions

Derek Smith

" The value of patents as competitive weapons and intelligence tools becomes most evident in the day-to-day transaction of business. "

Kevin G. Rivette and David Kline
Authors of *Rembrandts in the Attic:
Unlocking the Hidden Value of Patents*

Patent evaluation methodologies enable firms to make informed strategic business decisions by associating and revealing hidden information surrounding a patent. However, the value of a patent depends on a firm's capabilities and strategic direction; therefore, a patent evaluation requires the information to be properly related and aligned with a particular business consideration. This article reviews the literature on citation-based patent evaluation methodologies and develops a framework to help managers and entrepreneurs identify strategic groups of business considerations. The framework shows how categories of information can be interrelated to different strategic groups of business considerations, thereby providing a competitive advantage to the evaluating firm. The article includes recommendations for managers and entrepreneurs to help them make citation-based patent evaluation an ongoing business practice to enable strategic decision making.

Introduction

A patent can bring several well-known forms of potential value to a firm, primarily through the option for a 20-year monopoly to a patented technology. The monopoly represents other forms of value such as exclusive usage rights, licensing opportunities (with potential royalties), and proceeds from any future sale of the patent. These and numerous other forms of patent value can be categorized as bringing defensive, offensive, strategic/business, and technology leadership value to firms (de Wilton, 2011).

However, patents are expensive, and not all patents bring value. Moreover, a given patent may not have the same value to all firms, depending on their capabilities and strategic direction. So, whether a firm is evaluating its own patent portfolio or is considering a purchase involving intellectual property, the challenge lies in identifying the potential value of a patent to the firm.

Of particular importance are the hidden insights that relate to the strategic direction of the firm, because they may suggest new opportunities or business decisions, either now or in the future.

A patent evaluation allows managers or entrepreneurs to reveal insights concerning the value of a patent, or a portfolio of patents, within the context of their own firm. Patent evaluation methodologies generally assess three interrelated aspects of a patent: i) the new technology protected by a patent; ii) the old technology known before the patent; and iii) the associated commercial business information. Such an assessment ensures that other information associated with the patent, beyond the new technology solely described in the patent, is applied and considered in the assessment.

A key input to many patent evaluation methodologies examines the old technology information in the form of a prior art citations. Citations are a list of old technology that the patent office used to ensure that only new and non-obvious inventions become a granted patent. The government patent examiner seeks to identify and apply relevant citations against the patent application to ensure that old, uninventive technology does not issue as a patent. Citations may include both patent documents and academic literature. A citation-based patent evaluation may also consider other patent-related and business-related information, which may reveal strategic considerations such as potential joint ventures, mergers, or acquisitions.

The problem is, how can an entrepreneur or manager deal with the initial complexities of a patent evaluation? What are the business issues and potential opportunities facing a firm? What type of information is required for a specific business consideration? How does a firm relate the business issues and potential opportunities with relevant information to reveal insight that leads to better decisions concerning issues and opportunities?

Previous research on citation-based patent evaluation methodologies has focused on a single business issue or opportunity that may be grouped into the categories of strategic partnerships, identifying strategic innovation, or inventions and strategic linkages between firms and people. The information required is narrowly selected for that issue or opportunity. The previous approaches result in a fragmented and narrow view of evaluation requirements, strategic business considerations, and relevant information.

Understanding a larger group of strategic business options, issues, and opportunities both for and against a firm can lead to determining the potential value on a broader scale of evaluation methodologies. Understanding the information requirements enables entrepreneurs or managers to proactively plan and gather information to evaluate strategic business issues and opportunities. For example, an entrepreneur or manager could :

• select a business issue or opportunity from the group and identify the associated relevant information

• proactively track and gather this relevant information over time on an ongoing basis as part of a strategic business practice to ensure they have the relevant information when it is needed to evaluate the issue or opportunity

• be prepared to execute a patent evaluation methodo-

logy by evaluating the strategic option as a business consideration with relevant information in a patent evaluation methodology

This article identifies and groups four broader key strategic opportunities and associated information to conduct citation-based patent evaluations. It makes four contributions. First, this article provides a citation-based patent evaluation framework synthesized from the literature. The framework provides guidance to entrepreneurs and managers and provides a framework to understand four different strategic groups of business considerations with the required interrelated categories of information. This framework enables patent evaluation from the perspectives of identifying strategic partners, strategic innovation, and inventions and strategic linkages between firms and people. Second, this article identifies and groups business considerations into the four strategic groups of business considerations. Third, this article identifies categories of prior art, patent, and business information interrelated with each strategic group of business considerations to enable the patent evaluation. Finally, it provides four recommendations to entrepreneurs and managers for identifying specific opportunities and conducting patent evaluations.

The body of this article is organized into four sections. The first section reviews the literature about citation-based patent evaluation methodologies. This section also discusses the existing citation-based patent evaluation methodologies, business opportunities, and information required to conduct an evaluation. The second section describes the proposed citation-based patent evaluation framework and provides four example scenarios where it could be applied. The third section provides recommendations for entrepreneurs and managers, and a final section concludes the article.

A Review of Citation-Based Methodologies

Patent evaluation methodologies enable the assessment of technology, patent, metadata, and business opportunities to reveal hidden details and insight. A particular type of patent evaluation methodology focuses on the prior art citations. In such evaluations, citations are used for different types of measures, depending on the business consideration.

Prior art citations identify technology that was available before the filing date of the patent application; they list what was known, or the "state of the art", prior to the invention of the new technology. These citations create a link between the prior art and the new patent application. When a prior art citation refers to an existing *patent*, this technology coupling or link is made explicit in the patent. The new patent application creates a formal link back in time to the prior art – this is called a "cited citation". However, the older patent also inherits a citation forward in time to the new application – this is called a "citing citation". Thus, a given patent may have cited citations (i.e., backwards in time to prior art) and the patent may also be listed in the future as a citing citation (i.e., forwards in time, meaning the older patent itself has become prior art).

The objective of this literature review is to examine the current state of knowledge in citation-based patent evaluation methodologies. The relevant literature was located using a broad keyword search of scholarly journals in the Business Source Complete database (tinyurl.com/22teqry). The keywords were a combination of: "patent", "business", "citation", "evaluation", and "valuation". This search yielded 77 potential articles published between 1993 and early 2014. The abstracts and introductions of the 77 articles were examined closely, first with a focus on prior art patent citations, and then with a narrower focus on patent evaluation methodologies that required citations, either alone or in combination with other information. This step resulted in a list of 12 relevant articles related to the topic of citation-based patent evaluation methodologies. Specifically, these articles all reported on empirical research involving a range of firms in the integrated circuit manufacturing, pharmaceutical, and patent auction industries. The list only included firms having patents in the United States and Europe, and firms having inventors in Brazil, Russia, India, and China.

The articles covered different types of citation-based patent evaluation methodologies. Bapuki, Loree, and Crossan (2011) and Deng (2008) provided an evaluation of a firm's performance based on the relationship of knowledge between the citation (old technology) and the patent (new technology). Two articles provided an evaluation of a patent portfolio: Brietzman and Thomas (2002) used patent portfolio evaluation when considering the business of mergers and acquisition targeting, and Bapuki and colleagues (2011) targeted the business consideration of joint ventures and strategic alliances between firms. Chen and Chang (2010) used patent portfolio evaluation to measure a firm's performance. Four articles provided an approach to determine patent value. Fischer and Leidinger (2014) and Nair, Mathew, and Nag (2011) evaluated the value of a patent based on a patent auction price. Hall, Jaffe, and Trajtenberg

(2005) evaluated the value of a patent based on a firm's stock market price. Harhoff, Scherer, and Vopel (2002) used survey data to evaluate patent value. Hirschey and Richardson (2004) evaluated patent quality with a firm's stock market price. Reitzig (2003) provided an evaluation for the present value of a patent. Tseng (2009) provided an evaluation to compare the level of innovation between countries.

In summary, the literature review revealed the following nine types of citation-based patent evaluations:

1. Mergers and acquisition targeting

2. Joint venture targeting

3. Strategic alliance targeting

4. Firm performance based on knowledge flow or associated with a firm's patent portfolio

5. Patent value based on a sale price or a firm's stock market price and based on a portfolio of patents

6. Patent quality based on a portfolio of patents

7. Present value of a patent

8. A degree of invention based on a portfolio of patents

9. A range of comparisons based on knowledge flow

The literature was further inductively synthesized to identify trends across the body of literature from four specific perspectives, as outlined in Table 1. A first perspective is the overall business consideration, which identified a business issue or opportunity to investigate based on an evaluation of the patent, including strategic partnerships, strategic innovations, and inventions, as well as identifying potential leads to other firms and people.

A second perspective is citation information. This perspective relates to the use of prior art citations in the evaluation of a patent and includes the cited citation list of patents and the citing citation list of patents that depend on a particular evaluation need. Every one of the business considerations requires the use of citation information in the patent evaluation.

A third perspective is business information. This perspective relates to the type and makeup of business metrics required by patent evaluations in association with the overall business considerations. Some business considerations require the additional business metrics and others do not.

A fourth perspective is patent information, which relates to metadata associated with the patent and, again, some business considerations require the additional patent metadata and others do not.

Business Considerations

Four strategic groups of business considerations were synthesized from the literature review concerning citation-based patent evaluation methodologies. Respectively, these four groups concerned the strategies to identify: business partners, strategic innovation, strategic inventions, and strategic linkages between patents.

Table 1. Citation-based patent evaluation methodologies identified in the literature review

Perspective	Methodologies
Business Contribution	• Product portfolio management, joint ventures, and strategic alliances (Bapuki et al., 2011) • Targeting and due diligence in a mergers and acquisition process to identify key inventors, technology, higher impact patents, and technological compatibility (Brietzman & Thomas, 2002) • Measuring firm performance (Chen & Chang, 2010) • Measuring economic value of knowledge spillovers (Deng, 2008) • Identifying the geographic location of knowledge spillovers (Jaffe et al., 1993) • Determining the value or importance of a patent (Fischer & Leidinger, 2014; Hall et al., 2005) • Gauging a firm's inventive and innovative value (Hirschey & Richardson, 2004) • Determining the present value and inventiveness of a patent (Reitzig, 2003) • Comparing innovation on a country basis to identify fundamental, applied, incremental and radical innovation (Tseng, 2009)
Prior Art Information	• Knowledge flow; proxies for internal (self cited) and external (other cited) (Bapuki et al., 2011) • Patent quality (Brietzman & Thomas, 2002; Hall et al., 2005; Tseng, 2009); forward citations (Fischer & Leidinger, 2014; Hirschey & Richardson, 2004) • Patent value, forward and backward citations as a proxy (Harhoff et al., 2002) • Higher counts to other firms reveal more valuable patents (Chen & Chang, 2010) • Knowledge spillovers; cited citations from past to current technology (Deng, 2008; Jaffe et al., 1993) • Patent portfolio importance; citing citations as a proxy for importance (Deng, 2008; Jaffe et al., 1993) • Scientific advances; forward citations as a proxy (Hirschey & Richardson, 2004) • Research; non-patent citations as a proxy for research (Hirschey & Richardson, 2004) • Novelty and inventiveness; backward citations as a proxy (Reitzig, 2003) • Inventor and firm identification (Hall et al., 2005)
Patent Information	• Patent counts, patent growth, current impact, linkage to science, technology cycle time, R&D intensity, and market to book values (stock market value) (Brietzman & Thomas, 2002) • Patent share; relative patent position (Chen & Chang, 2010) • Patent family size as a proxy for economic relevance and IPC classes as a proxy for patent scope (Fischer & Leidinger, 2014) • Patent family size, opposition outcomes in Europe, and IPC classification as a proxy for scope of the patent (Harhoff et al., 2002) • Breadth of claims; degree of difficulty to design around; disclosure and position of a patent in a portfolio of patents as a proxy for patent value (Reitzig, 2003)
Economic Information	• Market value; optimal value of citations can positively increase market value (Chen & Chang, 2010) • Firm performance; sales as a proxy (Bapuji et al., 2011) • Market valuation (stock market value and book value); R&D ratio (Deng, 2008) • Stock market valuation of intangible assets (Hall et al., 2005) • Stock market prices; number of patents; value of R&D expenditures (Hirschey & Richardson, 2004) • Inventor and firm information as a proxy for geographic location (Jaffe et al., 1993)

Identifying strategic business partners requires the application of citation information and business economic information in the evaluation and is useful in product portfolio management, finding potential partners for joint ventures and strategic alliances (Bapuki et al., 2011), and finding potential partners based on a firm's performance (Deng, 2008).

Identifying strategic innovation requires the application of citation information, business economic information, and patent information in the evaluation. It leads to an evaluation of the patent or patents from the perspectives of intellectual property and business to reveal targets for mergers and acquisition (Brietzman & Thomas, 2002) or the value or importance of a patent (Fischer & Leidinger, 2014; Hall et al., 2005).

Identifying strategic inventions requires the application of citation information with patent information and leads to an evaluation of the patent or patents from an intellectual property perspective to reveal the present value of a patent (Reitzig, 2003), the degree of innovation (Tseng, 2009), or firm performance from an inventiveness perspective (Chen & Chang, 2010).

Finally, identifying strategic linkages between patents requires citation information and leads to an evaluation of the patent or patents from a technology perspective to compare the geographic location of knowledge spillovers (Jaffe et al., 1993), country-based innovation comparisons (Tseng, 2009), the inventiveness or "simplicity" of a patent (Reitzig, 2003), or incremental versus radical innovation (Tseng, 2009).

Citation Information

Prior art citations relate to the flow or exchange of knowledge (Bapuki et al., 2011) between old technology and the new technology described in the patent. Non-patent citations relate to a flow of knowledge between research (Hirschey & Richardson, 2004) and the new technology described in the patent. Prior art citations also reveal the names of inventors, entrepreneurs, and firms associated with a patent (Hall et al., 2005). As described earlier, citation information may include both backwards citations (i.e., cited citations referring to earlier records; may be part of the original patent or added later) and forwards citations (i.e., citing citations referring to later records; added after the original patent application). Citation-based evaluations may use cited citations or citing citations in three different ways. First, the evaluation may be based on cited citations to understand the relationship with the old prior art. Second,

the evaluation may be based on citing citations to understand the influence on the newer technology. Finally, the evaluation may be based on a combination of cited and citing citations. Through assignment of patent-ownership metadata associated with the patent, the citations also further identify when the citations are internal or external to the firm , which allows the evaluator to examine the citation relationships from the perspective of the firm or competitors to the firm.

Cited citations pertain to and indicate relative patent value (Chen & Chang, 2010), knowledge spillovers of old technology into a new technology (Deng, 2008; Jaffe et al., 1993) and novelty or inventiveness (Reitzig, 2003). In contrast, citing citations relate to patent quality (Fischer & Leidinger, 2004; Hirschey & Richardson, 2004), patent value (Chen & Chang, 2010), patent portfolio performance (Deng, 2008; Jaffe et al., 1993) and scientific advances (Hirschey & Richardson, 2004).

Business Information

Citation information may also be supplemented with business economic information that depends on the type of business contribution from the patent evaluation methodology. For example, business economic information is required in addition to citation information when the business consideration relates to strategic partner selection or identifying strategic innovation.

Citation information is supplemented with business economic information when the business consideration from the patent evaluation methodology relates to firm performance or economic value, joint ventures, strategic alliances, or a mergers and acquisition process. Business economic information includes sales information (Bapuki et al., 2011), market valuation information (Deng, 2008), stock market information (Hall et al., 2005; Hirschey & Richardson, 2004), and patent auction price (Fischer & Leidinger, 2014; Nair et al., 2011).

Patent Information

Citation information may also be supplemented with other patent-related information when the business contribution from the patent evaluation methodology relates to the patent or aspects surrounding the patent. Patent related-information includes:

• the number of patents, patent portfolio growth, current patent impact, linkages to science, the technology cycle time, R&D intensity (Brietzman & Thomas, 2002)

• the share of patents, relative patent position (Chen & Chang, 2010)

• the patent family size and international patent classification codes (Fischer & Leidinger, 2014)

• opposition outcomes in Europe (Harhoff et al., 2002)

• the breadth of the patent claims, the degree and difficulty to design around a patent, the patent disclosure and position of the patent in the portfolio (Reitzig, 2003)

Citation-Based Patent Evaluation Framework

Citation-based patent evaluation methodologies require a particular strategic focus. The evaluating firm must focus on a particular business consideration and provide links to relevant information. The citation-based patent evaluation framework was created through induction and synthesis of the ideas from the literature. The framework pulls all of this together with the associated linkages between the four key categories and is illustrated in Figure 1.

The citation-based patent evaluation framework synthesized in this research includes four constructs relating to citation information, business considerations, business information, and patent information. The main focus is business considerations and it connects with a subsequent citation-based patent evaluation methodology. The business considerations are grouped into four strategic groups: strategic partners, strategic innovation, strategic inventions, and strategic linkages between patents. These four strategic groups have very specific linkages and are interrelated to the information in the other three constructs as illustrated in Figure 1.

The "strategic partners" consideration relates to targeting higher-performance firms for joint ventures and strategic alliances. The evaluation requires both citation information and economic information. The "strategic innovation" consideration relates to targeting firms for a potential merger and acquisition or firms with higher-value, higher-quality patents. This type of evaluation requires citation information, economic information, and patent information. The "strategic in-

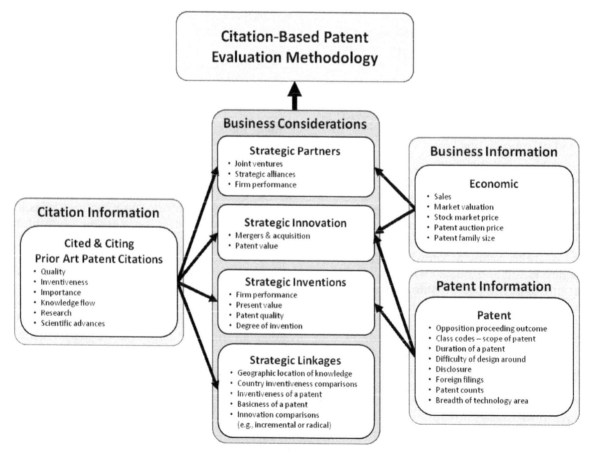

Figure 1. The citation-based patent evaluation framework

ventions" consideration relates to identifying a firm's more inventive assets. This could be the evaluating firm or a competitive firm, and it requires both citation information and patent information. Finally, the "strategic linkages" consideration relates to tracking knowledge flow for a range of comparisons concerning inventiveness and identifying more inventive firms and actors. This evaluation requires citation information.

Table 2 summarizes guidance for entrepreneurs and managers in the form of a checklist. It associates a citation-based patent evaluation methodology with each of the four strategic options of a business consideration and the information required by each of the four strategic options to conduct the evaluation.

The first step for entrepreneurs and managers in proactively preparing for an evaluation of a strategic opportunity is to identify the strategic focus from the four strategic groups of business considerations. Then, they identify and gather related citation information, economic information, and patent information based on the links to the strategic groups of the business considerations. The checklist will assist with this activity. Gathering the relevant information becomes an ongoing process to prepare the firm for any eventual citation-based patent evaluation of strategic opportunities.

In the subsections that follow, four example scenarios illustrate how the business considerations from Figure 1 and Table 2 can be applied in a citation-based patent evaluation.

Scenario 1: Strategic partners

Consider a firm that is interested in joining a business ecosystem and is seeking to identify a strategic partner from the firms in this ecosystem. This evaluation requires both citation information and economic information. First, the evaluating firm should identify the patent or patents of the target firms. Second, the firm should acquire the citation information, including the names of the inventors and associated firms. The citation information reveals whether the patents are based on knowledge that is internal or external to the firms. A patent based primarily on internal firm citation information suggests the associated firm has a higher capability for inventiveness. Next, the evaluating firm should acquire economic information is the form of sales information for the technology associated with the patent. Finally, the information may be compared on a firm-by-firm basis to identify target firms with higher or lower capability of inventiveness and higher or lower commercial success.

Scenario 2: Strategic innovation

Or, perhaps a publically traded company is interested in identifying a strategic innovation, either one of its own or that of a competitor. This evaluation requires citation, economic, and patent information. Again, the first steps are to identify the patent or patents of interest and then acquire the citation information. In this scenario, citation information includes the list of cited citations, the list of citing citations, and the date of the citations (older vs. newer). The citation information also includes the number of cited citations that are scientific, which reveals the degree to which the patent is based on scientific research or an early-commercialized technology. The number of citing citations reveals the degree of future value where the higher the number of citing citations, the higher the future value of the patent.

Finally, the company should acquire stock market information and the expenditure of the research and development efforts and the size or number of patents in the patent portfolio. The goal is to find the patents that have the highest number of citing citations based on scientific research and that are associated with the best economic information. This combination of information can reveal the strategic innovations.

Scenario 3: Strategic inventions

Consider a firm that is interested in identifying a relatively higher present value patent from a selection of patents that has not been commercialized. This evaluation requires both citation and patent information, so the firm should start by identifying the patent or patents of interest and gather cited citation information. A high number of cited citations suggests low inventiveness. Next, the firm should review the breadth of the claims in the patent and consider how easy it would be to "design around" the patent. The patent disclosure should be reviewed from a competitive perspective to assess the learning value to competitors. Finally, the relative value of the patent in a portfolio of patents should be examined. Conducting this type of evaluation on a patent-by-patent basis provides a relative comparison of the technological present value of the patent and helps identify strategic inventions with higher present value.

Scenario 4: Strategic linkages

Finally, consider a firm that is contemplating breaking into a new technology domain. Identifying strategic linkages based on the flow of knowledge between patents can help identify actors and firms associated with particular technology groups identified in the patents. So, the first step is to identify the key patents for evaluation. Then, both the cited citation and citing citation informa-

Table 2. Business consideration and information category checklist

Citation-Based Patent Evaluation Methodology	Business Consideration	Information		
		Prior Art Citation	Business	Patent
Breitzman and Thomas (2002) describe a method for evaluating a patent from the perspective of targeting firms for potential mergers and acquisitions. The method evaluates patent counts, patent growth, current impact, science linkages, technology cycle time, and R&D intensity with market to book values and stock market value.	Strategic Innovation	✓	✓	✓
Fischer and Leidinger (2014), Hall et al. (2005), Harhoff et al. (2002), and Nair et al. (2011) describe a method for evaluating a patent from the perspective of patent value. The methods evaluate auction data, patent quality (citing citations), economic relevance (family size), patent scope (IPC codes), stock market price, non-patent literature, outcome of opposition proceedings, and patent family size.	Strategic Innovation	✓	✓	✓
Hirschey and Richardson (2004) describe a method for evaluating patent quality. The method evaluates patent quality (citing citations) and stock market price, number of patents, and R&D expenditures.	Strategic Innovation	✓	✓	✓
Bapuki et al. (2011) describe a method for evaluating a patent from the perspective of a joint venture or strategic alliance targeting. The method evaluates internal knowledge, external knowledge, and sales information. External knowledge was found to have a negative effect on firm performance.	Strategic Partners	✓	✓	
Deng (2008) describes a method for evaluating firm performance. The method evaluates knowledge (citied citations), importance (citing citations), stock market value, and book value.	Strategic Partners	✓	✓	
Chen and Chang (2010) describe a method for evaluating firm performance. The method evaluates patent share, relative patent position, and knowledge.	Strategic Invention	✓		✓
Reitzig (2003) describes a method for evaluating a patent portfolio from the perspective of present value. The method evaluates the life of a patent, inventiveness (citied citations), breadth of claims, degree of difficulty to design around, the disclosure, position of a patent in a portfolio, and knowledge.	Strategic Invention	✓		✓
Tseng (2009) describes a method for evaluating the degree of innovation. The method evaluates quality (cited citations) and IPC codes.	Strategic Invention	✓		✓
Jaffe et al. (1993) describe a method for evaluating knowledge. The method evaluates patent citations (cited citations) from a knowledge-flow perspective in a citation network.	Strategic Linkages	✓		

tion should be obtained, including the names of the inventors and the names of the firms. Finally, for each key patent, links between the citations should be revealed and the actors and firms associated with each key patent should be identified.

Recommendations for Entrepreneurs and Managers

From a close reading of the published research on citation-based patent evaluation methodologies, and through induction and synthesis looking closely at business considerations, related information, and linkages between the business considerations and information, four recommendations are offered for entrepreneurs and mangers seeking to be prepared for strategic opportunities and business decisions by revealing valuable hidden details and insight surrounding a patent.

1. Make citation-based patent evaluation a differentiating business practice.
Citation-based patent evaluation methodologies provide an interesting opportunity to gain strategic advantage. This strategic advantage could relate to a firm's patent or portfolio of patents, or it could be with respect to another firm's patent or portfolio of patents. This competitive aspect is not well understood or known by entrepreneurs and managers; however, it can provide a strategic advantage to firms that identify and target strategic partners, innovation, inventions, and linkages in the citation network. This competitive aspect can become a differentiating business practice, thereby bringing strategic advantage to the firm.

2. Identify, understand, and use the four strategic options for citation-based patent evaluations.
The strategic options synthesized from a review of the extant literature with respect to business considerations reveals options that may be leveraged with specific interrelated information. Seeking out strategic partners, innovation, inventions and linkages provides relevant strategic advantage to a firm. Citation-based patent evaluation provides the means to realize this competitive advantage based on the citations, business economic, and patent information.

3. Make the gathering of patent evaluation information a core patent management activity.
The citation-based patent evaluation framework and checklist help identify the strategic options and key sources of information required by each option. Gather relevant information relevant to the opportunity based on these strategic options as part of a management process or activity. This prepares the firm for the moment when a patent evaluation is required.

4. Understand how to combine strategic options with relevant information.
The citation-based patent evaluation framework reveals specific links between the strategic options and the required interrelated categories of information. First, identify the strategic option and then gather the interrelated information. Finally, conduct the citation-based patent evaluation based on the literature identified in Table 2.

In summary, a key to the firm's success is leveraging the strategic options from the business considerations and interrelated information about the citations, business, and patents to reveal the hidden details surrounding their patent, or a competitor's patent, and make better strategic business decisions.

Conclusion

The citation-based patent evaluation framework and checklist that emerged from this research provide guidance and reveal the requirements for a set of nine different patent evaluation methodologies. The requirements are based on the four static options of business considerations, the information required by each consideration, and the associated links between the options and information to prepare for an evaluation.

Entrepreneurs and managers are able to prepare for strategic opportunities that include either a firm's patent or a competitive patent against the firm. They can identify strategic options, identify relevant information interrelated to the strategic options, and proactively gather this relevant information over time. This approach provides early and ongoing insight that enables strategic opportunities and decisions.

Further research should focus on refining the current strategic options and interrelated information, and expanding the citation-based patent evaluation framework. The research should examine other citation-based patent evaluation methodologies, business considerations, the interrelated information, and specifically the links between the considerations and interrelated information.

In practice, entrepreneurs and managers should identify their strategic options and proactively gather the information required by these options to reveal the valuable hidden details that enable strategic business decisions.

About the Author

Derek Smith is the founder and principal of Magneto Innovention Management, an intellectual property consulting firm that assists entrepreneurs and small businesses with difficult intellectual property issues. He is a registered patent agent in both Canada and the United States, and he has over 20 years of experience working as an intellectual property management consultant and patent agent for IBM Canada, Bell Canada, and Husky Injection Molding Systems where he was Director of Global Intellectual Property. Prior to entering the field of intellectual property, he was an advisory engineer at IBM Canada where he was involved in a variety of leading-edge software development projects. Derek holds an MASc degree Technology Innovation Management from Carleton University in Ottawa, Canada , for which he was awarded a Senate Medal for Outstanding Academic Achievement. Derek also holds a BEng degree in Systems and Computer Engineering, also from Carleton University.

Keywords: intellectual property, patent, patent citations, prior art citation, patent value, patent evaluation, citation-based patent evaluation, literature review

References

Bapuki, H., Loree, D., & Crossan. M. 2011. Connecting External Knowledge Usage and Firm Performance: An Empirical Analysis. *Journal of Engineering and Technology Management*, 28(4): 215–231.
http://dx.doi.org/10.1016/j.jengtecman.2011.06.001

Breitzman, A., & Thomas, P. 2001. Using Patent Citation Analysis to Target/Value M&A Candidates. *Research-Technology Management*, 35(5): 28–36.

Chen Y., & Chang, K. 2010. Exploring the Nonlinear Effects of Patent Citations, Patent Share and Relative Patent Position on Market Value in the US Pharmaceutical Industry. *Technology Analysis & Strategic Management*, 22(2): 153–169.
http://dx.doi.org/10.1080/09537320903498496

Deng, Y. 2008. The Value of Knowledge Spillovers in the U.S. Semiconductor Industry. *International Journal of Industrial Organization*, 26(4): 1044–1058.
http://dx.doi.org/10.1016/j.ijindorg.2007.09.005

de Wilton, A. 2011. Patent Value: A Business Perspective for Technology Startups. *Technology Innovation Management Review*, 1(3): 5–11.
http://timreview.ca/article/501

Fischer, T., & Leidinger, J. 2014. Testing Patent Value Indicators on Directly Observed Patent Value – An Empirical Analysis of Ocean Tomo Patent Auctions. *Research Policy*, 43(3): 519–529.

Hall, B. H., Jaffe, A., & Trajtenberg, M. 2005. Market Value and Patent Citations. *RAND Journal of Economics*, 36(1): 16–38.
http://www.jstor.org/stable/1593752

Haroff, D., Scherer, F. M., & Vopel, K. 2003. Citations, Family Size, Opposition and the Value of Patent Rights. *Research Policy*, 32(8): 1343–1363.
http://dx.doi.org/10.1016/S0048-7333(02)00124-5

Hirschey, M., & Richardson, V. 2003. Are Scientific Indicators of Patent Quality Useful to Investors? *Journal of Empirical Finance*, 11(1): 91–107.
http://dx.doi.org/10.1016/j.jempfin.2003.01.001

Jaffe, A. B., Trajtenberg, M., & Henderson R. 1993. Geographic Localization of Knowledge Spillovers as Evidenced by Patent Citations. *Quarterly Journal of Economics*, 108(3): 577–598.
http://dx.doi.org/10.2307/2118401

Nair, S. S., Mathew, M., & Nag, D. 2011. Dynamics between Patent Latent Variables and Patent Price. *Technovation*, 31(12): 648–654.
http://dx.doi.org/10.1016/j.technovation.2011.07.002

Reitzig, M. 2003. What Determines Patent Value? Insights From the Semiconductor Industry. *Research Policy*, 32(1): 13–26.
http://dx.doi.org/10.1016/S0048-7333(01)00193-7

Tseng, C. 2009. Technological Innovation in the Bric Economies. *Research and Technology Management*, 52(2): 29–35.

19

Mobile Convergence and Entrepreneurial Opportunities for Innovative Products and Services

Jeff Moretz and Chirag Surti

" Seriously, we are in the midst of the convergence of voice "
and data and that is challenging the infrastructure of
the telephone companies. There are huge commercial
interests in the basic technology, but even more so in
content delivery and control of content.

Steve Crocker
Visionary, inventor, and Internet Hall of Fame inductee

Our research on 2012 and 2013 Canadian wireless service pricing indicates that data was underpriced relative to traditional voice and text messaging services. Such a situation, while potentially disadvantaging consumers of traditional mobile services, created a market that favoured competitors pursuing innovative uses of mobile data. Although more competitive pressures in the telecommunications market would provide broader benefits to Canadian consumers and facilitate greater innovation in related services, a favorable pricing differential vis-à-vis data transmission provides useful incentives. Even with recent changes to the pricing of mobile services in Canada, we should expect continued development of services that substitute data for voice and text messaging, particularly for international communications, as well as more innovative uses of mobile data.

Introduction

The rapid expansion and improvement of digital wireless networks has created a sea change in the expectations among consumers regarding connectivity. Smartphones are becoming ubiquitous, and they are among the most rapidly adopted consumer technologies in history. DeGusta (2012) reported that smartphones were on pace to saturate North American and World markets in record time, and most US phones, including the vast majority of new phone purchases, are smartphones (Reed, 2013). Services such as Twitter and Vine were tailored for the mobile market from the start, and major industry players from Google to Facebook to Twitter have scrambled to stake their claim in the mobile space.

Yet, despite the rapid growth of this market, there is sometimes the perception that only the very large global competitors are able to compete in this new domain.

However, the success of Apple's AppStore and the more recent Google Play means that developers of software and associated services that leverage mobile technologies have the opportunity to reach millions of potential customers with relatively limited marketing and distribution budgets. In fact, the digital landscape makes it more rather than less feasible for upstarts to disrupt more established players (Davis, 2014), at least in many competitive domains. The AppStore alone generated $10 billion in sales in 2013 (Apple Press Info, 2014) across more than a million different apps (148Apps.biz, 2014). Google Play passed the 25 billion app download mark more than a year ago (Webster, 2013), and although revenues still lag behind the AppStore, the gap is narrowing (Perez, 2014).

All of this begs the question: what is the impact of Canada's uncompetitive telecommunications landscape on such entrepreneurship? It is well established that telecommunications services in Canada are not competitive, and that Canadian consumers pay more for less (Christopher, 2013), in large part due to the lack of effective competition (Surti & Moretz, 2013). However, there are some reasons for hope when it comes to telecommunications related entrepreneurship.

In order to detail the situation that pertains in the Canadian telecommunications market and the opportunities that this market presents for innovation, we first discuss the Canadian wireless market and examine the advertised pricing data of the three major service providers to infer the marginal cost of the various services. We then examine the pricing inefficiencies that arose under the pricing plans available to Canadian consumers in 2013 and the implications of these plans regarding incentives and substitution effects. We close with discussion of innovation opportunities provided by this market situation and by the infrastructure that has developed around smartphones and other mobile devices in particular.

The Canadian Wireless Market

Based on our analysis of the pricing of Canadian telecommunications services from 2012 to 2013, mobile data has been effectively cross-subsidized by the fees for voice calls and text messaging (i.e., short messaging service [SMS]). Thus, software and services that utilize the data stream of a mobile device were making use of a cheaper service option, giving such services an advantage in the marketplace and providing a stimulus for innovation and entrepreneurship in the Canadian mobile communications space.

Though such innovations have provided some relief for consumers, the Canadian telecommunications market remains uncompetitive, in part because of the high cost of entry for carriers. Telecom carries must invest enormous amounts of capital upfront in the acquisition of spectrum and development and maintenance of networks in order to provide sufficiently broad coverage. The cost of adding one more individual to the service is negligible in comparison to the costs of creating a viable network, and any calculation of the cost of providing services would need to amortize these fixed costs for many years across all of the customers served. However, even if we were to undertake such a calculation of service costs, we do not have access to the requisite detailed cost data. The telecommunications providers do not publish such data for strategic and competitive reasons. Thus, we must approach the problem from a different angle.

Although the data on the actual costs borne by the providers themselves is not readily available, we do have extensive access to consumer pricing information. Because the telecommunications providers operate an extensive retail operation, selling services directly to both individual consumers and small businesses, they make pricing information widely available as part of their marketing efforts. Using multiple linear regression (tinyurl.com/yqxx8v), we analyse 2012 and 2013 advertised pricing information across all retail plans offered by each of the "Big 3" Canadian telecommunications companies and their subsidiaries: Rogers (rogers.com), TELUS (telus.com), and Bell (bell.ca). The advertised price data were collected during the summer of 2012 and 2013 from their respective websites. We deliberately ignored short-term "teaser rates" and promotional pricing and instead focused on the published retail pricing that most consumers end up paying in the long run.

The use of multiple linear regression to estimate implied cost is a well-established approach in economics. For businesses that have very high fixed cost and negligible marginal cost of operation, it is possible to infer the cost component of each offering using advertised rates. In economics, this is referred to as the shadow price (tinyurl.com/24k7be). Given that the underlying telecommunications infrastructures used by the different providers are quite similar within each technological generation and all providers operate well above minimum efficient scale, such costs can be discounted as a source of cost differences between service providers. Therefore, by advertising information about their offerings and announcing the prices charged for variety of bundled options, the telecommunications companies reveal useful information about their cost structure for providing each of the three services to the consumer. The cost estimates of the service components for each of the three service providers are presented in Table 1. Here, we highlight the estimated cost of voice, text, and data implied by published pricing data along with advertised overage charges. This method allows us to estimate the implied marginal costs of one minute of voice, one text message, and one GB of data with statistical confidence (the p values and the F statistics were all significant at 95% level of significance). Although these values are indirect estimates of costs, we confirm them with reference to the data equivalent of voice transmissions.

In Table 1, we resolve the bundled telecom plan into its main cost components. Our analysis shows that there is a significant fixed cost component for simply connecting a customer to the network, as implied by the base

Table 1. Canadian mobile telecommunications main cost components (based on 2013 data)

Provider	Base Connection Fee	Voice		Text		Data	
		Per minute	Overage	Per message	Overage	Per GB	Overage
Rogers	$50.52	<$0.01	$0.45	$0.00	$0.20	$10.91	$21.25
TELUS	$58.95	<$0.01	$0.43	$0.00	$0.20	$9.19	$20.00
Bell	$44.86	<$0.01	$0.50	$0.00	$0.20	$10.85	$22.00

connection fee, or a monthly fee in industry parlance. Such a connection cost is to be expected in an industry with such an enormous fixed cost component. As the table shows, there are some substantial differences between the carriers in terms of the implied costs of building and maintaining the basic network infrastructure. These differences are perhaps due to historical accident, operational scale, technological sophistication, and market demographics, but they are not the focus of our discussion here. Without technological developments that radically reduce the costs associated with developing an extensive network of towers and switching equipment, this element of the pricing of service provision is unlikely to decline dramatically as a proportion of the overall cost structure, and it does little to elucidate the opportunity for mobile services innovation that we hope to see in the Canadian market.

Market Constraints, Inefficiencies, and Innovation

Because the marginal cost of voice calls and text messaging is negligible, once the consumer is connected to the network, the cost of providing additional voice and text services is negligible. The fact that voice minutes were limited by providers indicates a significant mark-up given the negligible cost of provision. In addition, consumers were heavily penalized for exceeding their allocated quota of voice and text; in our analysis, the overage charge mark-up on voice was approximately 4500% and for text it was almost 20,000%. For data however, in terms of overage charges, the mark-up on average was only 105%, substantially lower when compared to voice and text overage charge mark-ups. The fact that published prices imply limited cost for providing voice and text services coupled with the strong influence of data on plan prices indicates that the cost

structure is dominated by data volume. This finding from our analysis, coupled with the prevalence of limited voice minutes and text messages and the dramatic difference between the overage mark-up for voice and text relative to data, indicates an effective subsidy on data usage in the form of disproportionate mark-ups on voice and text services. Thus, consumers of voice and text are in effect cross-subsidizing heavy consumers of data. This subsidization might be especially true for lower-tier service plans or voice-only plans for which consumers pay significantly more than the implied cost to provide voice services, as well as for consumers who feel compelled to purchase plans with features and data allowances that they do not need in order to get the voice minutes they want.

Such cross-subsidization of data has significant implications for the development of software and services that utilize mobile data transmissions. Under such pricing schemes, mobile phone users who primarily make use of voice or text messaging are disadvantaged, while those consumers who use data services pay comparatively less for that aspect of service relative to the cost of provision. It is relatively easy and quite instructive to highlight the overpricing of voice minutes in the Canadian market. Assuming that the encoding used for proprietary mobile networks is similar to the G.711 standard (tinyurl.com/yoz6q5) used in telephony DS0 channels (tinyurl.com/kwaol8v), the conversion of voice to data would be: 64 kbps x 9.5367×10^{-7} gb/kb x 60 seconds = .003662 gbpm or 273 minutes per gigabit. Whereas a voice minute transmitted as overage would cost 46 cents, that same voice transmission using data overage would cost less than 8 cents/minute, making it substantially cheaper than voice overage. In fact, most wireless carriers used codecs similar to those used for Voice over Internet Protocol (VoIP), achieving low latency, high-quality transmission at data rates less than 10% those required by G.711 transmission. At 6.3 kbps, the higher data rate possible using G.723.1 (tinyurl.com/ 33hy5s), the data equivalent of one minute of voice would cost less than $0.01, which is precisely what our analysis shows. Overpricing of voice and text transmission by service providers, both globally and in Canada, has spurred the creation of a variety of innovative solutions by third-party developers to transmit voice and text messages using data.

Thus, entrepreneurs who developed software and services that leverage data transmission should experience a comparative advantage by virtue of the effective subsidy on data rates. The advantages to innovation of what amounts to a subsidy on mobile data proposed here are compatible with arguments regarding mobile web development proposed in Ville Saarikoski's (2006) PhD dissertation at the University of Oulu in Finland, in which he characterizes email specifically, and the mobile Internet more broadly, as disruptive technologies (cf. Bower & Christensen, 1995).

Saarikoski's dissertation argues that SMS or text messaging is far less efficient than email at creating scale-free networks. In essence, email connectivity (and communications via other technologies that use similar network connectivity approaches) requires fewer steps on average to connect any given node to another node. Saarikoski extends the insights related to scale-free networks to argue that value-added services (e.g., beyond traditional voice calling) could be increased in a mobile packet-based (digital) network. For example, NTT DoCoMo's i-mode service (tinyurl.com/nlkqtq) in Japan had achieved significant market success by adopting a packet switched network that facilitated non-voice communication and enabled extensive development of third-party services from which i-mode earned a revenue-sharing percentage (Mallon, 2013). However, carriers in Europe failed to adopt similar structures, which may have played a significant role in the slow growth of mobile data networks and associated services in the European market.

More importantly for our present argument, Saarikoski's dissertation also argues that the pricing associated with the European networks inhibited adoption in multiple ways, including connection costs and usage fees. DoCoMo's success was in part attributable to its decision to focus on the consumer market, where buyers were less conservative and more willing to experiment with new technologies than were many busi-

ness customers. Apple followed a similar path to market success with its line of i-products, with consumer adoption preceding eventual expansion into the business market. However, the success of i-mode is also intimately connected to its decision to leverage packet data and offer reasonable pay-per-use pricing to facilitate innovation in third-party services (Grech, 2003).

Opportunities for Innovation

Innovation is directly related to the application of ideas or methods in ways that provide greater value to society (McIntyre, 1982). Value, for both consumers and businesses, includes cost factors as well as benefits provided (Anderson & Narus, 1998; Ratchford, 1982). In the context of mobile telecommunications, applications that provide opportunities to substitute comparatively underpriced data for overpriced voice and texting services provide cost-focused value to consumers. However, the same innovations that provide those cost-saving opportunities also provide richer, more effectively integrated communications services that increase customer benefits.

Among the more famous of the app-based communications solutions are WhatsApp (whatsapp.com) and Viber (viber.com). Facebook recently acquired WhatsApp for $19 billion in cash and stock and Viber was purchased by Rakuten, a Japanese e-commerce company, for almost $1 billion. These transactions are testaments to the value of each solution's user bases, which number in the hundreds of millions. In addition to these more recent players, some of the early VoIP pioneers such as magicJack and Vonage have launched mobile apps that extend their service from simple landline telephony replacement into a mobile platform offering seamless voice communications. Such services can be very attractive to consumers because of the effective subsidization of data transmission by wireless service providers. These services also present opportunities for greater value creation through the integration of multiple forms of communication in a fashion that is not compatible with the traditional paradigm that voice communication is different than and separate from data.

Businesses may also substitute text data for voice communications when contacting customers. Businesses such as financial service providers, cable providers, water/power/gas utilities, and telecommunication service providers themselves can communicate upcoming bill payments, changes to account details, or upcoming planned outages of services via multiple channels including text messages. Such simple innovations with such significant potential to decrease costs, increase service quality, and dramatically improve overall profitability have remained virtually absent from Canadian marketplace, in part because of the consumer costs associated with their adoption. In India, where text messages are usually free and unlimited, most businesses, including financial services and utilities, make extensive use of SMS to communicate with customers. One substantial driver of the slower rate of adoption of such service innovations in Canada may be privacy and security concerns on the part of Canadian companies and the Canadian government, rendering such innovations infeasible. Yet, the fact remains that, from a cost-of-business point of view, such mechanisms represent significant efficiency improvement opportunities while also providing opportunities for enhanced customer service. Similarly, the success of online messaging services such as Skype, WhatsApp, and Viber bears testament to the fact that consumers have been very interested in alternatives to comparatively overpriced voice calling, text messaging (SMS), and multimedia messaging services (MMS).

Conclusion and Insights: Innovation Opportunities

The apps noted above represent but a small proportion of the explosion of apps that has arisen. The industry's shift from mobile phones with expanded capabilities to more flexibly functional mobile computing devices has changed the innovation landscape. The history of Research in Motion (RIM)/BlackBerry (blackberry.com) is informative. The Blackberry devices and their secured push-messaging service had enormous success because of their innovative solution to mobile communications problems, specifically reliable and secure transmission of email, avoiding the problems and excessive costs associated with mobile messaging (Gustin, 2013). Yet, RIM failed to expand its target market and neglected the benefits of broader innovation by third-party participants, particularly in the large consumer segment of the mobile market. As research has pointed out, Apple similarly neglected third-party developers at the initial launch of the iPhone but quickly moved to facilitate outside development when the market moved in that direction (West & Mace, 2010).

Although competition in the market for apps is fierce, particularly on Apple's closely managed AppStore (Lagorio-Chafkin, 2010), there are opportunities for smaller competitors to enter the industry. As of March

2014, there were more than 300,000 publishers of apps for Apple's products in the U.S. (148Apps.biz, 2014). In many respects, the AppStore and Google Play can be seen as a mechanism for lowering the obstacles to innovation by providing a platform that reduces the need for extensive investment in distribution and support capabilities. More broadly, the rise of the smartphone and similar mobile devices presents opportunities for substantial innovation in much more focused domains. Even where a robust market willing to purchase a tailored application is absent, businesses often find it desirable to create custom applications (cf. Apple Developer, 2014). This expansion of opportunities for customer-driven innovation is akin to the "user toolkits" concept promulgated by von Hippel (2001, von Hippel & Katz, 2002) among others. In the case of mobile telecommunications, the "smart" devices themselves may serve as the foundation for user-driven innovation with some additional support available through the distribution and support infrastructures of the device champions (e.g., Apple and Google).

Mobile commerce has also seen significant increase in interest as expanding mobile device capabilities make myriad approaches feasible (Ho & Kwok, 2003). Going forward, the growing success of phone- and text-based payment services such as mpessa in Asia and Africa, as well as increased use of virtual wallets using near field communication (NFC) technology and the rise of the "crypto currencies" may hasten the creation of more innovation in the West, which relies more extensively on data rather than voice and text.

Although the differences in pricing and the implied costs of service provision between various types of mobile telecommunications has historically presented some relative advantages for developers of digital products and services that utilize mobile data, we should note that the lack of competitiveness in the telecommunications sector still represents a significant obstacle to Canadian competitiveness in general and to innovation in the mobile space in particular. The structure of offerings in the consumer market may tend to offset such negative effects in certain domains by presenting consumers with data service at a price that is effectively subsidized by text and voice mark-ups, but innovation will still experience negative effects from the lack of a competitive market for mobile telecommunications.

Although there were potential advantages for innovators using mobile data under the pricing structures in place in 2012 and 2013, all innovative activities would benefit from lower prices and the spark to innovation in basic telecommunications provision that effective competition would provide. The recent simplification of mobile pricing plans (CBC News, 2014) is a small step toward a more consumer-friendly market, and to the extent that such changes encourage more extensive and intensive adoption of mobile data services, they will help foster innovation among third-party app developers and service providers. However, the fact that all plans are identical and involve substantial price increases shows that competition is lacking, with the threat of regulatory changes sparking the move to simpler pricing structures. Our analysis of the new plans reveal that in effect the data is priced at $6.21 per GB and the monthly access fee or the base fee is $60.95 and a phone subsidy of $20.00 is offered to consumers.

In fact, the revised plans, if anything, actually reduce the impetus to develop innovative products and services that utilize mobile data. If the mobile Internet is to live up to its potential as a disruptive technology, changing the nature of our interactions, we must foster the same kind of open innovation that has led to such incredible developments in the wired web. Although innovation is proceeding in mobile services, a more competitive market for basic mobile telecommunications service would greatly enhance opportunities for innovation that none of us can readily envision.

Thus, despite the lack of competitiveness of the Canadian telecommunications sector, a situation that deters innovation and the spread of potentially valuable services and capabilities, the structure of offerings may have served to counteract those negative effects for some products and services. There are many sectors of the Canadian economy that stand to benefit from more competitive pricing in mobile services in general and mobile data in particular. Mobile financial services are one area that has seen tremendous development globally, and the Canadian market now has its first open mobile wallet solution (CNW, 2013) using mobile phone data capabilities to manage payments and loyalty program points from President's Choice Financial and TD Bank Group. Mobile gaming, particularly games that require extensive data communications in order to facilitate real-time interactive gameplay, could also benefit from pricing rationalization. For example, Ingress (ingress.com) utilizes mobile data connectivity, GPS, etc. in order to create an integrated augmented-reality gaming environment. Games such as Shadow Cities (no longer available) and Parallel Kingdom (parallelkingdom.com) take a similar approach, and there are myriad other ways to enhance mobile gaming through data connectivity. Canada has a significant presence in the gaming domain, with major companies operating in Montreal, Toronto, Vancouver, and elsewhere across the country, and mobile gaming of all sorts could see more extensive adoption and development if given the opportunity to leverage cheap and reliable data connectivity.

More broadly, we should expect to see innovations in areas that are not receiving significant attention at present. The wonderful thing about market structures that foster innovation is that we all benefit from developments that few of us could predict and that many of us would discount, but that the energetic, creative, ambitious, and determined entrepreneurs among us are willing to bet on with everything they have. The best we can do for them is to provide an equable playing field.

Recommended Reading

- Global Technology, Media, Telecom Innovation Series (PricewaterhouseCoopers, 2014; tinyurl.com/pscsp2q)

- "Disruptive Technologies" (Manyika et al., 2013; tinyurl.com/nmbecug)

Acknowledgements

The authors wish to thank recent UOIT graduates, Darryl Hand and Kaileigh Peace, for collecting the data used in this study.

About the Authors

Jeff Moretz is Assistant Professor of Strategy and Entrepreneurship at the University of Ontario Institute of Technology (UOIT) in Oshawa, Canada. He obtained his PhD from the University of Texas at Austin, USA, and has an MBA and two undergraduate degrees from Michigan State University, USA. He is a recovering consultant, having worked for McKinsey & Company in Chicago after his MBA studies. Prior to joining the UOIT, he worked at University College Cork in Ireland, researching open source software communities and open innovation. His research interests focus on the impact of information, openness, and information technologies on innovation, business models, and strategies.

Chirag Surti is an Assistant Professor of Logistics and Supply Chain Management at the University of Ontario Institute of Technology (UOIT) in Oshawa, Canada. He earned a PhD degree from McMaster University in Hamilton, Canada, and a Master of Science in Industrial Engineering from the State University of New York in Buffalo, USA. His primary research interest is in the area supply chain management and understanding and analyzing the role process innovation can play in boosting productivity. He is a recipient of NSERC Discovery and SSHRC Partnership grants.

References

148Apps.biz. 2014. Apple iTunes App Store Metrics, Statistics and Numbers for iPhone Apps. *148Apps.biz.* June 1, 2014:
http://148apps.biz/app-store-metrics/

Anderson, J. C., & Narus, J. A. 1998. Business Marketing: Understand What Customers Value. *Harvard Business Review,* 76(6): 53–67.

Apple Developer. 2014. Develop Custom iOS Apps for Business. *Apple Developer.* June 1, 2014:
https://developer.apple.com/programs/volume/b2b/

Apple Press Info. 2014. App Store Sales Top $10 Billion in 2013. *Apple Press Info.* June 1, 2014:
http://www.apple.com/pr/library/2014/01/07App-Store-Sales-Top-10-Billion-in-2013.html

Bower, J. L., & Christensen, C. M. 1995. Disruptive Technologies: Catching the Wave. *Harvard Business Review,* 73(1): 43–53.

CBC News. 2014. Wireless Carriers Hike Prices Across Canada. *CBC News.* June 1, 2014:
http://www.cbc.ca/1.2575886

Christopher, D. 2013, July 16. Confirmed: Canadians Pay Some of the Highest Prices for Some of the Worst Telecom Service in the Industrialized World. *OpenMedia.ca.* June 1, 2014:
https://openmedia.ca/blog/confirmed-canadians-pay-some-highest-prices-some-worst-telecom-service-industrialized-world

CNW. 2013. PC Financial and TD Announce Ugo - Canada's First Open Mobile Wallet. *NewsWire.ca.* June 1, 2014:
http://cnw.ca/Mb9Ql

Davis, J. P. 2014. How To Create A "Killer App": A Guide For Entrepreneurs. *Forbes.* June 1, 2014:
http://www.forbes.com/sites/insead/2014/03/18/how-to-create-a-killer-app-a-guide-for-entrepreneurs/

DeGusta, M. 2012, Are Smart Phones Spreading Faster than Any Technology in Human History? *MIT Technology Review* (May). June 1, 2014:
http://www.technologyreview.com/news/427787/are-smart-phones-spreading-faster-than-any-technology-in-human-history/

Grech, S. 2003. Case: i-Mode Pricing. Seminar on Internet Pricing and Charging, S-38.042. Helsinki: TKK Networking laboratory, Helsinki University of Technology.
http://www.netlab.hut.fi/opetus/s38042/k03/topics/i-modepricing.pdf

Gustin, S. 2013. The Fatal Mistake That Doomed BlackBerry. *Time* (July). June 1, 2014:
http://business.time.com/2013/09/24/the-fatal-mistake-that-doomed-blackberry/

Ho, S. Y., & Kwok, S. H. 2002. The Attraction of Personalized Service for Users in Mobile Commerce: An Empirical Study. *ACM SIGecom Exchanges,* 3(4): 10–18.
http://dx.doi.org/10.1145/844351.844354

Lagorio-Chafkin, C. 2010. How to Make Money on iPhone Apps. *Inc.com.* June 1, 2014:
http://www.inc.com/guides/making-money-iphone-apps.html

Mallon, D. 2013. Where Are They Now? i-mode. *ZDNet.* June 1, 2014:
http://www.zdnet.com/uk/where-are-they-now-i-mode-7000021216/

Manyika, J., Chui, M., Bughin, J., Dobbs, R., Bisson, P., & Marrs, A. 2013. *Disruptive Technologies: Advances That Will Transform Life, Business, and the Global Economy.* New York, NY: McKinsey Global Institute.

McIntyre, S. H. 1982. Obstacles to Corporate Innovation. *Business Horizons,* 25(1): 23–28.
http://dx.doi.org/10.1016/0007-6813(82)90040-4

Perez, S. 2014. Google Play Still Tops iOS App Store Downloads, And Now Narrowing Revenue Gap, Too. *TechCrunch.* June 1, 2014:
http://techcrunch.com/2014/04/15/google-play-still-tops-ios-app-store-downloads-and-now-narrowing-revenue-gap-too/

PricewaterhouseCoopers. 2014. Global Technology, Media, Telecom Innovation Series. *PwC.* June 1, 2014:
http://www.pwc.com/tmtinnovators

Ratchford, B. T. 1982. Cost-Benefit Models for Explaining Consumer Choice and Information Seeking Behavior. *Management Science,* 28(2): 197–212.
http://dx.doi.org/10.1287/mnsc.28.2.197

Reed, B. 2013. Smartphones Now Account for Almost Two-Thirds of All Mobile Phones in the U.S. *BGR.* June 1, 2014:
http://bgr.com/2013/09/18/smartphone-adoption-united-states/

Saarikoski, V. 2006. *The Odyssey of the Mobile Internet - The Emergence of a Networking Attribute*. PhD Thesis. Oulu, Finland: University of Oulu.

Surti, C., & Moretz, J. 2013. Wireless is a necessity, so open the market. *Financial Post*. June 1, 2014: http://opinion.financialpost.com/2013/07/05/verizon-canada-wireless/

Von Hippel, E. 2001. User Toolkits for Innovation. *Journal of Product Innovation Management*, 18(4): 247–257. http://dx.doi.org/10.1111/1540-5885.1840247

Von Hippel, E., & Katz, R. 2002. Shifting Innovation to Users via Toolkits. *Management Science*, 48(7): 821–833. http://dx.doi.org/10.1287/mnsc.48.7.821.2817

Webster, S. 2014. Google Play Blows Past 25 Billion App Downloads. *AndroidGuys*. June 1, 2014: http://www.androidguys.com/2012/09/26/google-play-blows-past-25-billion-app-downloads/

West, J., & Mace, M. 2010. Browsing as the Killer App: Explaining the Rapid Success of Apple's iPhone. *Telecommunications Policy*, 34(5–6): 270–286. http://dx.doi.org/10.1016/j.telpol.2009.12.002

Keywords: mobile convergence, innovation, entrepreneurship, wireless pricing, mobile services, competition, Canada

20

Strengthening Innovation Capacity through Different Types of Innovation Cultures

Jens-Uwe Meyer

" There are two kinds of adventurers: those who go truly hoping "
to find adventure and those who go secretly hoping they won't.

William Least Heat-Moon (Trogdon)
Travel writer and historian

In times of increased market dynamics, companies must be capable of initiating and implementing innovation projects that vary greatly in type, speed, and degree of innovation. Many companies do not succeed. This article introduces Innolytics, an innovation management tool that allows companies to successfully face this challenge by analyzing their innovation culture and managing its development in the right direction. Analyzing empirical data from 200 staff members employed by German, Austrian, and Swiss companies using exploratory factor analysis, four types of innovation cultures were identified, each of which foster a different degree of organizational creativity. Proactive innovators (21%) promote organizational creativity at a high level and across all categories. Strategic innovators (26%) foster innovation by focusing on their strategy and their value system. Innovative optimizers (36%) promote more adaptive levels whereas operational innovators (16%) promote low levels of organizational creativity. Each type enables a company or a business unit to manage different degrees of innovation projects. The Innolytics tool introduced and described in this article will enable companies to better meet the challenges of rapidly changing markets.

Introduction

In dynamic markets, companies must manage a greater variety and a higher speed of innovations (Bjork, 2012). In the course of this effort, the different requirements for processes and abilities can quickly overstrain an organization's capacities (Benner & Tushman, 2002). The current understanding of innovation management is characterized by process-oriented approaches (cf. Cooper, 1994; Cooper & Kleinschmidt, 2001; Drucker, 1985) that focus on the establishment of innovation processes and the definition of roles as well as the establishment of key performance indicators (Cooper & Kleinschmidt 1996, 2001). These approaches nevertheless demonstrate their limits in dynamic market environments.

Processes gain great importance when managing complex projects with a diversity of participants, such as the development of innovative technologies (Cooper, 2014; Högman & Johannesson, 2013). Structured routines render advantages in terms of effectiveness but may hinder the development of something new (Junarsin, 2009). The strength of innovation processes appears to be in the ability to manage the innovation routine. Such a strategy of slow incremental change can be absolutely promising provided that the environment is stable or changes slowly (Tushman & O'Reilly III, 1996). Nevertheless, this strategy is not always the most productive approach to meeting the demands of dynamic markets because innovation is not necessarily a linear process (Rickards, 1996). The farther a project strays from this routine and the higher its degree of uncertainty, the greater the demand is for more encompassing instruments that promote more far-reaching forms of innovation.

Background

Numerous authors describe the influence of the innovation culture on the innovative capacity of companies and company units (e.g., Ekvall, 2006; Lin & Liu, 2012;

Naranjo et al., 2010). Category systems that outline the supporting framework conditions for creativity and innovation have been developed over recent years (e.g., Amabile et al., 1996; Khandwalla & Mehta, 2004; Robinson & Stern, 1997). These works assume that a company possesses an innovation culture to either a greater or lesser degree and that either a higher or lower innovative capacity can be derived from it (Dobni, 2008; Martins & Terblanche, 2003).

Nevertheless, different types of innovations require different framework conditions (Junarsin, 2009; Leifer et al., 2000). According to Ekvall (2006), different degrees in organizational creativity are required for the achievement of different innovation goals. And, according to Tushman and O'Reilly (1996), different cultures that promote different degrees of creativity can exist in a single company. But, current research does not provide a systematic and sufficiently deep understanding of the various cultural conditions that foster different levels of creativity as a prerequisite for being able to manage different degrees of innovation in highly dynamic markets. The purpose of this article is to develop an empirically-based comprehensive model in order to close this gap. For this purpose, the following hypotheses are established on the basis of a literature analysis:

Hypothesis 1: *There are several degrees of organizational creativity. Each degree promotes a specific quality, scope, and radicality of innovation.*

Hypothesis 2: *Organizational units with different degrees of organizational creativity can be determined on the basis of characteristics and can be summarized into innovation types.*

Hypothesis 3: *Through the establishment of a management model based on types of innovation, companies can increase their ability to simultaneously develop different levels of innovation at varying speeds.*

Theoretical foundations and classification
Up to the early 1990s, research had not yet provided broadly based scientific frameworks that explain the relationship between the work environment and creative achievements of staff members (Amabile, 1988; Woodman et al., 1993). A new research direction has since emerged as the field of organizational creativity that focuses less on the creative performance of an individual, but more so on the creative performance of an organization (e.g., Puccio & Cabra, 2010; Zhou & Shalley, 2008).

The number of studies on the subject of creativity has been continually accelerating over recent years (Runco & Albert, 2010). Kozbelt, Beghetto, and Runco (2010) provide a comparative review of creativity theories and divide them into 10 categories. This work is a convergence of psychometric theories, typological theories, and system theories. Psychometric theories are based on the assumption that creativity can be measured using criteria (Kozbelt et al., 2010). Typological theories assume that there are different types of creative individuals and working styles (Kirton, 1976, 1989; Kozbelt, 2008; Martinsen, 1995). System theories are based on the assumption that creativity can be influenced by the system surrounding it (Kozbelt et al., 2010).

This article examines the question of how companies and company units can influence their innovative capacity at a system level by developing typologies of organizational creativity with the support of psychometric techniques.

Definitions

Individual creativity
The foundational element in this article is Amabile's (1996) componential model, which includes three major components of creativity: expertise, creative thinking, and intrinsic task motivation. This definition of creativity may be limited because the level of creative efficiency appears to be additionally influenced by specific character traits:

• Independence, independent judgment, autonomy (Amabile, 1996; Barron & Harrington, 1981; Roth, 2001)

• Self-discipline or self-direction, highly achievement-motivated, perseverance in face of frustration, high energy (Amabile, 1996; Csikszentmihalyi, 2006; Kaufman & Sternberg, 2006; Roth, 2001)

• Orientation toward taking risks (Amabile, 1996; Farson & Keyes, 2002)

• Preference toward breaking the rules (Csikszentmihalyi, 2006)

• Largely unconcerned with regard to social acceptance (Amabile, 1996)

• Self-confidence (or self-efficacy) (Barron & Harrington, 1981; Hill et al., 2008; Prabhu et al., 2008)

For the purposes of this research objective, an expansion is made on Amabile's consideration of the relationship between creativity and intelligence (Amabile, 1996; Sternberg, 1996). According to Roth (2001), high creativity requires an above-average, particularly linguistic, intelligence. The concept of creative intelligence is applied within the literature (e.g., Buzan, 2001; Carr-Ruffino, 2001; Dewey et al., 2011). This intelligence may determine the degree of creative efficiency that moves between moderately creative achievements (Amabile, 1996) and truly creative breakthroughs (Feist, 2010).

Within the scope of this research project, individual creative potential is defined as a collection of creative abilities and character traits that enable achievements that are considered in a defined social context as new and useful and that the degree and the area of these creative achievements are strongly influenced by creative intelligence and individual expertise (Figure 1).

Definition of organizational creativity

Many terms are explored in the literature regarding innovation and creativity at a systemic level: innovativeness, organizational creativity, entrepreneurial creativity and corporate creativity, creative climate, innovation supportive culture, and innovation culture (e.g., Dobni, 2008; Ekvall, 1996; Robinson & Stern, 1997). A precise distinction between these terms is hardly possible on the basis of the present literature. The concept of innovation culture is defined within the scope of this article as the social environment that enables staff members to develop ideas and implement innovations. The concept of organizational creativity consists of two abilities: i) the ability to create this social environment as well as ii) the ability to utilize and exploit the resulting individual creativity of staff members.

Design and Methodology

For the analysis of the factors that promote organizational creativity referred to in the literature, authors have been selected who have followed the approach of listing all of the relevant factors and designating the factors that can be traceable and fully categorized:

• KEYS (Amabile et al., 1996)

• Six Factors Promoting Corporate Creativity (Robinson & Stern, 1997)

• Culture and Climate for Innovation (Ahmed, 1998)

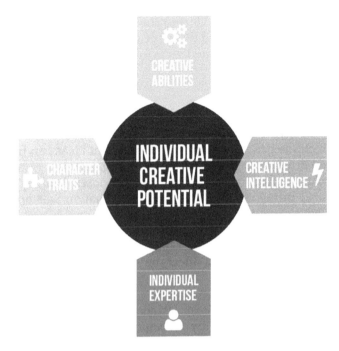

Figure 1. Individual creative potential and its influences

• Design of Corporate Creativity (Khandwalla & Mehta, 2004)

• Model of Engagement in Creative Action (Unsworth & Clegg, 2010)

• Key Issues Around Creating a Culture for Design, Creativity, and Innovation (von Stamm, 2005)

• Working Climate and Creativity (Ekvall & Tangeberg-Andersson, 1986)

• The Creativity Audit (Rickards & Bessant, 1980)

• Measuring the Perceived Support for Innovation in Organizations (Siegel & Kaemmerer, 1978)

• Organizational Creativity and Innovation (van Gundy, 1987)

• Needed Research in Creativity for Business and Industry Applications (Basadur, 1987)

• Exploratory Study for Creative Climate (Cabra et al., 2005)

• Measuring Climate for Work Group Innovation (Anderson & West, 1998)

• Characteristics of an Organizational Environment Which Stimulates and Inhibits Creativity (Soriano de Alencar & Bruno-Faria, 1997)

The 14 models include a total of 110 main categories – some of which are further divided into subcategories by the authors. These categories have been grouped into clusters applying Amabile's line of thought, after which the generation and development of ideas can be supported at multiple levels of an organization (Amabile et al., 1996). For classification purposes, Kromey's (2002) principle of operational interpretation was applied:

1. The organizational level includes factors of overriding importance that affect the entire organization or organizational unit.

2. The management level includes factors that can be directly influenced by the supervisor of an employee, such as the promotion of ideas by superiors.

3. On the employee level, creativity can be promoted in relation to the tasks and projects employees and teams are working on.

4. The level of the work environment includes factors that are perceived and interpreted by individuals in their personal working environment.

These four levels were associated with the 110 categories designated by the authors above as main categories. The categories were then grouped into the four levels with ten new categories and a total of 48 newly created items (Table 1).

A questionnaire was developed for the survey, and the collected data were coded on a scale from 1 to 6. After performing the factor analysis, the data were re-coded for clarity: values 1 to 3 were given the values -3 to -1 and the values of 4 to 6 were given the values 1 to 3. Incomplete datasets were removed from the analysis. All items were weighted equally. With the help of this questionnaire, nearly 200 staff members responsible for innovation in companies from Germany, Austria, and Switzerland were questioned as to the extent to which the characteristic features listed in Table 1 promote organizational creativity in their scope of action.

The base population from which the sample drawn is formed companies that are referred to as "innovation-active" by the Center for European Economic Research

(Rammer et al., 2011), a group that represents nearly 57% of all companies. The surveys were sent to staff members of these companies who deal with innovation due to their job description (e.g., idea manager, innovation manager, business development, research and development) or for another reason.

The survey fulfills the requirements of specific representativity (Moosbrugger & Kelava, 2012) as well as the quality criteria for objectivity, reliability, and validity.

Thirty-eight percent of the survey respondents are employed in companies that have between 51 and 1,000 staff members, 32% are in companies between 1,000 and 10,000 staff members, and 30% are employed in companies with more than 10,000 staff members. The majority (67%) is directly responsible for innovation. Fourteen percent of the interviewees belong to the management or the boards of directors. Nineteen percent come from the marketing and public relations (8%) departments, distribution (4%), product management (5%), or production (4%). Nearly two-thirds of the interviewees are executives.

To clarify the primary objective of this research project – to determine the extent to which different degrees of organizational creativity can be defined – the underlying data material has been analyzed with the aid of an exploratory factor analysis as a hypothesis-generating process (Moosbrugger & Schermelleh-Engel, 2012; Noack, 2007).

Findings

The results of the factor analysis show that there is a close relationship between the individual categories. Patterns could be found in the collected datasets. Respondents who, for example, evaluated their communication structures as being highly supportive of innovation almost always assessed their working climate and their risk culture as being equally supportive of innovation. There was also a strong correlation on the negative scale: respondents who evaluated their communication structures as being obstructive to innovation almost always assessed their working climate and their risk culture as being equally obstructive to innovation.

In evaluating the results of the exploratory factor analysis, four types of clusters were determined (Table 2). Their specific attributes, as evaluated on a scale from 1 to 6, can be described in the following way:

Table 1. Model levels, categories, and items *(continued on next page...)*

Level	Category	Items and Descriptions
Organization	**Strategy**	The goal formulated by the top management team to strive for and promote innovations.
		1. *Future strategy:* Offensive, future-oriented strategy from which innovation requirements are derived.
		2. *Innovation awareness:* The awareness of the need for innovation.
		3. *Innovation aspiration: The* aspiration to implement breakthrough innovations.
		4. *Engagement of the top management:* The degree to which the top managers develop their own innovation activities.
		5. *Sustainability:* The sense that the innovation strategy over a long period of time is a determining factor.
		6. *Strategy communication:* The magnitude to which the strategy is communicated and develops a leading influence.
	Values	Overriding factors: convictions and values.
		1. *Own responsibility:* The sense of being personally responsible for innovation.
		2. *Acceptance of contradictions:* To manage the attitude in spite of possibly contradicting information.
		3. *Lived philosophy:* The magnitude to which innovators show a personal conviction.
		4. *Value of creativity:* The degree to which new ideas as well as creative thinking and action are valued.
		5. *Courage for radical ideas:* The magnitude to which existing views are questioned and radical ideas are recognized.
		6. *Readiness for change:* The degree to which a readiness exists to accept changes concerning the structures and the scope of one's own duties.
Management	**Structures**	Creation of management structures with which creativity can be promoted.
		1. *Hierarchies:* Permeability of hierarchy levels in the company.
		2. *Management structures and organization structures:* Innovation-promoting management structures and organizational structures.
		3. *Control avoidance:* The possibility to work around the rules if required.
		4. *Decisive speed:* Speed of the decision-making processes.
		5. *Creativity-promoting practices and processes:* Practices and processes that actively promote creativity and innovation.
	Style	A management style that promotes creativity and innovation.
		1. *Innovation goals:* The measure to which concrete innovation goals are defined for individual staff members.
		2. *Active promotion:* The degree to which executives actively promote creative ideas and innovation projects.
		3. *Stimuli:* The magnitude to which executives expose staff members to stimulative influences.
		4. *Encouragement:* The encouragement of staff members to transcend the limits of what is currently feasible.
		5. *Autonomy:* The magnitude to which executives grant autonomy to their staff members.
	Resources	The granting of resources.
		1. *Temporal resources:* The granting of time freedoms.
		2. *Financial and material resources:* The granting of money and materials.
		3. *Internal synergies:* The possibility to fall back on the resources of other departments.
		4. *External resources:* Inclusion of external resources.
		5. *Training / tools:* The possibility for training.

Table 1. Model levels, categories, and items *(...continued from previous page)*

Level	Category	Items and Descriptions
Staff	**Team composition**	Composition and working style of teams.
		1. *Diversity:* The magnitude of technical and cognitive diversity.
		2. *Innovation-promoting staff:* The integration of innovation drivers and unconventional thinkers.
		3. *Criticism culture:* Discussions regarding the right course.
		4. *Mutual support:* The magnitude of mutual support.
	Incentives	The creation of incentives in order to expedite innovation.
		1. *Measurement of ideas:* The measurement of staff members in terms of the number and the quality of their ideas.
		2. *Career mechanisms:* Long-term career perspectives for creatively and innovatively managing staff members.
		3. *Reward of results:* To recompense the preference for results rather than compliance.
		4. *Reward of successful innovation:* The degree to which innovation success is recompensed.
Environment	**Communication**	Innovation-promoting communication.
		1. *Lateral communication:* Cross-divisional, lateral communication.
		2. *Internal informal networks:* The formation of informal networks.
		3. *External relationships:* The forming of external relationships.
		4. *Meeting culture:* The magnitude to which meetings serve the development of new ideas.
	Risk culture	Readiness to take risks.
		1. *Mistake acceptance:* The acceptance of mistakes.
		2. *Readiness to learn:* The readiness to learn from mistakes.
		3. *Mistake quality:* The distinction between different types of mistakes.
		4. *Unofficial projects:* The frequency of unofficial innovation projects.
		5. *Experimental readiness:* The magnitude to which experiments are carried out.
	Working climate	The personally perceived climate in the work environment.
		1. *Motivated environment:* The extent to which colleagues are motivated.
		2. *Informal contact:* Informal contact with one another.
		3. *Openness to problems:* Positive setting in the face of problems and difficulties.
		4. *Perceived dynamism:* The perceived degree of dynamism.

Table 2. The four innovation types revealed through factor analysis

Innovation Type	Organization Level	Management Level	Staff Level	Environment Level
Mean value of all interviewees	**1.0**	**1.1**	**0.9**	**0.6**
Standard divergence	± 2.1	± 2.0	± 2.0	± 2.1
Type 1	**2.0**	**1.9**	**1.9**	**1.6**
Standard divergence	± 2.4	± 2.3	± 2.4	± 2.5
Type 2	**1.5**	**1.2**	**1.0**	**0.7**
Standard divergence	± 1.9	± 1.9	± 1.6	± 2.0
Type 3	**0.7**	**0.8**	**0.7**	**0.1**
Standard divergence	± 1.9	± 1.9	± 1.9	± 2.0
Type 4	**0.0**	**0.5**	**0.4**	**0.0**
Standard divergence	± 1.9	± 1.9	± 1.8	± 1.8

1. Innovation Type 1 (21% of the interviewees) is characterized by clear evaluation tendencies as regards the features that strongly foster creativity: for all 10 items, statements that represent a culture that fosters organizational creativity achieved high values.

2. Innovation Type 2 (26% of the interviewees) ranks an average of 0.7 points lower than the first innovation type. Overall, the values fostering creativity are therefore assigned a lower, albeit not homogeneous, level. Of the 10 different categories, strategy, values, management styles, and team composition achieve higher values than the other categories.

3. For Innovation Type 3 (36% of the interviewees), the mean values on the evaluation scale are an average of 0.4 points lower than Innovation Type 2 and 1.1 points lower than Innovation Type 1. The evaluation level for the categories of strategy, values, management structures, team composition, and incentives is largely homogeneous.

4. Innovation Type 4 (16% of the interviewees) differs in all categories by 0.4 points from Innovation Type 3, by 0.8 points from Type 2, and by 1.5 points from Type 1. The categories of strategy, values, management structures, resources, incentives, communication, risk culture, and working climate are characterized by a largely homogeneous evaluation level on the lowest level.

The innovation aspiration (Figure 2) is valued at an average of 1.6 (± 2.6) for Innovation Type 1, but with Innovation Type 4, it is valued at 0.9 (± 1.8). Whereas Innovation Type 1 achieves high values with the courage for radical ideas (1.6 ± 2.5), the survey respondents who are assigned to the Innovation Type 4 see danger within radical ideas (0.4 ± 2.0).

Two questions of the survey were directly aimed at determining the degree of innovation the respondent aspires to achieve and the respondent's attitude to radical ideas. When comparing the values achieved by the different innovation types for both questions, a correla-

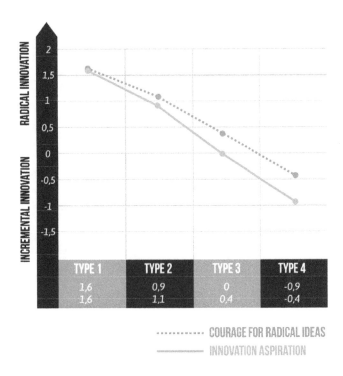

Figure 2. Continuous decrease in the targeted innovation degree

tion becomes apparent: the aim to establish ground-breaking new products on the market and the courage to adopt radical ideas decline steadily. Although Innovation Type 1 evaluates the aim to be the first to establish ground-breaking new products on the market with an average of 1.6 (± 2.6), Innovation Type 4 shows a clear tendency towards incremental innovations and improvements (-0.9 ± 1.8). Whereas Innovation Type 1 achieves high values with the courage for radical ideas (1.6 ± 2.5), respondents that are assigned to the Innovation Type 4 see a danger within radical ideas (0.4 ± 2.0).

Discussion

The types of innovation cultures were assigned names according to their defining characteristics:

1. Innovation Culture Type 1 is designated as "the Proactive Innovator". Proactive Innovators are entirely oriented toward innovation and can expedite more far-reaching innovations can develop innovations faster than the other innovation types.

2. Innovation Type 2 is designated as "the Strategic Innovator". Through the concentration on the organization level, Strategic Innovators can implement effectively. Through the strong top-down compon-

ent, they may adapt themselves more slowly to changed market circumstances than Proactive Innovators.

3. Innovation Type 3 is designated as "the Innovative Optimizer" due to the middle values in all categories. The Innovative Optimizer is oriented toward advancing incremental innovations.

4. Innovation Type 4 is designated as "the Operational Innovator" due to the below-average visionary orientation. This type is rather aligned toward the operational business.

Confirmation of the hypotheses
The culture of the companies that strive for a high degree of innovation differs significantly from those that aspire toward a lower degree of innovation. The perception that an organization's innovative capacity is only either low or high lacks dimension and is therefore limiting. In order to enable an organization's leadership to manage innovation in highly dynamic markets, it seems to be much more effective to think of suitable degrees of organizational creativity in relation to the specific innovation goals of a company. It can therefore be concluded that the idea that there is a consistent and clearly defined mechanism with which the management can positively impact the innovative capacity through organizational creativity does not sufficiently cover the many dimensions and variables of innovation itself.

Conclusion

The results of this research are of great practical relevance to the managers of companies. The innovation types developed in this research should enable managers to understand which mechanisms can be activated in different intensities to achieve defined innovation goals. The results should shift the focus in innovation management from the procedural consideration to the establishment of management models that envision company units with varying degrees of organizational creativity.

However, a limitation of this paper is the relatively small sample. One response per company does of course not properly describe the culture of that company. It is recommended to expand the sample and using a more complex process of investigation that covers statistically several management layers within the company. Moreover, future investigations on the subject of innovation should focus on the gradations of organizational creativity. The different degrees are insufficiently investigated in the literature.

For future research, it is encouraged that surveys similar to that conducted here are repeated – possibly with a higher number of participants. It would be a significant gain in knowledge to discover the extent to which more types of innovation can be defined. Due to the relatively low number of cases in this first research (200 interviewees), four innovation types naturally demonstrate a simplification.

In the meantime, on the basis of this preliminary study, a web-based analysis tool has been developed in German, and an English version will be available in 2015. This tool, which is called Innolytics (innolytics.de) – from "innovation analytics " – helps researchers and managers to measure, analyze, and continuously develop their own innovation capacity. For this purpose, the items discussed in this paper are converted into questions for different management levels and areas of expertise. This tool should help to enable the management of companies to identify and activate those factors that most efficiently improve the innovation capacity of different units. Given that different areas of expertise and business units within companies are usually subjected to different demands for innovation, Innolytics should help to enable the management to establish different innovation cultures in different divisions and business units.

Acknowledgements

An earlier version of this paper was presented at the first ISPIM Americas Innovation Forum in Montreal, Canada, on October 5–8, 2014. The International Society for Professional Innovation Management (ISPIM; ispim.org) is a network of researchers, industrialists, consultants, and public bodies who share an interest in innovation management.

About the Author

Jens-Uwe Meyer is Managing Director of Innolytics GmbH, a German consulting company that specializes in analyzing the innovation capacities and cultures of companies. He is author of eight books and numerous articles on the subject of innovation, and he is tutor for the Master's of Management and Innovation program at the Steinbeis SMI Berlin. He holds a doctorate degree in Business Sciences from the HHL Leipzig Graduate School of Management, and he holds an MBA from Steinbeis University in Berlin. In his dissertation, he focused on the topic of enhancing innovation capacity within corporations by establishing different cultures of innovation and reducing innovation barriers.

References

Ahmed, P. K. 1998. Culture and Climate for Innovation. *European Journal of Innovation Management*, 1(1): 30–42.
http://dx.doi.org/10.1108/14601069810199131

Amabile, T. M. 1996. *Creativity and Innovation in Organizations (Note: 9-396-239)*. Boston: Harvard Business School Publications.

Amabile, T. M. 1998. How To Kill Creativity. *Harvard Business Review*, 76(5): 77–87.

Amabile, T. M., Conti, R. Coon, H. Lazenby, J., & Herron, M. 1996. Assessing the Work Environment for Creativity. *Academy of Management Journal*, 39(5): 1154–1184.
http://dx.doi.org/10.2307/256995

Anderson, N. R., & West, M. A. 1998. Measuring Climate for Work Group Innovation: Development and Validation of the Team Climate Inventory. *Journal of Organizational Behavior*, 19(3): 235–258.
http://dx.doi.org/10.1002/(SICI)1099-1379(199805)19:3<235::AID-JOB837>3.0.CO;2-C

Barron, F., & Harrington, D. M. 1981. Creativity, Intelligence and Personality. *Annual Review of Psychology*, 32: 439–476.
http://dx.doi.org/10.1146/annurev.ps.32.020181.002255

Basadur, M. 1987. Needed Research in Creativity for Business and Industry Applications. In S. G. Isaksen (Ed.), *Frontiers of Creativity Research: Beyond the Basics*. Buffalo, NY: Bearly Ltd.

Benner, M. J., & Tushman, M. 2002. Process Management and Technological Innovation: A Longitudinal Study of the Photography and Paint Industries. *Administrative Science Quarterly*, 47(4): 676–706.
http://dx.doi.org/10.2307/3094913

Buzan, T. 2001. *The Power of Creative Intelligence*. London: Thorsons.

Cabra, J. F., Talbot, R. J. , & Joniak, A. J.. 2005. Exploratory Study of Creative Climate: A Case From Selected Colombian Companies and its Implication on Organizational Development. *Cuadernos di Administración*, 18(29): 53–86.

Carr-Ruffino, N. 2001. *Building Innovative Skills: The Creative Intelligence Model.* Boston: Pearson Custom Publishing.

Cooper, R. G., & Kleinschmidt, E. J. 1996. Winning Business in Product Development: The Critical Success Factors. *Research-Technology Management,* 39(4) 18–29.

Cooper, R. J., & Kleinschmidt, E. J.. 2001. *Stage-Gate Process for New Product Success.* Brøndby, Denmark: Innovation Management U3.

Cooper, R. G. 1986. *Winning at New Products.* Boston: Addison-Wesley.

Cooper, R. G. 1988. The New Product Process: A Decision Guide for Management. *Journal of Product Innovation Management,* 3(3): 238–255.
http://dx.doi.org/10.1080/0267257X.1988.9964044

Cooper, R. G. 1994. Perspective Third-Generation New Product Processes. *Journal of Product Innovation Management,* 11(1): 3–14.
http://dx.doi.org/10.1016/0737-6782(94)90115-5

Cooper, R. G. 2014. What's Next?: After Stage-Gate. *Research-Technology Management,* 57(1): 20–31.
http://dx.doi.org/10.5437/08956308X5606963

Csikszentmihalyi, M. A. 2006. Systems Perspective on Creativity. In J. Henry (Ed.), *Creative Management and Development:* 313-335. London: Sage Publications.

Dewey, J., Kallen, H. M., Tufts, J. H., Moore, A. W., Brown, H. C., Mead, G. H., Bode, B. H., & Stuart, H. W. 2011. *Creative Intelligence.* Calgary, AB: Teophania Publishing.

Dobni, C. 2008. Measuring Innovation Cultures in Organizations: The Development of a Generalized Innovation Culture Construct Using Exploratory Factor Analysis. *European Journal of Innovation Management,* 11(4): 539–559.
http://dx.doi.org/10.1108/14601060810911156

Drucker, P. F. 1985. The Discipline of Innovation. *Harvard Business Review,* 63(3): 67–72.

Ekvall, G., & Tångeberg-Andersson, Y. 1986. Working Climate and Creativity. A Study of an Innovative Newspaper Office. *Journal of Creative Behavior,* 20(3) 215–225.
http://dx.doi.org/10.1002/j.2162-6057.1986.tb00438.x

Ekvall, G. 1996. Organizational Climate for Creativity and Innovation. *European Journal of Work and Organizational Psychology,* (5)1: 105–123.
http://dx.doi.org/10.1080/13594329608414845

Ekvall, G. 2006. Organizational Conditions and Levels of Creativity. In J. Henry (Ed.), *Creative Management and Development:* 195-205. London: Sage Publications.

Farson, R., & Keyes, R. 2002. The Failure Tolerant Leader. *Harvard Business Review,* 80(8): 95–104.

Feist, G. J. 2010. The Function of Personality in Creativity. In J. Kaufman & R. J. Sternberg (Eds.), *The Cambridge Handbook of Creativity:* 113–130. New York: Cambridge University Press.

Hill, A., Tan, A., & Kikichi, A. 2008. International High School Students' Perceived Creativity Self-Efficacy. *Korean Journal of Thinking and Problem Solving,* 18(1): 105–115.

Högman, U., & Johannesson, H. 2013. Applying Stage Gate Processes to Technology Development – Experience From Six Hardware-Oriented Companies. *Journal of Engineering and Technology Management,* 30(3): 264–287.
http://dx.doi.org/10.1016/j.jengtecman.2013.05.002

Junarsin, E. 2009. Managing Discontinuous Innovation. *International Management Review,* 2(5): 10–18.

Kaufman, J. C., & Sternberg, R. J. 2006. The International Handbook of Creativity. New York: Cambridge University Press.

Khandwalla, P. N., & Mehta, K. 2004. Designs of Corporate Creativity. *Vikalpa,* 29(1): 13–28.

Kirton, M. J. 1989. A Theory of Cognitive Style. In M. Kirton (Ed.), *Adaptors and Innovators: Styles of Creativity and Problem Solving:* 1–33. New York: Routledge.

Kozbelt, A. 2008. Gombrich, Galenson, and Beyond: Integrating Case Study and Typological Frameworks in the Study of Creative Individuals. *Empirical Studies of the Arts,* 26(1): 51–68.
http://dx.doi.org/10.2190/EM.26.1.e

Kozbelt, A., Beghetto, R. A., & Runco, M. A. 2010. Theories of Creativity. In J. Kaufman & R. J. Sternberg (Eds.), *The Cambridge Handbook of Creativity:* 20–47. New York: Cambridge University Press.

Kromrey, H. 2002. *Empirische Sozialforschung. Modelle und Methoden der Datenerhebung und Datenauswertung.* 10. Aufl. Stuttgart, Berlin, Köln: UTB.

Leifer, R., McDermott, C. M., O'Connor, G. C., Peters, L. S., Rice, M., & Veryzer, Jr., R. W. 2000. *Radical Innovation: How Mature Companies Can Outsmart Startups.* Boston: Harvard Business School Press Books.

Lin, C. Y.-Y., & Liu, F.-C. 2012. A Cross-Level Analysis of Organizational Creativity Climate and Perceived Innovation: The Mediating Effect of Work Motivation. *European Journal of Innovation Management,* 15(1): 55–76.
http://dx.doi.org/10.1108/14601061211192834

Martins, E. C., & Terblanche, F. 2003. Building Organizational Culture That Stimulates Creativity and Innovation. *European Journal of Innovation Management,* 6(1): 64–74.
http://dx.doi.org/10.1108/14601060310456337

Martinsen, Ø. 1995. Cognitive Styles and Experience in Solving Insight Problems: Replication and Extension. *Creativity Research Journal,* 8(3): 291–298.
http://dx.doi.org/10.1207/s15326934crj0803_8

Moosbrugger, H., & Kelava, A. 2012. *Testtheorie und Fragebogenkonstruktion.* Berlin: Springer.

Moosbrugger, H., & Schermelleh-Engel, K. 2012. Exploratorische EFA und Konfirmatorische Faktorenanalyse CFA. In H. Moosbrugger & A. Kelava (Eds.), *Testtheorie und Fragebogenkonstruktion.* Berlin: Springer.

Naranjo, J., Valle, R. S., & Jiménez, D. J. 2010. Organizational Culture as Determinant of Product Innovation. *European Journal of Innovation Management,* 13(4): 466–480.
http://dx.doi.org/10.1108/14601061011086294

Noack, M. 2007. *Faktorenanalyse.* Institut für Soziologie, Universität Duisburg-Essen.

Prabhu, V., Sutton, C., & Sauer, W. 2008. Creativity and Certain Personality Traits: Understanding the Mediating Effect of Intrinsic Motivation. *Creativity Research Journal,* 20(1): 53–66.
http://dx.doi.org/10.1080/10400410701841955

Puccio, G. J., & Cabra, J. F. 2010. Organizational Creativity – A Systems Approach. In J. Kaufman & R. J. Sternberg (Eds.), *The Cambridge Handbook of Creativity:* 145–173. New York: Cambridge University Press.

Rammer, C., Aschhoff, B., Crass, D., Doherr, T., Hud, M., & Köhler, C., Peters., B., Schubert, T, & Schwiebacher, F. 2011. *Indikatorenbericht zur Innovationserhebung 2011,* Zentrum für Europäische Wirtschaftsförderung im Auftrag des Bundesministerium für Bildung und Forschung.

Rickards, T., & Bessant, J. 1980. The Creativity Audit: Introduction of a New Research Measure During Programmes for Facilitating Organizational Change. *R&D Management,* 10(2): 67–75. http://dx.doi.org/10.1111/j.1467-9310.1980.tb00014.x

Rickards, T. 1996. The Management of Innovation: Recasting the Role of Creativity. *European Journal of Work and Organizational Psychology,* 5(1): 13–27. http://dx.doi.org/10.1080/13594329608414835

Robinson, A. G., & Stern, S. 1997. *Corporate Creativity – How Innovation And Improvement Actually Happens.* San Francisco: Berrett-Koehler Publishers.

Roth, G. 2001. *Fühlen, Denken, Handeln. Wie das Gehirn unser Verhalten steuert.* Frankfurt: Suhrkamp.

Runco, M. A., & Albert, R. S. 2010. Creativity Research: A Historical View. In J. Kaufman & R. J. Sternberg (Eds.), *The Cambridge Handbook of Creativity:* 3–19. New York: Cambridge University Press.

Siegel, S. M., & Kaemmerer, W. F. 1978. Measuring the Perceived Support for Innovation in Organizations. *Journal of Applied Psychology,* 63(5): 553–562. http://psycnet.apa.org/doi/10.1037/0021-9010.63.5.553

Soriano Alencar, E. M. L. de, & Bruno-Faria, M. D. F. 1997. Characteristics of an Organizational Environment Which Stimulates and Inhibits Creativity. *Journal of Creative Behavior,* 31(4): 271–281. http://dx.doi.org/10.1002/j.2162-6057.1997.tb00799.x

Sternberg, R. J. 1996. *Successful Intelligence: How Practical and Creative Intelligence Determine Success in Life.* New York: Simon and Schuster.

Tushman, M. L., & O'Reilly III, C. A. 1996. Ambidextrous Organizations: Managing Evolutionary and Revolutionary Change. *California Management Review,* 38(4): 8–30. http://www.jstor.org/stable/41165852

Unsworth, K. L., & Clegg, C. W. 2010. Why Do Employees Undertake Creative Action? *Journal of Occupational and Organizational Psychology,* 83(1): 77–99. http://dx.doi.org/10.1348/096317908X398377

Van Gundy, A. Organizational Creativity and Innovation. 1987. In S. G. Isaksen (Ed.), *Frontiers of Creativity Research: Beyond the Basics:* 358–379. Buffalo, NY: Bearly Ltd.

von Stamm, B. 2005. *Managing Innovation, Design and Creativity.* Hoboken, NJ: John Wiley and Sons.

Woodman, R. W., Sawyer, J. E., & Griffin, R. W. 1993. Towards a Theory of Organizational Creativity. *Academy of Management Review,* 18(2): 293–321. http://dx.doi.org/10.5465/AMR.1993.3997517

Zhou, J., & Shalley, C. E. 2008. *Handbook of Organizational Creativity.* New York: Lawrence Erlbaum Associates.

Keywords: innovation management; innovativeness; innovation culture; innovation capacities; organizational creativity, corporate creativity

21

Widening the Perspective on Industrial Innovation: A Service-Dominant-Logic Approach

Heidi M. E. Korhonen

❝ Any existing structures and all the conditions of doing ❞
business are always in a process of change.

Joseph Schumpeter (1883–1950)
Economist and political scientist

The servitization of industry has progressed from services as add-ons to services as solutions. Today, industrial innovation needs an even broader perspective that moves towards service-dominant logic. This logic emphasizes value co-creation in actor-to-actor networks and requires new organizational structures and practices in industry. The article presents the case of a Nordic manufacturer of arc welding equipment that has gone through an extensive development program to become more customer and service oriented. An innovative offering created during the program is analyzed as an example in order to gain deeper insight about the concrete application of service-dominant logic in business. In addition to the outcome perspective, the article discusses the implications of the service-dominant logic for innovation practices. The article illustrates the behaviour of cutting-edge servitizing manufacturers and argues that similar behaviour can be expected to become a necessity in all industrial companies with large structural changes.

Introduction

There is a constant need for manufacturing to renew itself due to competition. Today, renewals are driven in particular by intangible assets such as human capital, intellectual capacity, and service provision. Since the end of the 1980s, manufacturing companies have added services to their offerings in order to create closer and more long-lasting relationships with their clients. However, it has been common to implement this practice – called "servitization" (Vandermerwe & Rada, 1988; Neely, 2008; Baines et al., 2009) – in a way that has not changed the basic view of the primary role of the provider in the emergence of value. Value has still been seen as something created in production and then delivered to clients (Michel et al., 2008). It was not until Vargo and Lusch (2004, 2008) presented their argument about the necessity of a new service-dominant logic that the central position of customers in value creation began to gain ground. According to service-dominant logic, this position is based on the fact that value is revealed only when goods and services are used and when

an individual good or service acquired from a single provider is linked to other goods and services acquired from other providers. The last mentioned process of resource integration is an indispensable part of value creation and is carried out by the user as well as the provider. Consequently, value is always co-created: the provider has to make its best effort to facilitate the emergence of value via purposeful goods and services, but the realization of value takes place in the use context.

Service-dominant logic links the value logic to the production of both goods and services. It considers the reciprocal nature of value creation a more crucial phenomenon than the production outputs in the form of individual goods and services. According to Vargo and Lusch (2004), goods and services are important, but value is not their inherent property; they are first and foremost conveyors of competences for the benefit of another party. Other authors, analyzing the implications of service-dominant logic from managerial viewpoints, have pointed out that this view should not lead to diminishing the importance of goods and services –

they do not go away. Rather, they must be designed around co-creation of human experiences through multi-sided interactions (Ramaswamy, 2009, 2011). In the service context, the formulation of value propositions is of particular importance because they are the entities based on which customers make purchasing decisions (Maglio & Spohrer, 2013). Finding a way to link the views of service-dominant logic with the concrete production outputs is essential for the current development in the servitization of manufacturing.

Although most innovation research has focused on product and process innovations, present discussion calls for a broader notion of innovation (Tidd et al., 2001). This discussion returns back to the definition of innovation by Schumpeter (1934), who laid the ground for studying innovation as a socioeconomic evolutionary process resulting in new combinations of resources. His categorization of innovations is wide and enables the analysis of renewals at different levels: products and methods of production; sources of supply and exploitation of new markets; and methods of organizing business. The service-dominant-logic view on innovation – based on value co-creation practices – has much in common with the Schumpeterian views. In addition to products and services, which manifest value co-creation practices, service-dominant logic advises firms to focus on the overall value-proposition design. This approach can be seen as a systematic search for business model innovation from the provider's perspective (Maglio & Spohrer, 2013).

This article studies: i) how the view of value as co-created can be applied to widen the perspective on industrial innovation and ii) what are the implications of this widening for the development of innovation practice. The study has been carried out as a single-case study of a Nordic welding equipment manufacturer that has gone through an extensive development program to increase its innovative capability in a more customer- and service-oriented direction. The program has led to the development of several offerings that represent a novel type of industrial service business.

To understand the current development in industrial innovation in detail, we will analyze the development of one specific offering in our case company. We will use this example to illustrate the relationships between industrial service innovations as add-ons, solutions-based innovations, and innovations based on service-dominant logic. We will then discuss innovation practices for systematically and efficiently producing innovations consonant with the view of value as co-created.

This article is structured as follows. We first explain the background and theory to better understand innovation as a co-development process and as novel outcomes and practices. We then describe our methodology and case selection. After this, we analyze the new innovative solution and discuss the innovation practices used in its creation. We finish our article by discussing the managerial implications of widening the perspective on industrial innovations.

Innovation in the Light of Service-Dominant Logic

In the history of manufacturing, innovation was seen primarily as a matter of technological development, and services were regarded as an unavoidable expense. The current synthesis approach suggests that service innovation brings neglected aspects of innovation to the fore (Coombs & Miles, 2000). Service-dominant logic is consistent with the synthesis approach, but it brings novel understanding to the discussion. It can be understood either as an innovation theory or as an approach for leveraging other discussions on innovation. In this article, we take the former viewpoint and point out its implications for the practice of innovation management.

Industrial companies often start servitization by developing services to support products (Oliva & Kallenberg, 2003). However, when their service business matures, they no more consider services as mere add-ons to products, but innovate services supporting customers (Mathieu, 2001). Customer centricity has often led to providing solutions, in other words, individualized and interactively designed offers for complex customer problems (c.f. Evanschitzky et al., 2011). In solutions, products and services are integrated and the relationship between the buyer and the seller is close. Instead of the traditional approach of managing services as a separate function, manufacturers may turn their entire business to service logic (Grönroos & Helle, 2010). The involvement of customers may take place both in the innovation process and in the joint creation of value.

Despite the change, servitization alone does not seem to represent a panacea for manufacturers (Baines et al., 2009). The service-dominant-logic approach includes the ideas of the synthesis perspective and solution business, but it widens the scope of the discussion. In particular, service-dominant logic broadens the view from a provider–customer dyad to a broader system of actors (Vargo & Lusch, 2011) – an approach that has been rare in service innovation research (Carlborg et al., 2013).

Also, in addition to operand resources that require action taken upon them to be valuable, service-dominant logic stresses the primacy of knowledge and technology because they are capable of acting on other resources to contribute to value creation (Vargo & Lusch, 2004). Further, service-dominant logic emphasizes the role of institutions – social rules and norms that both constrain and enable behavior – as resources that are needed for actors to co-create value. Markets can be seen as institutionalized solutions of resource application to human problems or needs. The way in which novelties become stabilized (i.e., institutionalized) in the markets is one of the most interesting issues in innovation according to service-dominant logic. Here, the view is very similar to the current emphasis of general innovation research on the diffusion (not only invention) of innovations.

These new insights are in line with innovation studies that highlight innovation as processes and practices (Gallouj, 2002; Lundvall, 2007). Innovation can be seen as a path dependent co-development process, and its outcomes include the adoption of new practices. We now use the service-dominant-logic theory in order to better understand the wide perspective on innovation from these points of view.

Innovation as a co-development process
Service-dominant logic emphasizes social institutions and therefore encourages the study of practices – "embodied, materially mediated arrays of human activity centrally organized around shared practical understanding" (Schatzki, 2005). Value co-creation takes place through the enactment of practices in systems at micro, meso, and macro levels (Akaka et al., 2013). These practices and systems cannot be created from nothing, but are recreated by integrating existing resources in novel ways. As Arthur (2009) puts it, novel technologies arise from existing technologies. In order to better understand the wide concept of innovation, technology should be understood in a broad way, as an operant resource and "as a set of practices and processes, as well as symbols, that contribute to value creation or fulfill a human need" (Akaka & Vargo, 2013). The most enduring and prevalent practices can be referred to as institutions (Giddens, 1984).

Value propositions are made about new practices for value co-creation, but it is in the use phase when the practices are enacted and come to being. Therefore, the resource integration for innovation occurs through both value proposition and value determination phases (Akaka & Vargo, 2013). There are parallels between value proposition and determination in service-dominant-logic theory and invention and innovation adoption in general innovation-diffusion theory (c.f. Rogers, 2003). Service-dominant logic strives to incorporate the issues of contextual value and multiple actors to the phenomenon. In most cases of industrial innovation, both the value proposition and determination involve multiple stakeholders instead of just one and are affected by the institutional landscape.

As has been described above, innovation is not a one-directional development activity by any single actor. Instead, it is co-development between the different actors of the service system. Innovation is a path-dependent and recursive process. It can be understood as mutual learning between actors and as the emergence of corresponding value co-creation systems, again implying that social capital matters – it has an important impact on a company' innovative capability.

In service-dominant logic, one of the most important operant resources is entrepreneurial spirit (Vargo & Lusch, 2006) – the mental capabilities for resource integration characteristic of entrepreneurs. Based on this, and in line with Schumpeter (1934), we accentuate that anyone can act entrepreneurially and stress its meaning for innovation. Innovative activity can be characterized as an actor's entrepreneurial search for new beneficial configurations for resource integration that emphasizes operant resources. Entrepreneurs search for change, respond to it, and exploit it as an opportunity (Drucker, 1964). This process of search and experimentation always involves uncertainty. Therefore, instead of trying to predict uncertain markets, experienced entrepreneurs co-develop novel markets with committed stakeholders (Read et al., 2009).

All humans participate in value co-creation through the repeated reproduction of institutionalized practices in their daily activities whether or not they do it entrepreneurially. The activity of co-development differs from this activity of co-creation. Co-development is proactive search for new actors, resources and configurations, making new kinds of value propositions and reciprocally assessing other actors' novel value propositions. It is a purposive activity aimed at transforming the structure of value co-creation in interaction with others. Actors can appreciate co-development either instrumentally through the appreciation of its aims or intrinsically through the appreciation of participating in the social interaction per se.

Innovations as novel outcomes

Scholars that study service-dominant logic are cautious when it comes to discussing innovation outcomes because such an approach easily leads to goods-dominant logic. Yet, goods and services, and activities and processes, still remain (Ramaswamy, 2011). Also, it is the resulting impact that determines whether innovation makes us better off or not. Therefore innovation as resulting novel practices and their concrete manifestations as, for example, products and services should not be ignored.

Edvardsson and Tronvoll (2013) see the results of innovation as new practices. They emphasize structuration (Giddens, 1984) and view innovation in service-dominant logic as changes in social structure that allows actors to co-create value. These changes stem from new configurations of resources or new knowledge of shared rules and norms. We agree with this view and characterize innovative outcomes as new value co-creation practices embedded in social structure. The new practices can either enable customers to attain something or relieve customers from something (Michel et al., 2008). They can address different benefits and even different level benefits than the old practices. The benefits may vary for different stakeholders. New levels of value are addressed, for example, when focus is shifted from efficiency to effectiveness or when the experiential and meaning-laden nature of value is emphasized. Service-dominant logic also stresses that operant resources such as skills and knowledge can be embedded in the offering with the purpose of making customers smarter.

The novel practices are often crystallized in concrete entities such as products, services, or technologies. Humans make observations through their physical senses, and they depend on their bodies as a means to act and participate in any social interaction. They have a limited view of the actions of others and of the consequences of their own actions and the actions of the actor-to-actor network as a whole. Products, services, and technologies are resources that aid humans by extending their senses and capability to act. They always have some physical manifestation that works as a medium enabling the human-to-human interaction for value co-creation. However, only an experience can be appreciated as an end itself (Holbrook, 1999). Therefore, value is not an inherent property of products, services, or technologies. Instead, they are manifestations and enablers of practices: configurations of resource integration that can be further integrated for enhancing value co-creation in social interaction.

All the forms of innovation originally proposed by Schumpeter (1934) can be considered to be *novel value co-creation practices*. Therefore, service-dominant logic as an innovation theory is wide enough to include all innovations, including new markets and reorganization of industries as well as new products and services.

Methodology and Case Company

Service-dominant logic is young as an innovation theory, and there is a clear need for more practically relevant knowledge about its implications for innovation management. In particular, we want to illustrate how it widens the perspective on industrial innovation and what effect this widening has for the innovation practice in industry. A case study is a suitable methodology for us because it fits especially well with answering "how" or "why" types of questions (Yin, 1994).

We first use our empirical case study to illustrate and concretize how to further widen the abstract idea of an innovation. We analyze the sample offering using service-dominant-logic theory to clarify the resulting innovations as novel value co-creation practices. Then, we further discuss the innovation practices used in creating this type of innovation.

Our case company is a Nordic manufacturer of arc welding equipment and a provider of solutions for highly productive welding. It has gone through an extensive development program to increase its innovative capability and to turn from an equipment company to a more customer- and service-oriented direction. It is an entrepreneurial and innovative company serving the high-end market. It has own offices in 15 countries and a strong dealer network with export to 80 countries. It has about 650 employees and its global revenue totals 120 million euros a year.

The company has developed services previously. We assess the company's earlier level of servitization as mainly a supplier of machines and add-on services, with some solutions for specific uses or user groups. During the development program, the company took clear steps to a more mature solutions-provider phase. These steps include development of customer centricity, incorporation of customers' voice, and the development of a wide range of new integrated product and service offerings focused on supporting customers' value creation processes. Service logic now better encompasses the entire company and proper attention has also been given to customer relationship management. In addition to these qualities of a solutions provider, the company has been able to develop certain level of preparedness and capabilities necessary for a company that wants to apply service-dominant logic in its innovation efforts.

Data collection

Our empirical data was collected from the company's extensive development program taking place during 2011-2013. The author, together with a larger research group, has been involved in the program since its beginning. Case data has been collected from various sources, including meeting notes, slide presentations, memos, process descriptions, conceptual descriptions, web pages, and observations. Every half a year, the author together with colleagues has written a thorough report about the progress of the development program, utilizing detailed material. These reports have also been used as data for study. In addition to the data collected as part of the development program, three company representatives in high management positions and two customer representatives were interviewed. The author has had a dual role in the process. The research group – including scholars in innovation management, service-dominant-logic and strategic renewal – has brought its expertise to the development program together with several other expert groups, and affected the change in the company's business and innovation practices.

Case Findings

In our theoretical discussion, we ended up with a view of innovations as novel value co-creation practices embedded in social structure. They come into being as customers and other relevant actors accept value propositions and enact them. In order to better understand industrial service innovations from this perspective, we now analyze a new offering created by the case company and then discuss our empirical findings on innovation management.

Analysis of a systemic industrial service offering

We find the offering an enabler of new value co-creation practices and summarize the main points of this analysis in Figure 1. The offering is a system for managing quality and productivity of welding work. It links together different modules or sub-offerings that fit together and can be used either together or separately. The modules are complementary, having the potential to become more valuable as more modules and actors are integrated together. The offering includes physical products such as welding machines and barcode readers, and services such as consultation and training, but it is best understood as a systemic, multi-actor value-proposition design capable of assisting customers in their value creation by making them "smarter" through the smart knowledge and connections it contains.

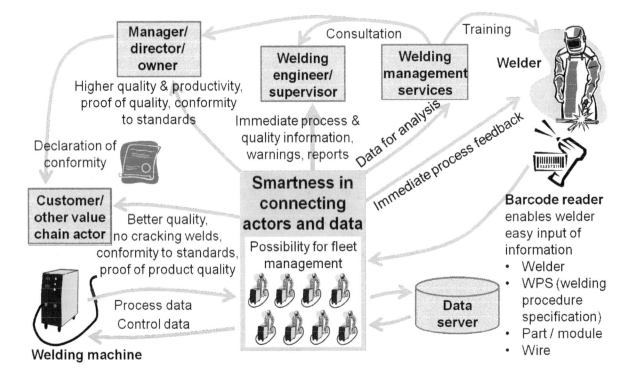

Figure 1. A systemic offering as an enabler of new value co-creation practices

We now discuss this value proposition by starting from the lower left corner of Figure 1 and moving counter-clockwise. We then further discuss institutions and other aspects of the offering not visible in the figure.

Welding machines are a basic product offering of the case company. They are physical manifestations of resource integration practices carried out by the case company. Customers integrate welding machines as resources in their own welding processes. However, value creation in welding work relies heavily on welders' competence and their compliance with welding procedure specifications. Welded joints are often safety critical, yet their metallurgic microstructures cannot be properly studied with non-destructive testing methods.

As a major benefit compared to welding machines alone, the systemic offering can be used to collect all welding data and to monitor compliance with welding procedure specifications for quality control. Because process data is collected and stored in *a data server*, it can be integrated with other information for quality and productivity improvements. An essential enabler of novel practices is *a barcode reader*. It allows *the welder* to easily input important quality parameters into the system. Due to the barcode technology, it is easy for the welder to adopt the new quality-control practices. The system also gives the welder immediate process feedback about their own work.

The data can also be used as a resource for the case company's *welding management services* production, such as training and consultation. The data and the different reports and services are also an important resource for *the welding supervisor* as the system facilitates and automates production management. At the company level, *the owner* benefits through better quality and improved productivity, which lead to reduced costs and higher throughput. For the company, it is also very important that welding quality and conformation to welding procedure specifications can be verified. Quality problems of safety-critical welded parts can cause substantial liabilities. *Customers* of the welding shop can further utilize the declaration of conformity while doing business with final customers. Welded parts and their quality can be tracked throughout the production chain. Naturally, customers also benefit directly through better quality and the resulting safety for people and their value creation processes.

The offering allows for new practices of fleet management on the shop floor, and even globally. It connects together different data resources and actor resources, which enables smart value co-creation practices in a networked business environment. Therefore, it is a systemic value proposition design.

The system draws on many institutionalized practices of welding industry as resources, including arc welding technology and the use of welding procedure specifications. It also utilizes the institutionalized practices of information technology such as barcodes. The servitization of industry is also an important norm and a resource for welding management services.

An especially important institutional change in the welding industry is the rapid spread of quality management practices as an industry norm. Welded seams are safety critical and there is a global trend of emphasis on safety issues. Accidents such as the Gulf of Mexico oil spill have had a major effect on the required safety precautions in many industries and especially in the offshore industry. Europe is adopting new quality standards for welding. CE marking will be required for all steel and aluminum structures sold within the European Economic Area. The offering facilitates conformity to the new standards. The institutional norm for quality management is further intensified by urbanization and the rapid growth of the Chinese market. Due to the high demand, there is a global shortage of well-trained welders. The quality management tools help welding companies to cope with the high demand when there is a shortage of personnel.

Institutional inertia often makes it difficult to induce changes in practices of systemic value co-creation. However, institutions not only constrain behaviour – they also enable it. The offering under study has been designed to meet the demand created by a major change in the institutional landscape of the welding industry. It does not try to fight major institutions, instead it utilizes them. For example, one of the first customers adopted this innovation in order to take proactive development steps, improve operations, and be well prepared for CE marking. Also, many of its large customers required operation almost at the level of the CE marking.

The offering can be viewed as designed around human value co-creation. Products, services, and technologies are an indispensable part of the design as enablers of human-to-human interaction. In this case, the main enabler of higher value creation is information technology that makes actions of the welder as well as functioning of the welding machine visible for other stakeholders across time and space. The offering embeds smart technology that helps each stakeholder utilize this knowledge and act smarter in his role.

As an important difference to the typically dyadic value propositions of solutions business, the novel offering represents a multi-stakeholder value proposition for welders, welding engineers, managers, customers of the welding shop, and the provider of welding management services. The offering supports the interactive value co-creation between the different stakeholders at least as much as it directly supports the value creation of each individual stakeholder.

As the stakeholders accept the value proposition and adopt the new value co-creation practices, an innovation emerges. The innovation is not the offering per se, but the enactment of new practices by the different stakeholders. The offering is an enabler. The new products and services are critical enabling components that need to be created before the innovation as novel practices can take place. However, products, services and technologies as such are not sufficient development targets. Development efforts need to be aimed at systemic value co-creation.

The example represents a gradual shift towards service-dominant logic. The offering differs from typical solutions offerings and resembles a service-dominant-logic offering due to its value proposition that supports joint value co-creation of multiple stakeholders and due to the way it utilizes the systemic market dynamics created by the wider institutional change. It also leverages knowledge and technology the way that is stressed by service-dominant logic.

The analysis of the offering illustrated how the adoption of service-dominant logic widens the perspective on innovation. We will now discuss the innovation practice used in its creation. Our elaboration on it is brief because, as a dynamic capability, it is a sensitive issue.

Understanding context and searching for win-win-win
A view of systemic complementarity between multiple actors instead of a provider-customer view becomes obvious in the offering example presented above. The search for such win-win-win is a complex and uncertain task for which theory suggests an entrepreneurial approach. For this search, the company has developed shared organizational capability for understanding customers and proactively utilizing this understanding for new offering development, as the following quotation from a senior manager at the start of the program tells us:

> *"It is not enough to know customers' present needs... Customer satisfaction surveys tell us about past*

and present... we need to go further in thinking and develop a proactive approach."

A consultative sales model is an important entrepreneurial element of the innovation process that was developed. Sales people learn about customers' different contexts and proactively widen the discussion on possible sources of value in their search for mutually beneficial solutions with customers. They need to have a certain level of consulting capability in order to sell the smart offerings and consulting services. It is not easy for all seasoned sales people to learn the new approach. However, sharing success stories helps sales people learn from each other's experiences and widen their minds to new creative value propositions. Special attention has been given to ensuring that all sales people have proper skills in consultative sales and on developing tools for learning the new skills.

When developing multiple-actor value systems, insight needs to be gained about stakeholders in multiple roles and how they experience value creation and value destruction. In our case these multiple roles include welder, welding engineer, owner, service provider, dealer, and the customer of the welding company. All these actors each have their individual context that has an influence on their service experience. A very important part of this context is the everyday practices of these actors. For example, the case company uses an ethnographic approach that is suitable for studying the everyday practices, contexts, and experiences of the different actors. Also, other methods such as questionnaires are used and integrated into the critical process points of the research, development, and innovation process. The front office is used for searching weak signals. The case company has also organized its innovation process so that it can create a very extensive and deep understanding of its customers on multiple levels, for example, an understanding of customer's people, customer's business, the tools used, and the context.

Co-developing value co-creation systems
Firms depend on their relationships with their external environment for innovation. This dependency emphasizes the importance of social capital and long-term relationships with other innovative agents. The case company has built extensive external networks and long-term relationships to support its innovation activity. It has carefully chosen strategic research partners to collaborate with and to tap into important information sources. As an example, the development program involved a multitude of research organizations and companies to provide rich expert knowledge.

The offering enables a change in the value co-creation system. From the provider's view, it can also be seen as a business model innovation. The idea is expressed in the following quotation from a senior manager discussing markets in different cultures:

> *"It is not the machines and their use, instead it comes more from business models and the whole system – how you offer support and how you do pricing. The machines are not that radically different and it accentuates contextual circumstances – the whole business model and how you approach through different channels – how the business runs."*

Technology, products, and services are not developed for their own sake; instead, they are developed to fill critical gaps so that value propositions can be made that fit the social context. In order to do this, the development program joined together technology development, business development, customer research, and organizational development. This approach proved to be a very successful research and development concept.

Conclusion

The servitization of industry has advanced from services as add-ons to services as solutions. The next logical step for industry is to widen its perspective on innovation based on the view of value as being co-created. It is a systemic and human-centered view that sees innovations as new practices in social interaction. First, this approach will be adopted by the advanced companies that want to be in the forefront of development. In the future, however, industry will face large structural changes, partly due to the positive forces of the knowledge society and new technologies such as the Internet of Things, robotics, and additive manufacturing – and partly due to more negative forces such as the coming shortage of resources and the need for a more sustainable economy. In the phase of large structural changes, a wider innovation concept that includes new market structures and the reorganization of industries is a necessity. Service-dominant logic can provide this wider innovation concept.

Companies that wish to adopt service-dominant logic in their innovation activities can start by aiming their innovation efforts at the development of new systemic value co-creation practices. New innovation capabilities are needed for creating a deep insight of multiple-stakeholder situations and an understanding of institutional forces. In addition to these new capabilities, practices of entrepreneurial search and co-development

need to be developed. Systemic change can be facilitated by identifying critical gaps of the system and developing technologies, products, and services to fill them. They are important enablers of human-to-human value co-creation and as such remain an integral part of innovation outcomes in service-dominant logic.

Acknowledgements

The author wishes to thank the case company's representatives, her dissertation advisor Professor Marja Toivonen, and her project companions Iiro Salkari and Tiina Apilo for participating in value co-creation. This article was written as part of the Finnish Metals and Engineering Competence Cluster's (FIMECC) Future Industrial Services program. It is based on a paper presented at the ISPIM 2013 Symposium.

About the Author

Heidi M. E. Korhonen is a professional in business development and research with a long experience of industrial and technology companies. She works as a Senior Scientist at VTT Technical Research Centre of Finland, in VTT's research area of business ecosystems, value chains, and foresight. She is also finishing her Doctoral Dissertation on industrial service innovation at Aalto University in Helsinki, Finland. Her research focus is on business development, innovation management, and value co-creation. Her current research interests cover service business, business ecosystems, business models, sustainability, open innovation, co-development, systems thinking, and customer and stakeholder orientation. She has published her research widely in international peer-reviewed journals, books, and conferences.

References

Akaka, M. A., & Vargo, S. L. 2013. Technology as an Operant Resource in Service (Eco)systems. *Information Systems and e-Business Management*, 1–18.
http://dx.doi.org/10.1007/s10257-013-0220-5

Akaka, M. A., Vargo, S. L., & Lusch, R. F. 2013. The Complexity of Context: A Service Ecosystems Approach for International Marketing. *Journal of International Marketing*, 21(4): 1–20.
http://dx.doi.org/10.1509/jim.13.0032

Arthur, W. B. 2009. *The Nature of Technology: What It Is and How It Evolves.* New York: Free Press.

Baines, T. S., Lightfoot, H. W., Benedettini, O., & Kay, J. M. 2009. The Servitization of Manufacturing: A Review of Literature and Reflection on Future Challenges. *Journal of Manufacturing Technology Management*, 20(5): 547–567. http://dx.doi.org/10.1108/17410380910960984

Carlborg, P., Kindström, D., & Kowalkowski, C. 2014. The Evolution of Service Innovation Research: A Critical Review and Synthesis. *The Service Industries Journal*, 34(5): 373–398. http://dx.doi.org/10.1080/02642069.2013.780044

Coombs, R., & Miles, I. 2000. Innovation, Measurement and Services: The New Problematique. In J. S. Metcalfe & I. Miles (Eds.), *Innovation Systems in the Service Economy:* 85–103. Boston, MA: Springer US.

Drucker, P. F. 1964. *Managing for Results.* New York, NY: HarperBusiness.

Edvardsson, B., & Tronvoll, B. 2013. A New Conceptualization of Service Innovation Grounded in S-D Logic and Service Systems. *International Journal of Quality and Service Sciences*, 5(1): 19–31. http://dx.doi.org/10.1108/17566691311316220

Evanschitzky, H., Wangenheim, F. V., & Woisetschläger, D. M. 2011. Service & Solution Innovation: Overview and Research Agenda. *Industrial Marketing Management*, 40(5): 657–660. http://dx.doi.org/10.1016/j.indmarman.2011.06.004

Gallouj, F. 2002. *Innovation in the Service Economy: The New Wealth of Nations.* Cheltenham, UK: Edward Elgar Pub.

Giddens, A. 1984. *The Constitution of Society: Outline of the Theory of Structuration.* Cambridge: Polity.

Grönroos, C., & Helle, P. 2010. Adopting a Service Logic in Manufacturing: Conceptual Foundation and Metrics for Mutual Value Creation. *Journal of Service Management*, 21(5): 564–590. http://dx.doi.org/10.1108/09564231011079057

Holbrook, M. 1999. *Consumer Value: A Framework for Analysis and Research.* London: Routledge.

Lundvall, B.-Å. 2007. Innovation System Research - Where It Came From and Where It Might Go. Globelics Working Paper Series, No. 2007-01.

Maglio, P. P., & Spohrer, J. 2013. A Service Science Perspective on Business Model Innovation. *Industrial Marketing Management*, 42(5): 665–670. http://dx.doi.org/10.1016/j.indmarman.2013.05.007

Mathieu, V. 2001. Product Services: From a Service Supporting the Product to a Service Supporting the Client. *Journal of Business & Industrial Marketing*, 16(1): 39–61. http://dx.doi.org/10.1108/08858620110364873

Michel, S., Brown, S. W., & Gallan, A. S. 2008. Service-Logic Innovations: How to Innovate Customers, Not Products. *California Management Review*, 50(3): 49–65. http://dx.doi.org/10.2307/41166445

Neely, A. 2008. Exploring the Financial Consequences of the Servitization of Manufacturing. *Operations Management Research*, 1(2): 103–118. http://dx.doi.org/10.1007/s12063-009-0015-5

Oliva, R., & Kallenberg, R. 2003. Managing the Transition from Products to Services. *International Journal of Service Industry Management*, 14(2): 160–172. http://dx.doi.org/10.1108/09564230310474138

Ramaswamy, V. 2009. Leading the Transformation to Co-Creation of Value. *Strategy & Leadership*, 37(2): 32–37. http://dx.doi.org/10.1108/10878570910941208

Ramaswamy, V. 2011. It's about Human Experiences... and Beyond, to Co-Creation. *Industrial Marketing Management*, 40(2): 195–196. http://dx.doi.org/10.1016/j.indmarman.2010.06.030

Read, S., Dew, N., Sarasvathy, S. D., Song, M., & Wiltbank, R. 2009. Marketing Under Uncertainty: The Logic of an Effectual Approach. *Journal of Marketing*, 73(3): 1–18. http://dx.doi.org/10.1509/jmkg.73.3.1

Rogers, E. M. 2003. *Diffusion of Innovations* (5th edition). New York: Free Press.

Schatzki. 2005. Introduction. In K. K. Cetina, T. R. Schatzki, & E. von Savigny (Eds.), *The Practice Turn in Contemporary Theory:* 50–63. London: Routledge.

Schumpeter, J. A. 1934. *The Theory of Economic Development: An Inquiry into Profits, Capital, Credit, Interest, and the Business Cycle.* New Brunswick, N.J: Transaction Publishers.

Tidd, J., Bessant, J., & Pavitt, K. 2001. *Managing Innovation: Integrating Technological, Market, and Organizational Change,* (Second Edition). Chichester, England: Wiley.

Vandermerwe, S., & Rada, J. 1988. Servitization of Business: Adding Value by Adding Services. *European Management Journal*, 6(4): 314–324. http://dx.doi.org/10.1016/0263-2373(88)90033-3

Vargo, S. L., & Lusch, R. F. 2004. Evolving to a New Dominant Logic for Marketing. *Journal of Marketing*, 68(1): 1–17. http://dx.doi.org/10.1509/jmkg.68.1.1.24036

Vargo, S. L., & Lusch, R. F. 2006. Service-Dominant Logic: What It Is, What It Is Not, What It Might Be. In R. F. Lusch & S. L. Vargo (Eds.), *The Service-Dominant Logic of Marketing: Dialog, Debate, and Directions:* 43–56. New York: M.E. Sharpe.

Vargo, S. L., & Lusch, R. F. 2008. Service-Dominant Logic: Continuing the Evolution. *Journal of the Academy of Marketing Science*, 36(1): 1–10. http://dx.doi.org/10.1007/s11747-007-0069-6

Vargo, S. L., & Lusch, R. F. 2011. It's All B2B...and Beyond: Toward a Systems Perspective of the Market. *Industrial Marketing Management*, 40(2): 181–187. http://dx.doi.org/10.1016/j.indmarman.2010.06.026

Yin, R. K. 1994. *Case Study Research: Design and Methods* (Second Edition). Thousand Oaks: SAGE Publications, Inc.

Keywords: systemic innovation, value co-creation, industrial service, practice, co-development

22

The Promoting Force of Technology for Service Innovation in High-Tech Industries

Silvia Gliem, Janny Klabuhn, and Nadine Litwin

" The advance of technology is based on making it fit in "
so that you don't really even notice it, so it's part of
everyday life.

Bill Gates
Former CEO and Chairman of Microsoft

This article focuses on the interaction between the development of technology and service innovation. It goes "back to the basics" by analyzing the first theoretical contributions to the service innovation literature from the late 1980s. These contributions were heavily technologically oriented: they aimed at bringing the results of technological innovation to the realm of services. More specifically, we focus on the model of "reverse innovation cycle" on one hand, and on the first innovation-specific categorization of services on the other. The latter introduced the division into supplier-dominated, production-intensive/scale-intensive, and science-based services. Our purpose is to examine in which ways these theoretical approaches could promote our understanding about the new phenomena of technology-service interaction in innovation. In the second part of the article, we apply these approaches in five case studies that originate from different service industries and that differ in size and technologies. The findings of the analysis demonstrate that the applicability of the approaches to the case studies depends on several factors including the kind of technology involved in the innovation activities, the stage of development of this technology, and the type of service.

Introduction

The field of service innovation has been acknowledged, amongst others, as an emerging field of research within service science, and it is considered to be autonomous from traditional innovation research conducted in the manufacturing industry (Hipp & Grupp, 2005; Miles, 2010; Toivonen & Tuominen, 2009). Nonetheless, the quantity and variety of contributions to the field of service innovation in comparison to traditional innovation research lag behind (Wang et al., 2010). Advances in understanding of service innovation would enable researchers and firms to design more appropriate and target-oriented service innovation processes (Rubalcaba et al., 2010). Vargo and Lusch (2004) went further by proposing a new perspective on service science in general. They argue that concepts of innovation research should not evolve from manufacturing indus-

tries. Instead, they emphasize the wide-ranging applicability of a service-centered perspective. For both a traditional and a service-centered perspective, there is no doubt that technology is one of the promoting forces that drive service innovation (Kandampully, 2002).

In this article, we depict the promoting force of technology towards service innovation in high-tech industries. Therefore, through this research, we ask: in what ways are service innovations driven by technology?

In answering these questions, the remainder of the article is structured as follows. First, we present two widely adopted and influential models of service innovation: i) the reverse innovation cycle model of Barras (1986a, 1986b) and ii) the typology of service innovation of Miozzo and Soete (2001). Next, we review literature that complements these two models. Then, for the purpose of evaluation, we map five case studies originating from the high-tech industry to the two models of service innovation. Finally, we discuss the managerial implications.

Barras' Reverse Innovation Cycle

Barras' model of the "reverse innovation cycle" has been generally regarded as the first actual theory on service innovation (Gallouj, 1998; Toivonen & Tuominen, 2009). Even though it is highly technologically biased, it has continuously aroused interest among those service researchers who have sought a strong linkage from service innovation to the general innovation theories. It is based on the "dynamic model of process and product innovation" by Utterback and Abernathy (1975), which shows the relationship between the forthcoming products of a firm from one product lifecycle stage to another and the adaption of a firms' innovative behaviour. The further a product proceeds in its lifecycle, the more likely it is that firms' focus on innovation activities shifts from product to process innovation. For service industries, Barras (1986a) predicts a reverse trajectory for this cycle, which is divided into three stages:

1. Firms adopt new technologies originating from a product innovation process and prove their spectrum of applicability. Mainly, their application results in incremental process innovations to increase efficiency and decrease costs.

2. Uncertainty concerning the adopted technology is eliminated. As a result, internal processes related to the application of the adopted technology are to be improved. Technology is still used for process innovations; however, in comparison to the first stage, the amount of incremental innovations declined, whereas radical process innovations aiming at quality improvement accumulate.

3. Product innovations are developed on the basis of the technology adopted in the first stage. If the development of product innovations is not done by firms themselves, it will be outsourced.

The reverse innovation cycle model of Barras was reviewed by several researchers (Gallouj, 1998; Tether & Howells, 2007; Uchupalanan, 2000) who raised four issues with the model, as described below.

First, the focus on technology as a single factor liable to influence service innovation is criticized (Gallouj, 1998). Other factors, such as experiences and knowledge accumulated during former innovation processes (Uchupalanan, 2000), were not taken into consideration. However, Barras includes these factors as drivers or restraints of the technology adoption process but not as influencing factors on service innovations (Barras, 1986a, 1990). Furthermore, by focusing on technology, Barras expels service innovations that do not contain technology, such as franchise systems.

Second, using Utterback and Abernathy's dynamic model of process and product innovation as a foundation, Barras adopted the differentiation between incremental and radical process innovation, and product innovation, which is considered problematic within the research community (Gallouj & Savona, 2009; Salter & Tether, 2014; Uchupalanan, 2000). Barras (1986a) addressed this problem and determined product innovations in services as "so different in nature and mode of delivery from more traditional forms of services that they can meaningfully be described as new service products." However, Barras only offers indications for determining whether a service innovation is a process or a product innovation (Gallouj, 1998). More precisely, Ettlie, Bridges, and O'Keefe (1984) state that "the strategy-structure causal sequence for radical innovation is markedly different from the strategy-structure sequence for incremental innovation." In other words, the extent to which an innovation makes organizational changes necessary, for example by the inclusion of customer learning, can be used as an indicator for the determination of the innovation type. This assertion is supported by Perks, Gruber, and Bo (2012), who characterize radical service innovations as powerful enough to cause fundamental changes in the structure, processes, and environment of an organization.

Third, focusing on information and communication technologies (ICT) as well as limiting the analysis to financial, business, and local government services creates doubts about the universal validity of the model (Tether & Howells, 2007).

Fourth, the reverse innovation cycle cannot be observed ex ante. Only if a service firm adopted a technology and went through all stages, can it be concluded (ex post) that the reverse innovation cycle was undergone. In addition, Barras (1990) himself acknowledged that the pace of technology adoption will vary between service industries, which makes analysis difficult. Further, the substitution of one technology by another and the outsourcing of research activities linked to the adopted technology will interrupt or stop an industry from undergoing the reverse innovation cycle (Gallouj,

1998). These assumptions are supported by Uchupalanan (2000) who found that the Barras' model is only one of many possible innovation trajectories.

Service innovations developed by firms outside the service sector are not encompassed by Barras' model. For these particular cases, Cusumano, Kahl and Suarez (2006) developed a model that builds upon Utterback and Abernathy's model by including a fourth stage, which displays the shift from process to service innovation. The role of technology for service innovation is not determined in this model. It can, but must not have an influence on service innovation because, apart from technology, service innovation can originate out of accumulated knowledge, for example, about the behaviour of customers.

The review of innovation cycle models showed that the influence of technology is manifold: technology can be seen as a requirement for developing service innovations. This requirement applies, for example, to firms in the manufacturing industry that offer maintenance or repair services for their products. Likewise, technology is a starting point for the initiation of service innovation processes.

Miozzo's and Soete's Typology of Service Innovation

Miozzo and Soete (1989, 2001) developed the first typology for innovation in service firms focusing on the influence of ICT. Their work is based on the taxonomy by Pavitt (1984, 1991), who analyzed innovations over three decades but did not assign services an appropriate role in innovation (de Jong & Marsili, 2006; Gallouj & Savona, 2009). Miozzo and Soete's typology consists of three types. The first type comprises firms of small size, including science-based firms and specialized suppliers. Software industry and business services are allocated to this type. Next, there is the supplier-dominated type, which is represented by public and social services, as well as services close to home. Finally, there is the scale-intensive type, which is divided into two subtypes: physical networks and information networks. Logistics and wholesale belong to the scale-intensive type using physical networks. Financial, insurance and communicational services represent the scale intensive type using information networks. The authors emphasize the interrelations between the manufacturing and service industries. Services using information networks influence the development of technologies by signaling future demands to manufacturing industries, especially in terms of technologies that improve their networks in

use. Furthermore, technology does not have to originate in manufacturing industries; for example, firms belonging to the science-based type and specialized suppliers can be developers of technology.

The typology of Miozzo and Soete (1989, 2001) was empirically validated by Evangelista (2000). His results show slight differences in comparison to the theoretically derived typology of Miozzo and Soete. The supplier-dominated type converted into a technology user consisting of logistics, waste management, retail sale, and tourism. Evangelista states that the allocation of logistics as scale-intensive, physical-networks-based type is also reasonable. Advertisement, banking, and insurance are considered to be interactive and IT-based instead of scale-intensive information network based. For these particular service industries, innovations neither originate from the adoption of technology nor from firms' own development. Instead, they are created on the foundation of obtained and accumulated knowledge. Science-based and specialized suppliers representing research and development and consulting services stayed the same.

De Jong and Marsili (2006) developed a corresponding taxonomy for small and medium-sized firms. They identified four types, but due to the objects analyzed, they introduced a resource-intensive type in place of a scale-intensive type. Firms belonging to the resource-intensive type often emphasize budget expenditure and effort for the development of innovation.

The taxonomy of Vence and Trigo (2009) divides the service sector into three types. There are industries of low innovation intensity, presented by wholesale, for example. Further, there are technology-intensive service industries of medium innovation intensity, such as financial services. Knowledge-intensive service industries, such as consultancy, are considered to be highly innovation intensive.

Taxonomies and typologies demonstrate the attempt to deal with the complexity and variety of services. However, the typology of Miozzo and Soete lacks the inclusion of non-technological innovations or at least the consideration of factors that are interrelated with technology and therefore potentially influential (Tether et al., 2001; Tether & Tajar, 2008).

Although the reverse innovation cycle model by Barras and the typology of service innovation by Miozzo and Soete were published more than ten years ago, our review demonstrated that they are frequently discussed models in the service innovation literature and provide the basis for many newer works. Both Barras as well as Miozzo and Soete focused their analysis on ICT. By this approach, they narrowed the validity of their models to a certain group of technologies and stage of development of these technologies. Applying these models to up-to-date ICT and other technologies, such as robotics, will expand the validity of the models, uncover potential for modification, and provide a revised starting point for the future development of new models of service innovation.

Research Methodology

A multi-case study method was chosen because it allows us to include and combine heterogeneous sources of information (Baxter & Jack, 2008), such as interviews and data from annual reports of companies. Further, processes that continue over time and might have had different starting points, such as development processes, can be examined in detail with this approach. Interconnections between processes also can be considered (Yin, 2003). The study of multiple cases should provide an insight into the diverse shapes and characteristics of one examined phenomenon and permit us to deduct robust conclusions (Eisenhardt, 1989; Yin, 2003). In this article, five cases are analyzed. The sources of information for making up the cases vary between personal interviews (Case 1 and Case 2), literature research (Case 3 and Case 4), and data from a university research project (Case 5). The technologies examined in the cases had different starting points of development and are interwoven. For instance, ICT started developing in the middle of the 20th century and operated as an enabler for the development of other technologies, such as robotics.

We analyzed the cases in three steps. First, we want to prove whether service firms are technology adopters when developing service innovations or technology developers. By this, we will clarify that technology actually is a force of promoting nature to service innovation. Second, the cases will be mapped to Barras' reverse innovation cycle model. Therefore, we need to differentiate between incremental and radical process innovation, and product innovation. Third, the applicability of the typology of Miozzo and Soete for service innovations and later modifications is to be evaluated focusing on the basis of the information obtained from the first and second steps of analysis. The focus is set on the congruency of the results of service innovation anticipated by the typologies and taxonomies and the actual results in the different case studies.

Case selection

The main selection criterion for the case studies was the application of a technology to or within a service process that was not used in this combination before. In other words, all service innovations analyzed within a case would not have been developed without technology or a combination of technologies. Further selection criteria included the context (i.e., business-to-business, business-to-consumer, or both), the size of firm, and the type of service industry. A selection of cases that differ from each other in the above-mentioned criteria was considered to be valuable according to the advantages of the multi-case method. The case selection covers a broad range of service firms and a wide variety of services.

The technologies considered as influential within the five cases range from robotics (two cases), automation technology (one case), information and communication technology (one case), and additive manufacturing (one case). All case studies are set in different high-tech industries, produce different services, and differ in size. Two of the firms are small (1–49 employees), one of the firms is medium-sized (50–249 employees), and two of the firms are large (>250 employees) (cf. Audretsch et al., 2009). Three cases are set in a business-to-business-context. These three cases also can be found in a business-to-consumer-context, but the firms presented in these cases offer their service exclusively to business customers. Two firms presented in the case studies provide their services to business and private customers. Table 1 provides an overview of the five cases, which are described in greater detail in the following section.

Case Descriptions

Case 1: Automation technology in car rental services

Customers of car rental services are often time-sensitive business travelers. At locations where many people wish to rent a car, for example, at the airport, delays can occur. With the help of automation technology, a worldwide car rental service developed an automatic car rental machine, which facilitated the car rental process in various ways. Customers can go directly to the car park where the machines are set up. Via touchscreen they initiate the rental process. The car keys can be taken out of the automatic car rental machine by pulling out a solid metallic cylinder. Customers returning the car go through a similar process.

Case 2: ICT in postal services

To most of us, email services are an essential part of our private and working lives. At the same time, customers

Table 1. Overview of the five case studies

	Case 1	Case 2	Case 3	Case 4	Case 5
Description	Automation technology in car rental services	ICT in postal services	Additive manufacturing in dentistry	Robotics in logistics	Robotics in industrial laundry services
Firm size	Large	Small	Small	Large	Medium
Operating context	B2B & B2C	B2B	B2C	B2B & B2C	B2C
Innovation	Automatic car rental machine (rental kiosk) for independent car rentals and returns	Email service for secure sending and receiving of legally binding emails and electronic documents	Stereolithography technology for manufacturing dental splints	Unloading robot for incoming freight containers	Service robot substituting manual operations
Type of innovation	Process	Product	Process	Process	Process
Motive for innovation	• Increase in competitiveness • Satisfaction of customer needs	• Expansion of the range of products • Adaptation to market conditions	• Satisfaction of customer needs • Process optimization	• Reduction of load on employees • Process optimization	• Reduction of risk of health and safety in the workplace • Process optimization
Development of innovation	• Internal	• Internal • Frame specified by government	• In collaboration with specialized suppliers	• Internal • In collaboration with research institutes	• In collaboration with specialized suppliers and research institutes
Type of technology	• Automation technology • ICT	• ICT	• Additive manufacturing • ICT	• Robotics • ICT	• Robotics • ICT
Sources of technology	• Specialized supplier	• Own research	• Specialized supplier	• Research institute • Specialized supplier	• Research institute • Specialized supplier

of email services are not aware of their privacy protection. Therefore, governments determined that some documents, such as tax assessment notices or articles of association, cannot be sent via email. Instead, they must be in written form. The German government decided that, in some cases, the obligatory written form can be substituted by a qualified electronic signature. The service firm presented in the case provides this special email service for firms. The email service contains several modules. Apart from a basic module consisting of the mailbox, additional modules can be obtained for end-to-end encryption, qualified electronic signature, and storage.

Case 3: Additive manufacturing in dentistry
People with bruxism or teeth grinding suffer from headaches, dental abrasion, and jaw pain (Carlsson et al., 2003). Therefore, the production of custom-fitting, indi-

vidual dental splints is gaining more importance in dentistry (Hoffmann, 2003). The traditional approach to fabricating dental splints is complex and time consuming; it begins with taking a dental impression of the client's teeth, which is then used to create a plaster cast, upon which the dental split is constructed (Polzin & Seitz, 2012). Additive manufacturing, or in this specific context stereolithography, is capable of facilitating this process significantly and further improving quality and fitting accuracy (Chengtao et al., 2006; Salmi, 2013; Van Noort, 2012). It constitutes a means of production that is crucial for the improvement of the whole service process that aims at the provision of patients with dental splints. Instead of taking a dental impression, additive fabrication begins with a computed axial tomography (CAT) scan of the client's teeth, which is used to create a 3D model of the dental splint, which is then printed using a stereolithography machine. Compared to the traditional approach, which takes from 4 to 10 days, the entire process of additive fabrication takes between 10 and 20 hours. The combination of additive manufacturing and ICT, presented by the CAT scan, permits to shorten the whole service process of producing a customized dental splint in terms of production time and feedback loops necessary to guarantee the proper fit of the splint.

Case 4: Robotics in logistics
In the packaging centre of a transport and logistics service provider, packages are sorted before being delivered to customers. Employees work in shifts 24 hours per day and 7 days per week to deliver packages as fast as possible. Cargo of incoming delivery trucks has to be unloaded by hand and put on a conveyor belt to be delivered to another delivery truck (Scholz, 2006; Vahrenkamp, 2005). Two issues threaten the health and safety of employees in their workplace (Echelmeyer et al., 2009; Schmidt & Rohde, 2010): i) large and heavy packages, such as automotive parts, have to be unloaded by hand and ii) stacks of packages can become unstable and fall onto employees. To confront these problems, a worldwide operating provider of transport and logistics services developed an unloading robot in collaboration with public research institutes. Once in position, a scanning system enables the unloading robot to recognize the exact location of the packages inside the truck and tells the robot where to grab them. The unloading robot is capable of unloading between 450 and 600 packages per hour (Echelmeyer et al., 2009).

Case 5: Robotics in industrial laundry services
Industrial laundries are well known for their automation systems (Vickery, 1972). Furthermore, radio-frequency

identification (RFID) technology has lately been widely implemented (Cangialosi et al., 2007). However, due to high levels of complexity and multiplicity, manual work is still required. Employees within industrial laundries servicing hospitals have to deal with heavy loads of laundry. Furthermore, they are exposed to highly contaminated and possibly infectious laundry items, especially when opening laundry bags by hand. A group of German researchers developed a service robot that partly substitutes manual work processes in industrial laundry services. For instance, the robot automatically opens laundry bags, reads RFID tags that are sewed in to the laundry items, and carries them to the conveyor belt. Heavy and wet laundry items can easily be processed, even during peaks of demand.

Case Analysis

In every case, technology was significant for service innovation. In fact, in four cases (1, 3, 4, and 5), a combination of two or more technologies formed the foundation for service innovation. ICT formed part of every one of these combinations. Although only five cases were considered and only one service innovation is based mainly on ICT (Case 2), the predominance of these technologies for service innovations is well represented in our study and coincides with the results of previous research (Higón, 2011; Jiménez-Zarco et al., 2011; Scupola & Tuunainen, 2011).

With regard to our research question, which concerned the ways in which service innovations are driven by technology, our cases indicate a variety of approaches. In Case 3, technology was adopted from the manufacturing industry, in particular from sectors dealing with mechanical engineering and frequently using prototypes, or other customized, prefabricated parts. In Case 1 and Case 2, technology incorporated in the service innovation was developed by the firms' own research and development departments. Two firms collaborated with public research institutions (Case 4 and Case 5). However, basic know-how of these technologies was adopted in each of the five cases. Robotics know-how (Case 4 and Case 5) was probably adopted from branches of industry using assembly devices, whereas know-how of automation technology (Case 1) was obtained from plant engineering and construction.

When applying the Barras model to our cases, we used the indicators included in the model, which led to debatable results. Our analysis will demonstrate that the indicators offered by Barras' model in some cases are not sufficient for determining whether an innovation is of an incremental or radical nature. According to Barras, the car rental services case can be characterized as a radical process innovation that significantly improves the quality of the service process, for example, by reducing waiting periods. At the same time, this innovation can be considered an incremental process innovation. It does not result in substantial changes for the car rental service firm nor does it require the acquisition of knowledge by the customer given that automation technology has surrounded our everyday life for more than two decades.

In the second case, service innovation was developed on the basis of information technologies that are considered to be highly diffused within the service industry (Djellal et al., 2013; Gago & Rubalcaba, 2007). By creating an email service with security options that facilitate sending and receiving emails with legal validity – in other words, improving the quality of the service – a radical process innovation was developed.

Again, this case demonstrates that Barras does not offer clear-cut criteria for assigning an innovation to one of the phases of his reverse innovation cycle. For this specific case, one can also argue that an email service with a qualified signature is not an innovation at all. Instead, it constitutes an example of adoption and implementation of earlier innovations.

The fabrication of dental splints via additive manufacturing (Case 3) represents an incremental process innovation in dentistry services. Improvements of quality for customers and providers, for example, by improved fitting accuracy, are achieved. Considering the past, this case reveals that the introduction of the CAT scanning technology might have been a radical process innovation to dentistry services as the handling of this new technology – for example, the scanning facility itself and the data processing software – have had to be learned by employees.

For laundry services as well as logistics, robotics is integrated into the overall operating systems. The determination of the process innovation type for these cases is highly dependent on the judge's point of view. For customers of an industrial laundry service, a laundry processing robot remains invisible. Improvements in quality will be marginal, whereas improvements in terms of efficiency will be noticed. Referring to the continuous threatening of employees' health, a laundry processing robot would stand for a significant improvement of health and safety in the workplace. For customers, logistics might improve on behalf of the delivery speed. Dependent on the extent to which delivery speed has increased, customers will perceive the service innovation as an incremental or radical process innovation. Although, one has to keep in mind, that the operation of an unloading robot remains invisible for customers. For employees, an unloading robot has visible advantages, including improved health and safety in the workplace. For both cases, the improvement can be perceived as an incremental or radical process innovation. The criterion of customer learning cannot be applied to both of the cases because, for customers, the innovations remain invisible.

The assignment of the cases to Miozzo and Soete's typology is summarized in Table 2. The typology covers all service industries presented in the cases. However, Case 5 is problematic because industrial laundry services are not considered services that are "close to home". Instead, they are assigned as public or social

Table 2. Assignment of cases to the typology of Miozzo and Soete (2001)

	Case 1	Case 2	Case 3	Case 4	Case 5
Description	Automation technology in car rental services	ICT in postal services	Additive manufacturing in dentistry	Robotics in logistics	Robotics in industrial laundry services
Types	Supplier-dominated OR Scale-intensive with physical networks	Knowledge intensive/ specialized supplier	Supplier-dominated	Scale-intensive with physical networks	Supplier-dominated
Innovation types	Process optimization	Innovative products	Process optimization	Process optimization	Process optimization

services. Both Case 4 and Case 5 used robotics and developed their service innovation in collaboration with public research institutions. Such a collaboration as a source of technology does not appear in the typology. However, in both cases, specialized suppliers originating in the manufacturing industry were granted a license to do further fabrication and maintenance.

Regarding the purpose of introducing a technology, the case data reflects Miozzo and Soete's expectations, except with Case 3, which does not fit. According to Miozzo and Soete's typology, Case 3 belongs to the knowledge-intensive type or specialized supplier.

Conclusion and Managerial Implications

Our case analysis demonstrated that technology has significant influence on the development of service innovations. Its characterization as a promoting force therefore is justified.

The reverse innovation cycle model of Barras, although not capable of displaying the dynamics of service innovation processes, demonstrates that service innovation and technology are interconnected. Further, the model indicates that the type of technology-service interaction results in different types of innovation. However, the indicators offered in the model of Barras are not sufficient.

A more precise approach to reflect the interconnections between service innovation and technology is the typology of Miozzo and Soete. It addresses the variety of the service sector and reveals technology-service interactions that are typical for certain service industries. Therefore, it enables managers to analyze and compare past technology-service interactions with present developments and conditions.

As the frontier between service and manufacturing firms blurs, future research has to deal with several fundamental questions referring to a service-dominant logic or the differentiation of process and product innovations and their characterization as incremental or radical. In this regard, the definition and measurement of intensity of innovation has to be reconsidered. At the same time, the measurement of productivity and quality of pre and post conditions of innovation has to be brought forward.

About the Authors

Silvia Gliem is a PhD student in Business Administration at Brandenburg University of Technology Cottbus-Senftenberg, Germany. She obtained her Bachelor's degree in International Business Administration from European University Viadrina in Frankfurt (Oder), Germany, and she holds a Master's degree in Business Administration from Brandenburg University of Technology in Cottbus, Germany. Her research interests focus on service productivity and service innovation research. She recently joined a research project that focuses on the improvement of health and safety in the workplace by means of a service robot. In the context of this project, she depicts the influence of physical surroundings and safety in the workplace on employees.

Janny Klabuhn is a PhD student in Industrial Engineering at Brandenburg University of Technology Cottbus-Senftenberg, Germany. She holds a diploma in Industrial Engineering from Brandenburg University of Technology in Cottbus, Germany. Her fields of research include human resource management, innovation management, and automation technology. She is part of a research project that aims at the development of a service robot to improve health and safety in the workplace. Within this project, she analyzes the transformational processes in human resources originating from the increasing application of automation technology in certain service industries.

Nadine Litwin is a PhD student in Business Administration at Brandenburg University of Technology Cottbus-Senftenberg, Germany. She received her diploma in Industrial Engineering from the Brandenburg University of Technology in Cottbus, Germany. Her research encompasses rapid prototyping, production processes, and disruptive innovation. In particular, she focuses on the diffusion of technologies that endanger firm's traditional competitive strategies, and the potential reorganization needs for manufacturing industries.

References

Audretsch, D., Horst, R. van der, Kwaak, T., & Thurik, R. 2009. First Section of the Annual Report on EU Small and Medium-sized Enterprises. Zoetermeer: EIM Business & Policy Research.

Barras, R. 1986a. Towards a Theory of Innovation in Services. *Research Policy*, 15(4): 161-173. http://dx.doi.org/10.1016/0048-7333(86)90012-0

Barras, R. 1986b. New Technology and the New Services – Towards an Innovation Strategy for Europe. *Futures*, 18(6): 748-772. http://dx.doi.org/10.1016/0016-3287(86)90125-4

Barras, R. 1990. Interactive Innovation in Financial and Business Services: The Vanguard of the Service Revolution. *Research Policy*, 19(3): 215-237. http://dx.doi.org/10.1016/0048-7333(90)90037-7

Baxter, P., & Jack, S. 2008. Qualitative Case Study Methodology: Study Design and Implementation for Novice Researchers. *The Qualitative Report*, 13(4): 544-559.

Cangialosi, A., Monaly, J. E., & Yang, S. C. 2007. Leveraging RFID in Hospitals: Patient Life Cycle and Mobility Perspectives. *IEEE Communications Magazine (Applications & Practice)*, 45(9): 18-23. http://dx.doi.org/10.1109/MCOM.2007.4342874

Carlsson, G. E., Egemark, E., & Magnusson, T. 2003. Predictors of Bruxism, Other Oral Parafunctions, and Tooth Wear over a 20-Year Follow-up Period. *Journal of Orofacial Pain*, 17(1): 50-57.

Chengtao, W., Shilei, Z., Xiaojun, C., & Yanping, L. 2006. A Novel Method in the Design and Fabrication of Dental Splints Based on 3D Simulation and Rapid Prototyping Technology. *The International Journal of Advanced Manufacturing Technology*, 28(9-19): 919-922. http://dx.doi.org/10.1007/s00170-004-2197-1

Cusumano, M., Kahl, S., & Suarez, F. F. 2006. Product, Process, and Service: A New Industry Lifecycle Model (Paper 228). Cambridge Massachusetts: MIT Sloan School of Management.

de Jong, J. P. J., & Marsili, O. 2006. The Fruit Flies of Innovations: A Taxonomy of Innovative Small Firms. *Research Policy*, 35(2): 213-229. http://dx.doi.org/10.1016/j.respol.2005.09.007

Djellal, F., Gallouj, F., & Miles, I. 2013. Two Decades of Research on Innovation on Services: Which Place for Public Services? *Structural Change and Economic Dynamics*, 27(2013): 98-117. http://dx.doi.org/10.1016/j.strueco.2013.06.005

Echelmeyer, W., Pallasch, A.-K. ,& Rohde, M. 2009. Die „Logistikfabrik der Zukunft" – ein ganzheitliches Konzept. *Industrie Management*, 25(5): 13-17.

Eisenhardt, K. M. 1989. Building Theories from Case Study Research. *Academy of Management Review*, 14(4): 532-550. http://dx.doi.org/10.5465/AMR.1989.4308385

Ettlie, J. E., Bridges, W. P., & O'Keefe, R. D. 1984. Organization Strategy and Structural Differences for Radical Versus Incremental Innovation. *Management Science*, 30(6): 682-695. http://dx.doi.org/10.1287/mnsc.30.6.682

Evangelista, R. 2000. Sectoral Patterns of Technological Change in Services. *Economics of Innovation and New Technology*, 9(3): 183-221. http://dx.doi.org/10.1080/10438590000000008

Gago, D., & Rubalcaba, L. 2007. Innovation and ICT in Service Firms: Towards a Multidimensional Approach for Impact Assessment. *Journal of Evolutionary Economics*, 17(1): 25-44. http://dx.doi.org/10.1007/s00191-006-0030-8

Gallouj, F. 1998. Innovating in Reverse: Services and the Reverse Product Cycle. *European Journal of Innovation Management*, 1(3): 123-138. http://dx.doi.org/10.1108/14601069810230207

Gallouj, F., & Savona, M. 2009. Innovation in Services: A Review of the Debate and a Research Agenda. *Journal of Evolutionary Economics*, 19(2): 149-172. http://dx.doi.org/10.1007/s00191-008-0126-4

Higón, D. 2011. The Impact of ICT on Innovation Activities: Evidence for UK SMEs. *International Small Business Journal*, 30(6): 684-699. http://dx.doi.org/10.1177/0266242610374484

Hipp, C., & Grupp, H. 2005. Innovation in the Service Sector: The Demand for Service-Specific Innovation Measurement Concepts and Typologies. *Research Policy*, 34(4): 517-535. http://dx.doi.org/10.1016/j.respol.2005.03.002

Hoffman, A. 2003. Die Aufbissschiene aus primosplint. *QZ – Quintessenz Zahntechnik*, 29(5): 626-634.

Jiménez-Zarco, A. I., Martínez-Ruiz, M. P., & Izquierdo-Yusta, A. 2011. Key Service Innovation Drivers in the Tourism Sector: Empirical Evidence and Managerial Implications. *Service Business*, 5(4): 339-360. http://dx.doi.org/10.1007/s11628-011-0118-6

Kandampully, J. 2002. Innovation as the Core Competency of a Service Organization: The Role of Technology, Knowledge and Networks. *European Journal of Innovation Management*, 5(1): 18-26. http://dx.doi.org/10.1108/14601060210415144

Miles, I. 2010. Service Innovation. In P. P. Maglio, C. Kieliszweski & J. C. Spohrer (Eds.), *Handbook of Service Science*: 511-533. New York: Springer. http://dx.doi.org/10.1007/978-1-4419-1628-0_22

Miozzo, M., & Soete, L. 2001. Internationalization of Services: A Technological Perspective. Technological *Forecasting and Social Change*, 67(2-3): 159-185. http://dx.doi.org/10.1016/S0040-1625(00)00091-3

Pavitt, K. 1984. Sectoral Patterns of Technical Change: Towards a Taxonomy and a Theory. *Research Policy*, 13(6): 343-373. http://dx.doi.org/10.1016/0048-7333(84)90018-0

Pavitt, K. 1991. Key Characteristics of the Large Innovating Firm. *British Journal of Management*, 2(1): 41-50. http://dx.doi.org/10.1111/j.1467-8551.1991.tb00014.x

Perks, H., Gruber, T., & Edvardsson, B. 2012. Co-Creation in Radical Service Innovation: A Systematic Analysis of Microlevel Processes. *Journal of Product Innovation Management*, 29(6): 935-951. http://dx.doi.org/10.1111/j.1540-5885.2012.00971.x

Polzin C., & Seitz H. 2012. 3D-Druck von Kunststoff-Medizinprodukten. *RTejournal*, 2012(9): 1-7.

Rubalcaba, L., Gago, D., & Gallego, J. 2010. On the Differences between Goods and Services Innovation. *Journal of Innovation Economics*, 5(1): 17-40. http://dx.doi.org/10.3917/jie.005.0017

Salmi, M. 2013. *Medical Applications of Additive Manufacturing in Surgery and Dental Care.* Doctoral Dissertation: Aalto University.

Salter, A., & Tether, B. S. 2014. Innovation in Services: An Overview. In K. Haynes & I. Grugulis (Eds.), *Managing Services: Challenges & Innovation:* 134-153. Oxford: Oxford University Press.

Schmidt, K. & Rohde, M. 2010. Low Cost Automation in der Logistik. *Zeitschrift für wirtschaftlichen Fabrikbetrieb,* 105(1-2): 91-95.

Scholz, E. 2006. Enthüllungsgeschichte: Ein Roboter packt aus. *Logistik & Fördertechnik,* 2006(12): 32-33.

Scupola, A., & Tuunainen, V. 2011. Open Innovation and Role of ICT in Business-to-Business Services: Empirical Evidence from Facility Management Services. Sprouts: Working Papers on Information Systems, 11(58).

Tether, B. S., Hipp, C., & Miles, I. 2001. Standardisation and Particularisation in Services: Evidence from Germany. *Research Policy,* 30(7): 1115-1138. http://dx.doi.org/10.1016/S0048-7333(00)00133-5

Tether, B. S., & Howells, J. 2007. Changing Understanding of Innovation on Services: From Technological Adoption to Complex Complementary Changes to Technologies, Skills and Organization (DTI Occasional Paper No. 9). DTI.

Tether, B. S., & Tajar, A. 2008. The Organisational-Cooperation Mode of Innovation and its Prominence amongst European Service Firms. *Research Policy,* 37(4): 720-739. http://dx.doi.org/10.1016/j.respol.2008.01.005

Toivonen, M., & Tuominen, T. 2009. Emergence of Innovation in Services. *The Service Industries Journal,* 29(7): 887-902. http://dx.doi.org/10.1080/02642060902749492

Uchupalanan, K. 2000. Competition and IT-Based Innovation in Banking Services. *International Journal of Innovation Management,* 4(4): 455-489. http://dx.doi.org/10.1142/S1363919600000238

Utterback, J. M., & Abernathy, W. J. 1975. A Dynamic Model of Process and Product Innovation. *The Omega,* 3(6): 639-656. http://dx.doi.org/10.1016/0305-0483(75)90068-7

Vahrenkamp, R. 2005. *Logistik – Management und Strategien* (5th Ed.). Munich: Oldenbourg.

Van Noort, R. 2012. The Future of Dental Devices is Digital. *Dental Materials,* 28(1): 3-12. http://dx.doi.org/10.1016/j.dental.2011.10.014

Vargo, S. L., & Lusch, R. F. 2004. Evolving to a New Dominant Logic for Marketing. *The Journal of Marketing,* 68(1): 1–17. http://dx.doi.org/10.1509/jmkg.68.1.1.24036

Vence, X., & Trigo, A. 2009. Diversity of Innovation Patterns in Services. *The Service Industries Journal,* 29(2): 1635-1657. http://dx.doi.org/10.1080/02642060902793631

Vickery, M.L. 1972. New Technology in Laundry and Cleaning Services. *Monthly Labor Review,* 95(2): 54-59. http://www.jstor.org/stable/41838539

Wang, W., Hsu, H. Y. S., Yen, H. R., Chiu, H.-C., & Wei, C.-P. 2010. Developing and Validating Service Innovation Readiness. *PACIS 2010 Proceedings,* 71.

Yin, R. K. 2003. *Case Study Research – Design and Methods* (3rd Ed.). Thousand Oaks: Sage.

Keywords: service innovation, technology, reverse innovation cycle, dynamic model of process and product innovation, typologies, case studies, technology adoption, technology development

Permissions

The contributors of this book come from diverse backgrounds, making this book a truly international effort. This book will bring forth new frontiers with its revolutionizing research information and detailed analysis of the nascent developments around the world.

We would like to thank all the contributing authors for lending their expertise to make the book truly unique. They have played a crucial role in the development of this book. Without their invaluable contributions this book wouldn't have been possible. They have made vital efforts to compile up to date information on the varied aspects of this subject to make this book a valuable addition to the collection of many professionals and students.

This book was conceptualized with the vision of imparting up-to-date information and advanced data in this field. To ensure the same, a matchless editorial board was set up. Every individual on the board went through rigorous rounds of assessment to prove their worth. After which they invested a large part of their time researching and compiling the most relevant data for our readers.

The editorial board has been involved in producing this book since its inception. They have spent rigorous hours researching and exploring the diverse topics which have resulted in the successful publishing of this book. They have passed on their knowledge of decades through this book. To expedite this challenging task, the publisher supported the team at every step. A small team of assistant editors was also appointed to further simplify the editing procedure and attain best results for the readers.

Apart from the editorial board, the designing team has also invested a significant amount of their time in understanding the subject and creating the most relevant covers. They scrutinized every image to scout for the most suitable representation of the subject and create an appropriate cover for the book.

The publishing team has been an ardent support to the editorial, designing and production team. Their endless efforts to recruit the best for this project, has resulted in the accomplishment of this book. They are a veteran in the field of academics and their pool of knowledge is as vast as their experience in printing. Their expertise and guidance has proved useful at every step. Their uncompromising quality standards have made this book an exceptional effort. Their encouragement from time to time has been an inspiration for everyone.

The publisher and the editorial board hope that this book will prove to be a valuable piece of knowledge for researchers, students, practitioners and scholars across the globe.

List of Contributors

Jesper Bank
New York University Stern School of Business, London School of Economics and Political Science, and HEC School of Management in Paris

Adnan Raza
Rotman School of Management at the University of Toronto, Canada

Chris McPhee
Technology Innovation Management from Carleton University in Ottawa

Risto Rajala
Department of Industrial Engineering and Management at Aalto University in Helsinki, Finland

Marja Toivonen
Aalto University in Helsinki, Finland

Mika Westerlund
Carleton University's Sprott School of Business in Ottawa, Canada

Asceline Groot
Institute of Management Research of the Radboud University Nijmegen, The Netherlands

Ben Dankbaar
Innovation Management at Radboud University Nijmegen, The Netherlands

Chris McPhee
Technology Innovation Management from Carleton University in Ottawa

Risto Rajala
Aalto University in Helsinki, Finland

Mika Westerlund
Carleton University's Sprott School of Business in Ottawa, Canada

Mervi Vuori
Department of Industrial Engineering and Management at Aalto University in Helsinki, Finland

Jukka-Pekka Hares
Aalto University School of Economics in Helsinki, Finland

Rabeh Morrar
Innovation Economics at An-Najah National University in Nablus, Palestine

Suchita Nirosh Kannangara
Technology Innovation Management (TIM) program at Carleton University in Ottawa, Canada

Peter Uguccioni
Technology Innovation Management (TIM) program at Carleton University in Ottawa, Canada

Finn Hahn
Product Development & Innovation from the University of Southern Denmark

Soren Jensen
University of Southern Denmark

Stoyan Tanev
Department of Technology and Innovation at the University of Southern Denmark, Odense

Doris Schartinger
Austrian Institute of Technology (AIT) in Vienna, Austria

Ian Miles
Manchester Institute of Innovation Research at Manchester Business School, United Kingdom

Ozcan Saritas
Manchester Institute of Innovation Research (UNIMAN) at Manchester Business School, United Kingdom

Effie Amanatidou
Manchester Institute of Innovation Research (UNIMAN) at Manchester Business School, United Kingdom

Susanne Giesecke
Austrian Institute of Technology (AIT) in Vienna, Austria

Barbara Heller-Schuh
Austrian Institute of Technology (AIT) in Vienna, Austria

Laura Pompo-Juarez
Antonio Nebrija University in Madrid, Spain

Gunter Schreier
Graz University of Technology in Austria

Bernardo Nicoletti
Master in Procurement Management at the Universita di Tor Vergata in Rome, Italy

Madeleine Gray

Mikael Mangyoku
Strate College in Sèvres, France

Artur Serra
i2cat Foundation in Catalonia, Spain

Laia Sanchez
Universitat Autonoma de Barcelona

Francesc Aragall
Design for All Foundation in Barcelona, Spain

Punit Saurabh
Indian Institute of Technology Kharagpur, India

Prabha Bhola
Indian Institute of Technology Kharagpur, India

Kalyan Kumar Guin
Indian Institute of Technology Kharagpur, India

Shiv S.Tripathi
Management Development Institute in Gurgaon, India

Stoyan Tanev
Integrative Innovation Management at the University of Southern Denmark, Odense, Denmark

Marianne Harbo Frederiksen
University of Southern Denmark

Erik Zijdemans
University of Southern Denmark, Odense

Stoyan Tanev
University of Southern Denmark, Odense

Tom Coughlan
School of Business at Mercy College in Dobbs Ferry, New York

Marit Engen
Lillehammer University College, Norway

Inger Elisabeth Holen
Lillehammer University College, Norway

Matthias Gotsch
Competence Center for Industrial and Service Innovations at the Fraunhofer Institute for Systems and Innovation Research ISI in Karlsruhe, Germany

Christiane Hipp
Technical University Cottbus, Germany

Mikael Laakso
Hanken School of Economics in Helsinki, Finland

Linus Nyman
Hanken School of Economics in Helsinki, Finland

Derek Smith
Technology Innovation Management from Carleton University in Ottawa, Canada

Jeff Moretz
University of Ontario Institute of Technology (UOIT) in Oshawa, Canada

Chirag Surti
University of Ontario Institute of Technology (UOIT) in Oshawa, Canada

Jens-Uwe Meyer
Steinbeis University in Berlin

Heidi M. E. Korhonen
VTT Technical Research Centre of Finland

Silvia Gliem
Brandenburg University of Technology Cottbus-Senftenberg, Germany

Janny Klabuhn
Brandenburg University of Technology Cottbus-Senftenberg, Germany

Nadine Litwin
Brandenburg University of Technology Cottbus-Senftenberg, Germany

Printed in the USA
CPSIA information can be obtained
at www.ICGtesting.com
JSHW051441221024
72173JS00006B/1545